DONABE

DONABE

Classic and Modern
Japanese Clay Pot Cooking

NAOKO TAKEI MOORE
KYLE CONNAUGHTON
Photography by Eric Wolfinger

TEN SPEED PRESS
California | New York

CONTENTS

RECIPE CONTENTS

Previous pages: Donabe from the late Edo Period to the
Meiji Period (late nineteenth to early twentieth centuries)

Dashi, Sauces, and Condiments 273

PREFACE

Donabe (doh-NAH-bay) is a storied type of clay cookware from Japan, with roots that go deep into Japanese history. It's often used for simmering one-pot dishes, especially popular in the wintertime.

In recent years, Japanese people have been rediscovering the remarkable utility of these traditional cooking vessels. As deep as donabe's history goes, it remains an everyday type of cookware used year-round. But donabe's potential goes way beyond comforting hot-pot cooking; it's perfect for making rice and braising meat. In addition, donabe ware brings warmth and beauty to the table. The communal nature of a donabe meal brings people together and invites conversation and bonding.

This book is all about creating these donabe experiences to be shared among family and friends.

NAOKO'S STORY

I grew up in Tokyo. I have always loved cooking and eating good food, thanks to my parents, but it was when I moved to Los Angeles in 2001 to study at Le Cordon Bleu in Pasadena that I became passionate about bringing Japanese food culture to America. Los Angeles is a big, multicultural city, but real Japanese home cooking—which is, after all, the core of Japanese food culture—is not so well known. I wanted to introduce authentic Japanese dishes and cooking styles to Americans and share the joy of cooking them.

Cooking with donabe has always been important to me, and close to my heart, but originally I used donabe for making hot pot dishes. On one of my trips back home many years ago, I tasted rice made in a double-lid donabe. It was one of the most striking food discoveries I've ever experienced. That simple, plain rice tasted so good I almost cried. An artisanal pottery company, Nagatani-en, based in Iga, Japan, had made that donabe. This family-owned company has been making authentic *Iga-yaki* (Iga-style) pottery since 1832—for eight generations.

So I bought a donabe for cooking rice from Nagatani-en and brought it home to L.A. I made this plain rice for my American friends, and they all loved it and started asking me where they could buy a donabe. I wrote to Nagatani-en and asked if they exported their donabe to the United States. They said no. So I wrote again and said I would like to import their donabe, and they said I could do so. Some months later, I went back to Japan and met the current generations running the Nagatani-en business. The family and I clicked immediately over an amazing donabe meal and sake. That was the very beginning of my relationship with the Nagatani family. Now, after countless visits back to Iga over the past seven years, the Nagatani family is like my real family.

Soon after the first visit to Nagatani-en in 2008, I began distributing donabe in the States. Meanwhile, my love for donabe cooking kept growing. I started collecting different, unique styles of donabe, including some made in a style similar to a Moroccan *tagine* pot, as well as steamers, soup and stew pots, and smokers. I found that they made my food taste better. I began to love cooking more and more. What I discovered was that donabe ware has the mysterious quality of bringing out the natural flavors of ingredients, helping them realize their higher potential.

There is actually a scientific explanation of this phenomenon: it's because of the natural characteristics of donabe, their porous bodies that promote higher heat retention, and a surface glaze that promotes natural far-infrared radiant heating. The effect is just like that of cooking on a grill using glowing charcoals, a process that cooks food gradually and traps flavors inside. Inspired, I gradually expanded the donabe lineup for my online donabe shop, (www.toirokitchen.com) and I also started hosting donabe cooking classes at home.

Originally, I thought my donabe shop and cooking classes would attract mainly Japanese and other Asians who were already familiar with clay-pot cooking. But to my surprise it has been mostly non-Asian people who have ordered donabe and come to my classes. I realized that donabe culture could be adapted to Western cooking traditions. The great thing is that so many of my students, regardless of cultural background, have become repeat customers of both my shop and my classes. Sometimes they send me photos of their original donabe dishes. My shop also has international customers—a customer in Sweden even sent me photos of his donabe reindeer stew! It looked so tasty. At that moment, I felt as if two completely different worlds had become connected.

In 2013, UNESCO designated *washoku*, traditional Japanese cuisine, as an Intangible Cultural Heritage of Humanity because of its respect for nature and for the proper seasoning of home cooking, passed down over centuries of shared mealtimes. Donabe is the perfect expression of Japanese home cooking. Now I feel even more responsible for the role I play as a Japanese cooking teacher and "donabe ambassador" living abroad. I'm on a mission to spread the word about the Japanese healthy lifestyle and authentic *washoku* home cooking.

Many typical donabe dishes require little or no fat and light seasoning, yet the results are very satisfying. Also, many donabe dishes are typically one-pot dishes, meant to be served at the table right out of the pot. As a result, preparation and cleanup tend to be easier compared with using other cookware. Donabe cooking is convenient for busy people who want to eat tasty, nourishing meals at home.

This cookbook features cooking in six styles of donabe pots: classic, rice cooker, soup and stew, steamer, *tagine* style, and smoker. My recipes are practical, home-style dishes that have been particularly popular among family, friends, and students from my donabe cooking classes. Through the recipes, I want to share *omotenashi*, the Japanese way of hospitality for various occasions. Whether it's a casual night with your family, an intimate meal with a partner, or a special dinner party with important guests, donabe cooking has a magical power to make everyone feel welcome. A donabe meal is meant for sharing, and sharing is at the heart of our *omotenashi* culture in Japan.

It also lets you create a beautiful tabletop presentation for home entertaining. You'll find here a variety of donabe serving ideas and seasonal variations, including an *izakaya-* (Japanese pub-) style donabe dinner party, a springtime temple-style donabe breakfast, and an outdoor donabe brunch. Through my *omotenashi* in this book, I am also excited to share the beauty of Iga pottery, whose casual beauty inspires feelings of warmth and welcome in those who are served from it. All the donabe and ceramic tableware you'll see on my recipe pages, including bowls, plates, and cups, is authentic *Iga-yaki* pottery handcrafted by Nagatani-en. It's made from the ancient clay around the city of Iga, which was a lake bed about four million years ago. What makes them special is the power of earth, fire, and history. In addition to recipes, I've included fundamentals about donabe and Iga, along with practical information about cooking with each specific type of donabe. I hope this book will be the essential guide for your happy donabe lifestyle.

It's my pleasure to help people from different cultures discover how great donabe cooking is and adapt it to their own cuisines. And my coauthor does just that with the California-inspired recipes he has included in this book. There are also recipes from some of the most respected chefs from the United States and Japan.

Donabe cooking is my heart and soul. And it makes people happy. I am extremely honored to share my passion with you through these pages, and hope this book will open the door to the rich everyday donabe lifestyle and *omotenashi* culture for you. My wish is that the recipes in this book will make you very happy.

Happy donabe life!

NAOKO TAKEI MOORE

Naoko and her mother, Mikiko, and sister, Tomoko

KYLE'S STORY

I've been fortunate to cook all over the world with chefs I respect and with other professionals who care deeply about food and hospitality. Having a passion for food is easy, but having a passion for hospitality and making people happy is something that can't be taught—it has to come from within. I discovered early on, well before I began my career as a chef, that great Japanese restaurants provided both in a way that spoke to me very deeply. My career has been built in a combination of Japanese, European, and California kitchens. I've been fortunate in my time to cook everything from rustic, seasonally focused cuisine with Los Angeles chef and restaurateur Suzanne Goin to very precise, science-oriented cuisine with British chef and restaurateur Heston Blumenthal. Through these varied experiences around the world, a few things have stayed constant: my love for Japanese cuisine and my passion for hospitality.

A dinner I had one night at a sushi bar in the mid-1980s, before sushi really took off in the United States, sparked a lifelong obsession with Japanese cuisine. I was nine years old. My dad took me to my first Japanese restaurant after coming back from Tokyo on business. I was fascinated by the postcards he'd sent and the stories he'd brought back. My parents supported my fixation by hosting Japanese foreign exchange students, traveling to Japan, and eating as much Japanese food as possible. Later, my wife and I—young, broke parents in our twenties—saved every penny we could to take trips to Japan to eat. I began going to language tutors and worked in Japanese kitchens in L.A., attending the California Sushi Academy and the Sushi Chef Institute with the great master sushi chef Andy Matsuda. Matsuda-sensei took me on a trip to Japan with him and dropped me off at his brother's sushi restaurant for an eye-opening apprenticeship.

These experiences only made me crave working in Japan more. While I cooked at my favorite restaurants in L.A. at night, my wife, young daughters, and I studied Japanese during the day. Finally, I landed a job working for Michel Bras at his new restaurant in Hokkaido. We moved our two young daughters to the rural, snowy northern island. There I spent a few years cooking in the Bras kitchen, as well as at some of the great restaurants of Japan that served classic and modern Japanese cuisine. The arctic weather of Hokkaido and our limited budget for heating fuel meant that most nights at home were spent huddled around a tabletop burner and a donabe. On my evenings off, the family came together for a hot pot of local seafood with miso or braised pork from the farmer families at our daughters' school. These are the experiences that stand out most in my mind when I think of our beautiful adopted home.

Later we moved to England for four years, where I was the research and development chef for Heston Blumenthal at The Fat Duck restaurant. That kitchen and our work there were centered on leveraging science in the kitchen and using technology to achieve precision and accuracy. That sounds very cutting-edge, but no chef I've ever met is as passionate about ancient cooking techniques as Heston. I started to piece together how both old and new technologies can be used together, all based on their merits and what's best for the job at hand. Heston used to say, "At one point, any cooking tool was considered new technology," and he is right. Donabe is an amazing and beautiful technology that has stood the test of time because of its unique functional properties.

When I returned to California after years abroad, I was so happy to reconnect with Naoko-san, whom I'd met while she was a culinary school student in Southern California. I saw her hard work and dedication to sharing donabe cooking with Western cooks and chefs. She began taking me with her on trips to Iga, where I joined her adopted Nagatani family. She has been my teacher and guide into the greater world of donabe, and we decided as a team to share this amazing world with you.

In this book, we share not only donabe recipes but also the functional properties of these beautiful vessels and ways you can incorporate them into your own cooking, whether at home or in a professional kitchen. Donabe can be used in all types of cuisines, as our guest chefs and I will show through our recipes. At home and in my professional kitchen, I use donabe for soups and braises to simmer vegetables, and to smoke meats. I hope that you, too, will bring donabe into your life and your kitchen, and share its communal hospitality with your family and friends.

KYLE CONNAUGHTON

Introduction

THE WORLD OF DONABE

What Is Donabe?

Donabe (doh-NAH-bay) is Japanese traditional earthen cookware. The Kanji characters that make up the word mean, literally, "clay pot": *do* (土) is "clay" or "earth," and *nabe* (鍋) is "pot." Donabe ware is versatile, and you can use it for a hot pot, soup, or stew; for steaming, making rice, or various other styles of cooking. It is designed to be used over a gas or open flame.

Over its long history, donabe has become an important part of Japanese cuisine and its food culture. You can almost call donabe the national cookware of Japan, and almost every household owns at least one of these vessels. In Japan, donabe is used both at home and in restaurants, whether for casual dishes or for special meals to entertain guests. The food can be served right out of the donabe at the table as a communal dish. The excitement of seeing and smelling the steaming-hot food when the donabe's lid is lifted never gets old and brings together everyone at the table.

A Brief History

One of the oldest extant documents in which clay pots are mentioned is from the eighth century. At the time, clay pots were referred to simply as *nabe* (pots), but as metal, iron, stone, and bronze pots were introduced to Japan over the next few centuries, it became necessary to distinguish clay pots from metal ones. Clay pots came to be known as donabe.

Later, in the eighteenth century (the middle Edo Period), serving a hot pot over a portable charcoal grill set on tatami floor mats or directly at a dining table became popular among residents in Edo, or what is now Tokyo. This style of serving is considered to be the origin of the hot-pot dishes we associate with donabe today, in which ingredients such as tofu, fish, meat, and vegetables are placed in the pot and cooked in a simmering broth at the table. At that time, however, a hot-pot dish was mostly served in small individual-serving-size pots. These dishes were mainly for adults to enjoy, rather than the whole family, and mostly iron pots were used for the convenience of fast heating.

It wasn't until much later, during the twentieth century, after the family dining style shifted from serving individual trays to family members and started dining by surrounding a table, that the Japanese people rediscovered donabe as the perfect cooking vessel for a communal hot-pot meal. When the strict patriarchal system in Japanese families—where fathers were normally served the best, or sometimes their own extra, portions—faded in the twentieth century, it became common for a family to share a meal communally. As a result, hot pot became a popular dish to share at home.

Donabe continues to evolve in quality and design. More specialized and improved functions of donabe, including *tagine*-style, steamer, and smoker donabe, serve different cooking purposes as people's lifestyles have become more modernized and food culture has been exposed to international influences. Donabe has evolved into a timeless cooking tool and continues to be loved by Japanese people for its utility and feel of earth and fire.

*Reference sources: *Bimi-Serai Magazine* (December 2011 issue), *Kibun Academy* (www.kibun.com), Donabegohan.com.

Donabe Culture in Japan

Today, donabe cooking brings family and friends closer together. In Japan, there is a common expression: *nabe o kakomu* ("surrounding a pot"). This expression evokes how sharing a hot-pot meal at the same table creates an intimate communal experience. The expression is used in ways like, "Let's go out and chat by surrounding a pot" or "I had a good time by surrounding a pot with" so-and-so. Also, when we say *nabe*, it not only refers to the cooking vessel itself, but also means "hot-pot dish." So you can just say, "Let's eat *nabe*." Such communal dining encourages participation and interaction at the table, so it's also often used to help people bond faster when they start a new relationship, whether business or personal.

At home, people make a simple one-pot meal by simmering meat or fish with vegetables on a regular day, or a more elaborate donabe dinner to entertain guests. Besides *nabe* (hot-pot dishes), donabe is also used for cooking other types of dishes, including rice or stews.

At restaurants, donabe dishes can be served in a variety of settings, from a humble *izakaya* (Japanese pub) to very elegant *ryotei* (luxurious Japanese restaurant). These restaurants can feature regional and seasonal dishes, or traditional or original cuisine, with diners gathered around a communal pot. For a special occasion, they might enjoy a *fugu-chiri* (blowfish hot pot) or a *kani suki*

(crab hot pot) dinner course. For a simple treat, some restaurants (many in Kyoto) serve traditional *yu-dofu* (simmered tofu) in donabe. Even rice snobs who frequent posh *izakayas* can choose from a long list of artisanal rice varieties and receive an individual-size donabe to order.

In the food culture of Japan, donabe cooking is constantly featured on television shows, in magazines, and on websites, as people crave new recipes and techniques. There are growing numbers of donabe cookbooks, too. As the donabe culture continues to evolve, donabe's possibilities are expanding into different methods of cooking in different cuisines—even beyond Asia. It's no longer surprising to see donabe used for making international dishes such as bouillabaisse, risotto, or pot roast.

Over thousands of years of donabe history, so many other kinds of cookware have become popular, and new kinds of high-tech cookware keep popping up in the market. But donabe still continues to have a strong presence in Japanese food culture. This longevity is due to the functionality and organic feeling of this earthenware, along with its ancient origin.

Advantages of Donabe Cooking

Many people who use donabe say it makes food taste better. The secret is the material: clay. Donabe takes a much longer time to build heat and cool down than other cookware, such as stainless steel. This characteristic is the key to all the natural flavor donabe can draw out of straightforward ingredients.

Because donabe builds heat slowly, it allows the flavors of a dish to build gradually. Donabe can help make your mushroom soup taste more savory and your rice taste sweeter. When a dish is higher in natural umami flavor, less seasoning and less fat are needed to complete the flavors. We like to say that donabe is a friendly cookware for health-conscious people.

Once the heat has built within the donabe, you can lower the flame and it will maintain a steady and gentle heat distribution. The donabe also works like a cushion for that heat, taking the direct flame from the stove and evenly distributing it across the surface and to the food. During cooking, donabe's glaze promotes natural far-infrared radiation, which is the same effect that glowing charcoal gives to food.

Donabe ware is known for its remarkable heat retention. It cools down slowly, so it stays warm on the table for a long time. This trait also makes it perfect for cooking with carryover heat. That's why donabe is ideal for slow-cooking. Donabe is an energy-efficient and eco-friendly cooking vessel because, once heated, it requires little energy to function.

What is umami?

The Japanese term *umami* (literally, "pleasant savory taste") has entered the English lexicon in recent years because there is no real Western equivalent that encompasses it. Like sweetness and saltiness, it is a basic flavor category recognized by the human taste buds, occurring naturally in foods ranging from dairy products to fish, meat, and vegetables. Umami doesn't usually stand alone but is experienced through the way it combines with other flavors to enhance them. In scientific terms, umami is the taste produced by various amino acids and nucleotides, including glutamate, guanylate, and inosinate. For the rest of us, it's enough to know that it makes food delicious.

Choosing Donabe

Especially if you are new to the world of donabe, choosing the right donabe is the first important step. It's wise to choose one that will have the most uses and last for a long time. Here are some tips for choosing a donabe that you can comfortably use every day.

Material. Coarse clay makes donabe with the highest heat-retention capability. Donabe can be made from all clay, but some are made from clay mixed with nonclay or artificial components. Some donabe are made from fine, smooth clay, which is easier to clean but doesn't retain heat as well. Donabe made from coarse clay, such as Iga clay, has an extra-porous body that retains and distributes heat the best.

Size. Smaller donabe are easier to handle, but larger donabe can be more flexible, as you can make either large or small portions in them. For cooking rice in donabe, consider whether you want to make mostly plain rice or will occasionally be making rice mixed with other ingredients. If the latter, you want to have enough extra space for the additional ingredients. It's more convenient to have two different sizes of donabe for different serving purposes.

Durability. Artisanal donabe can be more expensive than mass-produced donabe, but they are more likely to be made with higher-quality clay and with extra time and care taken to ensure durability and utility. It takes about two weeks to make an artisanal donabe such as Iga-yaki donabe, because it is fired twice at an extremely high temperature. Both the quality and the amount of glaze used can affect durability, too. Therefore, hand-crafted donabe is well worth the extra investment.

Shape and Style. A deeper donabe body holds broth best and works better in slow cooking, while a shallow, wide donabe—such as Kyoto-style donabe (see page 52) and *tagine*-style donabe (see page 214)—can provide more surface area for both cooking and presentation. This also means more surface area is exposed to receive benefit from the the far-infrared radiation effect, which cooks first the surface of the contents and then gradually penetrates inside.

There are also different styles for different functions of cooking. Beside the classic (standard) style of donabe, some are designed for specific purposes such as rice cooking, steaming, and smoking. So knowing what you plan to cook with your donabe will help you choose the right style. You don't have to buy one of everything. Some donabe can be used for multiple functions. For example, you can use a donabe rice cooker as a classic-style donabe for hot pots and stews.

Design. Of course, because donabe is something you not only cook with but also serve from at the table, for many people its aesthetics are important. Artisanal handmade types often carry different characteristics, depending on the artist or the region of manufacture. Some look rustic, while others are slick and modern.

All the recipes introduced in this book have been tested with *Iga-yaki* (Iga-style) donabe made by Nagatani-en in Iga, Japan. *Iga-yaki* donabe is very porous and is especially remarkable for its heat-retention ability, heat resistance, and durability. Of course, you can use different producers' donabe or other cooking vessels to make many of the recipes. Because some recipes require specific techniques such as high-intensity dry heating (heating while the pot is empty or heating with little or no fluid inside), read the manufacturer's instructions to ensure your vessel can handle such cooking techniques.

Different kinds of donabe can be found at larger Japanese markets, specialty stores, and online. For shopping information about the *Iga-yaki* donabe used in this book, see Resources on page 299.

Signature Characteristics

With use and age, the appearance of your donabe will change; donabe will develop a mature beauty as it's used. The more you use it, the more tiny crackles accumulate, like a leaf's thin veins, on the glaze inside. These cracks are called *kannyu* in Japanese. *Kannyu* occurs when a donabe repeatedly expands and shrinks during heating and cooling. While the clay itself can expand and shrink, the glaze is not as flexible as the clay, causing thin cracks to appear. *Kannyu* won't affect the function of the donabe. Rather, they enhance its strength, as the donabe body can expand and shrink more efficiently when the cracks give enough space. The cracks are highly appreciated as part of the *wabi-sabi* (art of "unfinished" or "incomplete" beauty) character of donabe.

Once you start using a donabe, the bottom changes color and black spots (like burned spots) could appear. That's another welcome maturing characteristic of the donabe. In Japan, it's something to be proud of if you've owned a donabe for a long time and the bottom looks dark and used. That's the sign of a grown-up donabe. However, if the bottom part turns black after a few uses, most likely the heat level you're using is too high.

Top: "Kannyu" crackles naturally appear after multiple uses of a Donabe

Bottom: The underside of the donabe becomes much darker after many years of use

Caring for Your Donabe

With proper care, donabe will develop personal characteristics and can last for decades. Once you understand donabe's basic characteristics, maintenance is a very easy task. Here are some useful tips on how to take care of your donabe, from seasoning it to washing and storing it.

Because donabe's clay body is porous, you must first season donabe by making rice porridge in it. As the starch of the thick gluelike porridge fills the tiny pores of the clay, it strengthens the body and helps prevent possible leaks and cracks during cooking. This process also creates a barrier to keep aromas from the food from penetrating the pores of the clay. It's a one-time step that will make your donabe last for a long time.

Donabe ware is not dishwasher-safe. Once you begin cooking with your donabe, use mild soap and a sponge to hand-wash it. Do not leave the donabe soaking in soapy water, as it could absorb the smell of the soap. Never plunge a hot donabe into cold water, as the acute heat change could cause cracking.

Once they are clean, make sure you dry all the pieces of the donabe. Place them upside down, at least overnight, to dry out. If you are storing a donabe for a while, leave it in a dry location. Storing a donabe in high humidity for a long time could cause mold to grow inside.

Donabe is not for storing food, as the clay body could absorb the smell if you leave food in it for many hours. Transfer leftovers to another container.

How to season donabe:

1. Fill the donabe about 70 percent full of water and add cooked rice equivalent to about one-fifth or more of the volume of water. You don't have to be nervous about the measurement, you can just eyeball the amount. For a medium-size (2.5-qt) donabe, it's about 7 cups (1.7 L) water plus 1½ cups (360 ml) or more cooked rice. Stir the water and rice thoroughly.

2. Cover and cook the rice over low to medium-low heat.

3. Once the porridge starts to simmer, uncover and cook over low heat until the porridge becomes almost like a paste. Stir occasionally to make sure the bottom does not burn. The cooking time varies depending on the size of the donabe. For a medium-size donabe, the cooking time could be about 1 hour.

4. Turn off the heat and let the donabe cool down for about 1 hour.

5. Remove the porridge completely. Wash the donabe thoroughly with a soft sponge and mild soap and dry completely before using it.

   Warning: Because the outer bottom is not coated in glaze, the exposed clay bottom is especially water-absorbent. If you set a donabe over heat while the outer bottom is wet, the moisture could expand in the donabe body and cause cracking. So always make sure the outer bottom is dry before heating.

Cooking Safety

There are dos and don'ts when using donabe. It's important to know the proper handling of donabe in order to cook safely.

Donabe is intended for cooking over an open flame or a gas stove top. It's also safe in the oven. Do not use it on an electric element, as the heat won't distribute the same way as with a flame. Donabe cannot be used on induction-heat cooktops either, unless you purchase an induction-safe donabe, with a treatment (such as a metal plate on the outer bottom) in the donabe body making it compatible with induction heat.

It's best to have at least one portable butane gas burner and butane cartridges at home. With a portable burner, you can enjoy tabletop communal-style cooking, whether indoors or out. Portable butane gas burners are widely available online and at Japanese and other Asian markets. We make some recommendations in the Kitchen Tools appendix (page 296) in this book.

In general, a donabe pot should not be heated when empty because it could crack, unless the manufacturer's instructions say it is safe to do so. Some types of donabe are made with extra heat-resistant clay or treated with a special glaze that allows them to be heated empty.

Donabe are not suitable for deep-frying. The porous body could absorb the oil and cause damage to the body or,

worse, a fire. You can, however, safely sauté ingredients in a little oil over moderate heat.

You shouldn't rapidly chill a hot donabe (such as by plunging it into cold water) or set a cold donabe over heat. Acute temperature changes can shock a donabe and cause cracking. Also, unless you know your donabe is extra heat-resistant, start the heat level at medium or lower so that you can prevent possible cracking from heat shock.

Troubleshooting

Even when you take good care of your donabe, mistakes can happen. Here are some tips for how to solve some of the possible problems:

Burned food. If you burn food in a donabe and it stains, fill it with warm water and scrape with a wooden spatula or scrub it gently with a soft-scrub sponge. Repeating the process will eventually help remove the stain completely. For very stubborn stains, boil water in the donabe for 5 to 10 minutes and let it cool down before scraping.

Minor cracks. Because donabe expands and shrinks during cooking, small cracks in the clay body (which are natural and even welcome) could expand further and cause leaking. This is rare, however. If the inside of the donabe has a small crack that causes leaking, don't panic. Repeat the seasoning procedure (see page 10) by making porridge in the donabe.

Strong odors. If a strong food smell remains after leaving pungent food inside the donabe, fill the donabe 80 percent full of water, add a small scoop of already steeped green tea leaves, and simmer for about 10 minutes. The used tea leaves can absorb the smell in the donabe.

Moldy odors. For a moldy smell caused by not drying the donabe properly, fill the donabe 80 percent full of water, add a few tablespoons of distilled vinegar, and simmer for about 10 minutes. Repeat the seasoning procedure by making porridge in the donabe (see page 8).

How to Use This Book

Heat levels indicated in the recipes are based on conventional home-kitchen gas stoves. For high-caloric stoves designed for professional use, adjust to a lower heat level (for example, if a recipe says to use medium-high heat, try medium or medium-low heat).

Play with the recipes and create your own style. Don't feel too constricted by the recipes. We hope you will feel free to adjust them to suit yourself. The stated ingredient amounts, cooking times, and heat levels are what work best for us in our kitchens. Everybody has different tastes when it comes to such things as salt level, heat level, and the consistency of sauces, so take these recipes as our suggestions and adjust them to your preferences.

Measurement and conversion charts. For rice measurement, we use the traditional Japanese measuring unit called *go* (we call it a "rice cup" in English). In Japan, this unit of measure has been used for hundreds of years and is still used today for measuring both sake and rice. Traditionally, a square wooden cup called *masu* was used. Now the *masu* is more commonly used simply as a cup for drinking sake. (You may have experienced drinking sake out of a square wooden *masu*, as it is very traditional.) The traditional Japanese rice measurement is 1 rice cup = US ¾ cup = 180 ml.

For other, nonrice measurements, this book uses US measurements with metric equivalents given in parentheses. Conversions are rounded up or down in the recipes. Teaspoons and tablespoons are standard for both US and metric measurements.

Many of the ingredients in the book may be new to you. There is an extensive glossary at the back (see page 288) that describes these ingredients and offers guidance on where you can buy them.

 VEGAN

 VEGETARIAN

IGA, HOME OF
AUTHENTIC DONABE

Iga, a historic province in a mountainous countryside, is situated in the present-day Mie Prefecture about 210 miles (340 km) southwest of Tokyo. It is one of the oldest and most prestigious pottery-making regions in Japan. The central district forms around Iga Ueno Castle (originally built in the late sixteenth century), which is surrounded by widespread, serene natural scenery. With its rich history and ecology, Iga offers a number of premium local artisanal specialties such as rice, sake, beef, pork, and rope making, in addition to its famous *Iga-yaki* (Iga-style) pottery.

Iga was the birthplace of Basho Matsuo (1644–94), the most revered haiku poet in history. Iga was also historically famous for mastery in the art of ninja and is a birthplace of Iga ninja clans. Ninja from Iga were considered to be among the most skilled elites during the age of samurai. There has been an ongoing rumor in past centuries that Bashō Matsuo, who traveled across the country in the late seventeenth century and wrote numerous haiku poems during his journey, was actually a ninja. He traveled about 1,500 miles (2,400 km) on foot in just six months at the age of forty-five, which was considered to be very old back when the average life expectancy for men was less than fifty years. Unless you were specially trained physically, completing such a rigorous journey at that age, including under some extremely harsh weather conditions, would have been almost impossible. The truth of the legend continues to be in question.

The history of *Iga-yaki* pottery dates back almost thirteen hundred years. *Iga-yaki* developed because the clay in this region has exceptional heat-resistant qualities when fired and because of the abundant red pine forests, which yielded ideal firewood for the kilns. The term *Iga-yaki* refers not only to the pottery made *in* Iga, but also to any pottery made from the clay of the region, known as "breathing clay."

About four million years ago, the region of Iga used to be part of the bed of Lake Biwa (today's Lake Biwa is still the largest lake in Japan), and clay for *Iga-yaki* pottery comes from this prehistoric layer of earth. This clay contains many fossilized microorganisms. When the clay is shaped and fired at extremely high temperatures, the microorganisms are completely burned to the point of carbonization, leaving behind tiny holes. Thus, *Iga-yaki* donabe is especially porous and has a higher capacity for heat retention. *Iga-yaki* donabe breathes, and fine bubbles come out through the *kannyu* (good cracks) of the glaze to circulate gently inside during cooking. Also, Iga's prehistoric clay is naturally very coarse. With all these remarkable characteristics, Iga's historic clay is considered to be the ideal clay for making donabe, and *Iga-yaki* donabe has been the top choice for many chefs and avid home cooks.

Iga-yaki donabe is famous for its bold, rustic beauty, attributed to the natural characteristics of the Iga clay. The surface can sometimes even appear cracked or chipped, but these "flaws" are part of its character. You can feel the power of the earth and the history of this pottery, which matures gracefully to improve with age. The more you use your donabe, the more you will come to admire and appreciate it—a stark contrast to many objects made today, which become less functional and less beautiful with use.

During the medieval era, *Iga-yaki* was renowned for its use in tea ceremonies. Tea masters revered the tea ceremony wares, especially for their "aesthetic of discord," an unevenness in the glaze caused by the ashes in the kiln. The exact form this unevenness takes is beyond

the artisan's control, though he or she can calculate and induce it to some extent. This "intentionally accidental" aesthetic, caused by the combination of Iga's coarse clay and the natural glaze, was called *keshiki* (scenery). *Keshiki* has been a leading factor in the Japanese way of appreciating pottery's beauty. It's caused by factors beyond a human's power to control, and is a part of what we call *wabi-sabi,* the appreciation of the beauty to be found in imperfection and unevenness.

Iga-yaki became widely popular for donabe and other everyday cookware during the Edo Period during the nineteenth century. Today, there are just over twenty *Iga-yaki* pottery producers, plus many individual artisans in the region, and *Iga-yaki* carries on its heritage to serve people with its authentic beauty and utility.

Nagatani-en is one of the oldest and most highly respected producers of Iga-yaki donabe and other pottery. Nagatani-en was established in 1832 and has been run by the Nagatani family for eight generations. Nagatani-en is situated in a quiet valley, surrounded by nature. The area is so pristine that visiting there can make you feel as if you had time-traveled hundreds of years into the past. It's a spiritual place with the strong power of earth.

The whole property of Nagatani-en is historical. On the hillside sits Japan's largest remaining historical connected climbing kiln (a traditional style of kiln in Japan, originally brought from China via Korea, with each kiln connected to another on a slope), designated as a tangible cultural property of Japan. The kiln has sixteen levels and was in active operation until the 1970s. Currently it is not in use, but another climbing kiln right next to it operates on special occasions a few times a year.

At Nagatani-en, artisans make numerous kinds of *Iga-yaki* pottery every day. Nagatani-en's donabe lineup is highly sought after for its beauty, utility, and durability. All its donabe are handcrafted, and it takes about two weeks to produce each one. Every donabe shows the true identity of *Iga-yaki,* and each is made to work to its full potential.

The person behind the creation of a number of unique donabe styles is Yuji Nagatani, the chairman of Nagatani-en and the seventh-generation of this family-run artisan pottery. He is a charismatic and energetic character. He loves to eat and drink, and his goal is to craft donabe that will make cooks and diners happy. Yuji feels that while it's important to carry on and preserve the traditions of *Iga-yaki* pottery, those traditions also need to evolve constantly to better serve people's changing needs. Just as every *Iga-yaki* donabe is unique and no two (even in the same design) are identical, every moment in life is a once-in-a-lifetime treasure (*ichigo-ichie,* a term used to explain both pottery and a philosophy). Every dish, every meal, every meeting, and every conversation happens once in a lifetime and is different the next time—if there is a next time. So as a pottery producer, Yuji's mission is to continue to make the kinds of donabe that meet people's needs, and he hopes to help make meals more enjoyable and something special each and every time.

Yuji Nagatani's oldest child, Yasuhiro, is now the president of Nagatani-en, and the rest of their children are also involved in Nagatani-en's operation, both in Iga and in Tokyo, with a mission to bring happy donabe life to people.

SAPPORO

SENDAI

KYOTO

TOKYO

OSAKA

IGA

Nagatani-en's seventh-generation chairman, Yuji Nagatani

Opposite: Nagatani-en's historic sixteen-level climbing kiln, built in the early nineteenth century

How Donabe Is Made

At Nagatani-en, the clay can be formed either entirely by hand on a wheel, or by using a plaster mold. The entire process takes about two weeks for each donabe to be made.

Here is the process of making hand-shaped donabe at Nagatani-en:

1. Kneading clay: It's called "chrysanthemum kneading" because the shape of the clay resembles chrysanthemum flower petals. This process creates texture and pushes out air.

2. Forming: Forming by hand on a wheel requires special expertise to achieve an even shape and thickness. Formed donabe is left to dry overnight.

3. Shaving: Each donabe is shaved with a plane to show the rough, porous surface and so that the surface area will become larger. This step ensures that a wider surface area will be in direct contact with the heat when the finished donabe is used for cooking. Shaved donabe is left to dry further for half a day.

4. Attaching knob and handles: The handles of donabe are called ears, and once they are shaped, they are glued to the clay.

5. Drying: Before the first firing, donabe is air-dried for about a week. Because *Iga-yaki* donabe has a thick body, it must dry slowly.

6. Initial firing: Donabe is fired in a kiln at 1,290°F (700°C) for about eight hours and then cooled down for more than twenty-four hours.

7. Glazing: This is done in two steps. After the initial glazing, a denser glaze is applied shortly after.

8. Final firing: Donabe is fired again in a kiln at 2,200°F (1,200°C) for about twelve hours and left in the kiln for an additional twelve hours or longer to cool down.

9. Out of the kiln: Even after twelve hours of cooling, these donabe are still very warm and must be allowed to cool further.

10. Inspection: Once completely cooled down, each donabe is carefully checked by expert eyes and then put in a box, ready to ship.

Donabe set out to dry
after shaping

Opposite: Forming a donabe

Attaching a handle to a donabe

Opposite: Attaching a knob to a donabe

Donabe drying before
initial firing

Opposite: Donabe ready
to be fired in the kiln

Glaze is applied before the
second firing of a donabe

Yuji Nagatani examining a newly
formed donabe handcrafted by one
of Nagatani-en's artisans

DONABE STYLE DINNERS

Donabe cooking is all about sharing. Whether it's at home or in a restaurant, a simple family meal, or a special dinner party with guests, donabe can make the experience more fun and memorable.

It's the communal dining experience that donabe creates, and it teaches the concept of *ichigo-ichie*—every moment is a once-in-a-lifetime treasure.

From Iga to Los Angeles, the following are some of our donabe experiences and serving ideas.

Donabe dinner with the Nagatani family in their 200-year-old house, Omoya (designated as a tangible cultural property in 2014)

**THE NAGATANI FAMILY'S
IGA-STYLE INOSHISHI NABE
(WILD BOAR HOT POT) DINNER**

Baby turnip, sautéed in sesame oil

Sun-dried vegetables, including hinona
daikon and *makomotake* mushrooms,
grilled and served with *shio-koji*
(salt-fermented rice *koji*) and *shoyu-koji*
(soy-fermented rice *koji*) condiments

Wild boar hot pot (recipe not included)

Rice and pickles

TEMPLE-STYLE VEGAN DONABE MEAL

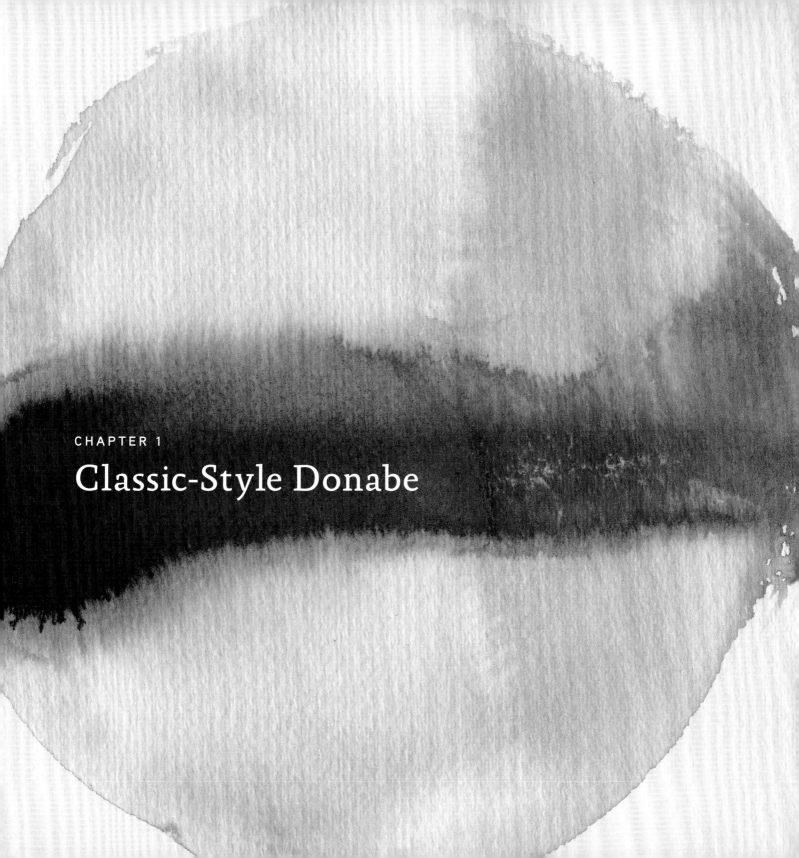

CHAPTER 1

Classic-Style Donabe

Classic-Style Donabe

The classic-style donabe is the most common style, the kind used for *nabe* (hot-pot) dishes, in which a family or group of friends shares a simmering pot of various ingredients cooked in a broth. The standard shape for these dishes is round and deep and comes in two pieces, the base (or bowl) and the lid. In Japan, especially during wintertime, *nabe* is a very popular way to eat.

If you are buying your first donabe, we recommend a medium-size one that will make enough for two to five people (a 2- to 2.5-quart/2- to 2.5-liter capacity). Unless otherwise noted, the recipes in this chapter can be made in a medium-size donabe.

For donabe collectors, there are various designs and sizes of classic-style donabe you can use, depending on the type of dish, style of presentation, and size of serving. If you want to make a long-simmered dish such as Napa Cabbage Hot Pot (page 75), a deeper-bodied standard shape would be easiest to use. For a dish like Simmered Tofu Hot Pot (page 57), a shallow-bodied (often called "Kyoto-style") donabe would make a more appealing presentation, and would make it easier to pick the ingredients from the broth, too. For a special occasion, you can show off an artisan's hand-designed donabe. Variations in shapes and designs are endless. There are even flat-bottomed, oval, and square donabe for different cooking, serving, or aesthetic preferences. But if you have one donabe of the standard shape, you can comfortably enjoy any of these classic-style donabe recipes.

Most important, it's about sharing a pot of food together at the table—the spirit of communal dining. You can either cook these dishes at a kitchen stove and then bring the donabe to the table to serve, or else set a portable gas burner on the dining table and cook and eat communally. For most of the hot-pot recipes in this chapter, we suggest that you cook and serve at the dining table.

DEEPER-BODIED CLASSIC-STYLE DONABE—the most common type, with a curved base. There are both thin-bodied and thick-bodied kinds. The thin-bodied kind is more suitable for quick simmers or making hot pots. The thicker body is more multipurpose, as not only can you use it for hot pots, but it can also work nicely for making stew, braising, or even making rice.

SHALLOW-BODIED CLASSIC-STYLE DONABE—often called "Kyoto-style" donabe because the shallow body is widely appreciated in Kyoto-style cuisine. This style is more suitable for quick simmering or when you want to make it easier to pick up the components without losing them deep inside the broth.

Ingredient Substitutions

With most of the hot-pot recipes, you don't need to stick to all the recipe ingredients exactly—you can use your own judgment when swapping out ingredients. For example, if a recipe doesn't call for tofu but you want to use it, just go for it. If you can't find *mitsuba*, use chives instead or simply omit the herbs altogether. Instead of *komatsuna*, you can use a different leaf vegetable including spinach, watercress, or dandelion.

Shime—The Finishing Course

Many of the hot-pot recipes in this chapter involve a *shime* (SHE-meh), a finishing course. After you finish most of the dish, save enough of the broth in the pot to cook rice or noodles in the fortified liquid. The leftover broth has a rich flavor after it has been reduced and infused with all the ingredients, and many hot-pot lovers look forward to this part of the meal as much as the main course. To cook a *shime* course, once you finish all or most of the ingredients cooked in the broth, return the broth to a simmer and add your choice of starch (suggestions are listed below). If the broth is not seasoned (such as in Dashi-Rich Shabu-Shabu on page 77 or Napa Cabbage Hot Pot on page 75), you can season the broth with a small addition of soy sauce or salt. This can be done either directly in the donabe before adding the starch, or everyone can season their own serving of broth to their individual preference at the table.

Here are some guidelines on cooking rice and noodles for the *shime:*

Rice *(Ojiya)*. Rice cooked in seasoned broth is called *ojiya* (see Glossary, page 288). To start, add warm or hot cooked rice to the simmering broth, about half to two-thirds of the broth by volume. Stir and return to a simmer. If you like (it's a must for most Japanese people), gradually pour in some whisked egg and cover the donabe. Cook for 1 to 2 minutes, or until the egg is cooked to your preferred doneness.

Noodles (Soba, Udon, Somen, Ramen or Rice Noodles). Precook the noodles in boiling water until they are still slightly firm. Drain, and rinse in cold water if instructed by package. Add to the simmering broth, up to about two-thirds of the broth by volume. If you use frozen soba, udon or instant dry ramen noodles, add them directly to the simmering broth and cook until ready (refer to the package instructions). The instant dry ramen absorbs more broth compared to fresh or dry kinds that require precooking, so adjust the amount of the broth to reserve accordingly.

SERVES 4
as part of a multicourse meal

EQUIPMENT:
One 1.5-quart/1.5 L or larger classic-style donabe

VARIATION:
For a version with an extra rich broth, start with 3¼ cups (800 ml) cold-infused Kombu Dashi (page 277), with the kombu used for infusion, instead of starting with water and kombu to soak for 30 minutes in the donabe.

Simmered Tofu Hot Pot

Yu-dofu

3¼ cups (800 ml) water

2 (4-inch/10 cm) square pieces kombu

2 tablespoons sake

1 teaspoon sea salt

5 ounces (150 g) enoki mushrooms, trimmed

¼ ounce (7 g) tororo kombu (thinly shaved seasoned kombu; optional), fluffed by hand to about 1 loose cup (240 ml)

1 (19-ounce/560 g) package soft tofu, cut into 6 pieces

About ¼ cup (60 ml) 3-2-1 Ponzu Sauce (page 279) or Umami-Rich Soy Sauce (page 285), for serving

Ground toasted white sesame seeds (see sidebar, page 58), for serving

Shichimi togarashi (Japanese seven-spice blend), for serving

This simple and satisfying dish is popular in homes across Japan. The basic style consists of only tofu, water, and kombu (kelp) and is enjoyed with ponzu sauce or your choice of condiments. My version includes enoki mushrooms and *tororo* kombu (thinly shaved seasoned kombu; see Glossary, page 288), which add layers of flavor to the broth. I highly recommend that you sip just the broth first before adding the ponzu, to appreciate its elegant, soothing flavor. Umami-Rich Soy Sauce (page 285) is also good with this dish in place of the ponzu.—Naoko

Combine the water and kombu in the donabe and let the kombu soak for 30 minutes. Set over medium heat, uncovered. Just before the broth comes to a simmer, remove the kombu and discard or save for another use. Add the sake and salt.

Pull apart the enoki mushrooms and add to the broth. Add the fluffed *tororo kombu* to the broth by spreading it over the surface. Add the tofu and cover. Bring to a gentle simmer, and then turn off the heat. Let it rest for 5 minutes.

Serve in individual bowls at the table with the condiments on the side.

continued

NOTE:
If you purchase already toasted sesame seeds, it's still best to toast them again, as the fragrance is much more aromatic when the sesame seeds are freshly toasted. Already ground sesame seeds are also available at markets, but for the same reason, it's recommended that you grind freshly toasted sesame seeds yourself.

Simmered Tofu Hot Pot, continued

How to Toast and Grind Sesame Seeds

To toast sesame seeds, I use a very convenient Japanese traditional sesame roaster called *horoku* (see page 296). I put the sesame seeds in it and toast them over medium-low to low heat, shaking often, for a couple of minutes, or until aromatic. If you don't have a *horoku*, it's fine to use a small sauté pan.

To grind sesame seeds, you can use a regular mortar and pestle, but for more effective grinding, a Japanese *suribachi* (mortar) and *surikogi* (pestle; see page 297) can be found at Japanese markets. You can then grind the sesame seeds to a coarse consistency for more texture, or to a fine consistency for more integration with the dish.

SERVES 4
*as part of a
multicourse meal*

EQUIPMENT:
One 1.5-quart/1.5 L or larger
classic-style donabe

Sun-Dried Mushroom and Tofu Hot Pot

Shojin Kinoko Nabe

7 ounces (200 g) enoki mushrooms

8 ounces (240 g) eryngii (king trumpet) mushrooms

5 ounces (150 g) shimeji mushrooms

3 cups (750 ml) water

1 (3 by 6-inch/7 by 15cm) square piece kombu

¼ cup (60 ml) sake

2 tablespoons mirin

2 tablespoons usukuchi shoyu (light-colored soy sauce)

1 (14-ounce/400 g) package soft tofu, cut into 8 pieces

5 ounces (150 g) mizuna (including stems), bottom ends trimmed and cut into 2-inch (5 cm) pieces

1 teaspoon thinly shredded yuzu rind or Meyer lemon rind

Shichimi togarashi (Japanese seven-spice blend), for serving

Whenever I serve this dish, guests are always surprised by how these few simple ingredients can produce such a rich and complex broth. The key is sun-drying the mushrooms for half a day to a full day, until they're semidried, before cooking. If you can't find a good outdoor space, use a sunny spot indoors to let the mushrooms sunbathe. The umami level of the mushrooms intensifies when they are dried in the sun, and the texture becomes meatier. If you can't find *enoki*, *eryngii*, or *shimeji* mushrooms, shiitake and *maitake* would also be good in this dish. Use at least two kinds of mushrooms.

Make sure you start heating the broth after adding the kombu and mushrooms, as the umami flavors are released from these ingredients during the slow heating process.—Naoko

To sun-dry the mushrooms, trim the enoki and pull them apart. Trim the *eryngii* mushrooms and cut them into ¼-inch (5 mm) slices. Leave the *shimeji* mushrooms whole, as it's easier to sun-dry them when they remain connected and trim them afterward.

Spread the mushrooms in baskets (or on trays) in an even layer only loosely overlapping. Leave the baskets in the sun outside, if possible, until the mushrooms have shrunk slightly and their surface is dry, 3 to 4 hours (on a hot summer day) to a full day (on a mild winter day) during the daytime. Turn the mushrooms over a couple of times

continued

during the drying period. When ready, rinse the mushrooms gently and quickly, and pat dry. Trim the *shimeji* mushrooms and pull apart.

Combine the water and kombu in the donabe and let the kombu soak for 30 minutes. Add the sake, mirin, soy sauce, and all the mushrooms. Cover and set over medium heat. Just before the broth comes to a simmer, remove the kombu.

Add the tofu and cover again. Bring to a gentle simmer and cook until the tofu is just heated through, 3 to 5 minutes. Add the mizuna and sprinkle with the yuzu rind. Let the mizuna wilt (about 1 minute or so), and then turn off the heat. Serve in individual bowls at the table and sprinkle with *shichimi togarashi*.

SERVES *4 to 6*
as part of a
multicourse meal

EQUIPMENT:
One 1.5-quart/1.5 L or larger
classic-style donabe

NOTE:
Nigari, a by-product of sea salt, is the extract of seawater.
In traditional tofu making in Japan, only *nigari* is used as
a coagulator of tofu, while commercial tofu may include
different kinds of coagulators. Liquid *nigari* can be found at
Japanese grocery stores and some online specialty stores.

Fresh Tofu

Yose-tofu

1 quart (1 L) pure, rich plain soy milk

2½ teaspoons (12.5 ml) liquid nigari
(see Note)

Umami-Rich Soy Sauce
(page 285),for serving

Ground toasted white sesame seeds
(see page 58), for serving

Extra-virgin olive oil, for serving

Flavored salt such as plum salt
(pickled-plum flavored salt) or
sea salt, for serving

As part of my donabe and Japanese cooking class, I also teach a tofu-making class. In the class, we first make soy milk from scratch, and from the soy milk we make fresh tofu. Although the steps are simple, the process of making soy milk requires quite a bit of labor and constant attention. The cleaning takes time, too. So in this recipe, we make it much easier and start with commercial soy milk. This way, you can easily make tofu for dinner after a long day at work or impress your guests at a dinner party without much hassle. Once you get your hands on good-quality soy milk (see Glossary, page 288), your fresh tofu will taste exceptional.—Naoko

Pour the soy milk into the donabe, cover, and set over medium heat. Stir every few minutes to make sure the bottom doesn't get burned. Once the soy milk reaches 176°F to 180°F (80°C to 82°C), turn off the heat and quickly stir in the liquid *nigari*. Cover the top of the donabe body tightly with foil and then cover with the lid (this will ensure that the seal is extra-tight). Let it rest for 30 minutes.

Serve immediately in individual bowls at the table. (Once the tofu has set, the longer you let it sit, the more the tofu tends to separate from the liquid. In that case, you can simply lightly drain the liquid out of the ladle as you scoop the tofu.) Enjoy with your choice of either Umami-Rich Soy Sauce and ground sesame seeds, or olive oil and salt.

Saikyo Miso

Saikyo miso is a type of sweet white miso from Kyoto, with a mild flavor that makes it extremely versatile in cooking. I use it for all different kinds of savory dishes, as well as in desserts such as ice cream and cookies.

It was first made in the early nineteenth century by Tanbaya Shigesuke, and specially presented at the Imperial Palace in Kyoto. Back then, it was simply called miso or white miso. In the high culture of the imperial court, this sweet white miso was extensively used in various traditional recipes, including ceremonial dishes.

Following the Meiji Restoration, Edo was renamed *Tokyo* (meaning "Eastern Capital"), and the capital was moved from Kyoto to Tokyo. Since then, Kyoto has been considered Saikyo ("Western Capital"), and consequently the sweet white miso from Kyoto has been called Saikyo miso. Saikyo miso has continued to be part of the traditional food culture of Kyoto. The imperial court culture's traditional *kyo-zoni* (Saikyo miso soup with mochi and vegetables) is now served as part of the celebration meal during New Year's holidays throughout Kyoto.

Kyle and I visited Honda Miso, the original Saikyo miso producer founded by Tanbaya Shigesuke in 1830. It has been run by the Honda family for eight generations. The shop is in their historic house, located near Kyoto's Imperial Palace. Junya Honda, the eighth generation of the family, took us to the production facility, surrounded by deep green forests and fields in Kyoto's Tanba region, about a two-hour drive away. The area is known for the purity of its water, which is essential in making high-quality miso. While the factory operation is very modern, with top-level quality and safety controls, the basic process of making Saikyo miso remains the same, and they say that the quality has actually improved thanks to the temperature-controlled facility.

Saikyo miso is known for its mild saltiness and rich sweetness. It is made from rice *koji* (malted rice), soy beans, and salt. While red miso (the most common type) is made from the same three ingredients, and contains 11 to 13 percent sodium, Saikyo miso's sodium content is only about 4.9 percent. More *koji* means sweeter miso, because during fermentation, enzymes in the *koji* work to turn carbohydrates into sugar. For Saikyo miso, the *koji*-to-soybeans ratio is 2:1, while for red miso, the ratio is usually about 1:1, or sometimes there is more soybean than *koji*.

The maturing period of Saikyo miso is only up to fourteen days, while red miso is aged from a few months to a few years. Therefore, Saikyo miso maintains mild and pure flavors, as well as a pale cream color.

In Japan, Saikyo miso is a protected brand name to be used only by its original producer, Honda Miso, and a few other producers who make the same traditional-style sweet white miso in Kyoto and are granted permission to use the name. Any miso made outside of Kyoto and labeled "Saikyo miso" is not the real thing.

True Saikyo miso can be found at Japanese markets in the United States. Although no substitute can impart the same flavor, you may, if necessary, substitute another sweet white miso for Saikyo miso. If you can only find regular white miso ("*shiro* miso"), which is less sweet and has a higher salt content, cut the quantity by one-half to two-thirds.—Naoko

Kyoto-Style Saikyo Miso Hot Pot
Saikyo Nabe

Pinch of sea salt

½ head green cabbage (about 10 ounces/300 g), cut into strips

1 medium carrot (about 3½ ounces/100 g), julienned into ⅛-inch (3 mm) strips

1 head broccoli (about 8 ounces/ 240 g), cut into bite-size pieces

1 russet or white potato (about 8 ounces/240 g), peeled and julienned into ¼-inch (5 mm) strips

1 pound (450 g) pork belly, cut into bite-size pieces

4 cups (1 L) Kombu and Bonito Dashi (page 274)

10 ounces (300 g) Saikyo miso or other sweet white miso

2 tablespoons white sesame paste (tahini is fine)

1½ teaspoons unseasoned rice vinegar, or more if desired

Karashi (Japanese mustard), for serving; can substitute Dijon mustard for a milder flavor

We tasted this *nabe* dish at the historic headquarters of the Saikyo miso maker Honda Miso in Kyoto, and we fell in love with the creamy broth and elegant flavor. The secret ingredient is a splash of vinegar, which adds a refreshing accent to the sweet miso flavor. You can also adjust the amount of Saikyo miso in this dish according to your taste.—Naoko

To cook the vegetables and meat: Bring a medium pot of water to a boil and add a generous pinch of salt. Add the cabbage and blanch until it's partly cooked but still crisp, about 30 seconds. Strain the cabbage out of the water and let it cool down. Using the same pot of water, repeat the process, first for the carrot and then for the broccoli, blanching each for 30 to 60 seconds. Finally, blanch the potato in the same pot of water for about 2 minutes, until slightly tender, and drain. Heat a sauté pan over medium and sauté the pork belly pieces just until the meat is cooked through, 2 to 3 minutes. Using a slotted spoon, transfer to a plate lined with paper towels to drain.

To make the broth: Pour the *dashi* into the donabe, cover, and set over medium-high heat. As soon as the broth starts to boil, turn down the heat to simmer. In a bowl, whisk together until smooth the Saikyo miso and sesame paste with a ladleful of broth from the donabe, and then stir the mixture into the donabe. Add the cabbage, potato, and pork belly, side by side, followed by the broccoli and carrot, pushing them between the other ingredients. Cover and bring back to a simmer and cook for another 3 to 5 minutes. Turn off the heat and drizzle with the vinegar.

Serve in individual bowls at table, with the *karashi* on the side.

EQUIPMENT:
One 2.5-quart/2.5 L or larger
classic-style donabe

SHIME (FINISHING COURSE) SUGGESTION:
Add either cooked or frozen udon
to the remaining broth.

Chicken Hot Pot

Tori-nabe

1 pound (450 g) boneless skinless chicken thighs, cut into large bite-size pieces

½ teaspoon sea salt

3 cups (720 ml) Chicken Dashi (page 278)

1 cup (240 ml) Kombu Dashi (page 277)

¼ cup (60 ml) sake

2½ to 3 tablespoons mirin

2½ to 3 tablespoons soy sauce

½ small head napa cabbage (about 10 ounces/300 g), cut into bite-size strips (separate the bottom and leafy parts)

2 negi (Japanese green onions), or 6 green onions (white and light green parts), thinly sliced on the diagonal

6 to 8 very small carrots, halved crosswise

8 ounces (240 g) assorted mushrooms

1 (14-ounce/400 g) package medium-firm tofu, cut into 8 pieces

5 ounces (150 g) mizuna (including stems), bottom ends trimmed and cut into 2-inch (5 cm) pieces

Yuzu-kosho, for serving

This *nabe* dish was made by Takako, the wife of Nagatani-en's chairman, Yuji, when we visited them in Iga. She blends Japanese chicken stock and kombu *dashi* for a complex yet clean flavor, but you can make it entirely with either kind of stock, if you like. Like most good cooks, she never measures or weighs the ingredients that go into this dish. So the measurements in this recipe are what I re-created from memory. The dish goes well with *yuzu-kosho* (see Glossary, page 288) as a condiment.—Naoko

Season the chicken all over with the salt. Let the chicken marinate for 15 to 30 minutes.

To make the broth: Combine the chicken *dashi*, kombu *dashi*, sake, mirin, and soy sauce in the donabe and add the bottom part of the napa cabbage. Cover and set over medium-high heat.

As soon as the broth starts to boil, turn down the heat to simmer. Add the chicken and the rest of the ingredients except for the mizuna. Cover again and bring back to a simmer. Simmer until everything is just cooked through, about 3 to 5 minutes. Add the mizuna and cook for 1 minute longer before turning off the heat. Serve in individual bowls at the table and enjoy with *yuzu-kosho*.

EQUIPMENT:
One 2.5-quart/2.5 L or larger
classic-style donabe

SHIME (FINISHING COURSE) SUGGESTION:
You can add cooked rice to the remaining broth and stir.
Then, once the rice is simmering, sprinkle a generous
amount of grated Parmesan cheese over it to finish. Freshly
ground black pepper is great with this course as well. *Sake-kasu*, Saikyo miso, and Parmesan cheese make a beautiful
marriage of Japanese and Western flavors.

Cod and Oysters in Sake Lees
Sake-kasu Nabe

A generous pinch of sea salt

1 medium russet potato, peeled and sliced into ⅓-inch (8 mm) rounds

4 cups (1 L) Kombu Dashi (page 277)

4 ounces (120 g) sake-kasu (sake lees paste)

2 ounces (60 g) Saikyo miso or other sweet white miso

5 to 6 leaves napa cabbage cut into bite-size strips (separate the bottom and leafy parts)

1 to 2 tablespoons usukuchi shoyu (light-colored soy sauce)

1 medium carrot (about 3 ounces/100 g), thinly-sliced

1 to 2 negi (Japanese green onions), or 3 to 4 green onions (white part only), thinly sliced on the diagonal

1 rectangular abura-age (fried tofu pouch), blanched and cut crosswise into 4 to 6 pieces (see Note page 104)

1 pound (450 g) black cod fillets

3 ounces (100 g) enoki mnushrooms, trimmed and pulled apart

8 ounces (250 g) freshly shucked or jarred oysters, rinsed thoroughly

5 ounces (150 g) mizuna, bottom ends trimmed and cut into 2-inch (5 cm) pieces

Yuzu-kosho (see page 295), for serving

Sake-kasu—sake lees—is a by-product of sake, the pressed mash that remains after sake is brewed. *Sake-kasu* is highly appreciated among Japanese people for its richness in both flavor and nutrition. It also contains a small percentage of alcohol. In Japan, it's commonly enjoyed as a drink by mixing with sugar and hot water in the wintertime, or used as an ingredient in a wide variety of dishes. *Sake-kasu* can be found in the refrigerated section of grocery stores. This hearty broth, made with *sake-kasu* and Saikyo miso, goes brilliantly with richly flavored ingredients such as cod and oysters.—Naoko

Bring a medium pot of water to a boil and add a generous pinch of salt. Add the potato slices and simmer until they are partially cooked, about 3 minutes. Drain and set aside.

In a bowl, combine a small ladleful of the kombu *dashi*, the *sake-kasu*, and the Saikyo miso and whisk together until smooth. Set aside.

Combine the remaining *Kombu dashi* and the bottom part of the napa cabbage in the donabe. Cover and set over medium-high heat. As soon as the broth starts to boil, turn down the heat to simmer. Whisk in the *sake-kasu* mixture and add the *usukuchi shoyu*.

Add the potato, carrot, remaining napa cabbage, *negi*, and *abura-age*. Cover again and bring back to a simmer. Cut the cod into 10-12 pieces and add to the donabe, simmer for a couple of minutes. Add the enoki mushrooms, oysters and mizuna. Cook until the oysters are plump and everything is cooked through, about 2 to 3 minutes, and then turn off the heat. Serve in individual bowls at the table and enjoy with *Yuzu-kosho*.

Prepared ingredients ready
to cook in a donabe

For *shime* (finishing course),
cooked rice and Parmesan
cheese are added to the broth.
It's like a creamy cheese risotto

EQUIPMENT:
One 2.5-quart/2.5 L or larger
classic-style donabe

NOTE:
Although it's optional, I highly recommend sun-drying the
napa cabbage leaves for half a day or so before cutting and
cooking. Just spread the leaves in a basket or tray and leave
it out under the sun. This gentle drying makes the napa
cabbage richer in umami flavor and natural sweetness.

Napa Cabbage Hot Pot

Pien-ro Nabe

4¼ cups (a little more than 1 L) water

4 medium dried shiitake mushrooms, quickly rinsed

1 (2 by 4-inch/5 by 10 cm) piece kombu

8 ounces (240 g) boneless skinless chicken thighs, cut into bite-size pieces

½ teaspoon sea salt, plus more for serving

¼ cup (60 ml) sake

About ⅓ to ½ head napa cabbage (about 1½ pound/700 g), cut into ⅓-inch (1 cm) strips crosswise (separate the bottom and leafy parts; see Note above)

8 ounces (240 g) thinly sliced pork belly, cut into bite-size pieces

3 ounces (100 g) enoki mushrooms, trimmed and pulled apart

1½ ounce (50 g) bean thread (cellophane noodles; see Note on page 76)

½ to 1 tablespoon toasted sesame oil

Ichimi togarashi (Japanese ground chiles), for serving

A renowned Japanese writer introduced this simple *nabe* dish, said to have originated in China, to *nabe*-loving home cooks in Japan. While the recipe has many manifestations, *Pien-ro nabe* is all about appreciating the natural flavors of its ingredients and broth. The most important rule is "Do not add anything extra," or it will become something else. It's the art of minimalism.

Infusing the kombu and dry shiitake overnight is also important to achieve the very rich flavor of the broth. The dish is not seasoned in the donabe (except that the chicken is lightly preseasoned in salt to concentrate its flavor), so you season it when serving, with salt and *ichimi togarashi* (Japanese ground chiles). The star ingredient of the dish is napa cabbage, so don't be overwhelmed by the amount of cabbage going into the donabe! After the long simmering, it becomes so sweet and tender, it almost melts in your mouth.

When I need to serve six to eight people, I just double the quantities and use a larger donabe. This dish is very easy to prepare, and it is always a crowd pleaser.—Naoko

Combine the water, dried mushrooms, and kombu in a large bowl. Cover and let it infuse for at least 6 to 24 hours (keep in the refrigerator if infusing overnight). Remove the rehydrated mushrooms, gently squeeze out the liquid into the bowl, and then cut off the mushroom stems and discard. Cut the caps in half and put them back in the bowl.

continued

NOTE:
Dry bean thread (cellophane noodles) can be added directly to the pot, but if you find the noodles are too long to fit the donabe, soak them in cold water for 5 to 10 minutes until soft enough to handle, and then cut into 4- to 6-inch (10 to 15 cm) lengths.

SHIME (FINISHING COURSE) SUGGESTION:
Season the broth with a drizzle of soy sauce to taste; add cooked rice and finish by gradually pouring in a couple of whisked eggs to make *ojiya*. Once the eggs are cooked to your desired consistency, garnish with a generous amount of minced green onion. Don't miss this *shime* course, as it's the real jewel of this dish. Quick-Pickled Kabu in Shio-Koji (page 282) can make a nice accompaniment for it.

Napa Cabbage Hot Pot, continued

Season the chicken with the salt. Let the chicken marinate for 15 to 30 minutes.

Transfer the infused water with the rehydrated mushroom caps and kombu into the donabe (strain first if there are any gritty particles left from the dried mushrooms); add the sake and the bottom of the napa cabbage. Cover and set over medium heat. Just before the broth comes to a simmer, remove the kombu. If a foam rises, skim lightly once. Turn down the heat to maintain a gentle simmer. Cover again and simmer gently until the napa cabbage is soft, about 20 minutes.

Add both meats and cover the surface entirely with the remaining napa cabbage. (You might think there is not enough broth at this point, but the napa cabbage will cook down and release a lot of moisture.) Cover with the lid and turn up the heat to medium-high. As soon as the broth starts to boil, turn down the heat. Simmer gently until the napa cabbage is very soft, about 20 minutes. Add the enoki mushrooms and bean thread. Cook for an additional 1 to 2 minutes. Turn off the heat and drizzle with the sesame oil.

To serve at the table, first, put a pinch each of salt and *ichimi togarashi* into each individual bowl and pour in a small ladleful of the broth, followed by the other ingredients cooked in the broth. Although it's very hard to resist, make sure you save a good amount of the broth after serving for the *shime*.

EQUIPMENT:
One 2.5-quart/2.5 L or larger
classic-style donabe

NOTE:
Paper-thin slices of meat for shabu-shabu or slightly thicker slices for sukiyaki can be found at Japanese markets. If your butcher cannot provide such a thin slice, you can partially freeze a block of meat (rib-eye or top sirloin for beef, never been frozen), and then try to slice it as thinly as possible.

For more complexity and a lighter-colored soy sauce, you can replace 2 tablespoons of the *usukuchi shoyu* with *shiro shoyu* (white soy sauce).

Dashi-Rich Shabu-Shabu
Dashi Shabu

3 ounces (100 g) burdock, peeled into thin strips (including outer peels; see page 288)

6 negi (Japanese green onions), or 2 bunches green onions (white part only), very thinly sliced on the diagonal

10 ounces (300 g) thinly sliced beef (see Note)

10 ounces (300 g) thinly sliced pork belly (see Note)

1 (14-ounce/400 g) package medium-firm tofu, cut into 8 pieces

1 medium carrot (about 3 ounces/ 100 g), peeled into thin strips

3 ounces (100 g) daikon, peeled into thin strips (outer peels discarded)

½ bunch spinach (about 5 ounces/150 g)

5 ounces (150 g) enoki mushrooms, trimmed and pulled apart

3 ounces (100 g) nira (garlic chives), bottom ends trimmed

continued

Shabu-shabu is a popular Japanese *nabe* dish in which you quickly swish paper-thin meat in simmering water and enjoy it with a dipping sauce. This is my version of shabu-shabu, which I like even more than the regular style that starts with just kombu and water for the broth and is served with ponzu sauce. In my version, I use my rich Kombu and Bonito Dashi (page 274) for the base broth and serve it with a soy- and mirin-based dipping sauce and a wasabi dipping sauce. I suggest you first cook only the *negi* and meat just briefly and enjoy it in a dipping sauce before adding the other ingredients. The flavor is quite sensational.—Naoko

Soak the burdock in cold water for a few minutes and drain. (This keeps the burdock from discoloring the broth.)

Set up a portable gas burner and arrange your vegetables, meat, and tofu on a platter at the table.

Make the soy and mirin sauce: Combine 1¼ cups (300 ml) *dashi*, mirin, and usukuchi shoyu in a saucepan and bring to simmer over medium heat. Remove from the heat and let it cool down completely. Transfer to a small pitcher or a bowl. Pour about 3 tablespoons per person into small serving bowls.

To make the wasabi and sesame oil sauce: For each person, pour about 1 tablespoon of the sesame oil into a small serving bowl and mix with about ¼ teaspoon of salt and a dab of wasabi paste. Adjust the amount of the wasabi according to your taste.

continued

SHIME (FINISHING COURSE) SUGGESTION:
Somen noodles are my favorite. You can lightly season the broth with soy sauce and mirin to taste before adding the somen, or simply season with salt and pepper in your bowl upon serving. Once it's ready, garnish with minced green onions.—Naoko

Ingredients, continued

9¼ cups (2.3 L) Kombu and Bonito Dashi (page 274), plus about 2 cups (500 ml) extra if needed for replenishment

3 tablespoons plus 1 teaspoon (50 ml) mirin

3 tablespoons plus 1 teaspoon (50 ml) usukuchi shoyu (light-colored soy sauce; see Note)

¼ cup (60 ml) or more toasted sesame oil

1 teaspoon or more sea salt

Wasabi paste

Dashi-Rich Shabu-Shabu, continued

Pour the remaining 8 cups of *dashi* into the donabe. Cover and bring to a high simmer over medium-high heat. To initiate, add some *negi* to the broth and spread evenly. Immediately add some beef or pork to spread over the *negi*. Pick up the meat and negi together as they are cooked, and enjoy with either dipping sauce.

From this point, continue to cook the remaining ingredients and enjoy with the dipping sauces as you cook. Skim the broth as necessary. If you want to cook different kinds of vegetables and have them ready at the same time, root vegetables like daikon and burdock take longer to cook (2 to 3 minutes), so you can time accordingly. If the broth is becoming too reduced, replenish with extra *dashi*.

SERVES 4

EQUIPMENT:
One 1.8-quart/1.8 L or larger
classic-style donabe

SHIME (FINISHING COURSE) SUGGESTION:
My top choice is soba, especially because duck and soba
is a classic combination in Japanese food. Once you taste
it, I'm sure you will understand why. You can heat the
cooked soba noodles in the broth and serve as a noodle
soup straight out of the donabe, or use the hot broth as
a dipping sauce for cold soba.

Duck and Tofu Hot Pot
Kamo Tofu Nabe

2 medium (about 1 pound/450 g total) duck
breast halves, excess skin trimmed

2 teaspoons sea salt

2¼ cups (540 ml) Kombu Dashi (page 277)

²⁄₃ cup (160 ml) sake

⅓ cup (80 ml) mirin

¼ cup (60 ml) soy sauce

1 negi (Japanese green onion), or 3 green
onions (white and green parts), thinly sliced
on the diagonal

1 (14-ounce/400 g) package soft tofu, cut
into 8 pieces

5 ounces (150 g) shimeji mushrooms,
trimmed

1 tablespoon finely grated peeled ginger

2 tablespoons kuzuko (kudzu starch) or
katakuriko (potato starch)

½ bunch watercress, bottom ends trimmed

Shredded yuzu rind or Meyer lemon rind,
for serving

Ground sansho (Japanese mountain
pepper; optional), for serving

**This recipe is inspired by a hot-pot dish I had in Kyoto many
years ago. The succulent duck and silky tofu in a slightly
thickened broth is both elegant and satisfying.—Naoko**

Using a paring knife, score the skin of the duck breasts crosswise at
¼-inch (6 mm) intervals. Be careful not to penetrate the meat. Season
the duck breasts all over with the salt. Let the breasts marinate in the
refrigerator for at least 1 hour and up to 24 hours.

Heat a sauté pan over medium heat. Pat both sides of the duck dry
with a paper towel and place the breasts, skin-side down, in the pan.
Immediately turn down the heat to lower medium-low and gradually
render the fat from the skin until the skin is lightly browned and crisp,
about 8 to 10 minutes. Be careful not to cook the breast meat. Transfer
the duck to a cutting board. Pat dry and slice the breast crosswise along
the scored lines.

Combine 2 cups (480 ml) of the *dashi* with the sake, mirin, and soy
sauce in the donabe. Cover and bring to a simmer over medium-high
heat. Add the *negi*, tofu and *shimeji*, and cover again. As soon as the
broth starts to boil, turn down the heat to simmer and add the ginger.
In a cup, whisk together the *kuzuko* and the remaining ¼ cup (60 ml)
dashi; gradually stir about three-quarters of the mixture (or more if you
like the broth to be thicker) into the broth.

Add the duck to the broth, and simmer for a couple of minutes or until
the meat is cooked half way, then add the watercress and yuzu rind to
cook for another minute or so. Turn off the heat. Serve in individual
bowls at the table, and sprinkle with some ground *sansho*, if you like.

SERVES 4
as part of a
multicourse meal

EQUIPMENT:
One 1.5-quart/1.5 L or larger
classic-style donabe

Niigata-Style Sake-Rich Hot Pot
Sake Nabe

1¼ cups (300 ml) Kombu and Bonito Dashi
(page 274)

2 tablespoons soy sauce

1 tablespoon mirin

4 to 5 leaves napa cabbage from a medium
head, cut into bite-size strips (separate the
bottom and leafy parts)

10 ounces (300 g) thinly sliced pork belly,
cut into 2-inch (5 cm) strips

1 negi (Japanese green onion), or 2 green
onions (white part only), thinly sliced on
the diagonal

3 ounces (100 g) shimeji mushrooms,
trimmed

3 ounces (100 g) enoki mushrooms,
trimmed and pulled apart

2 medium shiitake mushrooms,
trimmed and halved

2 ounces (60 g) carrots, julienned

2 ounces (60 g) nira (garlic chives),
bottom ends trimmed, then cut into
3-inch (7.5 cm) pieces

8 ounces (250 g) daikon, peeled, grated,
and lightly strained

About ½ cup plus 2 tablespoons
(150 ml) sake

A generous handful baby mizuna (optional)

Kanzuri (fermented chili paste from Niigata)
or yuzu-kosho, for serving

Niigata, a northern prefecture facing the Sea of Japan, is a famous rice- and sake-making region. When I visited Asahi Shuzo, maker of the famous sake Kubota, I had an opportunity to have a sake dinner with the brewery master. I was fascinated by the sake-rich *nabe* dish, which involved pouring a generous amount of freshly bottled sake directly into a donabe packed with meat and vegetables. A mound of grated daikon placed on top reminded me of the heavy snow of the region's long wintertime.

The key ingredient for this dish is sake, so I suggest using a freshly-opened, good quality bottle.—Naoko

Set a portable gas burner on the dining table. To make the broth, combine the *dashi*, soy sauce, and mirin in a small bowl.

Spread the bottom part of the napa cabbage in the bottom of a donabe, and then arrange the leafy parts of the napa cabbage, pork, negi, all the mushrooms, carrots and nira in an attractive pattern in a donabe. Top with a mound of grated daikon in the center. Pour in the broth.

Once your guests are seated, set the donabe over medium-high heat on the portable gas burner and pour the sake into the donabe. Cover, and as soon as the broth starts to boil, turn down the heat to simmer. Stir, and then simmer for a few minutes or until everything is cooked through. Add the mizuna and turn off the heat. Serve in individual bowls and enjoy with *kanzuri* or *yuzu-kosho*.

SHIME (FINISHING COURSE) SUGGESTION:
My recommendation is, of course, ramen, in recognition of its ramen roots. Add the ramen noodles to the remaining broth and serve. I like to serve this with a generous amount of minced green onions and freshly ground black pepper.

Chicken Meatballs in Hot Sesame Miso Broth
Tan Tan Nabe

1 pound (450 g) ground chicken

1 large egg

1 tablespoon katakuriko (potato starch)

¼ teaspoon sea salt

¼ teaspoon freshly ground black pepper

¼ cup (60 ml), plus 1 tablespoon sake

4 teaspoons finely grated peeled fresh ginger

1 tablespoon toasted sesame oil

1 clove garlic, finely grated

2 negi (Japanese green onion) or 4-5 green onions, minced (white part only)

1 teaspoon tobanjan (fermented chili bean paste)

3⅓ cups (800 ml) Chicken Dashi (page 278)

2 tablespoons miso (see page 291)

½ to 1 tablespoon soy sauce

4 to 5 leaves green cabbage, cut into 1-inch (2.5 cm) strips

7 ounces (200 g) medium-firm tofu, cut into 4 pieces

¼ cup (60 ml) white sesame paste (tahini is fine)

3 ounces (100 g) enoki mushrooms, trimmed and pulled apart

5 ounces (150 g) mung bean sprouts (crisp white part only)

1 negi (Japanese green onion), or 2 green onions (white part only), minced, for serving

Ground toasted white sesame seeds (see page 58), for serving

La-yu (chile oil)

Kurozu (Japanese black vinegar) or rice vinegar (optional), for serving

The broth in this *nabe* dish is inspired by the popular Japanese ramen dish *tan tan men,* which is derived from the Chinese *dan dan mein,* or *dan dan* noodles. While the original Chinese *dan dan mein* has no broth, the Japanese version typically has a spicy broth seasoned with rich sesame paste and topped with ground pork. I've adapted it to a hot pot, to cook chicken meatballs and a lot of vegetables.—Naoko

To make the meatballs: Combine chicken, egg, *katakuriko,* salt, pepper, 1 tablespoon sake, and 2 teaspoons ginger in a bowl and knead thoroughly by hand until smooth. Set aside.

Heat the sesame oil in a donabe and sauté the garlic, 2 teaspoons ginger, and half of the *negi* over medium heat until lightly aromatic, about 2 minutes. Push them to one side and add the *tobanjan* on the open side. Stir the *tobanjan* until aromatic, about 30 seconds. Add ¼ cup sake and *dashi.* Whisk in the miso and add the soy sauce. Cover and bring to a simmer.

Add the cabbage and tofu to the broth. Using two spoons, form the chicken mixture into balls about 1½ inches (3.5 cm) in diameter and drop into the broth. Cover and simmer until the meatballs are barely cooked through, about 3 to 4 minutes, and then stir in the sesame paste. Add the enoki mushrooms and bean sprouts, and cook for a minute or so. Sprinkle the remaining *negi* and some ground sesame seeds, then turn off the heat.

Serve in individual bowls with some splashes of *kurozu,* and *la-yu,* if you like, and enjoy.

EQUIPMENT:
One 1.8-quart/1.8 L or larger
classic-style donabe

SHIME (FINISHING COURSE) SUGGESTION:
You can lightly season the remaining broth with
soy sauce (or Asian fish sauce) and mirin to taste,
and then add cooked rice noodles and a garnish
of chopped green onion.

Gyoza Hot Pot
Gyoza Nabe

14 ounces (400 g) ground pork

1 tablespoon katakuriko (potato starch)

1½ teaspoons finely grated peeled
fresh ginger

1 tablespoon sake

2 tablespoons minced green onion

1 teaspoon toasted sesame oil

1 teaspoon soy sauce

¼ teaspoon freshly ground black pepper

25 to 30 gyoza wrappers (about
3½-inch/8.5 cm diameter)

4 cups (1 L) Kombu Dashi (page 277)

½ cup (120 ml) sake

3 to 4 leaves green cabbage, cut into
large bite-size pieces

6 medium shiitake mushrooms,
trimmed and halved

5 ounces (150 g) mung bean sprouts
(crisp white part only)

3 ounces (100 g) nira (garlic chives),
bottom ends trimmed, then cut into
3-inch (7.5 cm) pieces

Miso-Vinegar Dipping Sauce (page 283),
for serving

**The best way to enjoy this dish is to eat the gyoza as soon as they
are cooked. When I make gyoza *nabe*, we never have a problem
overcooking the gyoza; my guests become hungry hunters, and all
the dumplings are gone within a few blinks of an eye.—Naoko**

To make the gyoza: Combine the first eight ingredients for the gyoza in
a medium bowl. Knead by hand until the filling is smooth and shiny.
Cover with plastic wrap and let rest in the refrigerator for 30 minutes.
To fill the gyoza, mound about 1 tablespoon of the filling in the
center of a wrapper, and use water to wet the edges around half of the
wrapper's edge. Fold the wrapper in half by lifting the dry-edged side.
Pinch the edges tightly to seal and place the gyoza on the baking tray
lined with parchment paper. Repeat the process with the remaining
wrappers until the filling is gone. Cover the dumplings with a damp
paper towel until ready to cook. You can make them about 30 to
60 minutes in advance; any longer and the bottom of the gyoza
wrappers becomes soggy.

Combine the *dashi* and sake in a donabe. Cover and bring to a simmer
over medium-high heat. Add the ingredients in two batches: add half
the cabbage and cook until slightly tender, 30 to 60 seconds. Add half the
gyoza and half the shiitake; return to a simmer. Simmer for a couple
of minutes, and then add half the bean sprouts and half the *nira*. Cook
for another minute or until everything is cooked through, then remove
the gyoza and vegetables to a plate and repeat with the remaining
ingredients. Serve with Miso-Vinegar Dipping sauce.

SERVES *4 to 6*

EQUIPMENT:
One large (3-quart/3 L or larger)
classic-style donabe

Hokkaido-Style Seafood-Miso-Kimchi Hot Pot

¼ cup (60 ml) grapeseed oil or canola oil

2 ounces (60 g) minced peeled
fresh ginger

3 negi (Japanese green onions),
or 8 green onions

12 to 16 ounces (340 to 450 g) kimchi

6 ounces (180 g) miso (see page 291)
or your preference

¼ cup (60 ml) sake

¼ cup (60 ml) mirin

4 cups (1,000 ml) Kombu and Bonito Dashi
(page 274) or Crab Dashi (page 137)

1 tablespoon usukuchi shoyu (light-colored
soy sauce)

¼ to ½ small head napa cabbage,
cut into 2-inch (5 cm) pieces

6 to 8 shiitake mushrooms, stemmed
and halved or quartered

1 bunch shungiku (chrysanthemum greens)

8 to 12 whole small to medium live
clams or mussels

Hokkaido is the cold and snowy northern island of Japan, which experiences incredibly long winters and has absolutely amazing seafood. Living there for three winters, my family and I enjoyed cooking communal hot-pot dishes that not only warmed us up on a cold day but also heated the entire house! Hokkaido-style cooking is a very rustic style of cuisine that borrows heavily from the native people of the island, the Ainu. This dish combines classic elements of Japanese *nabe*-style cooking with the very popular Korean kimchi and a feel that is uniquely Hokkaido.

The seafood used varies depending on what is available and looks good that day. Salmon is at the heart of Hokkaido cooking and works really well cooked in a communal *nabe*, but feel free to mix and match seafood and vegetables to your taste. We prepare this dish at home in Sonoma using local seafood, vegetables, and seaweed that we forage along our coastline. In season, we use fresh Dungeness crab both for making the *dashi* and in the *nabe* itself. You can steam fresh crabs when available in a donabe steamer (*mushi nabe*) and then try your hand at making Crab Dashi following the instructions on page 137 to use in this dish.—Kyle

Heat a small sauté pan over medium heat and add the oil. Add the ginger and gently sauté, about 2 to 3 minutes. Wash, dry, and thinly slice one of the *negi* or 3 of the green onions into rings (white and light green parts only). Add the cut *negi* to the ginger and continue to lightly sauté until the mixture is soft and aromatic but not browned, about 2 minutes longer. Add half of the kimchi and continue to sauté for 2 more minutes, raising the heat slightly. Add the miso and sauté

SHIME (FINISHING COURSE) SUGGESTION:
Add rice to the reduced broth to make a rich,
fortified ojiya.

12 to 16 ounces (360 to 450 g) salmon
fillet, cut into 6 to 8 thick slices

8 to 12 ounces (240 to 340 g) firm
white fish (such as black cod, halibut,
or sea bass), cut into 4 to 6 thick slices

16 ounces (450 g) lump crabmeat or
whole shrimp, peeled and deveined

4 to 6 sea scallops

1 ounce (25 to 30g) dried nori or
wakame (optional)

for 1 minute, stirring constantly to incorporate it into the mix. Add the
sake and mirin and bring to a simmer to burn off the alcohol. Transfer
this mixture to the donabe, add the *dashi*, and begin to heat to just
below a simmer.

Once the *dashi* has been heated, taste for seasoning first and then add
the *usukuchi shoyu* as needed. Spread the cabbage evenly across the
bottom of the donabe. Add ingredients in layers to create a platform,
beginning with the shiitake mushrooms and *shungiku*. Cut the
remaining *negi* into 2-inch (5 cm) segments and layer those in as well.
Add the clams and then place the fish on top of the nest of vegetables
over on one side of the pot, overlapping the pieces slightly so they
cook evenly. On the other side of the pot, arrange the crab and scallops
to create a nice uniform presentation. Place the remaining kimchi and
the nori on top in one area and cover the donabe with the lid.

Heat the covered pot for 5 to 6 minutes over medium-high heat and
remove the lid. The seafood and vegetables should be just cooked
through. Lower the flame to just below a simmer and continue to
heat gently as you serve in the center of the table.

EQUIPMENT:
One 1.8-quart/1.8 L or larger
classic-style donabe

CHEF:
Namae Shinobu
RESTAURANT:
L'Effervescence
CITY:
Tokyo, Japan

Fried Scales-On Tilefish with Winter Melon Tagliatelle, Mussel Broth, Yuzu, and Kabosu

4 ounces (120 g) winter melon (white gourd), green skin peeled off, seeds scooped out, and sliced into thin strips (daikon can be substituted)

1 whole tilefish (about 1⅓ pounds/ 600 g), cleaned and filleted with the skin and scales on (or other white fish such as sea bream or sea bass, with scales removed)

1 tablespoon vegetable oil

1 tablespoon extra-virgin olive oil

3 ounces (100 g) mountain (brown) enoki mushrooms or enoki mushrooms, trimmed

1½ tablespoons unsalted butter

1 small shallot, minced

8 ounces (240 g) mussels

¼ cup (60 ml) white wine

½ cup (120 ml) water

Sea salt

1 yuzu or Meyer lemon, sliced ⅛ inch (3 mm) thick

1 kabosu citrus or Meyer lemon, sliced ⅛ inch (3 mm) thick

Tilefish has a rich and oily white meat, and its scales become super-crispy when fried. The rich umami profile of the mussel broth gently wraps the flavor of the delicate fish. With the aroma of the yuzu and *kabosu* citrus, and the different textures from winter melon and mountain enoki mushrooms, this dish can engage all your senses.

As a chef, I love donabe for many reasons. It's so important to bring a dish at its best stage to a customer, and with donabe's remarkable heat-retention ability, I can let the dish finish cooking right as it is served at the table. That way, a guest can enjoy the dish at its perfect temperature. Donabe's lid keeps the beautiful aroma of the food inside, so a guest can experience the "top note" of the aroma—imagine the smell of yuzu or herbs billowing out with steam when the lid is opened right at the table. This very moment is a beautiful surprise for a guest waiting in anticipation for a dish to arrive.—Namae Shinobu

Boil a pot of water and blanch the winter melon for 10 seconds. Drain the melon and transfer to a salted ice bath. Drain again and pat dry.

Pat dry the tilefish. In a sauté pan, heat the vegetable oil and place the fish fillets skin-side down. As soon as the scales stand up (or the skin becomes crispy, if you are using other white fish), turn the heat to low. Continue to cook without turning until the flesh is half cooked, about 2 to 3 minutes. Frying the scales over low heat will dehydrate them and make them crispy.

In a separate small pan, heat the olive oil over medium heat. Add the mushrooms and sauté until cooked through, about 4 to 5 minutes.

Heat 1 tablespoon of the butter in a shallow pot over medium heat. Add the shallot and sauté for 1 minute. Add the mussels, followed by the white wine and water. Cover and cook until the mussels open (discard any that do not open). Separate the mussels from the broth (do not discard). Take the meat out and discard the shells. Taste the broth and, if necessary, add more water to make it thinner. Season with salt.

Melt the remaining ½ tablespoon butter in a donabe over medium heat. Spread the yuzu and *kabosu* slices over the bottom and place the blanched winter melon on top of the yuzu. Lay the tilefish on top, skin side up, along with the mussels and mushrooms. Pour in the mussel broth and cover. As soon as the broth starts to simmer, about 3 to 5 minutes, remove from the heat and serve immediately in bowls at the table.

CHAPTER 2

Double-Lid Donabe Rice Cooker

Double-Lid Donabe Rice Cooker

Many people find both joy and comfort in a bowl of perfect rice. And the perfect rice can easily be achieved in donabe. When rice is cooked in a donabe, the result is that you can taste the texture of each individual grain. Donabe makes rice of exceptional quality because of its slow heat-building process, which brings out the natural sweetness in the rice. The shine and the ideal chewiness are achieved by its long period of heat retention during the resting time after the heat is turned off. If you cook it just a couple of minutes longer, you can also create that nice crispy bottom that your guests will fight over! Also, because of its porous body, donabe (especially *Iga-yaki* donabe) can absorb the moisture effectively, so rice cooked in donabe ware retains a chewy texture without becoming mushy after sitting a few hours. As a result, the leftover cool rice in a donabe can still taste surprisingly delicious.

For those who have never tried making rice in a donabe, it might sound like a complicated process. It's actually

very easy and rather fast. The approximate cooking time is only about 13 to 15 minutes for 2 to 3 rice cups (1½ to 2¼ U.S. cups) of rice, which can be a shorter time than a conventional electric rice cooker.

All the recipes in this chapter are cooked in a double-lid donabe rice cooker called Kamado-san. This unique type of donabe is particularly designed for cooking premium-quality rice without having to change the heat level during the process. The body of the Kamado-san is about one and a half times as thick as that of a conventional donabe. The extra-thick body allows the heat to build evenly and more gradually. It also allows the Kamado-san to retain its heat for a very long time after the heat is turned off. Its inner lid keeps the contents from boiling over and provides extra heat retention. If you have only a classic-style donabe, you can still enjoy the recipes in this chapter; however, see the note on page 96 before using it to make any of the following recipes. If you have an

alternative type of donabe rice cooker, you can apply this basic cooking method to the recipes in this chapter.

If you will be using your donabe rice cooker for the first time, we insist that you christen it by making plain rice in it! And choose a high-quality short-grain rice. That's the ultimate way to simultaneously appreciate the true, natural quality of the rice and what the donabe can do for the rice. Once you try plain rice, you can try different rice recipes with many variations. Whether it's plain rice or mixed rice with seasonal ingredients, making rice in a donabe is a joy, and there is a beauty to both the aesthetics of the finished dish and the process. The aroma of the steam puffing from the lid and the excitement when the perfectly cooked rice is revealed never get old.

This type of donabe can also be used for cooking other rice and grains, including jasmine, farro, quinoa, and wheat berries. (The grain-to-water ratios and cooking times may vary.) It can also be used like a classic-style donabe for hot pots, soups, and stews with only the upper lid. The extra-thick body of the donabe can work perfectly for slow-cooking dishes. It's a very versatile donabe for your kitchen.

About the Recipes in This Chapter

Before you get started, take a look at these useful reminders and information about cooking the recipes in this chapter.

There are different sizes of double-lid donabe rice cookers, and the size is distinguished by the amount of rice that can be cooked using the Japanese traditional rice measurement, the rice cup or *go*. One *go* is equivalent to U.S. ¾ cup (180 ml) of uncooked rice. The recipes in this chapter are made using a double-lid donabe rice cooker called Kamado-san with a 3-rice-cup capacity (about 1.5 quarts/1,500 ml). If using a smaller donabe rice cooker, adjust the recipe's ingredient amounts accordingly.

For all the recipes in this chapter, use both lids as instructed in the basic Plain White Rice method (see page 99) unless otherwise instructed. The cooking times in the recipes are approximate, and the steam from the lid can be used as an indicator. For best results, turn off the heat about 2 minutes after the steam starts puffing from the outer lid. (For example, if the steam starts puffing after 13 minutes, you cook an additional 2 minutes, for a total cooking time of 15 minutes.) To fluff the rice, we suggest you use a heat-resistant rice paddle (wood or plastic), unless otherwise instructed.

If You Don't Have a Double-Lid Donabe Rice Cooker

You can also use a classic-style donabe (with a capacity of between 1.5 quarts/1,500 ml and 3 quarts/3,000 ml) for the recipes in this chapter. When making rice in a classic-style donabe, you need to adjust the heat level during cooking (see the Plain White Rice and Plain Brown Rice recipes, pages 100 and 103). If a recipe asks for sautéing ingredients in oil, make sure that your donabe is suited for oil-sautéing. If not, use a sauté pan for such steps and transfer the contents to your classic-style donabe to continue with the rest of the recipe.

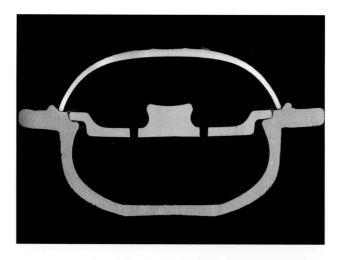

Cross-section view of Kamado-san. The body is especially thick to ensure effective rice cooking.

Choosing Rice

We use Japanese-variety short-grain rice in this book. Medium-grain rice can be used as a substitute. Make sure the rice grains are whole with few (ideally no) broken grains, as the broken grains can result in an undesirable starchy texture after the rice is cooked. Short-grain rice can be found at Japanese and other Asian grocery stores, as well as at specialty foods stores. (For more about rice, see Glossary, page 292.)

Water

For the best texture and flavor, either soft mineral water or filtered water is recommended. Hard (high-mineral-content) water tends to make drier and less chewy rice, as the calcium in the hard water gets in the way and prevents proper absorption, causing the rice to be cooked unevenly. The temperature of the water you use to wash and soak the rice should be cool to cold.

Cooking Liquid Variations

Water and *dashi* (stock) are used in the recipes in this chapter. Feel free to use your judgment in substituting another kind of stock or water in place of *dashi*. For example, if a recipe calls for Kombu and Shiitake Dashi (page 277), you can use Kombu and Bonito Dashi (page 274) or commercial vegetable stock instead, if you like.

Measuring Rice

For rice measurement, we use a traditional Japanese measure called the *go* or rice cup. Rice measuring cups can be found at Japanese markets. A level cup of it is 1 rice cup. As previously mentioned, 1 rice cup equals approximately ¾ cup US equals 180 ml.

Storing Dry Rice

The older rice becomes, the more the flavor deteriorates. This is because the surface of the rice oxidizes as it's exposed to air. If possible, it's better to buy rice that was polished and packaged close to the purchase date. Once you open the package, the best way to store the rice is to put it in a tightly sealed storage bag, making sure it's airtight (to prevent exposure to air and also keep out any insects). Once the bag is sealed, the best place to keep it is in the refrigerator. You can also store the bag in a cool, dry pantry. In that case, you want to use it up within two or three weeks for the best possible flavor. In the refrigerator or a very cold area, white rice can be stored without loss of quality for two to three months, while whole brown rice generally can keep up to a year.

Cooking White Rice

Rice-to-water ratio. The standard rice-to-water ratio is 9:10, so for every 1 rice cup (¾ cup/180 ml) rice, you need about ¾ cup plus 1 tablespoon/200 ml water. Depending on the brand or freshness of the rice, the ratio could vary slightly. For example, freshly harvested rice has a higher moisture content, and thus the rice-to-water ratio can be close to 1:1. You can adjust the ratio according to your preference.

To enhance the aromatic nuance. If you like, you can replace ½ to 1 tablespoon of the water with sake for each 1 rice cup of rice being made. The rice tends to become slightly shinier and more aromatic, but it won't be alcoholic.

For a crispy bottom. If you replace ½ to 1 tablespoon of the water with olive oil for each 1 rice cup of rice being made, you can get a crispier bottom layer of rice.

To cook a small amount. The smallest amount of rice you can cook in a 3-rice-cup Kamado-san is 1 rice cup (¾ cup/180 ml). If doing so, increase the water amount by 1 tablespoon or so for an optimal result.

Cleaning the rice: Before cooking the rice, it's important to thoroughly rinse it, to remove any dust or natural bran smell. However, you don't need to scrub hard, as that can break the grain. See rinsing procedure on the next page.

Rice-soaking time. In my home, 20 to 30 minutes of soaking is the standard. Some experts suggest that the rice should be soaked for 1 hour or even overnight. You can follow those guidelines you prefer. If you want to soak the rice for longer than 1 hour, use a separate bowl for soaking because the porous clay body of the donabe can absorb excess moisture, and transfer the contents to the donabe just before the rice is ready to cook. Soaking time may also vary depending on the type and freshness of the rice, season, and temperature of the water, too. But you don't need to get too nervous about it! For me, 20 minutes in cold to cool water always works.

Cooking speed is off. Even if you can't nail your stove's perfect heat level the first time, you can most likely discover it within a few tries. If the steam starts puffing in just 10 minutes or less, the heat level is too high. If it takes more than 15 minutes for it to start puffing, the heat level may not be high enough. You can adjust to find the perfect "medium-high" heat for your Kamado-san.

Leftover rice. Wrap leftover rice tightly in plastic wrap in single-serving portions and simply store in the freezer. The rice can be kept in the freezer up to three to four weeks. When ready to eat, heat the frozen wrapped rice in a microwave (make sure the plastic wrap is microwave-safe) for about 2 minutes.

SERVES **6** *to* **8**
to accompany
a meal

EQUIPMENT:
1 double-lid donabe
rice cooker (3-rice-cup size)

Plain White Rice
Hakumai

3 rice cups (2¼ cups/540 ml)
short-grain white rice

2½ cups (600 ml) cold filtered water
or low-mineral-content bottled water
(such as Volvic or Crystal Geyser)

Almost everyone who comes to our homes or work kitchens to try plain donabe rice for the first time is shocked by how "perfect" the rice tastes and how easy it is to cook in a donabe rice cooker. Because donabe lets the heat build slowly, the results are shiny and fluffy rice with a chewy, sweet taste. Good plain rice never gets old.—Naoko

First, rinse the rice. Combine the rice and enough cold water to completely cover the rice in a large bowl. Quickly swish the rice by hand in a circular motion several times so the water becomes cloudy. Immediately drain the rice in a colander. Repeat the process a few times until the water is mostly clear. Drain well in a colander.

Transfer the rice to the donabe and add the 2½ (600 mL) cups of water. Let the rice soak for 20 minutes.

Place both lids on the base so that the holes of the lids are positioned perpendicular to each other.

Set the donabe over medium-high heat. Once the steam starts puffing from the lid (11 to 13 minutes after you turn on the heat), allow the rice to cook an additional 2 minutes. If you like to have a nice crust on the bottom of the rice, extend the cooking time by another minute. After a couple of tries, you will know the best heat level for cooking rice on your stove; then you can just set a timer for 13 to 15 minutes and don't need to watch it for signs of steam.

When cooking rice in a double-lid donabe rice cooker, place an egg (right out of the refrigerator is fine) on top of the inner lid, making sure it doesn't cover the holes. Cover with the upper lid and cook the rice as instructed. After the rice has rested and is ready, your egg is ready, too. It will be medium-soft to hard-boiled.

You can make colorful multigrain rice by adding your choice of grains, such as quinoa, millet, barley, amaranth, or corn grits. For every 1 cup (¾ cup/ 180 ml) of rice, add 1 tablespoon of multigrains and increase the water amount by 1½ tablespoons. The multi-grains will give extra flavor, texture, and nutrients. There are also premixed multigrains (some are up to 16 different grains!) available at Japanese markets and some are even divided into small packets.

While rice is cooking in the donabe, eggs can be steamed in the upper compartment

Turn off the heat and let it rest undisturbed for 20 minutes. Uncover and fluff the rice.

If you do not have a double-lid rice cooker, you can still make rice in a classic-style donabe. After soaking the rice, cover with the lid and start with medium-high heat, bringing it to a boil, which will take about 7 to 8 minutes Turn down the heat to low and cook for 7 to 10 minutes longer, or until the water has mostly been absorbed (you can quickly open the lid to check, if necessary). When the water is absorbed and the rice is ready to rest, you will hear a subtle crackling sound inside (you need to bring your ear right up to the donabe—be careful not to burn yourself). Turn off the heat and let it rest undisturbed for 15 to 20 minutes. The cooking time is based on 3 rice cups (2¼ cups/540 ml) short-grain rice. The timing may vary depending on the amount of rice being cooked.

SERVES *6 to 8*
to accompany
a meal

EQUIPMENT:
One double-lid donabe
rice cooker (3-rice-cup size)

NOTES:
Adding a pinch of salt helps reduce the bitterness in brown rice.

If you are a novice at cooking brown rice in a donabe and worry about watery or undercooked rice, before turning off the heat, check the rice by quickly removing both lids. If the rice looks too wet, cover again and cook further until the rice absorbs most of the water.

Plain Brown Rice

Genmai

3 rice cups (2¼ cups/540 ml) short-grain whole brown rice

3¾ cups (900 ml) cold filtered water or low-mineral-content bottled water (such as Volvic or Crystal Geyser)

Pinch of sea salt

I have met many people who used to eat brown rice for health reasons but didn't necessarily like the taste of it. With donabe brown rice, I can't count how many have become brown rice fans. When brown rice is cooked in a donabe, the texture comes out nicely chewy with a natural sweetness, and without the common "heavy" or "mushy" mouthfeel. The cooking time is based on 3 rice cups (2¼ cups/540 ml) short-grain rice. The timing may vary depending on the amount of rice being cooked.—Naoko

In a bowl, combine the brown rice and the water. Add a pinch of salt. Allow the rice to soak for 6 to 12 hours.

Transfer the rice and the water to the donabe. Cover with both lids and cook over medium heat for 35 to 38 minutes. (The steam should start puffing from a hole in the top lid after about 20 minutes of cooking. You can continue to cook for an additional 15 to 18 minutes after it begins puffing.)

Turn off the heat and let it rest undisturbed for 30 to 40 minutes.

Uncover and fluff the rice.

If you are using a classic-style donabe, after soaking the rice and transferring it to the donabe, start with medium-high heat and bring to a boil. Turn down the heat to low and cook for 25 to 30 minutes, or until the water is mostly absorbed (you can quickly open the lid to check, if necessary). Turn off the heat and let it rest undisturbed for 30 to 40 minutes.

SERVES *4 to 6*
as part of a
multicourse meal

EQUIPMENT:
1 double-lid donabe rice
cooker (3-rice-cup size)

NOTE:
By blanching the *abura-age*, excess oil is removed
allowing it to absorb seasonings. To blanch,
spread the strips of abura-age in a single layer
across a wide-bottomed colander. Pour boiling
water over the strips. Allow them to cool, and then
gently squeeze out the excess moisture by hand.

Taro Rice

Sato-imo Gohan

2 rice cups (1½ cups/360 ml) short-
grain white rice, rinsed (see page 99)

1¼ cups (300 ml) Kombu and Shiitake
Dashi (page 277)

2 tablespoons sake

2 tablespoons mirin

2 tablespoons usukuchi shoyu
(light-colored soy sauce)

1 rectangular abura-age (fried tofu
pouch), blanched (see note), cut
crosswise into thin strips, then
halved crosswise

4 medium shiitake mushrooms,
trimmed and thinly sliced

10 ounces (300 g) taro, peeled and
sliced ¾ inch (1.5 cm) thick

When Kyle and I cooked together with the Nagatani family at
Nagatani-en, I made this dish with their home-grown taro root
(*sato-imo*), which I dug out of the ground myself. The freshly
harvested taro was especially moist and delicate in texture after
it was cooked. When fresh taro is cooked with rice, it becomes
nicely dense and creamy in texture. Taro is available all year
round at Japanese and Asian markets. However, it tastes
beautifully earthy and pure from autumn to winter, when
taro is in its prime season.—Naoko

In the donabe, combine the rice with the *dashi*, sake, mirin, and
usukuchi shoyu. Let the rice soak for 20 minutes.

Spread the *abura-age* over the rice, followed by the shiitake
mushrooms and taro. Cover with both lids and cook over medium-
high heat for 13 to 15 minutes. Turn off the heat and let it rest
undisturbed for 20 minutes.

Uncover and gently fluff the contents. Serve in individual bowls
at the table.

EQUIPMENT:
One double-lid donabe rice
cooker (3-rice-cup size)

Sea Bream Rice

Tai-meshi

1 medium-small (about 1 pound/450 g) whole sea bream, cleaned

1¾ teaspoons sea salt

1½ teaspoons extra-virgin olive oil

2 rice cups (1½ cups/360 ml) short-grain white rice, rinsed (see page 99)

1¼ cups (300 ml) Kombu and Bonito Dashi (page 274)

2 tablespoons sake

1 tablespoon usukuchi shoyu (light-colored soy sauce)

1 tablespoon peeled and very finely julienned fresh ginger

3 ounces (100 g) eryngii (king trumpet) mushrooms, sliced about 2 inches (5 cm) long and ¼ inch (3 mm) thick

1 rectangular abura-age (fried tofu pouch), blanched (see note on page 104), cut crosswise into thin strips, then halved crosswise

Chopped mitsuba (optional), for serving

Sea bream (also commonly called tai snapper) is a symbol of good fortune in Japan, and it is one of the most beloved fish among Japanese people. *Tai-meshi* is a very popular dish that will make both your eyes and your stomach happy. My friends Peggye and Richard, who run a seafood import company, brought me two large sea bream that had been caught in New Zealand and flown overnight to L.A. I decided to use my large 10-rice-cup Kamado-san to cook a special version of *tai-meshi* for a party on our patio. This donabe is so big that it can work only over an extra-large burner. It turned out to be the most decadent *tai-meshi* I'd ever made! For the recipe here, I've adjusted for a 3-rice-cup Kamado-san. If the fish is too large to fit in the donabe, you can cut off the head and cook just the body with the rice.—Naoko

Season all sides of the fish, including the cavity, with 1½ teaspoons of the salt. Set aside for 15 to 30 minutes. Pat the fish thoroughly dry with paper towels. Using a sharp knife, make three shallow crosswise incisions on each side of the fish. Drizzle the olive oil and rub on both sides (but not in the cavity) of the fish.

Wrap the tail with a piece of aluminum foil. Using either a hand torch or an oven broiler, lightly brown both sides of the skin, but do not cook the meat deeper than right under the skin (this step is optional). Remove the foil.

continued

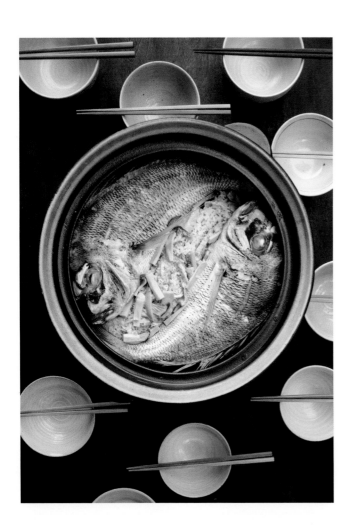

Sea Bream Rice, continued

Meanwhile, in the donabe, combine the rice with the *dashi*, sake, *usukuchi shoyu*, and remaining ¼ teaspoon salt. Let the rice soak for 20 minutes.

Scatter the ginger over the rice, followed by the *eryngii* mushrooms and *abura-age*. Carefully place the fish on top. If the tail doesn't fit, you can bend it to fit inside or cut it off. Cover with both lids and cook over medium-high heat for 13 to 15 minutes. Turn off the heat and let it rest undisturbed for 20 minutes.

Uncover and carefully transfer the fish to a plate. Remove the head and bones and discard. Transfer the fish back to the donabe and gently fluff by breaking up the fish with a spatula until all the components are mixed thoroughly. Serve in individual bowls at the table and garnish with chopped *mitsuba*.

SERVES *4 to 6*
as part of a
multicourse meal

EQUIPMENT:
One double-lid donabe rice
cooker (3-rice-cup size)

Turmeric Rice

1 tablespoon extra-virgin olive oil

1 teaspoon cumin seeds

2 rice cups (1½ cups/360 ml)
short-grain white rice, rinsed
(see page 99) and allowed to dry
in the colander 30 minutes.

Scant 1 teaspoon ground turmeric

1½ cups (360 ml) vegetable stock

½ teaspoon sea salt

When I make Japanese curry, I love making turmeric rice to serve
with it. It's easy to make and the result is always so fluffy and
aromatic. The color is beautiful, too. If you omit the turmeric
powder and increase the cumin seeds to 2 teaspoons in the recipe,
it's a nice simple cumin rice, which is also delicious with a curry
dish. In this recipe, you cook the rice over medium heat all the
way to the end.—Naoko

Heat the olive oil in donabe rice cooker over medium heat. Add the
cumin seeds and sauté until aromatic, about 1 minute. Add the rice
and continue to sauté until the rice is starting to turn translucent,
2 to 3 minutes. Add the turmeric and stir until the rice is evenly
coated in yellow.

Add the vegetable stock and salt. Cover with both lids and cook over
medium heat for 11 to 13 minutes. Turn off the heat and let it rest
undisturbed for 20 minutes.

Uncover and fluff the rice. Serve in individual bowls at the table.

SERVES *4 to 6*
as part of a
multicourse meal

EQUIPMENT:
One double-lid donabe rice
cooker (3-rice-cup size)

Buttered Scallop and Daikon Rice

½ teaspoon sea salt

8 large sea scallops (about 8 ounces/
240 g)

2 rice cups (1½ cups/360 ml) short-grain
white rice, rinsed (see page 99)

1¼ cups (300 ml) Kombu and Bonito Dashi
(page 274)

2 tablespoons sake

1 tablespoon plus 1 teaspoon (20 ml)
usukuchi shoyu (light-colored soy sauce)

4 ounces (120 g) daikon, peeled and cut
into ⅛-inch (3 mm) rounds and then
¼-inch (5 mm) strips

2 tablespoons unsalted butter

Chopped chives, for serving

Scallops and daikon make a beautiful combination and lend elegance to this dish. Daikon becomes tender and sweet in the donabe, and scallops bring a pure flavor. Once the rice is ready to fluff, break up the scallops with a spatula and mix thoroughly so you can enjoy the scallop flavor in every bite. I love that this dish is rich on the palate with the aroma of butter but still light in the stomach.—Naoko

Sprinkle the salt over both sides of the scallops. Set aside for 15 to 20 minutes. Pat dry.

Meanwhile, in the donabe, combine the rice with the *dashi*, sake, and *usukuchi shoyu*. Let the rice soak for 20 minutes.

Spread the daikon over the rice, followed by the scallops. Cover with both lids and cook over medium-high heat for 13 to 15 minutes. Turn off the heat and let it rest undisturbed for 20 minutes.

Uncover and add the butter. Gently fluff by breaking up the scallops with a spatula until all the components are mixed thoroughly. Serve in individual bowls at the table, and garnish with chopped chives.

EQUIPMENT:
One double-lid donabe rice
cooker (3-rice-cup size)

NOTE:
If you can't find low-sodium *shio-kombu*, regular *shio-kombu* is fine—just omit the *usukuchi shoyu* in the recipe. We suggest purchasing *shio-kombu* that doesn't include any added artificial flavors such as MSG. One of the most widely available brands in the United States is Kurakon; its low-sodium *shio-kombu* can be found at Japanese markets or online.

Salted Kombu and Ginger Rice

Shoga Shio-kombu Gohan

2 rice cups (1½ cups/360 ml) short-grain white rice, rinsed (see page 99)

1⅓ cups plus 1 tablespoon (330 ml) Kombu and Shiitake Dashi (page 277)

2 tablespoons sake

1 teaspoon usukuchi shoyu (light-colored soy sauce; optional)

1 teaspoon toasted sesame oil

1½ ounces (50 g) fresh ginger, peeled and very finely julienned

½ ounce (15 g) thinly shredded shio-kombu, low-sodium preferred (see Note)

Shio-kombu, a popular Japanese condiment, is sliced and cooked kombu seasoned with salt and other flavorings. It's so convenient that I keep it regularly stocked in my pantry. It's great in a salad, too. This is such a simple dish, made from simple ingredients, and it requires only one ingredient—the ginger—to be touched by a knife. The result is rich with the kombu's umami and refreshing with the ginger's bite. As a nonvegan option, I also like to add about 2 tablespoons *sakura ebi* (dried small shrimp).—Naoko

In the donabe, combine the rice with the *dashi,* sake, *usukuchi shoyu,* and sesame oil. Let the rice soak for 20 minutes.

Scatter the ginger over the rice, followed by the *shio-kombu.* Cover with both lids and cook over medium-high heat for 13 to 15 minutes. Turn off the heat and let it rest undisturbed for 20 minutes.

Uncover and gently fluff the contents. Serve in individual bowls at the table.

EQUIPMENT:
One double-lid donabe rice
cooker (3-rice-cup size)

NOTE:
Here are the simple steps to rehydrate dried *hijiki*. First, soak the *hijiki* in an ample
amount of water in a bowl for about 30 minutes. Make sure you don't oversoak the
hijiki, as it contains rich water-soluble fiber that could be lost, and the texture will
become too mushy. Gently transfer the *hijiki* by hand into a colander, trying to leave
most of the gritty stuff behind. Finally, rinse thoroughly under running water and
drain well.

Salmon and Hijiki Rice

SakeHijiki Gohan

2½ rice cups (2 cups minus 2 tablespoons/
450 ml) short-grain white rice, rinsed
(see page 99)

1⅔ cups (400 ml) Kombu and Bonito Dashi
(page 274)

2 tablespoons sake

2 teaspoons usukuchi shoyu (light-colored
soy sauce)

2 teaspoons toasted sesame oil

⅒ ounce (3 g; about 1 tablespoon) dried
hijiki seaweed, rehydrated (see Note)

7 ounces (200 g) Salt-Cured Salmon
(recipe follows), cut into 2 to 3 pieces,
or store-bought lightly salted salmon
(shio-jake)

Mixed chopped herbs and aromatics (such
as a handful of daikon sprouts; 1 green
onion, white and green parts; and 1 small
bunch mitsuba), tossed with a seeded and
thinly sliced dried red chile, or ½ teaspoon
red pepper flakes, for serving

Lemon wedges, for serving

I've been making this dish for years, and it's also one of the most
popular rice dishes in my cooking class. Because everything is
cooked together in a donabe, the salmon releases more flavors
as the dish is being cooked (just like making *dashi*), and *hijiki*
seaweed adds a nice mineral-rich taste. The preparation starts
a day before with the simple process of salt-curing the salmon
overnight, but if you have access to a Japanese market, you can
use already prepared lightly salted salmon (*shio-jake*) instead.
Once you plate the rice, I like to serve this dish with a generous
amount of mixed herbs on top and a good squeeze of lemon. The
dish is so refreshing that you can enjoy it like a salad.—Naoko

In the donabe, combine the rice with the *dashi*, sake, *usukuchi shoyu*,
and sesame oil. Let the rice soak for 20 minutes.

Spread the rehydrated *hijiki* over the rice and lay the salmon on
top. Cover with both lids and cook over medium-high heat for
13 to 15 minutes. Turn off the heat and let it rest undisturbed for
20 minutes.

Uncover, peel off the salmon skin (also remove the bones if using
store-bought salted salmon), and gently fluff by breaking up the fish
with a spatula until all the components are mixed thoroughly. Serve
in individual bowls at the table. Top with some mixed chopped herbs,
and serve with lemon wedges.

Salt-Cured Salmon

Shio-jake

2 tablespoons sea salt

1 pound (450 g) skin-on
salmon fillet, boned

Shio-jake is such a popular item in Japan that you can find a wide array of it at almost any local grocery store or department store year-round. It's most typically eaten simply grilled and served with rice, and is a popular filling for *onigiri* (rice balls), too. Making it at home is very easy, and you can adjust the saltiness to suit your preference. The cured salmon will keep for a few days in the refrigerator, tightly wrapped in plastic wrap.

To make Japanese-style grilled salmon, slice the cured fillet into four to six pieces and cook over a stove-top grill or pan-fry until done. You can also roast the whole fillet in the oven for 8 to 10 minutes at 450°F (230°C) and serve family style. Serve with grated daikon and lemon wedges as condiments, if you like.—Naoko

Rub the salt all over both sides of the fillet and wrap with two layers of plastic wrap.

Place the salmon on a tray and place another flat-bottomed tray on top of the fish. Place something that weighs 2 to 2.5 pounds (900 g to 1.25 kg) on the top tray. Refrigerate for at least 24 and up to 48 hours.

Remove the plastic wrap and wipe off the moisture and salt from the salmon with paper towels. Your cured salmon is ready to cook.

SERVES *4 to 6*
as part of a
multicourse meal

EQUIPMENT:
One double-lid donabe
rice cooker (3-rice-cup size)

Very Juicy Chicken-Wing Rice

Teba Gohan

8 medium chicken wings
(midsections with tips)

2 tablespoons sake

3 tablespoons soy sauce

1 tablespoon raw brown sugar

1 clove garlic, finely grated

2 rice cups (1½ cups/360 ml) short-
grain white rice, rinsed (see page 99)

1¼ cups (300 ml) Chicken Dashi
(page 278)

1 tablespoon peeled and very finely
julienned fresh ginger

2 teaspoons cooked sansho
(Japanese mountain pepper)
berries from a jar (optional)

1 teaspoon toasted sesame oil

Thinly sliced green onion, for garnish

Ground sansho (Japanese mountain
pepper; optional), for serving

This is not an ordinary chicken-and-rice dish, as you prepare the chicken wings boneless and cook them with the rice. When you bite into the chicken, the juice from the meat fills your mouth. With a very easy technique (I learned it from a Japanese TV science show), pulling the bones from the chicken wings takes just a little time and is completely worth the effort. The marinade infuses the meat and makes for chicken that is extra juicy and rich in flavor. I like to cook this dish with whole *sansho* (Japanese mountain pepper) berries, but since it's hard to find them in the United States, you can make it without them and the dish will still taste delicious. Just sprinkle on some ground *sansho* as an accent if you like.—Naoko

To remove the bones from the chicken wings, wear latex gloves so that the chicken won't slip from your hands. Using scissors, cut the connecting cartilage between the two bones at the cut end. Poke in the tips of the scissors along the side of the larger bone, which is connected to the skin. Cut off the connecting tissues by going to halfway deep. Be careful not to break the skin. Holding the tip with one hand, pick up the end of the larger bone with the other and squeeze to rotate it in one direction. Do not try to twist back and forth or push or pull the bone. Once the bone is loose, gently pull it out. It should pull out easily without force. Do the same thing with the other bone. Trim off the tips (you can discard them or save them for making stock).

continued

To make the marinade: Combine the sake, soy sauce, brown sugar, and garlic in a medium bowl and add the chicken. Cover and refrigerate for at least 3 hours and up to 24 hours. Remove the chicken from the marinade and set aside. Reserve the marinade.

In the donabe, combine the rice with the *dashi* and the reserved marinade. Let the rice soak for 20 minutes.

Spread the ginger over the rice, followed by the *sansho* berries. Place the chicken on top in one layer. Cover with both lids and cook over medium-high heat for 13 to 15 minutes. Turn off the heat and let it rest undisturbed for 20 minutes.

Uncover and drizzle the sesame oil. Transfer the chicken to a plate. Fluff the rice gently. Serve the rice in individual bowls at the table, topping each serving of rice with 1 to 2 chicken wings. Garnish with some green onion. If you didn't use *sansho* berries, sprinkle with some ground *sansho*, if you like.

NOTE:
To press-drain the tofu, set it in a shallow tray and place a flat-bottomed tray on top with a weight on top of the tray that is about equal to the weight of the tofu. Let it sit in the refrigerator for 30 minutes to drain, and then pour off the liquid and pat the tofu dry with a paper towel.

To rehydrate the dried wood ears, quickly rinse them under running water and then soak them in a medium bowl of cold to lukewarm water for 30 to 40 minutes. Drain and rinse again. (The rehydrated wood ear will become seven to ten times larger.)

VEGAN OPTION:
Substitute 1 tablespoon soy sauce for the oyster sauce, and omit the powdered chicken stock.

Tofu and Corn Rice

2 rice cups (1½ cups/360 ml) short-grain white rice, rinsed (see page 99)

¼ cup (60 ml) quinoa, rinsed

Generous 1¾ cups (430 ml) water

1½ tablespoons oyster sauce

1½ tablespoons soy sauce

1 tablespoon sake

1 teaspoon Asian chicken stock powder (optional, see Glossary, page 288)

¼ teaspoon sea salt

¼ teaspoon freshly ground black pepper

1 tablespoon toasted sesame oil

1 clove garlic, minced

7 ounces (200 g) medium-firm tofu, press-drained (see Note)

Kernels from 1 ear of corn

½ cup (120 ml; about 0.2 ounce/5 g) rehydrated wood ears, cut into small bite-size pieces (see Note)

This mixed rice is one of my summer favorites, and it's also nutritious. Quinoa is cooked right in with the rice. Meanwhile, tofu is sautéed with corn and seasoned with oyster sauce. For an extra layer of flavor, I like to use Asian chicken stock powder (see Glossary, page 288), an instant stock that is available at Japanese markets, but it's totally optional. Wood ears are mushrooms that are sold in dried form at Asian markets. Sautéed or scrambled tofu with corn is also lovely as a filling for a lettuce-wrap appetizer. As a variation, shelled edamame can make a nice substitute for the corn.—Naoko

In the donabe, combine the rice with the quinoa and water and let soak for 20 minutes.

Cover with both lids and cook over medium-high heat for 13 to 15 minutes. Turn off the heat and let it rest undisturbed for 20 minutes.

Meanwhile, make the sauce: in a small bowl, combine the oyster sauce, soy sauce, sake, chicken stock powder, salt, and pepper. Set aside.

Heat the sesame oil in a sauté pan and sauté the garlic for 1 minute over medium heat. Break the tofu into smaller pieces by hand and add it to the pan. Stir, continuing to break up the tofu with a wooden spatula. Cook for 3 to 4 minutes, or until the tofu is lightly browned. Add the corn and wood ears and sauté for another minute or so.

Add the sauce to the pan and turn up the heat to medium-high. Sauté until the liquid is almost gone, 2 to 3 minutes. Remove from the heat and set aside.

As soon as the rice has finished resting, uncover and gently fold in the corn and tofu mixture. Serve in individual bowls at the table.

SERVES *4 to 6*
as part of a
multicourse meal

EQUIPMENT:
One double-lid donabe rice
cooker (3-rice-cup size)

Tomato-Flavored Fava Bean and Hijiki Rice

¾ cup (180 ml) salt-free tomato juice

¾ cup (180 ml) Kombu and Shiitake Dashi
(page 277)

2 tablespoons sake

1 tablespoon usukuchi shoyu
(light-colored soy sauce)

½ teaspoon sea salt

Generous pinch of sea salt

1½ cups (360 ml; about 8 ounces/240 g)
shelled medium to large fava beans

1 tablespoon extra-virgin olive oil

2 cloves garlic, minced

2 rice cups (1½ cups/360 ml) short-grain
white rice, rinsed (see page 99) and dried
in the colander for at least 30 minutes

¹⁄₁₀ ounce (3 g; about 1 tablespoon)
dried hijiki seaweed, rehydrated
(see note on page 114)

I like to make this dish when fava beans are in season during
the spring. You can add the blanched fava beans after the heat
is turned off, and they cook perfectly with the carryover heat of
the donabe. By using tomato juice, the tomato flavor doesn't
overpower the delicate sweetness of the fava beans.—Naoko

To make the broth: Place the tomato juice, *dashi*, sake, *usukuchi shoyu*,
and ½ teaspoon salt in a bowl and stir to combine. Set aside.

Bring a medium pot of water to a boil and add a generous pinch of
salt. Add the fava beans and blanch for 1 minute. Drain and allow
them to cool down. Peel and pat dry with a paper towel. Set aside.

Heat the olive oil in the donabe over medium heat and sauté the
garlic for 1 minute. Add the rice and continue to sauté until the rice
is starting to turn translucent, 2 to 3 minutes.

Add the broth mixture and stir. Spread the *hijiki* on top. Cover with
both lids and cook over medium heat for 11 to 13 minutes. Turn off
the heat, quickly uncover, and spread the fava beans over the rice.
Immediately cover again and let rest undisturbed for 20 minutes.
Uncover and gently fluff the contents. Serve in individual bowls
at the table.

SERVES *4 to 6*
as part of a
multicourse meal

EQUIPMENT:
One double-lid donabe rice
cooker (3-rice-cup size)

English Peas and Yuba Rice
Mame Yuba Okowa

1 rice cup (¾ cup/180 ml) short-grain
white rice, rinsed (see page 99)

1 rice cup (¾ cup/180 ml) sweet
rice, rinsed

1½ cups (360 ml) Kombu and Shiitake
Dashi (page 277)

2 tablespoons sake

1½ tablespoon usukuchi shoyu
(light-colored soy sauce)

1 teaspoon sea salt

⅔ ounce (20 g) dried yuba (tofu skin)

1 cup (240 ml) shelled English peas

Just like fava beans, English peas taste great with rice when they are in season (late spring to early summer) and cook nicely with the carryover heat of the donabe. *Yuba* (tofu skin; see Glossary, page 295) adds a nice delicate flavor to the dish, but if you can't find dried *yuba*, you can simply omit it or substitute thinly sliced *abura-age* (fried tofu pouch; see note on page 104). This dish is all about celebrating the pure sweetness of English peas. I use half short-grain rice and half sweet rice for a result that is nice and sticky but not too heavy. If you don't have sweet rice, you can simply make it entirely with short-grain rice.—Naoko

In the donabe, combine both kinds of rice with the *dashi*, sake, *usukuchi shoyu*, and salt. Let the rice soak for 20 minutes.

Break the *yuba* into coarse pieces by hand and spread over the rice. Cover with both lids and cook over medium-high heat for 13 to 15 minutes. Turn off the heat, quickly uncover, and spread the English peas over the rice. Immediately cover again and let it rest undisturbed for 20 minutes.

Uncover and gently fluff the contents. Serve in individual bowls at the table.

SERVES *4 to 6*
as part of a
multicourse meal

EQUIPMENT:
One double-lid donabe rice
cooker (3-rice-cup size)

Orange Butter Rice

1 medium orange (such as navel)

3 rice cups (2¼ cups/540 ml) short-grain
white rice, rinsed (see page 99)

2¼ cups (540 ml) water

3 tablespoons unsalted butter, cut into
3 slices, at room temperature

3 tablespoons usukuchi shoyu
(light-colored soy sauce)

Freshly ground black pepper

It may be hard to imagine how the flavor combination of steamed
rice with orange, butter, and soy sauce could work, but it's delicious
to the point of being irresistible. While this dish is good on its own,
I combined it with Smoke Duck Breast with Creamy Wasabi-Green
Onion Dipping Sauce (page 256) in one of my cooking classes,
and it became a great hit. Smoked duck and orange butter rice . . .
brilliant pairing! It's also great as a side dish for grilled meat or
fish.—Naoko

Using a paring knife or a peeler, slice off the zest from the orange in
long strips ¾-inch (1.5 cm) wide. Be sure to remove just the top layer
of the skin, not the white pith. Cut crosswise into very finely julienned
pieces. Set aside. Reserve the peeled orange for another use.

In the donabe, combine the rice with the water. Let the rice soak for
20 minutes. Cover with both lids and cook over medium-high heat
for 13 to 15 minutes. Turn off the heat and let it rest undisturbed for
20 minutes.

Uncover and add the butter, *usukuchi shoyu*, and orange zest. Gently
fluff the contents and serve in individual bowls at the table. Grind
some black pepper on top and enjoy.

SERVES *4 to 6*
as part of a
multicourse meal

EQUIPMENT:
One double-lid donabe
rice cooker (3-rice-cup size)

Yuzu-Kosho Pesto Rice

2 rice cups (1½ cups/360 ml) short-grain white rice, rinsed (see page 99)

1½ cups (360 ml) water

3 tablespoons pine nuts

1 clove garlic

2 cups (480 ml) medium-packed fresh basil leaves

¼ cup (60 ml) extra-virgin olive oil

⅔ to 1 tablespoon yuzu-kosho

1 tablespoon usukuchi shoyu (light-colored soy sauce)

1 tablespoon freshly squeezed lemon juice

¼ cup (60 ml) grated Parmesan cheese

This is my Japanese-Italian-style rice dish, made with pesto seasoned with *yuzu-kosho* (see Glossary, page 295). It's very aromatic with a spicy-hot finish. I especially like this dish for eating outdoors, or you can form it into rice balls (*onigiri*) and take it to a picnic. The rice tastes delightful at room temperature, and the kick of the *yuzu-kosho* is refreshing. This *yuzu-kosho* pesto is also great with grilled chicken, vegetables, or pasta—just like a classic pesto. The amount of yuzu-kosho pesto made in this recipe is more than enough to mix with the recipe amount of the rice; keep the extra for two or three days in the refrigerator.—Naoko

Preheat the oven to 350°F (180°C).

In the donabe, combine the rice with the water. Let the rice soak for 20 minutes. Cover with both lids and cook over medium-high heat for 13 to 15 minutes. Turn off the heat and let it rest undisturbed for 20 minutes.

Meanwhile, make the pesto: Spread the pine nuts on a baking sheet. Roast in the oven for 5 minutes. Remove from the oven and let cool. In a food processor, combine 1 tablespoon of the toasted pine nuts with the remaining pesto ingredients. Process until they become a smooth paste.

As soon as the rice has finished resting, uncover and add about ¼ cup (60 ml) of the pesto, the remaining toasted pine nuts, and the Parmesan cheese. Gently fluff the contents. Add more pesto if you like. Serve in individual bowls at the table.

SERVES *4 to 6 as*
part of a multicourse
meal (makes 6 to
8 rice balls)

EQUIPMENT:
One double-lid donabe rice
cooker (3-rice-cup size)

NON-VEGAN OPTION:
Add 2 tablespoons dried *sakura ebi* (small shrimp) when
you add the sesame and kombucha powder; see Glossary,
page 293.

Green Tea Rice Balls

Matcha Onigiri

2 rice cups (1½ cups/360 ml) short-grain
white rice, rinsed (see page 99)

1½ cups (360 ml) water

2 teaspoons matcha (powdered Japanese
green tea)

1 tablespoon warm water

1 tablespoon toasted white sesame seeds
(see page 58)

2 teaspoons plum-flavored or regular
kombucha powder (seaweed tea powder),
or ⅔ teaspoon salt

Sakura no shio-zuke (pickled cherry
blossoms, rinsed; optional), for garnish

While this rice dish can be served in bowls, the bright green color
of matcha (powdered Japanese green tea) makes it especially
pretty when it's formed into balls and garnished with preserved
cherry blossoms. I also add plum-flavored *kombucha* powder
(seaweed tea powder, see Glossary, page 290; not to be confused
with the sweetened fermented tea drink), but you can simply
substitute an extra ⅔ teaspoon sea salt instead. For more on
sakura no shio-zuke (pickled cherry blossoms), see Glossary,
page 293.—Naoko

In the donabe, combine the rice with the water. Let the rice soak for
20 minutes. Cover with both lids and cook over medium-high heat
for 13 to 15 minutes. Turn off the heat and let it rest undisturbed for
20 minutes.

Meanwhile, whisk together the matcha and warm water in a cup.

As soon as the rice has finished resting, uncover and add the dissolved
matcha, sesame seeds, and *kombucha*, and gently fluff with the rice.

Transfer one-sixth to one-eighth (up to about ¾ cup/180 ml) of the
rice to a small rice bowl. If the rice is too hot to handle, let it cool
down slightly. Wet both palms lightly. Gently invert the bowl into one
hand, and then use both hands to shape the rice into a ball by gently
press the rice in a quick motion. Be careful not to burn your hands.
Repeat with the remaining rice. Garnish each ball with a pickled
cherry blossom, if you like.

SERVES *4 to 6*
as part of a
multicourse meal

EQUIPMENT:
One double-lid donabe rice
cooker (3-rice-cup size)

Azuki Sticky Rice
Azuki Okowa

½ cup (120 ml) dried azuki beans

1 rice cup (¾ cup/180 ml) short-grain
white rice, rinsed (see page 99)

1 rice cup (¾ cup/180 ml) sweet
rice, rinsed

½ rice cup (¼ cup plus 2 tablespoons/
90 ml) black rice, rinsed

2 cups (480 ml) water

1½ tablespoons mirin

1 teaspoon sea salt

Azuki is one of the types of beans I always stock in my pantry. These red beans don't require presoaking, and they cook in a short time. They are rich in flavor as well as vitamins, protein, and fiber, and I like them for both sweet and savory dishes. In Japanese culture, because red symbolizes good luck and happiness, azuki are often used in festive dishes, so eating azuki simply makes me happy by association. In addition to regular short-grain white rice, two more kinds of rice are blended in. The sweet rice is used to give a nice sticky texture, and black rice to adds a beautiful purple color as well as nutty flavor and texture to the finished dish. If you don't have black rice, increase the amount of the sweet rice.—Naoko

In a saucepan, combine the azuki beans with about 2½ cups (600 ml) water. Set over medium-high heat and bring to a boil. Reduce the heat and simmer for 3 minutes. Drain and rinse the beans in warm running water.

In the same saucepan, combine the drained azuki beans with about 2½ cups (600 ml) water. Set over medium-high heat and bring to a boil. Reduce the heat and simmer for 30 minutes, or until the beans are almost tender. Drain and let cool.

In the donabe, combine all three rices with the 2 cups (480 ml) water, the mirin, and the salt. Let the rice soak for 20 minutes. Spread the azuki beans over the rice. Cover with both lids and cook over medium-high heat for 13 to 15 minutes. Turn off the heat and let it rest undisturbed for 20 minutes.

Uncover and gently fluff the rice. Serve in individual bowls at the table.

SERVES *4 to 6*
as part of a
multicourse meal

EQUIPMENT:
One double-lid donabe
rice cooker (3-rice-cup size)

Crab Rice with Charred Green Onion, Tatsoi, and Sesame

3 rice cups (2¼ cups/540 ml) short-grain white rice, rinsed (see page 99)

2¼ cups (540 ml) water or leftover Crab Dashi (recipe follows)

2 bunches green onions

¼ cup (60 ml) grapeseed or canola oil

1 tablespoon toasted sesame oil

¼ cup (60 ml) mirin

⅓ cup shiro shoyu (white soy sauce) or usukuchi shoyu (light-colored soy sauce)

4 ounces (120 g) baby tatsoi leaves (about 2 cups loosely packed; can substitute baby spinach leaves, turnip greens, mizuna, or pea tendrils)

Crabmeat reserved from the Crab Dashi, or 1 pound (450 g) lump crabmeat

1 cup (240 ml) Crab Dashi (recipe follows) or Kombu and Bonito Dashi (page 274)

1-2 tablespoons toasted white sesame seeds (see page 58)

Sea salt or soy sauce (optional)

Ichimi togarashi (Japanese ground chiles), for garnish

With so many possible variations, it's difficult to choose which rice dish recipes to share. This is a satisfying and relatively easy one that makes a complete meal with only a small amount of crabmeat. I like to make this dish on the Sonoma Coast of California, using local Dungeness crabs when they are in season; however, most varieties of crab will work just fine.

Buying whole crabs will yield you the shells and all the meaty flavors that come with them. The shells can be used to make the crab *dashi*, which can be used in place of the water when cooking the rice to give a deeper, more complex umami flavor. The *dashi* instructions here make much more than the recipe requires, so you can enjoy the rest by trying the Hokkaido-Style Seafood-Miso-Kimchi Hot Pot (page 88) or by serving it as a clear soup to accompany this dish. To make a soup from it, combine the *dashi* with just a bit of reserved crabmeat and a few of the tatsoi leaves, and add a sprinkle of salt, soy sauce, or *shiro shoyu* (white soy sauce).

Once you feel comfortable with the techniques in this dish, you can easily customize it to suit your tastes and the seafood you have on hand. We enjoy adding different types of kimchi to this dish, as well as ginger, braised kombu, gingko nuts, mushrooms, and a variety of vegetables.—Kyle

In the donabe, combine the rice with the water. (If you have made the crab *dashi* and have at least 3¼ cups, you can substitute 2¼ cups for the water here. Just make sure you have 1 cup left over to use later.) Let the rice soak for 20 minutes. Cover with both lids and cook over medium-high heat for 13 to 15 minutes. Turn off the heat and let it rest for 20 minutes.

continued

Crab Rice with Charred Green Onion, Tatsoi, and Sesame, continued

Meanwhile, working in batches, lay the green onions in a large dry sauté pan and char over medium-high heat, turning regularly, for 2 to 3 minutes. The green onions will begin to steam in their own moisture and char on the outside. Remove from the sauté pan and lay the green onions all facing the same direction on a cutting board. Trim the root end and a few inches of the green tops and discard. Slice the green onions into ¼-inch (6 mm) rounds and reserve.

Wipe out the sauté pan and heat the grapeseed oil over medium heat. Add the charred green onions and sauté for 1 minute, stirring frequently. Add the sesame oil and the mirin and scrape the pan to deglaze. Allow the alcohol to evaporate (1 to 2 minutes) and remove the pan from the heat. As the pan is cooling, swirl in the *shiro shoyu.* Set the green onions aside.

Prepare a bowl of ice water and set aside. Bring a medium to large pot of salted water to a boil. Blanch the tatsoi leaves for 10 seconds and transfer the tatsoi immediately to the ice water. Once chilled, remove the leaves from the ice water, drain, and reserve.

To finish the dish, fold the crabmeat into the rice (reserving some nice lump pieces for garnish), 1 cup (240 ml) of the crab *dashi* (or other *dashi*), the charred green onion mixture, the tatsoi leaves, and the toasted sesame seeds. Cover the rice cooker and gently heat over a medium flame for 3 to 4 minutes to heat thoroughly and perfume the rice with the crab aroma. Season with salt or additional soy sauce if desired, and garnish with the reserved lump crab pieces, additional sesame seeds, and *ichimi togarashi.*

Crab Dashi

1 whole Dungeness or stone crab

1 (4-inch/10 cm) square kombu

2 quarts (2 L) water, soft (low-mineral-content) preferred

1 ounce (30g) loosely packed katsuobushi (dried bonito flakes)

If you can't get a whole crab, forgo making this *dashi* and substitute 1 pound (450 g) lump crabmeat and 1 cup Kombu and Bonito Dashi (page 274) in the rice recipe.

If using live crab, steam for 15 minutes, until cooked through, and then chill the whole crab before separating the meat from the shell. (If you have a donabe steamer, follow the basic steaming instructions on page 179.) Chill thoroughly in an ice bath or the refrigerator. Clean the crab by separating the meat from the shells and reserve the meat for making the Crab Rice (page 135). Remove any lungs, eyes, or apron using scissors, and discard. If you like a richly umami "sea flavor," mix in any of the cooked brown sections of the crab with the meat, or keep them with the shells for a deeper-flavored stock. Reserve some of the nice lump pieces of meat for garnish on top of the final rice dish.

In a medium pot, combine the reserved shells with the kombu and cover with the water. Heat gently and maintain the low heat below a simmer for 1 hour to infuse the crab and kombu into the stock. Remove the kombu and raise the heat slightly, still just below a simmer. Add the *katsuobushi* and turn off the heat. Steep for 5 minutes and strain through a fine-mesh sieve. Reserve 1 cup (240 ml) of strained stock for the final rice dish. Use the remaining stock to make a clear crab soup (see page 164) or for cooking the rice, if desired.

CHAPTER 3

Donabe for Soup and Stew

Donabe for Soup and Stew

A simple steamy soup is a luxury, especially when it's accompanying a perfect bowl of rice. And there is nothing like a hearty stew to make you feel at home.

With donabe's remarkable heat-retention abilities, hot soup stays hot for a long time at the table. And because a donabe heats up and cools down slowly, it's the perfect vessel for stews and other braised dishes, regardless of whether they're from Japanese or Western cuisine.

The recipes in this chapter are all soups, stews, and braises. The ideal type of donabe for making these dishes has a very round shape and extra-thick body, for even slower heating and extra heat retention. The donabe used is called Miso-Shiru Nabe. Just like a classic-style donabe, a Miso-Shiru Nabe comes in two pieces: a base (bowl) and a lid, but with its extra-thick and round body, with the upper open side that tapers inward, a Miso-Shiru Nabe is made especially for slow cooking and long heat retention.

When making soup in a Miso-Shiru Nabe, you can bring the donabe to the table and keep it there through second servings without reheating. This donabe is perfect for making miso soup, for which the aroma is very important. Because the aroma of miso is very delicate, reheating the soup would cause the aroma to be lost.

The thick, round body of this donabe gives a very steady and even heat distribution, which is perfect for stews or slow-braising dishes, including meat and legumes. When you cook a stew in a thick-bodied donabe like the Miso-Shiru Nabe and turn off the heat, you can still hear it simmering for a while after. As the donabe cools down slowly, the gentle cooking process continues and flavors are effectively integrated even after it's off the heat. And because this type of donabe ware can be heated empty, you can also dry-sauté or toast ingredients in it. It works great in the oven, too. It donabe is truly a versatile tool in the kitchen.

Even if you have only a classic-style donabe, however, you can still enjoy most of the recipes in this chapter; but see the note on page 141 for tips on adapting your classic donabe for these recipes.

We hope you enjoy these very comforting donabe recipes, from quick soups to slow-cooked stews to oven-braised delights.

About the Recipes in This Chapter

Before you get started, take a look at these useful reminders and information about cooking the recipes in this chapter. The recipes here are all made in a soup and stew donabe called Miso-Shiru Nabe. We use the large size (1.6-quart/1.6 L capacity).

Cooking Liquid Variations

You can replace the *dashi*/stocks called for in the recipes in this chapter with different kinds of *dashi*/stock if you like—for example, if a recipe calls for Chicken Dashi (page 278), it's okay to use vegetable stock instead. Please use your judgment on which kind will work with a particular recipe.

If You Don't Have a Miso-Shiru Nabe

Most of the dishes in this chapter can be made entirely with a classic-style donabe, a donabe rice cooker like the Kamado-san (without using the inner lid), or a donabe steamer like the Mushi Nabe (without using the steam grate). Please note that the cooking times may vary with different types of donabe. If a recipe asks for sautéing ingredients either dry or in oil, check the manufacturer's information to make sure your donabe is suited for oil-sautéing or dry-heating. If it isn't, use a pan for such steps and transfer the contents to the donabe afterward to continue with the rest of the recipe. If you are using a smaller size donabe, adjust the recipe's ingredient quantities accordingly.

SERVES *4 to 6*
as part of a
multicourse meal

EQUIPMENT:
One large (1.6-quart/1.6 L)
soup and stew donabe

NOTE:
To blanch *konnyaku* (see page 290),—including *shirataki*,—noodles, place them in a colander and rinse under running water. Cut them first, if necessary. Bring a medium pot of water to a boil; add the rinsed *konnyaku* and boil for about 3 minutes. Drain. Blanching helps remove the earthy smell of the *konnyaku* and lets it absorb flavors better when cooked with seasonings.

Oven-Braised Soybeans and Vegetables

Daizu no Gomoku-ni

1 cup (240 ml) (about 7 ounces/200 g) dried soybeans, rinsed and soaked in about 1 quart (1 L) water for 12 hours

1 tablespoon toasted sesame oil

7 ounces (200 g) shirataki noodles (konnyaku noodles), blanched (see Note) and cut into 2-inch (5 cm) pieces

1/10 ounce (3 g; about 1 tablespoon) dried hijiki seaweed, rehydrated (see page 114)

4 medium dried shiitake mushrooms, rehydrated (see Note, page 144), trimmed and diced

2 ounces (60 g) (about 2 to 3 medium) carrots, diced

1/4 cup (60 ml) sake

1½ tablespoons mirin

1½ teaspoons sugar

3 tablespoons soy sauce

About 3/4 cup (180 ml) Kombu Dashi (page 277)

Sea salt

In Japan, soybeans are called "meat from the garden" because they are so high in protein. Soybeans are also one of the prime ingredients in Japanese Buddhist temple vegan cuisine (*shojin ryori*). This dish is a traditional *shojin ryori* recipe and a popular home-cooked meal in Japan. When cooked in a donabe, beans become tender and flavorful without getting mushy. *Shirataki* noodles (see Glossary, page 293) add the nice bouncy texture and also soak in the rich flavors from the broth. For this dish, once you set the donabe in the oven you can simply just forget about it until it's ready. To achieve an even more integrated flavor, let the cooked dish rest for a few hours or refrigerate (after transferring to a different container) overnight. Reheat to serve or enjoy at room temperature.—Naoko

Place the soybeans and their soaking water (or you can replace it with fresh water if you prefer) in a saucepan. Set over medium-high heat. Bring to a boil and then turn down the heat to simmer. Simmer for 45 minutes, or until the beans are crisp-tender. (Add more water if the cooking water falls below the beans.) Skim as necessary to remove any floating bean shells or scum. Drain and rinse the beans with warm water.

Preheat the oven to 350°F (180°C).

continued

Oven-Braised Soybeans and Vegetables, continued

In the donabe, heat the sesame oil over medium-high heat. Add the *shirataki*, rehydrated *hijiki*, rehydrated shiitakes, carrots, and soybeans. Sauté for 2 to 3 minutes, or until the ingredients are well coated in oil.

Add the sake, mirin, sugar, and soy sauce. Gradually add the *dashi* (you can replace up to half of it with the reserved soaking liquid from the shiitakes, if you like) until it's almost covering the ingredients. Bring to a boil and then turn off the heat. Cover the surface of the contents with a drop lid (*otoshibuta*; see Kitchen Tools, page 296) or a piece of aluminum foil, then cover with the lid, and transfer to the oven. Cook for 1 hour, or until the beans are tender and the broth is reduced by more than half. Add a pinch or more of salt to adjust the seasoning, if necessary. If the mixture is still quite brothy, transfer back to the stove and reduce over medium-high heat. Once it's off the heat, let it rest for 15 to 30 minutes, covered, or more ideally for 2 to 3 hours. Serve in individual bowls at the table, passing the salt around.

EQUIPMENT:
One large (1.6-quart/1.6 L)
soup and stew donabe

Simmered Pork Shoulder
Ni-buta

1 tablespoon sea salt

2½ pounds (1.2 kg) pork shoulder, halved

1 cup (240 ml) sake

1 negi (Japanese green onion),
or 3 green onions (green part only)

3 cloves garlic, lightly smashed

1½ tablespoons sliced fresh ginger

½ teaspoon black peppercorns

¼ cup (60 ml) sake

¼ cup (60 ml) raw brown sugar

¼ cup (60 ml) soy sauce

½ cup (120 ml) strained broth from
cooking the pork

2 teaspoons katakuriko (potato starch)

1 tablespoon water

Very finely julienned negi or green onion
(white part only), for garnish

Shichimi togarashi (Japanese seven-spice
blend), for serving

When I host a dinner party at my house, *ni-buta* is on the short list of the dishes I like to make. It's a crowd-pleaser, and I can basically just leave the donabe to do most of the work, rather than having to spend a lot of time tending it. Once the meat has simmered in the donabe and the heat is turned off, it's further cooked by carryover heat and rests for about an hour. When it's time to serve, I make a quick sauce and slice the meat. Be sure to start the night before, though, to give the meat time to marinate.

While this dish tastes great at gentle warm temperature right out of the donabe, if you'd like to serve it hot, you can simply reheat the donabe and slice the meat after it has warmed through. I highly recommend you strain and save the cooking broth, as it makes a wonderful soup for ramen after adjusting the seasoning with some salt or soy sauce. Of course, you can top this ramen with some slices of *ni-buta*, if you are lucky enough to have any left over.—Naoko

Rub the salt all over the pork. Put the halves in a resealable plastic bag and seal tightly, pushing all the air out. Let the pork marinate in the refrigerator overnight. Return to room temperature before cooking.

Remove the pork from the bag and place it in the donabe along with all the aromatics. Add the cup of sake and just enough water to barely cover the surface of the meat. Cover with the lid and set over medium-high heat. As soon as the broth starts to boil, turn down the heat to low. Skim as necessary. Cover the surface of the contents with a drop

continued

Simmered Pork Shoulder, continued

lid (*otoshibuta*; see Kitchen Tools, page 296) or a piece of aluminum foil. Cover with the lid again and simmer very gently for 45 to 60 minutes, or until clear juice runs out when a skewer is inserted into the center of the pork. Turn off the heat and let it rest, covered, for 1 hour. If the kitchen is cold, wrap the donabe with a large towel to help insulate it.

To make the sauce: Combine the sake, brown sugar, soy sauce, and pork broth in a saucepan and set over medium-high heat. Bring to a boil, and then turn the heat down to simmer for 5 minutes. In a small bowl, whisk together the *katakuriko* and water. Gradually stir the mixture into the sauce and stir until thickened. Remove from the heat and set aside.

To serve, transfer the pork to a cutting board and cut into thin slices. Arrange the slices on a large plate and drizzle with the sauce. Garnish with some *negi* and sprinkle with *shichimi togarashi.*

SERVES 4
*as part of a
multicourse meal*

EQUIPMENT:
One large (1.6-quart/1.6 L)
soup and stew donabe

Kabu Miso Soup

Kabu no Miso-shiru

4 medium kabu (Japanese turnips) with greens

3⅓ cups (800 ml) Kombu and Shiitake Dashi (page 277)

4 medium shiitake mushrooms (or the leftover shiitakes from making the dashi), trimmed and sliced

3½ tablespoons miso (see page 291)

The *kabu* (Japanese turnip) is a versatile vegetable, and it can be served in a wide variety of ways, including raw, pickled, stewed, or roasted. I always enjoy a simple miso soup with *kabu*, as the white bulb becomes sweet and tender and complements the mellow miso flavor very well. Unless you get extremely fresh *kabu*, it's a good idea to peel its skin because the texture could become fibrous. The bulbs cook quite fast, so make sure you cook them just long enough to reach your desired texture. The leaves are much richer in vitamins and minerals than the bulb, so save any left over for another use. Simply sautéing the leaves can make a very tasty side dish.—Naoko

Separate the greens from the *kabu* bulbs and reserve half of them for a later use. For the remaining half, trim off the very thick end of the stems and cut both the stems and the leaves into ¼-inch (6 mm) slices. You should have a little over 1 cup (240 ml) of greens total. Peel and halve the bulbs and slice into ¼-inch (6 mm) rounds.

Combine the *dashi*, shiitake mushrooms, and *kabu* bulb slices in the donabe. Cover and set over medium-high heat. As soon as the broth starts to boil, turn down the heat to a gentle simmer. Simmer gently until the *kabu* is just tender, about 3 to 4 minutes.

Gently whisk in the miso and immediately turn off the heat. Add the *kabu* greens and let rest, covered, for 1 to 2 minutes. Serve in individual bowls at the table.

SERVES *4 to 6*
as part of a
multicourse meal

EQUIPMENT:
One large (1.6-quart/1.6 L)
soup and stew donabe

Simmered Hijiki Salad

Hijiki no Gomoku-ni

1 tablespoon toasted sesame oil

1 ounce (30 g) dried hijiki seaweed, rehydrated (see Note page 114)

3 medium dried shiitake mushrooms, rehydrated (see page 144), trimmed and thinly sliced

1 rectangular abura-age (fried tofu pouch), blanched (see Note page 104), cut crosswise into thin strips, then halved crosswise

3 ounces (90 g) lotus root, thinly shaved (see page 288)

1½ ounces (50 g) (about ½ medium) carrots, julienned into 1¼-inch (3 cm) strips

2 tablespoons sake

2 tablespoons mirin

2 tablespoons raw brown sugar

⅔ cup (160 ml) Kombu Dashi (page 277) or water used for soaking the dry shiitake mushrooms

3 tablespoons soy sauce

Hijiki seaweed has been eaten by Japanese people for thousands of years. It's like a jewel from the ocean, and we appreciate it for its flavor as well as its extremely rich nutritional value. Simmered *hijiki* is one of the classic Japanese home-cooked dishes, and it can be enjoyed hot, warm, or cool. It's also a great dish to bring to a picnic. It can keep for a few days in the refrigerator, so you can make a large batch and enjoy it for the next few days. Make sure you cook it until the liquid has almost evaporated for a more integrated flavor and to make the *hijiki* less perishable. Also, be sure to sauté the *hijiki* first before adding the other ingredients, as cooking it in oil in the beginning helps it to absorb flavor better.—Naoko

Heat the sesame oil in the donabe and sauté the *hijiki* for a couple of minutes over medium-high heat. Add the rehydrated shiitake, *abura-age*, and lotus root and continue to sauté for a couple more minutes. Add the carrot and stir. Add the sake, mirin, and sugar and stir for 1 to 2 minutes. Add the *dashi* (you can replace half of it with the reserved soaking liquid from the shiitakes, if you like) and soy sauce. Cover and bring to a boil, then turn down the heat to simmer. Cover the surface of the contents with a drop lid or a piece of aluminum foil and then cover this with the donabe lid. (*otoshibuta*; see Kitchen Tools, page 296) Simmer for 20 to 25 minutes, or until the liquid is almost gone, stirring a couple of times.

Remove from the heat and let it rest, covered, for at least 15 to 30 minutes, or more ideally 2 to 3 hours. Serve in individual bowls at the table.

EQUIPMENT:
One large (1.6-quart/1.6 L)
soup and stew donabe

Miso Keema Curry

1 tablespoon extra-virgin olive oil

1 tablespoon unsalted butter

1½ teaspoons cumin seeds

1 medium yellow or sweet onion, minced

1 clove garlic, finely grated

1½ teaspoons finely grated peeled
fresh ginger

1¼ pound (600 g) ground beef (pork can
be substituted)

1 medium carrot (about 3½ ounces/100 g),
peeled and cut into ¼-inch (5 mm) cubes

2 tablespoons curry powder

1½ teaspoons paprika (preferably hot)

1½ tablespoons Hatcho miso (red miso
can be substituted)

1¾ cups plus 2 tablespoons (450 ml)
vegetable stock

3 tablespoons tomato ketchup

2 bay leaves

1 to 2 teaspoons kurozu (Japanese black
vinegar) or rice vinegar (optional)

½ teaspoon sea salt, plus more if needed

Freshly ground black pepper

7 ounces (200 g) okra, trimmed
and sliced crosswise

Keema curry is a minced meat curry from India. This is my Japanese-style *keema* curry, with a small addition of Hatcho miso (malted soybean miso), which is very dark in color and has a more pronounced flavor. If you can't get Hatcho miso, you can substitute regular red miso. The recipe should comfortably serve four people unless you are serving someone like my husband, Jason, who can eat almost the full donabe of curry, along with Plain Rice or multigrain rice (see variation 2 page 101).—Naoko

Heat the olive oil and butter in the donabe and sauté the cumin seeds over medium to medium-low heat for 1 to 2 minutes, or until aromatic. Add the onion and a pinch of salt and continue to sauté for 20 to 25 minutes, or until the onion is light golden and very soft. Stir often and be careful not to burn the onion. Cover with a lid when not stirring. Add the garlic and ginger and stir for 1 minute, or until aromatic. Turn up the heat to medium-high, and add the beef. Sauté until the beef is almost cooked through. Add the carrot and stir. Add the curry powder and paprika and stir for 1 minute.

Whisk the miso with a half ladleful of the stock in a small bowl. Set aside. Add the remaining stock, ketchup, and bay leaves to the donabe. As soon as the broth starts to boil, turn down the heat to simmer. Skim as necessary. Cover the surface of the contents with a drop lid (*otoshibuta*; see Kitchen Tools, page 296) or line the surface with a piece of aluminum foil. Cover with the lid and simmer for 10 minutes.

Stir in the miso mixture, vinegar, salt, and some black pepper. Adjust the seasoning with more salt, if necessary. Add the okra and simmer for 5 minutes. Turn off the heat and let it rest, covered, for 5 to 10 minutes. Serve in individual bowls at the table.

EQUIPMENT:
One large (1.6-quart/1.6 L)
soup and stew donabe

NOTE:
Dry-sautéing *shirataki* helps it to absorb
the seasonings better.

Simmered Beef with Shirataki and Potatoes
Gyu Shigure-ni

10 ounces (300 g) shirataki noodles
(konnyaku noodles), blanched (see page
144) and cut into 2-inch (5 cm) pieces

1 tablespoon toasted sesame oil

7 to 8 small (about 1½-inch/3.5 cm
diameter) potatoes, peeled and halved
(about 7 ounces/200 g)

⅓ cup (80 ml) sake

¼ cup (60 ml) mirin

2 tablespoons black sugar
or raw brown sugar

¼ cup (60 ml) soy sauce

10 ounces (300 g) thinly sliced beef
for sukiyaki (see page 77), cut into
bite-size pieces

2 tablespoons very finely julienned peeled
fresh ginger, or more to taste

Ground sansho (Japanese mountain
pepper; optional), for serving

In this comforting Japanese dish, thinly sliced beef is simmered
with bouncy *shirataki* noodles and potatoes in a sweet soy-based
seasoning. Ginger gives a gentle accent to the rich beef flavor.
If you have access to a Japanese market, *sukiyaki*-thin beef is
suggested, or the less-expensive *kiriotoshi* beef cut (odds and ends
of often high-quality meat), which would be perfect also. —Naoko

Place the *shirataki* noodles in the donabe and dry-sauté over medium
heat for 4 to 5 minutes to remove the excess moisture. Add the sesame
oil and potatoes and continue to sauté for a minute or so. Add the
sake, mirin, black sugar, and soy sauce and turn up the heat to medium-
high. As soon as the broth starts to boil, turn down the heat to simmer.
Cover the surface of the contents with a drop lid (*otoshibuta*; see
Kitchen Tools, page 296) or line the surface with a piece of aluminum
foil. Cover with the lid and simmer for 10 minutes or until the broth
is reduced by half or so.

Meanwhile, bring a medium pot of water to a boil. Add the beef
and blanch for 10 to 15 seconds, or until it changes color. Drain and
immediately transfer to a bowl of ice water to stop the cooking. Drain
well again.

Add the beef and ginger to the donabe and stir. Cook for 5-10 minutes,
or until the broth is reduced to a very small amount. Turn off the heat
and let it rest, covered, for 15 to 30 minutes. Serve in individual bowls
at the table and enjoy with sprinkles of *sansho*, if you like.

EQUIPMENT:
One large (1.6-quart/1.6 L)
soup and stew donabe

Tomato Curry with Chicken and Eggplant

1 pound (450 g) boneless skinless chicken thighs, cut into large bite-size pieces

1 tablespoon Shio-Koji (page 280; can substitute 1 teaspoon sea salt)

4 medium Japanese eggplants, a few stripes peeled lengthwise using a peeler, and then cut oblique into 1 inch (2.5 cm) thick pieces

¼ cup (60 ml) extra-virgin olive oil, plus more as needed

1 tablespoon unsalted butter

1½ teaspoons cumin seeds

1 large yellow or sweet onion, minced

1 clove garlic, finely grated

1½ teaspoons finely grated peeled fresh ginger

2 ounces (60 g; about 1 small) carrot, cut into ¼-inch (5 mm) cubes

2 to 3 teaspoons curry powder

1 teaspoon paprika (mild or hot)

8 ounces (240 ml) canned tomato sauce

1½ cups (360 ml) vegetable stock

2 bay leaves

continued

My sister, Tomoko, is a wonderful home cook, and every time I go back to Japan, I look forward to eating her food. This curry with tomatoes, eggplant, and chicken is one of my favorites of her specialties. The sauce is smooth and mildly spicy, and the chicken and eggplant are so tender. I tweaked her recipe with slightly different ingredients to make it my own. Chicken marinated in Shio-Koji (page 280) makes the dish taste even richer, but you can simply substitute salt and the dish will still be delicious. A splash of the cider vinegar lifts the flavors nicely. You can serve it with Turmeric Rice (page 109) or freshly baked naan, which is what she does.—Naoko

Combine the chicken and *shio-koji* in a bowl and mix well by hand. Cover with plastic wrap and let it marinate in the refrigerator for at least 30 minutes and up to overnight.

Soak the eggplant slices in a bowl of water for 5 minutes. Drain and pat dry. Set aside.

Heat 1 tablespoon of the olive oil and the butter in the donabe over medium-low heat and sauté the cumin seeds for 1 to 2 minutes, or until aromatic. Add the onion and continue to sauté for 35 to 45 minutes, or until the onion has caramelized to deep golden brown and is slightly pasty. Stir often and be careful not to burn the onion. Cover with a lid when not stirring. Add the garlic and ginger and stir for 1 minute. Add the carrot and stir; add the curry powder and paprika and stir for 1 minute. Add the tomato sauce, stock, and bay leaves and turn up the

continued

Ingredients, continued

2 tablespoons all-purpose flour

1 teaspoon Asian fish sauce
or soy sauce

½ teaspoon garam masala (optional)

1½ teaspoons cider vinegar
or rice vinegar

Freshly ground black pepper

Sea salt (optional)

Tomato Curry with Chicken and Eggplant, continued

heat to medium-high. Cover and bring to a boil, and then turn down
to simmer gently for 5 minutes.

Meanwhile, dust the chicken all over with the flour. Heat 1 tablespoon
of the olive oil in a sauté pan over medium-high heat and add the
chicken. Cook both sides until golden brown (you don't have to cook
the meat through), about 2 minutes per side. Turn off the heat and
transfer the chicken to the donabe. Cover the surface of the contents
with a drop lid (*otoshibuta*; see Kitchen Tools, page 296) or a piece of
aluminum foil. Cover with the lid and simmer gently for 10 minutes.
Stir in the fish sauce, garam masala, vinegar, and some black pepper.
Adjust the seasoning with some salt, if necessary.

Meanwhile, wipe the grease from the sauté pan with a paper towel.
Heat the remaining 2 tablespoons olive oil (or more if necessary) in
the pan over medium to medium-high heat and sauté the eggplant
by turning occasionally until it's soft and golden brown, about 3 to
5 minutes. Transfer to a plate lined with paper towels to drain the
excess grease. Add the eggplant to the donabe and stir. Turn off the
heat and let rest, covered, for 5 to 10 minutes. Serve in individual
bowls at the table.

SERVES *4 to 6*
as part of a
multicourse meal

EQUIPMENT:
One large (1.6-quart/1.6 L)
soup and stew donabe

Soy-Flavored Simmered Ground Chicken over Rice
Tori Soboro Gohan

¼ cup (60 ml) sake

¼ cup (60 ml) soy sauce

1½ tablespoons raw brown sugar

1½ tablespoon mirin

¼ cup (60 ml) water

1 pound (450 g) ground chicken
(preferably dark meat)

2 tablespoons very finely julienned
peeled fresh ginger

1½ teaspoons kuzuko (kudzu starch)
or katakuriko (potato starch)

4 to 6 large eggs

Plain White Rice (page 100)

Very popular among Japanese people of all ages, this juicy simmered ground chicken is cooked in simple seasonings of soy sauce, sake, mirin, and sugar, and is typically served over plain rice. My version has the accent of a generous amount of shredded ginger to stimulate your appetite. I like to serve it with a very soft-boiled egg (with runny egg yolk) over freshly cooked donabe rice. You can also enjoy it as a topping for steamed kabocha, asparagus, or tofu.—Naoko

Combine the sake, soy sauce, sugar, mirin, 3 tablespoons of the water, and the chicken in the donabe. Bring to a simmer over medium heat, stirring constantly to crumble the chicken. Simmer for 10 to 15 minutes, stirring frequently, until the broth is reduced by half or so. Add the ginger and stir.

Whisk together the *kuzuko* and remaining 1 tablespoon water in a small cup. Gradually stir into the donabe and stir until the chicken mixture thickens, 1 to 2 minutes. Turn off the heat.

To make soft-boiled eggs with very runny egg yolks, bring a medium pot of water to a boil. Pierce a tiny hole in the bottom of each cold egg (right out of the refrigerator) with a safety pin. Place the eggs carefully in the boiling water and cook for 7 minutes. Immediately transfer the eggs to a bowl of cold water to cool down. Peel the eggs carefully, as they will be quite soft and fragile.

To serve, scoop some rice into each bowl, spoon some simmered chicken over the rice, and place an egg on top or on the side.

SERVES *4 to 6*
as part of a
multicourse meal

EQUIPMENT:
One large (1.6-quart/1.6 L)
soup and stew donabe

NOTE:
Beveling is a traditional Japanese technique
(called *mentori*) to smooth the edges and
keep them from crumbling during cooking.

Braised Spicy Kabocha

1½ pounds (650 g; about ½ large)
kabocha squash

2 tablespoons sake

¼ cup (60 ml) water

2 tablespoons black sugar
or raw brown sugar

1½ teaspoons soy sauce

½ teaspoon sea salt

1 teaspoon toasted sesame oil

½ teaspoon tobanjan (fermented
chili bean paste)

Braised kabocha is a Japanese classic, here given a spicy kick.
As the dish tastes so good at room temperature, it is great for
a potluck or a picnic. With the gentle heat distribution of the
donabe, the kabocha becomes nice and tender without falling
apart or getting mushy. If you don't care for the spicy flavor, you
can simply omit the *tobanjan* (fermented chili bean paste), and
add another pinch of salt. For more information about *tobanjan*
and black sugar, see Glossary, pages 294 and 288.—Naoko

Slice off only the very rough part of the skin of the kabocha squash,
and cut the flesh into 1½-inch (3 cm) cubes. Then, if you wish, trim
(bevel) the skin-side edges (see Note).

Place the kabocha squash, skin-side down and preferably in a single
layer, in the donabe. Add the sake, water, sugar, soy sauce, and salt.
Cover the surface of the contents with a drop lid (*otoshibuta*; see
Kitchen Tools, page 296) or a piece of aluminum foil. Cover with
the lid and bring to a gentle simmer over medium heat. Simmer for
10 minutes, or until the kabocha is tender when tested with a skewer
and the liquid has reduced to a very small amount.

Stir together the sesame oil and *tobanjan* in a small cup. Drizzle
over the kabocha. Turn off the heat and let it rest, covered, for
10 to 15 minutes. Serve in individual bowls at the table.

SERVES *4*
as part of a
multicourse meal

EQUIPMENT:
One large (1.6-quart/1.6 L)
soup and stew donabe

Salmon Chowder with Miso Soy-Milk Broth

1 pound (450 g) salmon fillet (skin removed), cut into 1½-inch (4 cm) cubes

Sea salt

4 ounces (120 g) broccoli florets, cut into bite-size pieces (from 1 small head)

2 tablespoons unsalted butter

½ medium yellow or sweet onion, minced

2 tablespoons all-purpose flour

2 tablespoons sake

1¾ cups (400 ml) vegetable stock

1 medium carrot (about 3½ ounces/ 100 g), cut into ⅛-inch (3 mm) rounds

7 ounces (200 g) satsuma-imo (Japanese sweet potato), peeled, cut into ⅓-inch (8 mm) rounds, and the rounds halved

½ cup (120 ml) Saikyo miso or sweet white miso

1¾ cups (400 ml) pure, rich plain soy milk or whole milk

5 ounces (150 g) shimeji mushrooms, trimmed

Shichimi togarashi (Japanese seven-spice blend)

This Japanese-style chowder can make a perfectly nutritious one-pot meal with salmon, a variety of vegetables, and mildly flavored Saikyo miso (sweet white miso). Soy milk adds a rich, savory character (see page 294), or you can substitute whole milk. Enjoy with freshly cooked Plain White Rice (page 100) or a crusty baguette to dip into the chowder.—Naoko

Season both sides of the salmon lightly with sprinkles of salt. Set aside for 15 to 30 minutes. Pat dry.

Bring a medium pot of water to a boil and add a generous pinch of salt. Add the broccoli and blanch until it's partly cooked and crisp, about 30 seconds. Drain well and let it cool down. Set aside.

Heat the butter in the donabe over medium heat and sauté the onion until very soft but not colored, 10 to 15 minutes. Cover with a lid when not stirring. Add the flour and stir for about 1 minute to cook it. Add the sake and stir again. Gradually add the stock, stirring so that the mixture won't become lumpy. Add the carrot and *satsuma-imo* and cover. As soon as the broth starts to boil, turn down the heat to simmer gently until the vegetables are just tender, about 4 to 6 minutes.

In a bowl, whisk together the Saikyo miso and soy milk. Stir the mixture into the donabe. Bring back to a gentle simmer. Add the salmon and *shimeji* mushrooms and bring back to a gentle simmer again. Simmer gently for 3 to 4 minutes, or until the salmon is barely cooked through. Adjust the seasoning with a pinch of salt or more, if necessary. Add the broccoli and turn off the heat. Let it rest, covered, for a few minutes. Serve in individual bowls at the table and enjoy with some sprinkles of *shichimi togarashi* on top.

SERVES 4
*as part of a
multicourse meal*

EQUIPMENT:
One large (1.6-quart/1.6 L)
soup and stew donabe

Crab and Napa Cabbage Soup

1 tablespoon toasted sesame oil

1½ teaspoons finely julienned peeled
fresh ginger

1 green onion, thinly sliced crosswise
5 to 6 leaves medium napa cabbage, cut
into ⅓-inch (8 mm) strips (separate
the bottom and leafy parts)

2 medium shiitake mushrooms,
trimmed and thinly sliced

2 tablespoons sake

2½ cups (600 ml) Chicken Dashi
(page 278)

1 teaspoon sea salt

½ teaspoon usukuchi shoyu (light-colored
soy sauce)

1 tablespoon katakuriko (potato starch)

1½ tablespoons water

4 ounces (120 g) lump crabmeat, coarsely
broken apart by hand

2 ounces (60 g; about ⅙ bunch) spinach,
bottom ends trimmed and leaves cut into
2-inch (5 cm) pieces

1 (14-ounce/400 g) package soft tofu, cut
into 4 to 6 cubes

Freshly ground black pepper, for serving

Kurozu (Japanese black vinegar) or rice
vinegar, for serving

La-yu (chile oil), for serving (optional)

This dish was inspired by a soup I fell in love with at a Chinese restaurant in Tokyo. The elegantly rich flavors of the crabmeat and napa cabbage, a classic combination found in Chinese cuisine, complement each other so well, and the silky tofu is gently wrapped with the slightly thickened broth. If you want to take a shortcut, instead of heating the tofu separately, you can simply cut the tofu into smaller cubes and add it directly to the donabe to heat through before serving.—Naoko

Heat the sesame oil in the donabe over medium heat and sauté the ginger and green onion for a couple of minutes. Add the bottom part of the napa cabbage and shiitake mushrooms, and sauté for 2 to 3 minutes.

Add the sake, *dashi*, and remaining napa cabbage and cover. As soon as the broth starts to boil, turn down the heat to simmer. Simmer for 10 to 15 minutes, or until the napa cabbage is very soft. Season with the salt and *usukuchi shoyu*. In a small cup, whisk together the *katakuriko* and water, and gradually stir the mixture into the broth. Stir until the broth is slightly thickened. Add the crabmeat and spinach. Stir and bring back to a simmer. As soon as the spinach has wilted, turn off the heat.

While the soup is simmering, get the tofu ready. Bring a medium pot of water to a boil and add the tofu. Turn down the heat to low. Wait until the tofu is just heated through and turn off the heat.

To serve, using a slotted spoon, divide the tofu evenly among individual bowls and bring to the table. Pour the soup over the tofu at the table and enjoy with some sprinkles of black pepper, a splash of *kurozu*, and some *la-yu*.

SERVES *4 to 6*
as part of a
multicourse meal

EQUIPMENT:
One large (1.6-quart/1.6 L)
soup and stew donabe

Pork and Vegetable Miso Soup

Tonjiru

1 tablespoon toasted sesame oil

½ medium yellow or sweet onion,
thinly sliced

5 ounces (150 g) medium daikon, peeled,
sliced into ⅛-inch (3 mm) rounds, and
the rounds quartered

2 ounces (60 g) (about ½ large-size)
carrot, sliced into ⅛-inch (3 mm) rounds
and the rounds halved

4 medium shiitake mushrooms, trimmed
and quartered

8 ounces (240 g) thinly sliced pork belly,
cut into 2-inch (5 cm) strips

2 tablespoons sake

3⅓ cups (800 ml) Kombu and Bonito
Dashi (page 274)

4 ounces (120 g) satsuma-imo (Japanese
sweet potato), peeled, cut into ¼-inch
(6 mm) rounds, and the rounds quartered

7 ounces (200 g) medium-firm tofu, cut
into ¾-inch (2 cm) cubes

3 to 3½ tablespoons light brown
or red miso

1 tablespoon Saikyo miso or sweet
white miso (can substitute with up
to ½ tablespoon of the other miso)

Shichimi togarashi (Japanese seven-spice
blend), for serving

This very classic Japanese dish can easily be the main item in
your meal, satisfying your body and nutritional needs. I always
feel nicely recharged after eating my *tonjiru*. While there is no
special seasoning other than miso and a small amount of sake,
tonjiru tastes so rich and complex because of the wide variety of
ingredients cooked in the broth. My version of *tonjiru* has very
thinly sliced onion that is sautéed until very soft, so it becomes
sweet in the soup and melts in the mouth. You can omit Saikyo
miso and increase the amount of the other miso to taste, if you
prefer.—Naoko

Heat the sesame oil in the donabe over medium heat and sauté the
onion for 5 to 10 minutes, or until soft. Add the daikon, carrot, and
shiitakes and sauté for 1-2 minutes. Add the pork belly and continue
to sauté until the pork is more than half-way cooked.

Add the sake and *dashi* and cover. Bring to a boil, and then turn down
to a gentle simmer. Skim as necessary. Add the *satsuma-imo* and simmer
for 8-10 minutes, or until all the vegetables are tender.

Add the tofu and gently whisk in both kinds of miso. Just before
the broth comes back to a gentle simmer, turn off the heat. Serve in
individual bowls at the table and sprinkle some *shichimi togarashi* on top.

SERVES 4
as part of a
multicourse meal

EQUIPMENT:
One large (1.6-quart/1.6 L)
soup and stew donabe

Grilled Steak with Buddha's-Hand Kosho and Ponzu Vinaigrette

8 ounces (240 g) Buddha's Hand citron, diced

3 ounces (90 g) yellow chiles (yellow wax peppers), stemmed, seeded, and coarsely chopped

1½ teaspoons sea salt

⅓ cup (80 ml) freshly squeezed lemon juice or Meyer lemon juice

8 to 12 ounces (240 to 360 g) beef rib-eye, New York strip, or filet steak

Sea salt and freshly ground black pepper

¼ cup (60 ml) grapeseed or canola oil, plus more for searing the steak

2 negi (Japanese green onions), or 6 green onions, sliced on the diagonal (white and light green parts only)

½ cup (120 ml) Yuzu Ponzu (page 279) or store-bought ponzu sauce

Toasted white sesame seeds (see page 58), for garnish

Thinly sliced green onions (white and green parts), for garnish

Young leaves of spicy greens (such as mustard greens, mizuna, wasabi, or arugula) or onion, garlic, or chive blossoms, for garnish

Sous vide is a technique that has been used for several decades, though it has become more popular among restaurant chefs and home cooks over the past ten years. The name means "under vacuum," referring to the vacuum-sealed bags most sous vide foods are cooked in. While this is very important for even heat transfer, the most important part of the technique is controlling the precise temperature to get consistent and even doneness in foods. When applied to steak, the sous vide technique creates a tender and very reliable medium-rare steak. If the technique is done correctly, you have a perfect steak without a gray layer of overcooked meat toward the surface.

With its extra-thick body made from very porous clay, a soup and stew donabe like the Miso-Shiru Nabe is particularly suited to this technique. The water in the donabe transfers heat through the plastic and in turn into the meat. Over the cooking process, the meat temperature stabilizes to a perfect medium-rare.

I serve this dish with a condiment called Buddha's-Hand *kosho*, which we developed with our friends at the Cultured Pickle Shop in Berkeley, California. Our goal was to take the idea of Japanese *yuzu-kosho* (see Glossary, page 295) and create a similar product but using our own California citrus varieties. The result is a mildly acidic condiment that you can also make from Meyer lemons. Please note that the condiment needs to be made a few weeks before this dish can be prepared.—Kyle

continued

Grilled Steak with Buddha's-Hand Kosho and Ponzu Vinaigrette, continued

To make the kosho: Combine the citron, chiles, and salt in a mortar or
food processor. Grind with a pestle or pulse until the mixture becomes
homogeneous but remains coarse. Add the lemon juice and stir to
combine. Spoon into a jar and close the lid, but not tightly. Allow to
ferment in a cool, dark place for 9 days. Remove the lid, stir, and reseal
the lid. Refrigerate for several days to weeks before using.

To prepare the steak, fill the body of the donabe with water and
cover with the lid. Place a digital thermometer through the hole and
begin heating the water over medium-low heat. Meanwhile, season
the steak with salt and pepper and vacuum-seal in a plastic bag rated
for cooking. When the water reaches 125°F (51.5°C), adjust the heat
to keep a constant temperature between 124° and 126°F (51°C and
52°C). Remove the lid and add the steak to the water, making sure
it is completely submerged. Cover again. After the temperature has
stabilized, maintain for 1 hour.

In a sauté pan, heat the oil over medium heat and add the *negi*. Heat
gently to soften, 5 to 6 minutes. Remove from the heat and allow to
cool slightly. Swirl in the ponzu.

To finish, remove the steak from the water and the plastic and pat
dry. Sear over high heat with a small amount of oil in a pan or on a
grill. Let rest for 3 to 4 minutes before slicing. Spoon the ponzu-*negi*
mixture onto a platter. Slice the steak and lay it over the mixture.
Spoon the *kosho* in various areas so that each slice receives some.
Offer the garnishes alongside the platter at the table.

EQUIPMENT:
1 large (1.6-quart/1.6 L)
soup and stew donabe

Pacific Saury with Tomato Sauce and Oven-Dried and Fresh Tomatoes

5 pounds (2.25 kg) ripe, red heirloom or beefsteak tomatoes

Sea salt

2 cloves garlic, thinly sliced lengthwise

2 tablespoons extra-virgin olive oil

6 to 8 ounces (180 to 240 g) komatsuna (mustard spinach), mustard greens, spinach, or mizuna leaves, separated

Sea salt

¼ cup (60 ml) grapeseed or canola oil

16 to 18 ounces (450 to 500 g) Pacific saury, mackerel, or sardine fillets

4 to 6 ounces (120 to 180 g) small cherry and/or teardrop tomatoes (preferably a mix of colors)

Freshly grated yuzu zest, for garnish

Chrysanthemum petals or flowers from spicy greens, for garnish

The tomato sauce is the heart of this dish. It was inspired by work we did at The Fat Duck from a study Fat Duck chef and owner Heston Blumenthal had conducted with Reading University and the Umami Information Center. This study compared the levels of glutamates (the proteins responsible for umami taste) in the outer flesh of the tomato against that of the center. It was discovered that the center of a tomato is much higher in these glutamates, and concentrating the tomato centers increases the umami taste even further. So for this recipe I cook the tomato centers down to create umami-rich sauce on par with that of a sauce based on those high-umami Japanese ingredients, miso, *dashi*, or soy sauce. The body shape and clay of a soup and stew donabe like the Miso-Shiru Nabe are perfect to concentrate these flavors and brown the sugars in the tomato along the edges to develop a deep, rich flavor. With this in mind, try cooking other tomato sauces for pasta dishes such as Bolognese and see the difference a donabe can make! The leftover flesh of the tomato in my recipe is oven-dried as another way to concentrate the glutamates.

I made this recipe in Iga in the kitchen of the Nagatani family using *sanma* (Pacific saury), but it will also work well with sardines or fresh mackerel.—Kyle

To prepare the sauce: Core the tomatoes and bring a large pot of water to a boil. Prepare a large ice bath with more ice than water. Blanch the tomatoes in the boiling water for 5 seconds and transfer to the ice bath to stop cooking. Once they have cooled, peel the skins from the tomatoes and discard. Cut the tomatoes in half lengthwise and scoop out the centers into the donabe. Divide the tomato halves into 2 pieces

continued

each and cut away the interior of the tomato from the outer flesh using a paring knife. Place the interior of the tomato in the donabe. Reserve the exterior of the tomatoes, that will now resemble petals. Place the donabe over medium heat and bring the tomato centers to a simmer. Simmer uncovered for about 1 hour, stirring regularly and scraping down the sides.

Meanwhile, preheat the oven to 275°F (135°C). Line a baking sheet with parchment paper or a silicone baking mat and lay the tomato petals, insides up, in a single layer on the sheet. Sprinkle with a little salt and lay one slice of garlic on each petal. Drizzle with the olive oil and place in the oven. Turn the tray every 15 minutes, until the tomatoes are dry but still jammy (tomatoes should bake for a total of about 45 minutes). Set aside to cool.

Bring a pot of water to a boil and blanch the greens briefly until just tender, 5 to 10 seconds. Drain in a colander and allow to cool at room temperature. Sprinkle with a small amount of salt.

Once the tomato sauce has cooked down to a sauce consistency and is beginning to concentrate, prepare the fish. In a sauté pan, heat the oil over medium-high heat. Place the fish skin-side down in the pan and sprinkle with salt. Cook on the skin side only until crisped and just cooked through, about 1 minute. Transfer to paper towels to drain.

Cut the cherry tomatoes into quarters. Taste the sauce and season with salt if needed; gently fold in the cherry tomatoes, dried tomatoes, and greens (reserving some of each to place on top). Cut the fish into strips about 3 inches (7.5 cm) long. Combine with the sauce and garnish the top with greens, dried tomatoes, fresh tomatoes, yuzu zest, and chrysanthemum petals.

SERVES 4

EQUIPMENT:
One large (1.6-quart/1.6 L)
soup and stew donabe

CHEF:
Josef Centeno
RESTAURANT:
Bäco Mercat
CITY:
Los Angeles, CA

Braised Shio-Koji Beef Brisket with Sunchokes, Radishes, Celery, and Coffee

2 tablespoons coffee beans, finely ground

½ tablespoon smoked paprika

½ tablespoon yellow mustard powder

2 tablespoons freshly ground black pepper

2 tablespoons Aleppo pepper

1 teaspoon ground ginger

1 teaspoon chili powder

1 pound (450 g) beef brisket (or belly), cut into 8 to 10 equal pieces

8 cipollini onions, peeled and halved

1 clove garlic, thinly sliced

3 tablespoons Shio-Koji (page 280)

1½ teaspoons Saikyo miso or sweet white miso

2 tablespoons extra-virgin olive oil

3 sprigs rosemary

3 sprigs thyme

6 sprigs mitsuba

3 cups (750 ml) beef or chicken stock or water

6 French Breakfast radishes, stemmed and halved or quartered lengthwise

8 shishito (or padrone) chiles, stemmed

12 ounces (360g) sunchokes, sliced 1½ inches (4 cm) thick

2 ribs celery, sliced 1½ inches (4 cm) thick

1 tablespoon shiro shoyu (white soy sauce) or soy sauce

2 tablespoons freshly squeezed yuzu or Meyer lemon juice

1 cup (240 ml) loosely packed fresh basil leaves

1 cup (240 ml) loosely packed shiso (perilla) leaves, loosely packed

1 clove garlic, peeled

3 tablespoons finely grated pecorino romano cheese

¼ teaspoon Shio-Koji (page 280)

3 to 5 tablespoons extra-virgin olive oil

2 large eggs

This dish is a pot roast done in a Japanese style. First the brisket is dredged with a coffee-chile rub—a nod to the way I often prepare steaks—and then it is cooked in a donabe, resulting in tender, flavorful beef. Autumn vegetables add earthiness and are seasoned with Shio-Koji (page 280). The stewlike dish would be delicious served with steamed short-grain white rice.—Josef Centeno

To prepare the rub: Place in a small bowl the ground coffee, paprika, mustard powder, both peppers, ginger, and chili powder and stir to combine.

Combine the beef, onions, garlic, 1 tablespoon of the *shio-koji*, 1 to 2 tablespoons of the coffee rub (save the remaining for another use), and miso in a bowl and toss to coat evenly. Cover and refrigerate for 1 hour to marinate.

Heat a sauté pan over high heat and add the olive oil. Working in batches, sear the beef on all sides until just browned, about 1 minute on each side. Remove from the pan and place in the donabe. Add the onions to the pan and lower the heat to medium. Caramelize the onions for 3 to 5 minutes until deeply browned. Using a piece of string or twine, tie together the rosemary, thyme, and mitsuba. Transfer the onions to the donabe and add the bouquet of herbs. Add the stock and cover with the lid.

Preheat the oven to 350°F (175°C). Over medium heat on the stove top, bring the beef mixture to a low simmer. Transfer to the oven and cook for 1 hour.

Remove the donabe from the oven and skim any excess fat from the top using a spoon or ladle. Add the radishes, chiles, sunchokes, celery, the remaining 2 tablespoons of the *shio-koji*, *shiro shoyu*, and yuzu juice. Cover again and return to the oven until both meat and vegetables are tender, about approximately 3 more hours.

While the beef dish is cooking, prepare the puree: Bring a large pot of water to a boil and prepare an ice bath. Blanch the basil and shiso leaves for 3 seconds and transfer to the ice bath to cool. Drain and pat dry. Combine the leaves, garlic, cheese, and *shio-koji* in a blender and puree until it resembles a chunky pesto, drizzling in the olive oil in a steady stream while blending. Remove the basil-shiso puree and set aside.

Remove the donabe from the oven. Uncover and stir in 2 tablespoons of the puree (save the remaining for another use). Crack the eggs and add to the top of the dish. Cover and set over medium-low heat. Cook for 3 to 5 minutes until the eggs have just set but the yolks are still runny. Serve in individual bowls at the table.

CHAPTER 4

Donabe Steamer

Donabe Steamer

Steam cooking is an integral part of Japanese cuisine. While a steamed course of the Japanese *kaiseki* (traditional multicourse meal) prepared by a highly trained chef can be something seasonal and extremely elaborate, steamed dishes at home are often something simple and fast. Steaming is also considered a healthy cooking option, as the ingredients tend to retain more of their nutrients compared to when they are simmered in water.

We love steaming with a donabe steamer because you can enjoy both cooking and eating steamed dishes right at the table—just like hot-pot dishes made in the classic-style donabe. You can use a donabe steamer only in the kitchen if you like, but it is truly designed for communal family-style cooking and dining. When you prepare a family-style donabe-steamed meal at the table, there is no travel time from the kitchen to the table. Everybody can pause and see the freshly cooked ingredients when the lid is lifted. Another benefit of donabe steaming is that with the intense steam and far-infrared radiation effect of donabe, ingredients can cook even faster while retaining not only their nutrients but also their texture. The rapid steaming also keeps the flavor of each ingredient locked inside.

The setup is very easy. A donabe steamer comes in three pieces. It's essentially a classic-style donabe (with a bottom bowl and a lid), with the addition of a steam grate to set inside. Without the steam grate, a donabe steamer can be used as a classic-style donabe, so you can also make hot pots, soups, stews, and more in it. From a classic *chawanmushi* (steamed savory custard) such as Crab and Wakame Savory Egg Custard (page 184) and dim sum–style dumplings such as Steamed Tofu and Shrimp Gyoza (page 196) to unique Steamed Yellowtail Shabu-Shabu (page 183), you can even make several recipes one after another to create a multicourse meal with just one donabe!

About the Recipes in This Chapter

Before you get started, here are some useful reminders and information about cooking the recipes in this chapter.

These recipes are made in a large donabe steamer called Mushi Nabe. The vessel consists of a base (bowl), steam grate, and lid. The capacity of the base is about 3 quarts (3 L), and the steam grate is about 10 inches (25 cm) in diameter. If you're using a smaller donabe steamer and need to make less, simply adjust the recipe's quantities.

If You Don't Have a Mushi Nabe

Other types of steamers (such as metal steam pots or bamboo steamers with a wok) can be used for most of the recipes in this chapter. Cooking times may vary depending on the type of cooking vessel.

Basic Steaming

Unless otherwise instructed, for all the recipes in this chapter you can follow the same basic steaming instructions:

1. Fill about 70 percent of the donabe body with water.

2. Set the steam grate in place and cover with the lid. Bring to a boil over medium-high to high heat.

3. Once the donabe steamer is ready, simply place the ingredients either directly atop the grate or on a plate or a bed of napa cabbage, green leaf lettuce, green cabbage, or bean sprouts. (This will help prevent the ingredients from sticking to the grate without clogging the holes, thus easier cleaning after use, and

you can eat the bed, too!) Cover and cook until done. Other options for lining the steam grate are a sheet of parchment paper punched with holes, or a mat of bamboo leaves.

Useful tips

Do not clog the holes of the steam grate. Be sure to keep enough space for the steam to get through the holes and to circulate effectively.

If you are using the donabe steamer for multiple courses, between each course make sure there is enough water to steam in the donabe and replenish as necessary. Clean the steam grate between courses if necessary.

When you cook multiple ingredients, start with items that take a longer time to cook, and add those items that take less time to cook later during the steaming.

Shime (Finishing Course)

Instead of using plain water to create the steam, you can try using your choice of *dashi* or seasoned stock instead. Cooking with stock steam imparts an aroma to the steamed ingredients. After you've enjoyed your steamed food, simply remove the lid and the steam grate, and you can add rice or noodles to create your own *shime* course (see chapter 1, page 55). Flavorful drippings from steamed ingredients such as meat and seafood can add even more flavor and richness to the reduced broth.

SERVES 4
as part of a
multicourse meal

EQUIPMENT:
One large (3-quart/3 L) donabe steamer

Seasonal Steamed Vegetables

SPRING SELECTION

4 small waxy potatoes (peeled or unpeeled), quartered

3 to 4 small carrots, sliced on the diagonal ¼ inch (6 mm) thick

5 ounces (150 g) cauliflower florets, cut into large bite-size pieces

4 medium shiitake mushrooms, trimmed and halved

5 ounces (150 g) asparagus, trimmed

5 ounces (150 g) sugar snap peas

AUTUMN SELECTION

5 ounces (150 g) or about ¼ small kabocha squash, cut into ¾-inch (2 cm) wedges

5 ounces (150 g) satsuma-imo (Japanese sweet potato), unpeeled and sliced into ⅓-inch (1 cm) rounds

2 large or 3 medium kabu (Japanese turnip) bulbs, peeled and cut into ¾-inch (2 cm) wedges

5 ounces (150 g) lotus root, sliced into ⅓-inch (1 cm) rounds

½ cup (120 ml) Karashi Peanut Butter Sauce (page 282), for serving

½ cup (120 ml) Saikyo Miso Aioli (page 283), for serving

The first time you try donabe steaming, I really want you to try these simple steamed vegetables, which showcase how donabe-steamed vegetables can taste extremely pure and delicious. In fact, they taste so good that you can enjoy them with just salt and olive oil, or even without any seasoning! But here, we suggest my Karashi Peanut Butter Sauce (page 282) and Kyle's Saikyo Miso Aioli (page 283). You can use the vegetables listed here or make your own selection of seasonal ingredients. We have included the combinations from our spring and autumn donabe meals in the recipe. For a summer menu, you could try cherry tomatoes, okra, eggplant, zucchini, bell pepper, and corn; and for winter options, perhaps brussels sprouts, daikon, taro, burdock, *negi* (Japanese green onion), and *yama-imo* (Japanese mountain yam).—Naoko

Prepare the donabe according to the basic steaming instructions on page 179. Arrange the vegetables on the steam grate, cover, and steam over upper medium-high heat until done. You can start with the ingredients that take a longer time to cook and add the rest of the ingredients in a staggered order so that everything will be done at the same time.

For the spring ingredients, start with the potatoes, and once the potatoes are almost tender (after about 6 to 8 minutes), add the carrots and cauliflower and cook for about 2 minutes. Finally, add the shiitakes, asparagus, and sugar snap peas and cook for about 2 minutes longer.

For the autumn ingredients, arrange all the ingredients on the grate and steam until everything is cooked through, about 6 to 8 minutes.

Serve immediately at the table with your choice of the dipping sauces.

Steamed Yellowtail Shabu-Shabu

Buri no Mushi Shabu

10 ounces (300 g) daikon, peeled and julienned

2 negi (Japanese green onions), or 6 green onions very thinly sliced on the diagonal

1 pound (450 g) yellowtail fillet, sliced ¼ inch (6 mm) thick

Yuzu Ponzu (page 279) for serving

I love the simplicity of this dish, and the flavor never fails! You can slice the ingredients thinly to steam in a very short time. The delicate steamed yellowtail with the thinly sliced negi and daikon pair very well together. Homemade Yuzu Ponzu (page 279) is a nice condiment to dip in for this dish, but you can serve it with other dipping sauces of your choice. When I get a sashimi-grade fillet of yellowtail, I like to serve part of it as a simple sashimi and the rest as a steamed shabu-shabu—this way I can enjoy the same fish in two preparations. You can also try this method with different types of fish such as salmon or sea bream (also known as tai snapper).—Naoko

Prepare the donabe according to the basic steaming instructions on page 179. Spread half of the daikon over the steam grate. Cover and steam over upper medium-high heat for 1 to 2 minutes. Add half of the *negi* and spread over the daikon, followed by half of the yellowtail slices. Cover again and cook for 1 to 2 minutes, or until the fish is medium-rare to barely cooked through (make sure you don't overcook the fish).

To serve, provide each person with about 2 tablespoons of the ponzu in a bowl. Pick up the fish and vegetables and dip in the ponzu to enjoy. Once the first batch is finished, repeat the process to finish the remaining ingredients.

EQUIPMENT:

One large (3-quart/3 L) donabe steamer

One heat-resistant bowl (ceramic or glass) that can fit on the steam grate with the lid on and has a capacity of about 3⅓ cups (800 ml), or is about 8 inches (20 cm) in diameter and 2½ inches (6 cm) high

Crab and Wakame Savory Egg Custard

Kani Wakame Chawanmushi

2 large eggs

1½ cups (360 ml) Kombu and Bonito Dashi (page 274)

2 teaspoons usukuchi shoyu (light-colored soy sauce)

⅓ cup (80 ml; about 1 tablespoon dried) rehydrated wakame seaweed (see page 295), cut into bite-size pieces

3 ounces (90 g) lump crabmeat

¼ cup (60 ml) coarsely chopped mitsuba

½ cup (120 ml) Kombu and Bonito Dashi (page 274)

1½ teaspoons mirin

1½ teaspoons usukuchi shoyu (light-colored soy sauce)

Generous 1 teaspoon kuzuko (kudzu starch) or katakuriko (potato starch), dissolved in 2 teaspoons extra dashi or water

Chawanmushi is a very popular traditional dish in Japan. It's a steamed savory custard with a base of *dashi*, egg, and a small amount of seasoning. The key to a delicious *chawanmushi* is the quality of the *dashi*. In order to focus on the elegant flavor of the *dashi*, seasoning is kept at a minimum (sometimes only a pinch of salt). *Chawanmushi* is commonly prepared in individual serving bowls, but this version is made in a large bowl to serve family-style for a more casual setting. My friend Mikizo Hashimoto, a great Japanese chef, taught me that you can prepare the batter in advance and let it rest for several hours and even up to one day, and this helps the batter taste more integrated and richer when it's cooked. That's a win-win for me when I plan a dinner party. I can get the batter ready a day before, and all I need to do at the dinner is steam it with the rest of the ingredients to serve.—Naoko

To make the batter: Whisk the eggs in a bowl and gradually add the *dashi* as you continue to whisk. Add the *usukuchi shoyu* and stir. You can make the batter up to 1 day in advance and keep it refrigerated. Make sure to bring the batter back to almost room temperature before starting to cook.

Prepare the donabe according to the basic steaming instructions on page 179. Spread the wakame in the heat-resistant bowl, followed by the crabmeat and *mitsuba* (save some of the crabmeat and *mitsuba* for garnish, if you like). Gradually pour the egg batter through a

fine-mesh sieve into the bowl. Cover the bowl with plastic wrap and gently place the bowl on the steam grate. Cover and turn down the heat to low. Cook for 20 to 25 minutes, or until the custard is set. (You should see very gentle steam constantly coming out of the lid's hole during steaming.) If the heat is too high, it will cause air bubbles on the surface of the custard. When the custard is set, turn off the heat, remove the bowl from the donabe, and take off the plastic wrap.

While the dish is being steamed, make the sauce: Combine the *dashi*, mirin, and *usukuchi shoyu* in a small saucepan and bring to a simmer over medium heat for 2 to 3 minutes. Turn down the heat to a gentle simmer and gradually stir in the *kuzuko* solution until the sauce has thickened slightly, about 30 to 60 seconds. Transfer to a small serving bowl.

If you saved some crabmeat and *mitsuba*, scatter them on top of the *chawanmushi*. To serve, spoon the *chawanmushi* into individual bowls and pour some warm sauce over each at the table.

SERVES 4
*as part of a
multicourse meal*

EQUIPMENT:
One large (3-quart/3 L) donabe steamer

One heat-resistant bowl (ceramic or glass), about 8 inches (20 cm) in diameter that can fit on the steam grate with the lid on and has a capacity of about 3⅓ cups (800 ml), or is about 8 inches (20 cm) in diameter and 2½ inches (6 cm) high.

NOTE:
This dish is great cold, too. To enjoy cold *chawanmushi*, chill both the *chawanmushi* and the sauce completely before serving.

VEGETARIAN OPTION:
Substitute Kombu and Shiitake Dashi (page 277) for the Kombu and Bonito Dashi.

Savory Steamed Soy Custard with Saikyo Miso Sauce
Tofu Chawanmushi

2 large eggs

2 cups (480 ml) pure, rich plain soy milk (see page 294)

⅓ cup (80 ml) Kombu and Bonito Dashi (page 274)

Scant 1 teaspoon sea salt

⅓ cup (80 ml) Kombu and Bonito Dashi (page 274)

2 tablespoons Saikyo miso or other sweet white miso

⅔ teaspoon kuzuko (kudzu starch) or katakuriko (potato starch), dissolved in 2 teaspoons extra dashi or water

This dish is made from a few simple ingredients and tastes like extra-silky fresh tofu with an extra-rich flavor. Just like classic *chawanmushi* (steamed savory custard), make sure you steam over very low heat in order to achieve a very smooth texture. Saikyo miso sauce adds a subtle sweet-and-savory flavor to complete the dish.—Naoko

To make the batter: Whisk the eggs in a bowl and gradually add the soy milk, *dashi*, and salt as you continue to whisk until smooth.

Prepare the donabe according to the basic steaming instructions on page 179. Gradually pour the egg batter through a fine-mesh sieve into the heat-resistant bowl. Cover the bowl with plastic wrap and gently place the bowl on the steam grate. Cover and turn down the heat to low. Cook for 20 to 25 minutes, or until the custard is set. (You should see very gentle steam constantly coming out of the lid's hole during steaming.) If heat is too high it will cause air bubbles on the surface of the custard. Turn off the heat, remove the bowl from the donabe, and take off the plastic wrap.

While the dish is being steamed, make the sauce: Combine the *dashi* and Saikyo miso in a small saucepan and whisk until smooth. Bring to a simmer over medium heat. Turn down the heat to a very gentle simmer, and gradually stir in the *kuzuko* solution until the sauce has thickened and is smooth, about 15 to 30 seconds.

To serve, spoon the *chawanmushi* into individual bowls and pour some warm sauce over each at the table.

EQUIPMENT:
One large (3-quart/3 L) donabe steamer

Steamed Pork Belly and Cabbage

4 to 5 leaves green cabbage, cut into strips

4 ounces (120 g) mung bean sprouts (crisp white part only)

8 ounces (240 g) thinly sliced pork belly, cut into 3-inch (7.5 cm) strips

About ½ cup (120 ml) Sesame Dipping Sauce (page 285) or Yuzu Ponzu (page 279), for serving

Sliced pork belly and cabbage is a classic combination in Japanese cooking, and you can never go wrong pairing them. This dish is something you can make on a lazy day, as all you need to do is pile the cabbage, bean sprouts, and pork belly on the steam grate, steam, and enjoy. The vegetables are infused with juicy pork flavors, while the excess grease is drained through the steam grate. I love it with either the Sesame Dipping Sauce (page 285) or Yuzu Ponzu (page 279).—Naoko

Prepare the donabe according to the basic steaming instructions on page 179. Spread the cabbage on the steam grate and mound the bean sprouts on top of the cabbage. Arrange the pork slices radially from the center, slightly overlapping, to cover the bean sprouts. Cover and steam over upper medium-high heat for about 5 to 6 minutes, or until the pork is cooked through.

Serve with your choice of the dipping sauces at the table.

Pork Snow Balls

Shiro-mushi Dango

1 rice cup (¾ cup/180 ml) sweet rice, rinsed (see page 294)

1 tablespoon sake

½ teaspoons sea salt

1 pound (450 g) ground pork

1 large egg

3 medium dried shiitake mushrooms, rehydrated (see page 144), trimmed, and diced small

¼ cup (60 ml) finely minced yellow or sweet onion

1 small clove garlic, finely grated

1 teaspoon finely grated peeled fresh ginger

2½ tablespoons katakuriko (potato starch)

2 tablespoons sake

1 teaspoon soy sauce

¼ teaspoon sea salt

¼ teaspoon freshly ground black pepper

1 teaspoon toasted sesame oil

Yuzu-kosho, for serving

These hearty dumplings look like shiny snowballs, and they make me feel festive every time I make them. Pork meatballs are covered in sweet rice and steamed until the rice is perfectly sticky and the meat is fluffy. I like it with a tiny dab of *yuzu-kosho* (see Glossary, page 295) for accent. Or you can serve them the more classic way, with soy sauce mixed with karashi (Japanese mustard) or ponzu.—Naoko

In a medium bowl, soak the sweet rice with enough water to cover the rice completely for 2 hours. Drain well and transfer it back to the bowl. Add the sake and salt and mix thoroughly.

To make the pork meatballs: Combine all the ingredients in a bowl. Knead by hand until the mixture is shiny and smooth. Cover tightly with plastic wrap and let it rest in the refrigerator for 30 minutes.

Divide the pork mixture into 16 portions and shape them into balls (about 1½ inches/3.5 cm in diameter) by hand. Dip each ball into the sweet rice and, using your hands, coat it completely with rice. Press down lightly on the rice so that it sticks.

Prepare the donabe according to the basic steaming instructions on page 179, lining the steam grate with one of the suggested liners. Arrange the dumplings on the lining. Cover and steam over upper medium-high heat for about 20 minutes, or until the meat and rice are cooked through. Serve with *yuzu-kosho* at the table.

Shrimp and Tofu Two Ways (1): Steamed Shrimp on Tofu

4 ounces (120 g) peeled and deveined shrimp, rinsed, patted dry, and coarsely minced

1 teaspoon katakuriko (potato starch)

1 tablespoon egg white

1 teaspoon sake

Pinch of sugar

Pinch of sea salt

Freshly ground white pepper

1 (19-ounce/400 g) package soft tofu, sliced into 6 rectangular pieces

Katakuriko (potato starch), for sprinkling

2 tablespoons minced green onion (white and green parts)

1 teaspoon finely grated peeled fresh ginger

1 clove garlic, finely grated

1 teaspoon sugar

½ teaspoon thinly sliced dried red chile or red pepper flakes

2 tablespoons toasted sesame oil

1½ tablespoons soy sauce

1 tablespoon sake

In my multicourse donabe dim sum meal, I like to do "Shrimp and Tofu" two ways, because guests are always delighted by how these two ingredients can make two completely different styles of steamed dish. The first version is this elegant appetizer, which can be prepared in a few simple steps. The shrimp topping looks like a shiny jewel on a silky pillow of tofu when it's cooked.—Naoko

To make the shrimp topping: Combine all the ingredients for the topping in a bowl and knead by hand thoroughly until smooth.

Prepare the donabe according to the basic steaming instructions on page 179. Lay the tofu pieces, wider side up, on a tray. Pat the upper surface dry with a paper towel. Use a tea strainer to sprinkle a small amount of *katakuriko* over the upper surface of each piece. Mound one-sixth of the shrimp topping on each tofu piece. Arrange the shrimp-tofu pieces on the steam grate. Cover and steam over upper medium-high heat until the shrimp is just cooked through, 7 to 8 minutes.

In the meantime, make the sauce: Combine the green onion, ginger, garlic, sugar, and dried chile in a heat-resistant bowl. In a small saucepan, heat the sesame oil over medium-high heat until it starts smoking, about 1 to 2 minutes. Remove from the heat and pour into the bowl immediately to flash-fry the ingredients. (Be careful, because it will sizzle and might splash a little.) Immediately add the soy sauce and sake to the same saucepan to cook in the residual heat. Stir well. Pour into the bowl.

Divide the steamed shrimp-tofu pieces among individual plates at the table. Pour the sauce over each and enjoy.

Shrimp and Tofu Two Ways (2): Steamed Tofu and Shrimp Gyoza

7 ounces (200 g) medium-firm tofu, press-drained (see note, page 121)

4 ounces (120 g) peeled and deveined shrimp, rinsed, patted dry, and coarsely minced

2 tablespoons minced negi (Japanese green onion) or green onions (white part only)

1 teaspoon finely grated peeled fresh ginger

1 tablespoon sake

1 teaspoon usukuchi shoyu (light-colored soy sauce)

1 teaspoon toasted sesame oil

¼ teaspoon Asian chicken stock powder (optional, see Glossary, page 288)

1 tablespoon katakuriko (potato starch)

½ teaspoon sea salt

¼ teaspoon ground sansho (Japanese mountain pepper) or freshly ground white pepper

25 to 28 gyoza wrappers (about 3½ inches/8.5 cm in diameter)

About ¼ cup (60 ml) Yuzu Ponzu (page 279), for serving

About ¼ cup (60 ml) Chunky La-yu (page 287), for serving

The filling of tofu and shrimp makes these gyoza taste light yet very savory and satisfying. The shrimp is coarsely minced, so you can also enjoy its springy texture alongside the fluffy tofu in each dumpling. You can substitute ground chicken for the shrimp, if you like.—Naoko

To make the filling: Combine the first eleven filling ingredients in a bowl. Mash the tofu by first squeezing it by hand, and then kneading it thoroughly with the other ingredients until smooth. Cover tightly with plastic wrap and let it rest in the refrigerator for 30 minutes.

To fill the gyoza, mound about 1 tablespoon of the filling in the center of a wrapper and use water to wet about two thirds of the area around the edges. Fold the wrapper in half by lifting the dry-edged side. Pinch the edges tightly to seal and place the gyoza on the baking tray. Repeat the process with the remaining wrappers until the filling is gone. Cover the dumplings with a damp paper towel until ready to cook. You can make the dumplings about 30 to 60 minutes in advance, but any longer and the bottom of the gyoza wrappers will start to become too wet.

Prepare the donabe steamer according to the basic steaming instructions on page 179, lining the surface of the steam grate with one of the suggested liners. Arrange half of the gyoza on the lined steam grate, cover, and steam over upper medium-high heat for 5 minutes, or until the filling is cooked through.

Serve immediately with the ponzu and *la-yu* at the table. Repeat the process with the remaining gyoza.

SERVES 4
*as part of a
multicourse meal*

EQUIPMENT:
One large (3-quart/3 L) donabe steamer

Crab and Pork Shumai

6 ounces (180 g) lump crabmeat

5 ounces (150 g) ground pork

1 tablespoon finely minced shallot

1 green onion, thinly sliced crosswise

1 teaspoon finely grated peeled
fresh ginger

1 tablespoon sake

1 teaspoon usukuchi shoyu
(light-colored soy sauce)

1½ tablespoons katakuriko
(potato starch)

½ teaspoon sea salt

¼ teaspoon raw brown sugar

¼ teaspoon white pepper

15 to 18 small wonton wrappers
(2¾-inch/7 cm squares)

Soy sauce, for serving

Rice vinegar, for serving

Karashi (Japanese mustard; optional),
for serving

Shumai is the Japanese name for a popular Chinese dim sum dish called *shao mai* that has been adapted to Japanese home cooking. It's an open-face wrapped dumpling and is very easy to make. This recipe is full of rich crab flavors and has a nice juicy texture.—Naoko

To make the filling: Combine the first eleven filling ingredients in a bowl and knead by hand until smooth. Cover tightly with plastic wrap and let it rest in the refrigerator for 30 minutes.

To make the *shumai*, mound about 1½ tablespoons of the filling in the center of a wonton wrapper. Gather up the edges of the wrapper, leaving the top of the filling open. Lightly squeeze the neck of the wrapper with your thumb and index finger to form pleats. Rub the bottom flat with your other hand. Set it on the tray and repeat the process with the remaining wrappers until the filling is gone. Cover with a damp paper towel until ready to cook. You can make the *shumai* about 15 to 30 minutes in advance, but any longer and the bottom of the wonton wrappers will start to become too wet.

Prepare the donabe steamer according to the basic steaming instructions on page 179, lining the surface of the steam grate with one of the suggested linings. Arrange all the *shumai* on the lined steam grate, cover, and steam over upper medium-high heat for 6 to 8 minutes, or until the filling is cooked through.

To serve, have each person mix a dipping sauce to taste in a saucer. The standard ratio is about 1.5:1, soy sauce to rice vinegar. Put a small amount of the *karashi* on the side of the saucer. Dip the *shumai* in the sauce and top with a dab of *karashi*, if you like.

EQUIPMENT:

One large (3-quart/3 L) donabe steamer

One shallow heat-resistant bowl (ceramic or glass), about 8 inches (20 cm) in diameter

Steamed Black Cod in Fermented Black Bean Sauce
Gindara Tochi Mushi

1 pound (450 g) black cod fillets (either skin on or skin off is fine), cut into 4 to 6 pieces

1 teaspoon sea salt

1 tablespoon Chinese fermented black beans, minced

1 clove garlic, minced

2 teaspoons minced peeled fresh ginger

1 teaspoon raw brown sugar

1 teaspoon soy sauce

1 tablespoon sake

1½ to 2 tablespoons toasted sesame oil

1 negi (Japanese green onion), or 3 green onions, julienned into hair-thin pieces (white part only)

Shredded or sliced dried red chile (optional), for garnish

Buttery black cod is covered with an aromatic mix of Chinese fermented black beans (*douchi*; see Glossary, page 288), garlic, and ginger and then steamed with sake. Sizzling sesame oil completes the dish for a bold and complex taste. The sizzling effect is fun to watch, and I believe it stimulates guests' appetites at the table. I originally made this dish with traditional Japanese fermented black beans, called *hama-natto*, which actually have their origin in Chinese fermented black beans and have a very similar flavor. They are both pungent and similar to a concentrated, chewy miso, so a small amount can give a very nice accent to the dish.—Naoko

Season the cod all over with the salt and set aside for 15 to 30 minutes. Pat dry with a paper towel.

To make the bean sauce: Combine black beans, garlic, ginger, brown sugar, soy sauce, and sake in a bowl and stir well. Set aside.

Prepare the donabe steamer according to the basic steaming instructions on page 179. Place the fish fillets in a single layer in the heat-resistant bowl. Spread the sauce over the fish. Set the bowl on the steam grate. Cover and steam over upper medium-high heat until the fish is cooked through, about 5 to 7 minutes. Turn off the heat.

As soon as the fish is ready, heat the sesame oil in a small saucepan over medium-high heat just until it starts smoking, about 1 to 2 minutes. To serve, mound the *negi* over the fish. Remove the pan from the heat and immediately drizzle the smoking oil over the *negi* to flash-fry at the table. (Be careful because it will sizzle and might splash a little.) Garnish with some chile.

SERVES 4
*as part of a
multicourse meal*

EQUIPMENT:
One large (3-quart/3 L) donabe steamer

One shallow heat-resistant bowl (ceramic or glass), about 8 inches (20 cm) in diameter

Peel-and-Eat Shrimp with Green Tea and Shochu

14 ounces (400 g) shell-on large shrimp, shells cut open on the back side and shrimp deveined

1 tablespoon Shio-Koji (page 280), or 1 teaspoon sea salt

2 teaspoons fine-quality sencha green tea leaves

1 tablespoon shochu (preferably rice shochu; can substitute with sake)

1 tablespoon very finely julienned peeled fresh ginger

About 1 tablespoon Yuzu-Scented Sweet Vinegar Seasoning (page 286; optional), for serving

The combination of *Shochu* (a distilled drink made from rice), green tea, and shio-koji make this peel-and-eat steamed dish aromatic and flavorful. Make sure you use fine-quality *sencha* tea leaves for the best results.—Naoko

In the heat-resistant bowl, season the shrimp all over with the shio-koji. Let them marinate for 30 minutes.

Place the tea leaves in a small cup. Bring some water to a boil and cool down slightly, and then measure out 1 tablespoon and pour over the tea leaves. Let the tea steep for a few minutes, and then add the *shochu*.

Prepare the donabe steamer according to the basic steaming instructions on page 179. Mix the shrimp with the ginger, and the green tea and *shochu* mixture. Set the bowl on the steam grate. Cover and steam over upper medium-heat for about 10 minutes or until the shrimp are cooked through. Meanwhile after half-way cooking, turn the shrimp once to ensure even-cooking.

Remove the bowl from the steamer. Drizzle with the sweet vinegar seasoning, if you like. Serve warm.

EQUIPMENT:
One large (3-quart/3 L) donabe steamer

NOTE:
Paper-thin slices of meat for shabu-shabu can be found at Japanese markets. If your butcher cannot provide such a thin slice, you can partially freeze a block of meat (rib-eye or top sirloin for beef, never been frozen) and try to slice it as thinly as possible.

Steamed Enoki Mushrooms Wrapped in Beef
Enoki Gyu-maki Mushi

7 ounces (200 g) enoki mushrooms, trimmed

10 ounces (300 g) beef, sliced thinly into 12 to 14 slices for shabu-shabu (see Note)

Katakuriko (potato starch), for dusting

12 to 14 shiso (perilla) leaves

4 large leaves napa cabbage (leafy upper half only), quartered

About ⅓ cup (80 ml) Negi and Shio-Koji Dipping Sauce (page 281)

Enoki mushrooms are wrapped in thinly sliced beef and steamed briefly on a bed of napa cabbage. These pretty rolls are easy to pick up and dip into an umami-rich sizzling negi and *shio-koji* dipping sauce. The mushrooms absorb the flavor of the succulent beef and taste incredibly juicy. Napa cabbage is a nice part of this dish, as it also absorbs the flavors from the beef. These steamed rolls are perfect as an *izakaya-* (Japanese pub-) style course to share. You can substitute pork shoulder or belly for the beef for another flavorful result.—Naoko

Pull apart the enoki mushrooms into 12 to 14 pieces, depending on how many slices of meat you have. To make a wrap, lay a slice of the meat on a work surface vertically in front of you and lightly dust it with the *katakuriko* through a tea strainer. This will seal the meat more effectively and help keep the juices inside when it's cooked. Place a shiso leaf at the end of the meat closest to you, followed by a piece of enoki on top of the shiso horizontally and positioned so that only the end side sits on the meat. Tightly roll the meat at a slight angle to wrap the shiso and enoki so that the meat overlaps partially and leaves the upper end of the shiso and enoki exposed. Place it on a tray and repeat the process with the remaining beef, shiso, and enoki.

Prepare the donabe steamer according to the basic steaming instructions on page 179, using the napa cabbage to line the grate. Arrange all the wrapped beef packets on the napa cabbage. Cover and steam over upper medium-high heat until the meat is just cooked through, about 2 to 3 minutes. Serve immediately with the dipping sauce at the table.

EQUIPMENT:

One large (3-quart/3 L) donabe steamer

One rectangular metal mold with removable inner tray (about 6 by 5¼ by 1¾ inches/ 15 by 13.5 by 4.5 cm) or small baking pan

NOTE:

For a subtle nutty taste, replace about 1⅓ ounces (40 g) of the all-purpose flour with almond flour.

Green Tea Steam Cake

Matcha Mushi Cake

3½ ounces (100 g; about ¾ cups) all-purpose flour (see Note)

2 teaspoons matcha (powdered Japanese green tea)

1 teaspoon baking powder

¼ teaspoon sea salt

1½ ounces (45 g; about 3 tablespoons plus 2 teaspoons) unsalted butter

1 large egg, at room temperature

2 ounces (60 g; about ⅓ cup) raw brown sugar

¼ cup plus 1 tablespoon (75 ml) heavy cream

Sweet, spongy, and very moist, these rustic steam cakes make Japanese adults feel nostalgic and are appealing to all ages. I serve these as a dessert or sometimes send them home with visitors as take-away gifts. They take a very short time to prepare, as the ingredients only need to be assembled and then whisked for a short time. I use a classic Japanese metal mold with a removable inner tray called a *nagashi-kan* (see the Kitchen Tools page 297) to make this, but you can use a small baking pan that will fit on the steam grate with the lid on. The cakes will keep fresh in a tightly sealed container in a cool space for three to four days.—Naoko

Prepare the donabe according to the basic steaming instructions on page 179. Line the inside of the metal mold with a piece of parchment paper cut to fit.

Sift together the flour, matcha, baking powder, and salt into a bowl. Set aside.

Melt the butter in a small saucepan over low heat. Remove from the heat and let it cool down slightly. In a separate bowl, whisk together the egg and sugar until smooth. Gradually whisk in the butter and then the heavy cream, combining thoroughly. Fold in the flour mixture gently and quickly with a rubber spatula. Immediately pour the batter into the parchment-lined mold and smooth the surface with an offset spatula.

Place the mold on the steam grate. Cover and steam over upper medium-high heat for 14 to 16 minutes, or until a skewer inserted into the cake comes out clean. Turn off the heat and remove the mold from the donabe. Let it cool down enough to handle. Remove the cake from the mold.

EQUIPMENT:

One large (3-quart/3 L) donabe steamer

One rectangular metal mold with removable inner tray (about 6 by 5¼ by 1¾ inches/ 15 by 13.5 by 4.5 cm) or small baking pan

NOTE:

For a subtle nutty taste, replace about 1⅓ ounces (40 g) of the all-purpose flour with almond flour.

Black Sesame and Sugar Steam Cake
Ganzuki

3½ ounces (100 g; about ¾ cups) all-purpose flour (see Note)

1 teaspoon baking powder

¼ teaspoon sea salt

1½ ounces (45 g; about 3 tablespoons plus 2 teaspoons) unsalted butter

1 large egg, at room temperature

2 ounces (60 g; about ⅓ cup) black sugar (see Glossary, page 288) or raw brown sugar

¼ cup plus 1 tablespoon (75 ml) heavy cream

1½ tablespoons black sesame seeds, toasted (see page 58)

Prepare the donabe according to the basic steaming instructions on page 179. Line the inside of the metal mold with a piece of parchment paper cut to fit.

Sift together the flour, baking powder, and salt into a bowl. Set aside.

Melt the butter in a small saucepan over low heat. Remove from the heat and let it cool down slightly. In a separate bowl, whisk together the egg and sugar until smooth. Gradually whisk in the butter and then the heavy cream, combining thoroughly. Fold in the flour mixture along with the black sesame seeds gently and quickly with a rubber spatula. Immediately pour the batter into the parchment-lined mold and smooth the surface with an offset spatula.

Place the mold on the steam grate. Cover and steam over upper medium-high heat for 14 to 16 minutes, or until a skewer inserted into the cake comes out clean. Turn off the heat and remove the mold from the donabe. Let it cool down enough to handle. Remove the cake from the mold.

Slice the cakes to serve. You can enjoy them while they're still warm or at room temperature.

CHEF:
David Kinch
RESTAURANT:
Manresa
CITY:
Los Gatos, CA

Abalone and Mushroom Rice

4 live red abalone (about 4 ounces/120g), each about 2½ inches/9 cm long

3 matsutake mushrooms, cleaned and very hard bottom end trimmed

10 ounces (300 g) short-grain white rice, rinsed (see page 99)

A few drops of neutral oil such as grapeseed

Soft mineral water like Volvic (see page 97)

1 to 2 teaspoons shiro shoyu (white soy sauce)

5 shiso leaves, halved

3 to 4 spring onions, split in half lengthwise

Pinch of sea salt

4 sprigs of amaranth leaves

It was at home, not at the restaurant, that I learned a lot about my donabe cooking. Cooking simple meals at home on my days off turned into "Donabe Mondays" for quite a while. Abalone scraps from the restaurant, especially with spring onions, was a favorite, but adding matsutakes during their short season took it to another level. Though some might think of this as gilding the lily, the fragrance of this earth and sea combination is hard to beat. The key to this dish is creating that small amount of "cuisson" at the bottom of the pot by slowly stewing the abalone pieces.—David Kinch

Remove the abalones from their shells with a spoon. Using kitchen shears, remove the viscera. Rinse the abalones thoroughly in running water. Put abalone in a container with a cover and add enough 100°F (38°C) water to cover. Cover the container and place in a warm spot to maintain temperature and allow to rest for 45 minutes.

Place the abalones between two kitchen towels with the foot side facing up and pound with a meat mallet. Place in a covered container and refrigerate overnight.

Reserve one of the abalones whole and slice the other three as thinly as possible. Quarter two of the *matsutake* and cut one in half.

Place the rice in a colander, place the colander in a bowl, and gently fill the bowl with enough water to cover the rice without pouring the water directly on top of the rice. Let the rice sit anywhere from 25 to 40 minutes. Taste the rice periodically between your teeth. You

are waiting for the brittleness to go away and have the rice break off cleanly between your teeth. When ready, lift the colander out of the bowl and drain.

Warm up a few drops of the neutral oil up in the base of the donabe steamer over low heat. Add the sliced abalones and stir gently until the edges just start to curl. Remove the donabe from the heat.

Weigh out the soaked rice, note the weight, and measure out 90 percent of the rice weight in soft water. Add the rice to the abalones, pour the water over, add the quartered matsutake, and mix well. Add a teaspoon or two of *shiro shoyu* to suit your taste and push the shiso leaves below the surface of the water into the rice. Lay all but 3 of the spring onion halves on the surface of the rice. Place the steam grate on top and place the remaining spring onions, the matsutake halves, and the whole abalone on top of the grate. Season with a pinch of salt.

Cover and place the donabe steamer over medium-high heat. When it starts to simmer (steam will come through the hole), turn up the heat to high. Set a timer for 9 minutes.

After 9 minutes, remove the lid, scatter the amaranth leaves on top of the steam grate, and cover again. Let rest with the lid on for 2 minutes.

Remove the lid and the grate and fold the rice gently. Thinly slice the abalone from the grate along with the mushrooms and spring onion. Serve the rice into bowls and top with the sliced abalone, mushrooms, spring onion and amaranth leaves.

Fold the rice gently with a spatula and serve.

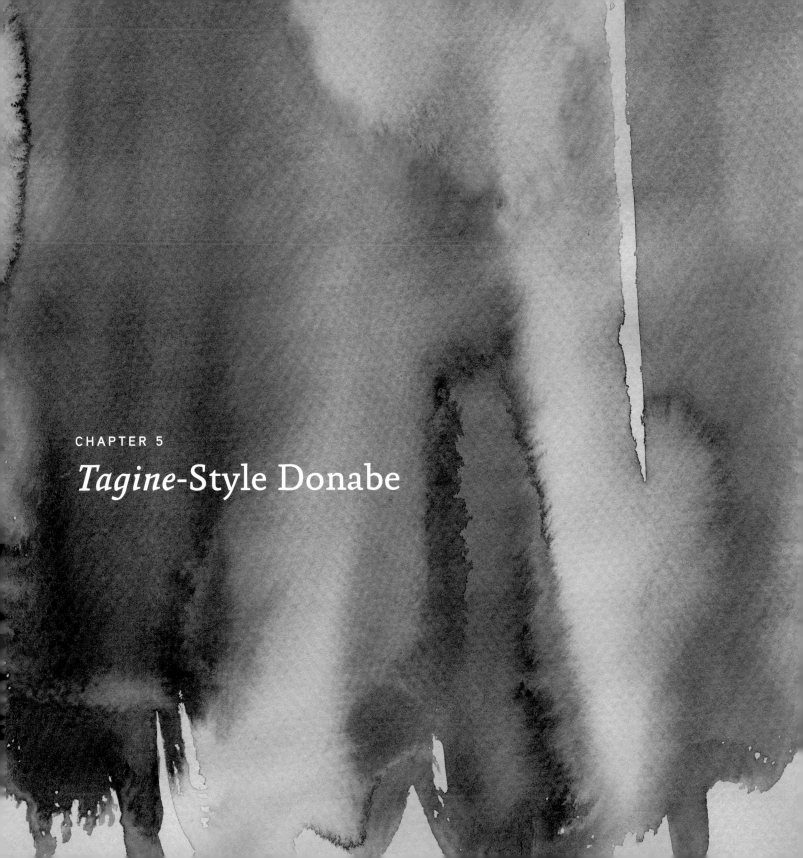

CHAPTER 5

Tagine-Style Donabe

Tagine-Style Donabe

The donabe producer Nagatani-en in Iga, Japan, has been carrying on the tradition of Iga pottery for almost two hundred years. But that doesn't mean that the donabe ware has remained unchanged. The company also applies creativity to tradition. The historic Iga clay and artisanal techniques are presented in new designs and functions. One such unique style is a *tagine*-style donabe with a shape inspired by a Moroccan *tagine* pot, a traditional ceramic cooking pot with a tall cone-shaped lid (the word *tagine* also refers to the stewlike food that's cooked inside the vessel). This *tagine*-style donabe is called Fukkura-san, and it takes full advantage of the characteristics of Iga's storied clay and craftsmanship. This donabe combines the same functions as a traditional Moroccan *tagine* with enhancements that include extra heat retention and durability.

Fukkura-san's lid looks like a tall dome. The uniquely shaped lid with no hole creates circulation inside and handles the steam effectively. This helps preserve the internal moisture during cooking because the steam is trapped inside the insulated body and it condenses back into liquid, so the ingredients cook with a little added moisture. You can even enhance the steam effect by simply filling the inside of the lid with water and letting it rest for a few minutes, draining before use. Fukkura-san's porous clay lid is naturally water-absorbent, so doing this can create extra steam during cooking as the damp lid releases extra steam. Additionally, the glaze on the wide surface of the lid promotes far-infrared radiation effectively, so the ingredients inside tend to be cooked faster and more evenly.

The *tagine*-style donabe's base is shaped like a shallow skillet instead of a bowl. The skillet is heat-resistant enough that it can be heated to a high temperature even while it's empty. Its skillet can work for sautéing or pan-frying. The skillet part is called *toban,* which means "ceramic skillet" in Japanese. Even if you are not familiar with *tagine*-style donabe, you might have already seen or tasted a dish called *toban-yaki,* which is a pan-fried dish made and served directly in a *toban.* Many dishes are as easy as assembling all the ingredients, covering, and heating, and the results are eye-opening one-pot dishes to share. This donabe also works for serving things cold, as it insulates the cold air inside and can work like a portable mini-fridge. Before using, fill the inside of the lid with water, let sit for a few minutes, and drain. Then spread ice cubes in the skillet portion. Place food directly over the ice or on a tray on top of the ice and cover with the lid. It's perfect for serving cold noodles or sashimi outdoors in the summertime. If you turn over the beautiful tall dome-shaped lid of the *tagine*-style donabe, it can work as a serving bowl at your table.

About the Recipes in This Chapter

Before you get started, take a look at these useful reminders and information about cooking the recipes in this chapter.

The recipes here are made in a large-size *tagine*-style donabe, called Fukkura-san; the skillet is about 12½ inches (31.5 cm) in diameter, and this donabe is 7 inches (17.5 cm) tall with the lid on. The capacity of the skillet is about 2 cups (500 ml). The vessel consists of a bottom skillet (*toban*) and a dome-shaped lid, with a grate insert that can be used for roasting. If you are using a smaller *tagine*-style donabe, adjust the recipe's ingredient amounts accordingly.

Creating an Extra-Steam Effect

Many of the recipes in this chapter take advantage of the Fukkura-san's unique design, which enables dry-heating (heating with little or no liquid inside), stir-frying/pan-frying, and sizzling, combined with the creation of steam when the lid is used. In order to enhance the effect of steaming, we recommend that you fill the inside of the lid with water, let it rest for 3 to 5 minutes, and drain. This will allow the porous lid to absorb moisture before use and create extra steam during cooking. When you use the lid, because of the steam that was created inside the insulated body of the donabe, simmering, sautéing, and roasting techniques naturally turn into steam-simmering, steam-frying, and steam-roasting. Though highly recommended, the process of wetting the lid before use is optional unless instructed otherwise in a recipe.

High-Heat Cooking

Some recipes in this chapter use high heat during the course of cooking. Because the skillet base of the *tagine*-style donabe can radiate heat from the flame and can stay very hot for a long period of time after the heat is turned off, be extra-cautious with the heated donabe at all times. Make sure your stove-top surface (especially a glass top) doesn't get too hot to withstand the heat from the skillet.

If You Don't Have a Fukkura-san

Because many of the recipes in this chapter take advantage of the Fukkura-san's unique ability to work as a skillet for both sautéing and dry-heating (heating with little or no liquid inside) combined with high heat, most other types of donabe, including classic-style donabe, are not suitable for the recipes in this chapter. Another brand's large ceramic or cast-iron *tagine*, or other cookware such as heavy-bottomed cast-iron or ceramic skillets with a lid can be used for most of the recipes in this chapter, if they are suited for oil-sautéing or dry-heating over high heat. Cooking times may vary with different types of cooking vessel.

SERVES *4* to *6*
as part of a
multicourse meal

EQUIPMENT:
One large *tagine*-style donabe
(12½ inches/31.5 cm in diameter)

Sizzling Tofu and Mushrooms in Miso Sauce

3 tablespoons miso (see page 291)

3 tablespoons sake

1½ teaspoons toasted sesame oil

1 clove garlic, thinly sliced

1 tablespoon finely julienned peeled fresh ginger

5 ounces (150 g) eryngii (king trumpet) mushrooms, trimmed and thinly sliced

5 ounces (150 g) shimeji mushrooms, trimmed and broken apart by hand

3½ ounces (100 g) enoki mushrooms, trimmed, broken apart by hand, and halved

1 (14-ounce/400 g) package soft tofu, drained

1 thinly sliced green onion for garnish

Chunky La-yu (page 287) or La-yu (chile oil), for serving

A combination of mixed mushrooms and tofu is simply piled up, seasoned with an easy miso sauce and steam-fried in sesame oil. The aroma of sizzling miso always stimulates my appetite. Once you bring the donabe to the table, coarsely break apart the tofu and quickly mix it with the mushrooms in front of the guests. The sizzling sound and savory aroma make a wonderful presentation. You can make this dish with other types of mushrooms of your choice, but it's good to have a few different varieties for more complexity in flavor and texture.—Naoko

Whisk together the miso and sake in a small bowl. Set aside.

Pour the sesame oil into the skillet of the donabe. Scatter in the garlic and ginger. Add all the mushrooms and spread them out so that there is a well in the center where the tofu can sit nicely. Place the tofu in the center. Drizzle the miso and sake mixture over the mushrooms.

Cover and set the donabe over medium heat. Cook for 8 to 10 minutes, or until everything is cooked through and sizzling. Turn off the heat and let it rest, covered, for 2 to 3 minutes.

Uncover at the table and immediately break up the tofu coarsely with a large spoon and mix with the other ingredients inside. Garnish with some green onion. Serve in individual bowls and enjoy with a drizzle of some *la-yu*.

SERVES *6 to 8*
as part of a
multicourse meal

EQUIPMENT:
1 large *tagine*-style donabe
(12½ inches/31.5 cm in diameter)
with a metal grate

Steam-Roasted Fingerling Potatoes

1½ pounds (650 g) small fingerling potatoes, unpeeled

2 teaspoons sea salt

¼ cup (60 ml) crème fraîche

1½ teaspoons chopped fresh chives

½ ounce (15 g) caviar

1 ounce (30 g; a generous ⅓ cup) walnuts

½ teaspoon raw brown sugar

1 tablespoon miso (see page 291)

½ teaspoon Shio-Koji (page 280) or ¼ teaspoon soy sauce

2 to 3 tablespoons Kombu Dashi (page 277) or water

These simple steam-roasted potatoes taste so good that this dish is a huge hit whenever I make it. I love the light yet crisp texture of the potato skin with the creamy interior. Enjoy on their own or with the dipping sauce.—Naoko

Fill the lid of the donabe with water and let it sit for 3 to 5 minutes to allow it to absorb moisture for the extra steaming effect during cooking. Add the potatoes to the water in the lid to rinse them. Drain well and toss the rinsed potatoes with the sea salt while the potatoes are still moist.

Line the skillet of the donabe with aluminum foil and set a grate in the skillet. Place the potatoes on the grate in a single layer. Cover and cook over upper medium-high heat for 30 to 35 minutes, or until the potatoes are tender. The potatoes are ready when a skewer can easily pierce them. Turn off the heat and let it rest for 5 to 10 minutes.

Preheat the oven to 400°F (200°C).

To prepare the caviar and crème fraîche: Mix the crème fraîche with the chopped chives in a small bowl. Transfer to a serving cup. Set it at the table next to the caviar.

To make the dipping sauce: Spread the walnuts out on a baking sheet. and roast in the oven for 8 minutes. Remove and let cool. Transfer to a food processor and pulse until the walnuts are coarsely ground. Add the sugar, miso, shio-koji, and *dashi* and process until they form a smooth paste. Transfer to a serving cup and set at the table.

Serve the potatoes right out of the donabe with your selection of the condiments.

EQUIPMENT:
One large *tagine*-style donabe
(12½ inches/31.5 cm in diameter)

NOTE:
Here's a fast way I use to clean clams and get rid of their sand and grit. Rinse and scrub the clams in cold water first and set aside. Fill a large bowl with very warm water (make sure the temperature is between 118°F and 126°F/ 48°C and 52°C) and submerge the clams for a few minutes. The clams will naturally purge their sand and grit. Drain, and rinse again in cold water.

If you are not going to use the clams immediately, spread them on a tray and cover with a damp paper towel or newspaper. You can store the fresh clams for 1 to 2 days in the refrigerator. Be sure to bring them back to room temperature before use.

Sake-Steamed Clams

Asari no Sakamushi

1 tablespoon unsalted butter

1 clove garlic, minced

1½ teaspoons minced peeled fresh ginger

2 dried red chiles, seeded

2 medium shiitake mushrooms, trimmed and thinly sliced

1 negi (Japanese green onion), or 2 green onions (white part only), thinly sliced on the diagonal

½ cup (120 ml) sake

2 pounds (900 g) littleneck clams, rinsed and scrubbed (see Note)

5 ounces (150 g) broccolini, cut into 2-inch (5 cm) pieces

1½ to 2 teaspoons shiro shoyu (white soy sauce) or Asian fish sauce

½ lemon, cut into 4 wedges

Clams and sake are a beloved combination, and steaming clams in sake is a very popular method of cooking in Japan. It's easy and almost error free, as long as you don't overcook them. I sauté the aromatics and add the sake to reduce it before adding the clams to finish. The broth becomes beautifully enriched with the aromatics and juices released from the clams. You can soak donabe-cooked Plain White Rice (page 100) in the broth or dip crusty bread into it, if you like. It's a sake-flavored dish, but I also like to pair it with an aromatic dry Riesling from Alsace.—Naoko

Heat the butter in the donabe over medium heat; add the garlic, ginger, and dried chiles and sauté until aromatic, about 1 minute. Add the shiitakes and *negi* and stir until the shiitakes are soft, about 1 minute. Add the sake and simmer until it's reduced by more than half, about 3 minutes.

Add the clams and spread out evenly. Add the broccolini and spread over the clams. Cover and cook for 4 to 5 minutes, or until all the clams have opened (discard any that do not open). Turn off the heat, drizzle in the *shiro shoyu*, and stir gently. Serve in individual bowls at the table, with lemon wedges on the side.

EQUIPMENT:
One large *tagine*-style donabe
(12½ inches/31.5 cm in diameter)

Sake-Lover's Ginger Pork Sukiyaki

¼ cup plus 2 tablespoons sake (60 ml)

1 pound (450 g) thinly sliced pork belly, cut into 1½-inch (4 cm) strips

½ cup (120 ml) Kombu and Bonito Dashi (page 274)

¼ cup (60 ml) soy sauce

1 tablespoon toasted sesame oil

1 medium yellow or sweet onion, thinly sliced

1 clove garlic, thinly sliced

1 tablespoon finely julienned peeled fresh ginger

6 medium shiitake mushrooms, trimmed and thinly sliced

7 ounces (200 g) shirataki noodles (konnyaku noodles), blanched (see page 144) and cut into 2-inch (5 cm) pieces

1 green onion, very thinly sliced on the diagonal, for garnish

Chunky La-yu (page 287), for serving

Unlike a traditional *sukiyaki,* no sugar or mirin is used in this recipe. The dish tastes savory with a hint of natural sweetness from the onion. I named this dish Sake-Lover's Ginger Pork Sukiyaki because sake drinkers in Japan typically prefer less-sweet dishes to pair with dry sake. My sake-loving friends tell me that this dish makes them want to drink more sake. I like to make it with thinly sliced pork belly, but pork butt slices or even chicken thighs (cut into bite-size pieces) can work very nicely as well.—Naoko

In a bowl, splash 2 tablespoons sake over the pork and lightly toss by hand. Let it marinate for 15 to 30 minutes.

To make the sauce: combine the *dashi,* remaining ¼ cup sake and soy sauce in a bowl. Set aside.

Heat the sesame oil in the donabe over medium heat; add the onion, garlic, and ginger and sauté for a couple of minutes. Add the shiitakes and sauté for an additional couple of minutes, or until the shiitakes are soft. Add the pork and continue to sauté until the meat is almost cooked through, about 3 to 4 minutes. Add the *shirataki* noodles and stir well.

Add the sauce. Cover and bring to a simmer. Cook for 7 to 8 minutes, or until the sauce is reduced by one-third or so, stirring a couple of times. Turn off the heat and let it rest, covered, for 3 to 5 minutes.

Uncover at the table and garnish with the green onion. Serve in individual bowls with *la-yu* on the side.

SERVES *4 to 6*
as part of a
multicourse meal

EQUIPMENT:
One large *tagine*-style donabe
(12½ inches/31.5 cm in diameter)

NOTE:
Depending on the vegetables you choose, you might want to cut them into similar sizes so that they can be cooked with the same timing. Or you can start with the ingredients that will take a longer time to cook (such as thicker-cut potatoes) and add the ones that cook faster (such as cherry tomatoes, asparagus, and sliced zucchini) near the end.

Steam-Fried Vegetables with Creamy Sesame-Tofu Dipping Sauce

7 ounces (200 g) medium-firm tofu, press-drained (see note, page 121)

2 tablespoons white sesame paste (tahini is fine)

2 tablespoons barley miso or white miso

1 teaspoon raw brown sugar

½ teaspoon toasted sesame oil

1 tablespoon rice vinegar

Sea salt

1½ tablespoons extra-virgin olive oil

6 ounces (180 g) cauliflower florets, cut into small bite-size pieces

4 ounces (120 g) lime radishes or daikon, peeled and cut into ¼-inch (5 mm) rounds

4 ounces (120 g) eryngii (king trumpet) mushrooms, trimmed and cut ⅓ inch (8 mm) thick

2 tablespoons water

4 ounces (120 g) broccoli rabe (rapini), trimmed

2 ounces (60 g) shelled English peas

Regardless of whether you love vegetables, I hope this dish will prove to you that simple cooked vegetables can taste exceptionally good. Many people who have tasted this dish have commented that they would be happy to make a meal out of it. All you do is place your choice of vegetables with a small amount of water in an oiled *tagine*-style donabe and cover to cook. The donabe sizzles and steams the vegetables to crisp-tender. You can use the vegetables here or choose your favorites. While the creamy tofu dipping sauce is our favorite accompaniment for this dish, the Walnut-Miso Dipping Sauce on page 218, or just salt and olive oil can go wonderfully with this dish too.—Naoko

To make the dipping sauce: Place the tofu in a food processor. Add the sesame paste, miso, sugar, sesame oil, and vinegar and blend until smooth. Adjust the seasoning with a pinch of salt or more, if necessary. If using a *suribachi* (mortar) and *surikogi* (pestle), mash the tofu until smooth, then add the rest of the ingredients and mix until smooth. Transfer to a serving cup and set at the table.

Pour the olive oil into the donabe and add the cauliflower, radishes, and eryngii in an even layer. Pour in the water, cover, and set over medium-high heat. Cook for 4 to 6 minutes, or until the ingredients are more than halfway cooked through. Check a couple of times, and if the bottom becomes too dry, add more water. Add the broccoli rabe and peas, and cook for a couple of more minutes or until everything is barely cooked through. Turn off the heat and let rest, covered, for 2 to 3 minutes. Serve with the dipping sauce at the table.

SERVES *4 to 6*
as part of a
multicourse meal

EQUIPMENT:
One large *tagine*-style donabe
(12½ inches/31.5 cm in diameter)

Crunchy Lotus Root in Black Vinegar Sauce

2 tablespoons sake

2 tablespoons kurozu (Japanese black vinegar) or rice vinegar

1 tablespoon soy sauce

1 tablespoon oyster sauce

1 tablespoon toasted sesame oil

1 pound (450 g) lotus roots, peeled and cut oblique into large bite-size pieces

1 tablespoon toasted white sesame seeds (see page 58)

1 dried red chile, seeded and thinly sliced, or ¼ teaspoon red chile flakes

This dish is all about lotus root, simply steam-fried in sesame oil and seasonings. The deep savory character of the *kurozu* (Japanese black vinegar; see Glossary, page 290) wraps the lotus root and tastes brilliant whether the dish is served hot or cool. This makes an ideal shared appetizer, or you can also take it to a picnic.—Naoko

To make the sauce: Combine the sake, *kurozu*, soy sauce, and oyster sauce in a small bowl. Set aside.

Heat the sesame oil in the donabe over medium heat. Add the lotus root and sauté for 1 to 2 minutes. Add the sauce mixture and stir. Cover and cook for 8 to 10 minutes, or until the liquid is almost gone and the lotus is crisp-tender, stirring a couple of times. If the sauce has reduced too quickly, add a small amount of water to keep the ingredients (and skillet) from burning.

Add the sesame seeds and chile. Stir. Turn off the heat and let it rest, covered, for 3 to 5 minutes. Serve directly out of the donabe at the table or transfer to a serving bowl.

EQUIPMENT:
One large *tagine*-style donabe
(12½ inches/31.5 cm in diameter)

Steam-Fried Salmon and Vegetables in Miso Sauce
Chan Chan Yaki

1 teaspoon sea salt

1 pound (450 g) salmon fillet (either skin on or off is fine), cut into 6 to 8 pieces

¼ cup (60 ml) miso (see page 291)

2 tablespoons sake

1 tablespoon mirin

1½ teaspoons raw brown sugar

1½ tablespoons unsalted butter

½ medium yellow or sweet onion, thinly sliced

1 clove garlic, thinly sliced

1½ teaspoons finely julienned peeled fresh ginger

4 to 5 leaves green cabbage, cut into coarse strips

5 ounces (150 g) shimeji mushrooms, trimmed

1 small carrot, peeled and julienned

4 ounces (120 g) mung bean sprouts (crisp white part only)

1½ teaspoons toasted sesame oil

4 lemon wedges, for serving

About ¼ cup (60 ml) Chunky La-yu (page 287), for serving

Chan chan yaki is a regional specialty from Hokkaido, the northern island of Japan. It's typically made in a large skillet in which salmon is cooked with vegetables in butter and miso and served right out of the skillet. The name is said to come from the sound of the metal spatulas and skillet clinking when the ingredients are mixed. It sounds like "Chan! Chan!" and *yaki* means "to grill" or "to bake." I always chant "Chan! Chan!" as I mix the salmon with the vegetables to finish, and the table laughs.—Naoko

Sprinkle the salt on both sides of the salmon pieces and leave for 15 minutes. Pat dry with a paper towel. Set aside.

To make the sauce: Whisk together the miso, sake, mirin, and brown sugar in a small bowl to combine. Set aside.

Heat 1 tablespoon of the butter in the donabe over medium heat and sauté the onion, garlic, and ginger for about 2 minutes. Add the cabbage and spread out in an even layer. Place the salmon on top of the cabbage. Pull apart the *shimeji* into smaller clusters by hand and place among the salmon pieces followed by the carrot. Pour in the miso sauce and cover. Cook for 4 to 6 minutes, or until the salmon is more than halfway cooked.

Add the bean sprouts and the remaining ½ tablespoon butter. Cover again and cook for an additional few minutes, or until everything is just cooked through. Turn off the heat and let rest for a few minutes. Uncover at the table and drizzle with the sesame oil. Quickly mix all the ingredients inside, coarsely breaking the salmon apart with a large spoon and integrating it into the rest. Serve in individual bowls with lemon wedges and *la-yu* on the side.

SERVES *4 to 6*
as part of a
multicourse meal

EQUIPMENT:
One large *tagine*-style donabe
(12½ inches/31.5 cm in diameter)

Steam-Fried Burdock and Carrot

Kimpira Gobo

2 tablespoons sake

2 tablespoons mirin

2 tablespoons raw brown sugar

¼ cup (60 ml) soy sauce

2 tablespoons water

3 tablespoons toasted sesame oil

1 pound (450 g) burdock, julienned into
3-inch (7.5 cm) pieces

4 ounces (120 g; about 1 large)
carrot, peeled and julienned into 3-inch
(7.5 cm) pieces

1½ tablespoons toasted white sesame
seeds (see page 58)

1 dried red chile, seeded and thinly
sliced, or ¼ teaspoon red chile flakes

This is a very traditional dish in Japanese homes, and I have loved it since I was a child. In typical *kimpira gobo*, sliced burdock (see Glossary, page 288) and carrots are cooked in a soy-based seasoning. I like to cut both the burdock root and the carrot into very thin matchstick slices for better flavor integration as well as texture. The dish can be served hot, cold, or at a room temperature. The flavors will meld and it will taste even better after a few hours or overnight in the refrigerator. You can enjoy it for the next few days. My favorite way to eat *kimpira gobo* has always been over plain rice. If you're not good with heat, you can simply omit the chile.—Naoko

To make the sauce: Combine the sake, mirin, brown sugar, soy sauce, and water in a bowl and whisk to blend. Set aside.

Heat the sesame oil in the donabe over medium heat, add the burdock, and stir for a couple of minutes. Add the sauce, cover, and continue to cook for 10 minutes. Add the carrot, cover again, and cook for an additional 10 minutes, or until the liquid is almost gone, stirring a couple of times. If the sauce has reduced too quickly, add a small amount of water to keep the ingredients (and skillet) from burning.

Add the sesame seeds and chile. Stir, cover again, turn off the heat, and let it rest for 10 to 15 minutes. Serve on individual plates at the table or transfer to a serving bowl.

SERVES *2 to 4*
as part of a
multicourse meal

EQUIPMENT:
One large *tagine*-style donabe
(12½ inches/31.5 cm in diameter)

NOTE:
To scrub the oysters, use a scrub brush
and remove any weeds or debris on the
shell under cold running water.

Steam-Roasted Oysters

10 to 12 medium whole oysters, rinsed
and scrubbed (see Note)

Lemon wedges, for serving

Naosco (page 281), for serving

Yasuhiro, who is an eighth-generation member of the Nagatani family, once told me that nothing makes him feel better than ice-cold stout with steam-roasted oysters right out of a Fukkura-san after a long day of work. It sounds very good, indeed. You just place whole oysters in the *tagine*-style donabe and let the donabe do the work for you. The result is super-plump and steamy, juicy oysters. Be careful that your stove-top surface (especially a glass top) doesn't get too hot to withstand the heat; if it does, turn off the heat immediately and let it cool down for a while. *Naosco* (page 281) is a combination of *yuzu-kosho*, vinegar, and *shio-koji*.—Naoko

Line the surface of the donabe's skillet with aluminum foil. Set it over high heat and preheat for 5 minutes.

Place the oysters with the flat-side up in a single layer on the aluminum foil. Cover and cook for 10 to 15 minutes, or until the shells are open (discard any that do not open). Turn off the heat, uncover at the table, and remove the upper shells. If a shell is only slightly open, use an oyster knife or small table knife and insert it into the open space, pushing up the upper shell. Serve immediately at the table with lemon wedges or *Naosco*.

SERVES **6**
as part of a
multicourse meal

EQUIPMENT:
One large *tagine*-style donabe
(12½ inches/31.5 cm in diameter)

VEGAN OPTION:
Omit the egg yolks.

Japanese-Style Sizzling Bibimbap

6 egg yolks

About ½ cup (120 ml) Umami-Rich Soy Sauce (page 285)

1½ teaspoons extra-virgin olive oil

6 medium shiitake mushrooms, trimmed and thinly sliced

1½ teaspoons sake

Sea salt

Freshly ground black pepper

Several pinches of toasted white sesame seeds (see page 58)

4 ounces (120 g) soybean sprouts

1 to 1½ tablespoons plus several splashes of toasted sesame oil

5 ounces (150 g; about ⅔ bunch) fresh spinach

2 small carrots; 4 ounces (120 g), thinly sliced on the diagonal

6 servings Plain White Rice (page 100; two-thirds to full recipe amount)

2 tablespoons Naokochujang (page 284), plus more as needed

Bibimbap is one of the signature dishes from Korea, and it's also very popular in Japan. This is a party-size *bibimbap* with a generous amount of vegetables. To mix with the rice, instead of the traditional *gochujang* (Korean fermented hot chile paste) I make my own *Naokochujang* , which includes a good amount of Japanese miso (page 280). You can vary your mix of vegetables, as well as the amount of chile paste, to suit your taste.

The tagine-style donabe's skillet makes the perfect crust on the bottom of the rice. All the vegetable toppings can be prepared a few hours in advance. Soy-marinated egg yolk is served individually, and it's up to you whether you mix it with your rice in the bowl with extra hot paste or break it on top of the rice and let it ooze like a sauce over the rice.—Naoko

To make the soy-marinated egg yolks: Gently place the yolks in a flat-bottomed container and pour in just enough of the soy sauce to barely cover the surface. Place a piece of plastic wrap onto the surface. Let the yolks marinate in the refrigerator 5 hours or overnight.

To prepare the shiitake, heat the olive oil in a sauté pan over medium; add the shiitakes and sauté until they are soft, about 2 to 3 minutes. Add the sake and continue to sauté until the mushrooms are cooked through, about 1 to 2 minutes. Season with a pinch each of salt, pepper, and sesame seeds. Stir again. Turn off the heat and transfer to a plate.

Bring a medium pot of water to a boil. Add the soybean sprouts and cook until they are just tender, about 2 minutes. Drain well and let them cool down slightly. Transfer to a bowl and season with a splash

continued

of the sesame oil and a pinch each of salt, pepper, and sesame seeds. Gently toss by hand.

Prepare a bowl of ice water and bring a medium pot of water to a boil. Lightly salt the water, add the spinach, and cook until it's wilted, about 10 seconds. Drain and immediately transfer the spinach to the bowl of ice water. Drain again and squeeze out the excess moisture. Trim the bottom ends (if any), and cut the spinach into 2 inch (5 cm) pieces. Place in a bowl and season with a splash of the sesame oil and a pinch each of salt, pepper, and sesame seeds. Gently toss by hand.

Bring a medium pot of water to a boil. Lightly salt the water, add the carrots, and cook until crisp-tender, about 1 minute. Drain well and let it cool down.

Set the donabe over medium-high heat and preheat for 3 minutes. Add 1 to 1½ tablespoons of the sesame oil and turn down the heat to medium. Add the rice and spread evenly. Place the shiitakes, soybean sprouts, spinach, and carrots over the rice. Cover and cook for 4 to 5 minutes, or until the bottom of the rice is light golden to golden brown. You can check the doneness by gently scooping the bottom of the rice. Uncover, immediately add about 2 tablespoons *Naokochujang* in the center, and mix all the ingredients together using two large spoons at the table. Add more *Naokochujang* if you like. Serve in individual bowls and top each bowl with a soy-marinated egg yolk, if you like.

SERVES *4 to 6*
as part of a
multicourse meal

EQUIPMENT:
One large *tagine*-style donabe
(12½ inches/31.5 cm in diameter)

Steam-Fried Black Cod with Crisp Potatoes, Leeks, and Walnut-Nori Pesto

½ cup (120 ml) walnuts

2 cloves garlic, minced

2 teaspoons sea salt

¼ cup (60 ml) shredded Parmesan cheese

2 full square sheets nori

5 cups (1 L) loosely packed fresh basil leaves (about 3 large bunches)

¾ cup (180 ml) grapeseed oil

¼ cup (60 ml) extra-virgin olive oil

Steam-Roasted Fingerling Potatoes (page 218)

¼ cup (60 ml) grapeseed oil

2 leeks, trimmed and dark green parts removed, cut into ¼-inch (6 mm) rounds

2 teaspoons sea salt

1½ pounds (650g) black cod fillet, skin and bones removed, cut into 8 to 12 pieces

Black cod, also known as sablefish, is a wonderfully rich and buttery fish. It has become a popular dish in restaurants, most often cooked in a sweet miso sauce, but it's incredibly versatile. You can substitute sea bass or halibut here; however, the black cod lends itself exceptionally well to the unique cooking process in the *tagine*-style donabe. This dish incorporates the Steam-Roasted Fingerling Potatoes (page 218), which are then crisped and steam-fried with the leeks and black cod.—Kyle

To make the pesto: Preheat the oven to 350°F (175°C). Place the walnuts on a baking sheet and toast in the oven for 7 to 10 minutes. Let cool slightly. Combine the garlic, salt, and toasted walnuts in a food processor and pulse until the nuts are pureed but still crumbly. Add the cheese and pulse several times. Take each sheet of nori individually and toast it over an open flame, passing it back and forth several times. Tear the nori sheets into small pieces, add to the processor, and pulse several times. Meanwhile, bring a large pot of water to a boil and prepare an ice bath. Add the basil to the boiling water and blanch for 3 seconds; drain the basil and transfer to the ice bath. Drain the basil again and pat dry. Add the basil to the processor and puree until the mixture becomes homogeneous but still coarse, drizzling in both oils while pureeing. Check the seasoning and adjust if necessary.

continued

Steam-Fried Black Cod with Crisp Potatoes, Leeks, and Walnut-Nori Pesto, continued

Prepare the Steam-Roasted Fingerling Potatoes according to the recipe instructions on page 218, up to the point where they are allowed to rest for 5 to 10 minutes.

When the potatoes are cool enough to handle, cut them in half and discard the aluminum foil. Pour the oil into the skillet of the donabe and heat over medium-high heat. Add the potatoes, cut-side down, and cook until crispy and brown on the cut sides, about 4 minutes. Push the potatoes to one side and add the leeks to the oil. Cover and lower the heat to medium. Allow to cook for 3 minutes. Uncover and season the leeks and potatoes with 1 teaspoon of the salt.

Add the fish pieces in a single layer over the leeks (to keep the potatoes crispy) and season with the remaining 1 teaspoon salt. Cover and cook the fish for 4 minutes, or until the fish is cooked through. Turn off the heat. Uncover at the table and spoon the pesto over the fish, leeks, and potatoes.

EQUIPMENT:
One large *tagine*-style donabe
(12½ inches/31.5 cm in diameter)

NOTE:
For a prettier presentation,
trim (bevel) all of the edges
of each daikon.

VEGAN OPTION:
Replace the butter with olive oil
and omit the *katsuobushi*.

Daikon Steak

1 medium (about 1¾ pounds/800 g) daikon, peeled and cut into 1-inch (2.5 cm) rounds

½ cup (120 ml) water

1½ tablespoons unsalted butter

3 tablespoons mirin

3 tablespoons soy sauce

1 teaspoon toasted sesame oil

Handful of katsuobushi (dried bonito flakes; preferably the hair-thin type), for garnish

Ground sansho (Japanese mountain pepper; optional), for serving

Whether raw or cooked, daikon is an essential and beloved item in Japanese kitchens all year round. Daikon steak is very simple to make and so rich in flavor. Sprinkle on the *katsuobushi* (dried bonito flakes) while the daikon is still hot, so they will move as if they are dancing happily.—Naoko

To prepare the daikon, score an X across the surface on each side of each daikon disk, slicing one-third to almost halfway through. This will help the daikon absorb the sauce more throughout the cooking.

Add the water to the donabe and place the daikon inside in one layer. Cover, set over medium heat, and cook for 15 to 17 minutes, or until the daikon disks are almost tender but the center is still slightly firm when you insert a skewer. Check while it's cooking and add more water if the water evaporates too soon. Turn off the heat and transfer the daikon to a plate. Drain any leftover water from the donabe and wipe with a paper towel.

Return the donabe to the stove over medium heat and add the butter and daikon. Cover, and cook for 3 to 5 minutes or until the daikon is lightly browned. Flip the daikon over and add the mirin and soy sauce. Cover again and cook for about 8 minutes, or until the sauce has reduced by more than half. Flip them over again and drizzle in the sesame oil. Stir gently, so that the daikon pieces are nicely coated with the sauce. Let the sauce reduce further for a few minutes, until it has thickened. Turn off the heat and let it rest, covered, for 3 to 5 minutes.

Uncover at the table and garnish with the *katsuobushi*. Serve on individual plates and sprinkle with *sansho*, if you like.

EQUIPMENT:
One large *tagine*-style donabe
(12½ inches/31.5 cm in diameter)

Drunken Steam-Fried Drummettes in Shochu Sauce

1½ pounds (650 g) chicken drumettes

1 teaspoon sea salt

3 green onions, halved crosswise
(white and green parts)

1 tablespoon thinly sliced peeled
fresh ginger

¼ cup (60 ml) shochu (Japanese distilled
drink), preferably rice shochu

3 tablespoons soy sauce

2 tablespoons raw brown sugar

1½ teaspoons kurozu (Japanese black
vinegar) or rice vinegar

4 to 5 green cabbage leaves

Minced chives, for garnish

Ichimi togarashi (Japanese ground
chiles), for serving

This simple dish is ideally suited to casual *izakaya* (Japanese pub)-style get-togethers. I find that *shochu* (a Japanese distilled drink; see Glossary, page 294) tends to make the chicken more tender and also gives it a nice aroma. I use rice *shochu*, but other types of *shochu* or even sake can work with this dish, too. Just put the ingredients in a *tagine*-style donabe and let it do the work for you.—Naoko

Season the chicken all over with the salt and allow to marinate for 30 minutes, or cover and refrigerate overnight.

Spread the green onions and ginger in the donabe. Add the chicken and spread out in a single layer. Add the shochu, soy sauce, brown sugar, and vinegar over the chicken.

Spread out the cabbage to cover the chicken entirely. Cover with the lid and set over medium-high heat. Cook for 5 minutes. Turn down the heat to medium-low and cook for 25 to 30 minutes longer, or until the sauce has reduced by half or more, stirring occasionally. Turn off the heat and let it rest for 5 to 10 minutes.

Serve in individual bowls at the table and sprinkle with chives and *ichimi togarashi*.

EQUIPMENT:
One large *tagine*-style donabe
(12½ inches/31.5 cm in diameter)

CHEFS:
Nick Balla and Cortney Burns
RESTAURANT:
Bar Tartine
CITY:
San Francisco, CA

Roasted Shio-Koji Chicken

1 (about 4-pound/1.8 kg) whole chicken

½ cup (120 ml) Shio-Koji (page 280), ground to a smooth paste

2 pounds (900 g) button mushrooms, trimmed

2 dried shiitake mushrooms

Sea salt

1 (3 by 6-inch/7.5 by 15 cm) piece kombu

2 small (6 to 8 ounces/180 to 240 g each) satsuma-imo (Japanese sweet potatoes), or 1 large one, halved, skin brushed to remove any dirt

2 tablespoons chicken fat or butter,

8 ounces (240 g) maitake (hen-of-the-woods) mushrooms, trimmed and whole clusters halved, or substitute with large shiitake mushrooms

12 ounces (360 g) gai lan (Chinese broccoli), stems peeled

3 to 4 green onions, sliced thinly on the diagonal, for garnish

Shichimi togarashi (Japanese seven-spice blend), for serving

This recipe makes use of two techniques that give a simple roast chicken a flavor that cannot be obtained in any other way. The recipe begins with Shio-Koji (page 280), the fermented mixture of salt and *koji* (malted rice) that gives sake, soy sauce, and miso their unique flavors. The chicken is cooked in a *tagine*-style donabe, its radiant heat browning the skin and leaving the interior tender. The *shio-koji* makes the chicken slightly sweet and intensely flavorful. Note, plan this recipe ahead, it requires one day of marinating and ten hours to bake.—Nick Balla and Cortney Burns

To marinate the chicken, rub the chicken with the *shio-koji* and refrigerate for 24 hours. Remove from the refrigerator and wipe off the *koji* paste. Allow the chicken to come to room temperature for at least 1 hour before continuing.

Preheat the oven to 180°F (82°C).

Grind the button mushrooms in a food processor until they are thoroughly minced. Place the dried shiitake mushrooms on the bottom of a baking pan and cover with the minced button mushrooms and a pinch of sea salt. Cover the pan with a tight-fitting lid and place in the oven for 10 hours. Add the *kombu* and return to the oven for 1 hour. Remove the mixture from the oven and strain through a fine-mesh sieve. Taste the mushroom broth for seasoning. If using the broth immediately, reserve at room temperature. This broth can also be made ahead and stored in a refrigerator for up to 3 days.

Heat the oven to 450°F (230°C).

To assemble the dish, rub each of the *satsuma-imo* with 1 tablespoon of the chicken fat and a pinch of sea salt. Place the skillet of the donabe in the oven for 10 minutes; remove from the oven and test that it is hot enough by flicking a drop of water on the surface. If the water sizzles on contact, it is ready to roast the chicken. Place the chicken in the center of the skillet with the breast side facing up. Place a *satsuma-imo* on either side of the chicken. Return the skillet to the oven with the lid next to it to heat it. Cook the chicken and *satsuma-imo* for 20 minutes, or until they just start to brown. Place the lid over the skillet and return to the oven for 25 minutes.

Remove the donabe from the oven to check that the chicken and *satsuma-imo* have finished cooking. The chicken should be about 155°F (68°C) and the *satsuma-imo* should be tender when a skewer is inserted. Return to the oven and cook longer if needed. Transfer the chicken and *satsuma-imo* in a shallow baking dish and cover with a lid to keep them warm while finishing the dish. Place the skillet over low heat on top of the stove. Place the *maitake* mushrooms cut-side down and the peeled *gai lan* in the bottom of the vessel and pour the mushroom broth over the top. Simmer for 5 minutes, until the mushrooms and gai lan are tender.

While the vegetables are simmering, carve the chicken and slice the *satsuma-imo*. Arrange the chicken and *satsuma-imo* over the broth with the mushrooms and *gai lan*. Garnish with the green onions and serve immediately. Place the *shichimi togarashi* on the side for guests to use on the chicken as desired.

CHAPTER 6

Donabe Smoker

Donabe Smoker

Smoked food appeals to people for its diversity of styles. At the same time, many people may perceive smoking as intimidating or impractical to do at home. People often assume that it requires special techniques or is a long process that takes from a full day to sometimes weeks. Others are afraid of the amount of smoke that will be released if trying it at home and think smoking is something to be done only with special equipment outdoors.

But the donabe has made it easy to smoke foods at home. The donabe we introduce in this chapter is specially designed for hot-smoking. It's called Ibushi Gin, and you can enjoy quick smoking with virtually no smoke released. This donabe smoker can be used even in a tiny kitchen in a closed space, and you can serve the freshly smoked food right from the donabe at the table. If you have a portable burner, it's great for dinner parties, either indoors or out. With this donabe, you can enjoy a whole new smoking experience with no fuss.

Ibushi Gin is an invention of Yuji Nagatani, the chairman of Nagatani-en. The idea first arose from necessity. As a lover of both sake and smoked food, Yuji wanted to make a donabe that could smoke foods at the table to be enjoyed communally, just like other types of donabe. This donabe has a thick round body with extra space inside for better smoke circulation. There are three tiers of metal grates that can be set inside. You place the smoke chips on the bottom and the ingredients on the grates, cover, and set the donabe over high heat. The thick, porous body of Iga clay and tightly sealed lid trap both the heat and the smoke inside the donabe. The average smoking time over heat is only 12 to 15 minutes (and you don't need to change the heat level while it's cooking), followed by an average 20 minutes of resting time after the heat is turned off. So the whole smoking process, including resting time, is just about 30 to 35 minutes, and the result is a beautiful and flavorful dish. We will explain the step-by-step basic donabe smoking procedures later in this chapter.

Donabe smoking has its own magic. You throw regular ingredients, ranging from simple fillets of fish and meat to mushrooms and vegetables or nuts and cheese, into a donabe smoker and they transform in no time at all into something special. Once you familiarize yourself with the donabe smoker and the recipes in this chapter, you can stretch your creativity to experiment with different variations of smoke aromas (combining smoking wood with herbs, tea leaves, and so on) or new ingredients you are interested in trying. While you might make a few small mistakes along the way (some ingredients work better in the smoker than others), you will discover new favorites—and that's always a joy. You can become a proud smoker!

About the Recipes in This Chapter

Before you get started, here are some useful reminders and information about cooking the recipes in this chapter.

The recipes are made in a large donabe smoker (about 10¾ inches/27 cm in diameter and 8 inches/20 cm tall) called Ibushi Gin. This donabe has a base (bowl) and a lid with no hole. The rim of the base has a reservoir all around. When the cover is placed on the base, you fill the reservoir with water, creating a water seal that traps the smoke inside. There are three tiers of metal grates that can be set inside the base, on which you place the ingredients to smoke. If you're using a smaller donabe smoker, adjust the recipe's ingredient quantities accordingly. Ibushi Gin should not be used for purposes other than smoking.

If You Don't Have an Ibushi Gin

Other heat-smoking cookware can be used for these recipes. Follow your product's instructions to adapt the recipes to your cookware.

Smoke Chips

Wood smoke chips are used in the recipes in this chapter. The wood chips should be fine (small) so that they can heat and start to release smoke faster. These chips don't need to be soaked in water before use. The following are some of the types of wood chips we recommend. Fine-cut wood chips can be found at housewares stores or online shops (see Resources, page 299). In this chapter, we use cherry-blossom wood chips because we particularly like the elegant smoky character these chips provide, but you can try different kinds of smoke chips of your preference.

Cherry-Blossom (called *sakura* in Japanese): This is the most popular type of smoke wood in Japan. Cherry-blossom wood chips provide a mild and elegant aroma with a hint of sweetness. The color these chips impart to the ingredients is medium-dark.

Apple: Also popular in Japan. Apple wood chips impart a relatively lighter color. The flavor is mild and slightly acidic with a hint of sweetness.

Walnut: These chips provide a light and elegant aroma, but they tend to give a darker color to the ingredients. They're especially popular for smoking white meat or fish.

Hickory: A popular smoke wood in the United States, hickory has a rich aroma and is popular for meat. The color it imparts tends to be dark, too.

You can combine the smoke chips with about a teaspoon of raw brown sugar, which will give the ingredients more color and shine.

Other items you can mix with the smoke chips include tea leaves (such as *hojicha*, oolong, or Earl Grey) and fresh herbs (such as sprigs of rosemary or thyme), which will add another layer of flavor. For the tea leaves, use about a teaspoon; for the fresh herbs, a few sprigs are enough. Play around with different combinations and enjoy the variations of smoke aromas.

Basic Smoking

1. Line the bottom of a donabe smoker with a piece of aluminum foil (about a 6-inch/15 cm square). Make sure that the foil is pressed firmly into the bottom. Place a handful of dry smoke chips (about ⅓ ounce/ 7 to 10 g) spread in a large ring shape atop the foil. If the ingredient(s) have a high fat or moisture content, place another, slightly larger piece of foil very loosely over the smoke chips in order to catch the drippings and keep the smoke chips from getting wet. Make sure there is room for the smoke to escape between the two layers of foil.

2. Cut the ingredients of your choice into the desired size. Each ingredient should not be thicker than about 1 inch (2.5 cm). Lightly season fish fillets with salt and pepper and let rest (30 to 60 minutes for small cuts, 1 to 2 hours for large fillets); lightly season meat with salt and pepper and let rest for 1 to 2 hours or longer. For other ingredients, such as vegetables, season with salt and pepper if you desire. Pat dry all the ingredients before smoking to remove any excess moisture.

3. Set the grates inside the smoker one by one, placing ingredients on each grate before adding the next. The ingredients should not overlap one another. The lower grate tends to become hotter, as it's closer to the flame, so if you are smoking different ingredients at the same time, place the thicker ingredients on the bottom grate.

4. Set the donabe smoker, uncovered, over high heat. Once the smoke chips start to release smoke, about 7 to 8 minutes, cover with the lid. If the heat is too high (i.e. the smoke chips start to release smoke too soon), the ingredients can overcook and also taste bitter.

5. Fill the reservoir in the rim of the base a little over half full with water. Smoke for 7 to 9 minutes over high heat, and then turn off the heat. Cooking times may vary depending on the ingredients and their sizes. Experiment and see what works best for you. For thin-sliced ingredients, the smoking time after heating dish has been covered can be 5 minutes or even less. For thicker cuts, especially meat, it can be 9 minutes or longer.

6. Let it rest undisturbed for 20 minutes. Uncover, and the smoked items are ready to eat.

It's very important to pat each ingredient's surface dry before smoking so that it can absorb the smoke effectively.

SERVES *4 to 6*
as part of a
multicourse meal

EQUIPMENT:
One large donabe smoker
(about 10¾ inches/27 cm in diameter)

NOTE:
Octopus for sashimi is already boiled;
it can be found at Japanese markets.

Smoked Medley: Smoking with Assorted Ingredients

6 medium chicken wings,
middle joint only

Sea salt

Freshly ground black pepper

5 ounces (150 g) octopus legs for
sashimi, cut into bite-size pieces
(see Note)

3 large eggs, chilled

Handful of smoke chips (your choice)

6 asparagus tips

3 ounces (100 g) eryngii (king
trumpet) mushrooms, sliced
lengthwise ¼ inch (6 mm) thick

About 2 tablespoons Naosco
(page 281), for serving

In this recipe, various ingredients are smoked in a donabe smoker and uncovered at the table, revealed layer by layer amid the guests' excited oohs and ahs. The yolks of the very soft boiled eggs stay magically soft while the outsides absorb the nice smoky aroma. I serve it with my own sauce I call *Naosco* (page 281), a combination of *yuzu-kosho*, vinegar, and *shio-koji*, or you can serve with just lemon wedges on the side, too. This dish is a great introduction to smoking with donabe.—Naoko

Season the chicken wings lightly with salt and pepper. Let them rest, uncovered, for 1 to 2 hours in the refrigerator. Remove them about 30 minutes prior to smoking to bring them close to room temperature. Pat dry with a paper towel.

Meanwhile, season the octopus legs lightly with salt and pepper. Let them rest for 30 to 60 minutes in the refrigerator. Pat dry with a paper towel.

Bring a small pot of water to a boil. Pierce a hole in the bottom of each cold egg (right out of the refrigerator) with a safety pin. Place them carefully in the boiling water and cook for 7 minutes. Immediately transfer the eggs to a bowl of cold water to cool down. Carefully peel the eggs and pat dry with a paper towel. The yolks should still be runny.

Set the smoke chips in the donabe according to the basic smoking instructions on page 250. Set up the grates inside the donabe, placing the chicken wings on the bottom grate, the asparagus and *eryngii*

mushrooms on the middle grate, and the eggs in the center of the top grate surrounded by the octopus.

Set the donabe, uncovered, over high heat. Wait until the smoke chips start to release smoke, about 7 to 8 minutes. Cover, and fill the reservoir in the rim of the base a little over half full with water. Smoke for 9 to 10 minutes over high heat, and then turn off the heat. Let rest undisturbed for 20 minutes.

Transfer the items to a large serving plate or serve directly on individual plates at the table, with the *Naosco* on the side.

EQUIPMENT:
One large donabe smoker
(about 10¾ inches/27 cm in diameter)

NOTE:
Depending on the size of the sausages, cooking time
may vary. For a thicker sausage (up to 1 inch/2.5 cm
thick), smoke for 9 to 10 minutes after the lid is put on,
and let it rest for 20 minutes after the heat is turned off.

Smoked Sausages

1 pound (450 g) fresh uncooked sausages
(different sizes are okay)

Handful of smoke chips (your choice)

Coarse-ground mustard, for serving

Such a simple ingredient as sausage upgrades to something special
when smoked in a donabe. When we have a casual party, I like
to serve this with coarse-ground mustard as a condiment and
alongside ice-cold beer. Guests often rave about them as if they
had never tried sausages before! When I'm out of town, this is
what my husband, Jason, likes to make, too. If you can find a large
coiled sausage, it makes a wonderful presentation at a party. Use
whatever type of sausage you like best.—Naoko

If the sausages have been kept in the refrigerator, remove them about
30 minutes prior to smoking to bring them close to room temperature.
Pat dry the sausages with a paper towel.

Set the smoke chips in the donabe according to the basic smoking
instructions on page 250. Set the grates inside the donabe one by one,
placing sausages on each grate.

Set the donabe, uncovered, over high heat. Wait until the smoke
chips start to release smoke, about 7 to 8 minutes. Cover, and fill the
reservoir in the rim of the base a little over half full with water. Smoke
for about 7 minutes over high heat and then turn off the heat. Let rest
undisturbed for 20 minutes.

Transfer the items to a large serving plate or serve directly on
individual plates at the table, with the mustard on the side.

SERVES *4 to 6*
as part of a
multicourse meal

EQUIPMENT:
One large donabe smoker
(about 10¾ inches/27 cm in diameter)

Smoked Duck Breast with Creamy Wasabi–Green Onion Dipping Sauce

4 medium (about ¾ inch/2 cm thick) duck breast halves, excess skin trimmed

Sea salt

Freshly ground black pepper

Handful of smoke chips (your choice)

½ cup (120 ml) crème fraîche

1 to 1½ teaspoons wasabi paste

2 teaspoons usukuchi shoyu (light-colored soy sauce)

1 green onion, thinly sliced

1 to 1½ teaspoons freshly squeezed lemon juice

This dish is so popular among my friends that when someone hosts a potluck dinner, I often receive requests to bring my donabe smoker and make this dish on location. The duck breast is seasoned with salt and pepper and dry-marinated in the refrigerator overnight. This process enhances the umami flavor of the meat and makes it tender when smoked. Scoring the skin releases excess fat and lets the meat absorb the deep smokiness. Add *hojicha* (roasted green tea leaves; see Glossary, page 289) to the smoke chips before starting the smoking process for a flavor variation. The fresh, tangy crème fraîche in the sauce paired with the hot wasabi flavor complements the rich smoked duck. If you don't have wasabi paste, horseradish will work as well.—Naoko

Using a sharp paring knife, score the skin of the duck breast at ⅓-inch (8 mm) intervals crosswise. Score it again at about ½-inch (1 cm) intervals lengthwise. Be careful not to penetrate the meat. Lightly season both sides of the duck breast with salt. Set the breasts skin-side up on a plate, uncovered, and let rest in the refrigerator for 12 to 24 hours. Remove from the refrigerator about 30 minutes prior to smoking to bring them close to room temperature. Pat dry with a paper towel.

NOTE:
As shown in the picture below, I also like to serve this dish over Orange Butter Rice (page 126).

Set the smoke chips in the donabe according to the basic smoking instructions on page 250. Set up the bottom and middle grates with the duck breasts skin-side up on each. The thicker pieces should go on the bottom tier. Set the donabe, uncovered, over high heat. Wait until the smoke chips start to release smoke, about 7 to 8 minutes. Cover, and fill the reservoir in the rim of the base a little over half full with water. Smoke for 9 to 10 minutes over high heat, and then turn off the heat. Let rest undisturbed for 20 minutes.

Meanwhile, make the sauce: Whisk together the crème fraîche and wasabi paste in a medium bowl until smooth. Add the *usukuchi shoyu* and green onion and stir. Gradually stir in the lemon juice. Adjust the seasoning with a pinch of salt, if desired.

Transfer the duck breast to a cutting board and slice crosswise along the scored lines (or thinner if you like). Serve with the dipping sauce on the side.

SERVES *4 to 6*
as part of a
multicourse meal

EQUIPMENT:
One large donabe smoker
(about 10¾ inches/27 cm in diameter)

NOTE:
Be careful to not overheat or overcook the
Camembert as this can result in it curdling
(becoming almost solid).

Smoked Camembert, Nuts, and Dried Figs
with Rosemary

1 (8-ounce/240 g) good-quality
Camembert cheese

Handful of smoke chips (your choice)

4 to 6 dried figs, halved

10 to 12 unsalted walnut halves

10 to 12 dry-roasted unsalted pistachios
in their shells

2 to 3 sprigs rosemary

Camembert, walnuts, pistachio, and dried figs . . . these are all
good on their own, yet with a quick smoke in a donabe, they
become a special tasty treat. No preseasoning or resting is
necessary; you can just place them in the donabe smoker and they
are ready in a short time. Camembert becomes warm, gooey, and
smoky. Walnuts become even nuttier, and the sweetness of the
figs blends nicely with the smoky aroma. The scent of rosemary
gently wraps the entire dish. Enjoy with crackers or a sliced
baguette.—Naoko

Remove the Camembert from the refrigerator 30 minutes before using.
Place the Camembert on a piece of aluminum foil and wrap it so that
only the top half is exposed.

Set the smoke chips in the donabe smoker according to the basic
smoking instructions on page 250. Place the rosemary lightly over
the smoke chips in the center. Set up the middle and top grates with
the ingredients, placing the dried figs on the middle grate and the
Camembert, walnuts, and pistachios on the top grate. Set the donabe,
uncovered, over high heat. Wait until the smoke chips start to release
smoke, about 7 to 8 minutes. Cover, and fill the reservoir in the rim
of the base a little over half full with water. Smoke for 5 minutes
over high heat, and then turn off the heat. Let rest undisturbed for
10 minutes. Transfer the cheese, nuts, and figs to a serving plate and
serve immediately.

EQUIPMENT:

One large donabe smoker
(about 10¾ inches/27 cm in diameter)

Smoked Chicken Tender Salad with Kurozu Vinaigrette

1 small clove garlic, finely grated

1 teaspoon finely grated peeled fresh ginger

½ teaspoon tobanjan (fermented chili bean paste; optional)

2 tablespoons kurozu (Japanese black vinegar) or rice vinegar

2 tablespoons soy sauce

1½ teaspoons honey

1 tablespoon toasted sesame oil

1 tablespoon plus 1½ teaspoons extra-virgin olive oil

5 ounces (150 g) chicken tenders (3 to 4 pieces)

¼ teaspoon sea salt

2 green onions (white and light green parts only), cut into 2-inch (5 cm) lengths on the diagonal

Handful of smoke chips (your choice)

¼ cup (60 ml) unsalted almonds

¼ cup (60 ml) shelled fava beans

5 ounces (150 g) mixed greens

4 radishes, halved

Freshly ground black pepper (optional)

Fresh vegetables are tossed with torn smoked chicken tenders, almonds, and green onions in a *kurozu* (Japanese black vinegar) vinaigrette. The result is a very satisfying salad with layers of flavor. I like the smoked chicken tenders not only in the salad but also as a topping for soup or noodles. To bring out extra sweetness, green onions are lightly charred in a pan before being smoked, but you can skip that step and they will still taste delicious.—Naoko

To make the vinaigrette: Whisk together the garlic, ginger, tobanjan, kurozu, soy sauce, and honey in a small bowl. Gradually add the sesame oil and 1 tablespoon olive oil while whisking; continue whisking until smooth (can be prepared several hours in advance and kept in a cool place or refrigerated).

Season the chicken all over with the salt. Let it rest, uncovered, for 30 to 60 minutes. Pat dry with a paper towel.

Heat the remaining olive oil in a sauté pan over medium heat. Add the green onions and spread them in a single layer. Cook for 1 to 2 minutes on each side until lightly browned. Transfer to a plate to cool down and then pat dry.

Set the smoke chips in the donabe according to the basic smoking instructions on page 250. Set up the middle and top grates with the ingredients, placing the chicken on the middle grate and the green onions and almonds on the top grate. Set the donabe, uncovered,

continued

over high heat. Wait until the smoke chips start to release smoke, about 7 to 8 minutes. Cover, and fill the reservoir in the rim of the base a little over half full with water. Smoke for 5 minutes over high heat, then turn off the heat. Let rest undisturbed for 20 minutes. Transfer the smoked ingredients to a plate. Shred the chicken into small bite-size pieces by hand.

While the smoked ingredients are resting, bring a small pot of water to a boil and add a generous pinch of salt. Add the fava beans and blanch until tender, 2 to 3 minutes. Drain and let cool. Peel and pat dry with a paper towel.

In a large bowl, combine the fava beans, mixed greens, radishes, and all the smoked items. Pour over the vinaigrette and toss well. Add some black pepper, if you like. Transfer to a serving plate.

EQUIPMENT:
One large donabe smoker
(about 10¾ inches/27 cm in diameter)

Smoked Heirloom Tomato Salad with Smoked Tomato Vinaigrette

Handful of smoke chips (your choice)

1½ pounds (680 g) red heirloom or plum tomatoes, cut into ¾-inch (2 cm) wedges

Sea salt

2 tablespoons rice vinegar

¾ cup (180 ml) extra-virgin olive oil

Freshly ground black pepper

Handful of smoke chips (your choice)

1½ pounds (680 g) heirloom tomatoes, various colors and types, cut into ½-inch (1 cm) wedges

Sea salt

1 cup (240 ml) thinly sliced cucumber

2 avocados, peeled, pitted, and diced

6 ounces (180 g) fresh sheep's-milk feta, ricotta, or burrata cheese

1 tablespoon toasted white sesame seeds (see page 58)

12 to 16 ounces (360 to 450 g) mixed greens (such a purslane, baby arugula, and mizuna)

4 French Breakfast radishes, sliced thin and curled in ice water, for garnish

Nasturtium and borage flowers, for garnish

This salad is a smoky version of a California summer favorite that we look forward to with the onset of tomato season. The combination of other vegetable and cheese elements is flexible with the base of both smoked and fresh tomato. The smoke from the donabe smoker applied to the tomatoes allows the light, fresh flavors of the other ingredients to show through without being overpowered.—Kyle

To make the vinaigrette: Set the smoke chips in the donabe smoker according to the basic smoking instructions on page 250. Place the tomato wedges in a single layer on the middle and top grates. Set the donabe, uncovered, over high heat. Wait until the smoke chips start to release smoke, about 7 to 8 minutes, before covering. Cover, and fill the reservoir in the rim of the base a little over half full with water. Smoke for 5 minutes over high heat, and then turn off the heat. Let rest undisturbed for 10 minutes. Transfer the smoked tomatoes from the donabe to a plate. Allow to cool slightly and remove the skins from the wedges.

Place the smoked tomatoes in a blender and season with a pinch of salt. Pulse the blender and remove the seeds by passing the mixture through a fine-mesh strainer. Discard the seeds and return the tomato puree to the blender. Add the vinegar and puree on low speed. Slowly drizzle in the olive oil and adjust the seasoning with salt and pepper. Cool completely and refrigerate until ready to use.

continued

Smoked Heirloom Tomato Salad with Smoked Tomato Vinaigrette, continued

Set the smoke chips in the donabe according to the basic smoking instructions on page 250. Place half the tomato wedges in a single layer on the middle and top grates. Set the donabe, uncovered, over high heat. Wait until the smoke chips start to release smoke, about 7 to 8 minutes,. Cover, and fill the reservoir in the rim of the base a little over half full with water. Smoke for 5 minutes over high heat, and then turn off the heat. Let rest undisturbed for 10 minutes. Transfer the smoked tomatoes to a plate and sprinkle with sea salt. Allow to cool slightly and remove the skins from the wedges.

Combine the smoked and fresh tomatoes in a bowl with the cucumber, avocados, cheese, and sesame seeds. Pour in the vinaigrette (adjust the amount as necessary to avoid overdressing the salad) and toss the mixture. Then toss with the greens. Mound the salad in a serving bowl and garnish with the radishes and flowers.

SERVES *4*
as part of a
multicourse meal

EQUIPMENT:
One large donabe smoker
(about 10¾ inches/27 cm in diameter)

Smoked Calamari Salad in Black Sesame Vinegar Sauce

8 ounces (240 g) calamari legs, cut into large bite-size pieces

⅔ teaspoon sea salt

3 tablespoons ground toasted black sesame seeds (see page 58)

1 teaspoon raw brown sugar

1 teaspoon mirin

1 tablespoon soy sauce

1 tablespoon rice vinegar

1⅓ tablespoons extra-virgin olive oil

Handful of smoke chips (your choice)

½ cup (120 ml) baby shungiku (chrysanthemum greens) or chopped mitsuba

As a small course, I sometimes make poached calamari that is tossed in a light sauce of toasted and ground black sesame seeds and vinegar. It's really delicious, and one day when I made it, I thought the dish would be even better if I smoked the calamari instead of poaching it. So I made it, and I was right! Add some baby greens and the dish becomes a nice salad. In order to make it easier for the calamari to absorb the smoke and become tender, it's good to let it rest uncovered in the refrigerator overnight after it is seasoned. Smoked calamari is also great on its own with a little drizzle of soy sauce and olive oil.—Naoko

Season the calamari all over with the salt. Set aside in the refrigerator, uncovered, for a few hours or preferably overnight. Remove from the refrigerator about 30 minutes prior to smoking to bring them close to room temperature. Pat dry with a paper towel.

To make the sauce: Stir together the sesame seeds, brown sugar, mirin, soy sauce, and vinegar in a small bowl. Add the olive oil and stir until smooth. Set aside.

Set the smoke chips in the donabe according to the basic smoking instructions on page 250. Set up the middle and top grates with the calamari. Set the donabe, uncovered, over high heat. Wait until the smoke chips start to release smoke, about 7 to 8 minutes. Cover, and fill the reservoir in the rim of the base a little over half full with water. Smoke for 4 minutes over high heat, and then turn off the heat. Let rest undisturbed for 15 minutes.

In a bowl, combine the smoked calamari, sauce, and baby *shungiku* and toss. Transfer to a serving plate.

SERVES **6**
as part of a
multicourse meal

EQUIPMENT:
One large donabe smoker
(about 10¾ inches/27 cm in diameter)

Smoked Shrimp, Scallops, and Sweet Chestnuts

6 large shrimp, peeled except for
the tail and deveined

6 large sea scallops

Sea salt

12 peeled sweet roasted whole chestnuts
(from a package)

Soy sauce

Extra-virgin olive oil

Handful of smoke chips (your choice)

Here's another dish that proves how simply smoked ingredients in a donabe can taste so special. Choose large shrimp and scallops so that they absorb the nice smoky aroma while staying juicy. Already peeled sweet roasted chestnuts are available at Asian markets and are convenient to use. They are a tasty snack right out of the package, but become nutty and tender after being smoked. This dish is simply served with a little drizzle of soy sauce and olive oil. Wasabi can also be nice on the side as well.—Naoko

Season the shrimp and scallops lightly with salt. Let them rest, uncovered, for a few hours in the refrigerator. Remove from the refrigerator about 30 minutes prior to smoking to bring them close to room temperature. Pat dry with a paper towel.

Set the smoke chips in the donabe according to the basic smoking instructions on page 250. Set up the middle and top grates with the ingredients, placing the shrimp on the middle grate and the scallops and chestnuts on the top grate. Set the donabe, uncovered, over high heat. Wait until the smoke chips start to release smoke, about 7 to 8 minutes. Cover, and fill the reservoir in the rim of the base a little over half full with water. Smoke for 5 minutes over high heat, and then turn off the heat. Let rest undisturbed for 15 minutes.

Transfer the smoked items to a serving plate. Splash a small amount of soy sauce over the shrimp and scallops, followed by a good drizzle of olive oil to your taste.

SERVES *4 to 6*
as part of a
multicourse meal

EQUIPMENT:
One large donabe smoker
(about 10¾ inches/27 cm in diameter)

NOTE:
If you have *shiso* leaves, it's also nice to put
a dab of wasabi on the tofu slice and then
wrap with a *shiso* leaf.

Smoked Miso-Marinated Tofu

½ cup (120 ml) miso (see page 291)

1½ tablespoons plain yogurt

1½ tablespoons honey

1 (14-ounce/400 g) package medium-firm
tofu, cut in half and press-drained (see note
on page 121)

Handful of smoke chips (your choice)

Wasabi paste

I regularly make miso-marinated tofu and like to slice and serve
it fresh, but when it's smoked in a donabe, it becomes a whole
other delicious dish. Miso and smoke flavors work magically
together, and the tofu becomes very rich in taste. The tofu needs
to be marinated in the miso sauce for at least three days, so plan
ahead.—Naoko

Whisk together the miso, yogurt, and honey in a small bowl. Pat dry the
tofu very well. Wrap each tofu half with a piece of cheesecloth. Place a
piece of plastic wrap on a work surface. Spread over about 2 tablespoons
of the miso marinade. Place a tofu half (wrapped in cheesecloth) on the
miso, and then spread about 3 tablespoons of the miso marinade on top
of the tofu with a spatula. Wrap tightly with the plastic wrap and make
sure the tofu is completely covered in the sauce by lightly pressing with
your fingers. Wrap again with another piece of plastic wrap. Repeat the
process with the other tofu half. Place both in a resealable plastic bag
and let them marinate in the refrigerator for 3 to 5 days.

Unwrap the tofu carefully and discard the marinade. Pat the tofu dry.
Cut each block in half crosswise, and then cut each of those halves
into four slices crosswise.

Set the smoke chips in the donabe according to the basic smoking
instructions on page 250. Set up the middle and top grates with the
tofu slices. Set the donabe, uncovered, over high heat. Wait until the
smoke chips start to release smoke, about 7 to 8 minutes. Cover, and
fill the reservoir in the rim of the base a little over half full with water.
Smoke for about 5 minutes over high heat, and then turn off the heat.
Let rest undisturbed for 20 minutes. Transfer to a serving plate and
serve with a small mound of wasabi on the side.

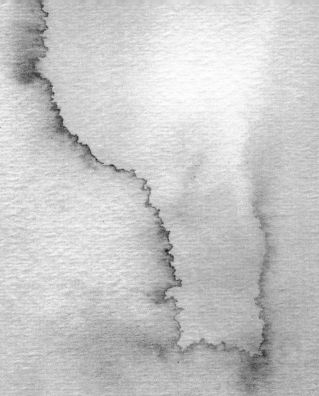

CHAPTER 7

Dashi, Sauces, and Condiments

With good *dashi*, sauces, and condiments, simple dishes can shine and make your food more inspired. Many of the recipes in this chapter can be prepared in advance, and can be used in a wide variety of dishes. I've also included tips for making your *dashi* easier to make and even tastier.

Kombu and Bonito Dashi

MAKES ABOUT 7 cups (1.8 L)

2 quarts (2 L) water, low mineral content preferred (see Note)

3 (4-inch/10 cm) square pieces kombu (about ⅔ ounce/20g)

1 ounce (30 g) katsuobushi (dried bonito flakes)

This is a basic *dashi* that can be used in a wide variety of Japanese dishes. It's commonly called *awase dashi* (blend *dashi*) or *ichiban dashi* (first *dashi*). Once you have dried kombu and bonito in your pantry, you can easily make it whenever you need it. I just love the smell of *dashi* in my kitchen. Freshly made *dashi* is perfect for a simple clear soup, allowing you to really appreciate its delicate umami taste. I even drink cold *dashi* straight just to charge me up in warm weather. I have included notes about different variations of *dashi* making, from more elaborate (longer) versions to shortcuts. So, you can stick to a single way that fits you the best, or you can use different methods in accordance with how rich you want to make your *dashi* and how much time you have. You can also adjust the amount of kombu and/or *katsuobushi* to your preference. Don't worry too much about the measurement of the ingredients or how long to infuse especially for your everyday cooking! Just make sure to get the high quality ingredients.

Kombu and Bonito Dashi can keep for a few days in the refrigerator. For convenience, you can make a large batch to use over several days, though there is nothing better than the flavor of freshly made *dashi*.—Naoko

Combine the water and kombu in a donabe and let the kombu soak for 30 minutes. The kombu will reconstitute and double in size.

Set the donabe, uncovered, over medium heat. Just before the broth comes to a simmer (after about 20 to 25 minutes), remove the kombu. Then quickly turn up the heat to bring to a simmer; immediately turn off the heat. Add the *katsuobushi* all at once.

Wait until the *katsuobushi* settles in the bottom of the donabe, about 2 minutes. Strain into a bowl through a fine-mesh sieve lined with a double layer of damp cheesecloth or a thin cotton cloth. Let the *dashi* strain by gravity or press very gently. Do not press hard or squeeze, as doing so will add a slight fishy flavor to the *dashi*.

For everyday use at home, I actually strain *dashi* directly through a fine-mesh strainer without lining it with a cloth. It's less fuss! The residue will settle at the bottom, so when I need to use the very clear *dashi*, I just scoop gently from the top without stirring it.

When I'm really short on time and need only a small amount of *dashi*, here's a good shortcut: I sometimes use a tea bag–style *dashi* for convenience. There are slight variations depending on the brand, but essentially you simply infuse a *dashi* tea bag in simmering water for a few minutes, and it's ready. There are many different brands of really tasty *dashi* tea bags available in Japan, and some are imported to the United States. When choosing tea bag–style *dashi*, I suggest you choose a kind that includes only natural ingredients (no MSG or artificial flavors).

Enriched Dashi

My standard ratio for water to kombu and water to *katsuobushi* is between 100:1 and 100:1.5 by weight. In other words, for every 4 cups (1 L) of water, use ⅓ to ½ ounce (10 to 15 g) each of kombu and *katsuobushi*. For richer *dashi,* you can adjust the ratio to about 100:3—that is, for the same amount of water, use up to 1 ounce (30 g) each of kombu and *katsuobushi*. Once you familiarize yourself with the standard ratio of kombu and bonito *dashi*, it's also fun to try using different ratios to taste the flavor differences. Once you become your own *dashi* expert, you can even adjust the ratio dish by dish to your preference. For some dishes, you might prefer an extra-rich flavor of *katsuobushi* or a very light flavor.

Here are some other (more economical) ways to make richer (higher-umami-level) *dashi*, using the same amount of kombu. Use just one, or combine them:

1. Increase the soaking time of the kombu in the water to a few hours or even overnight (cold infusion). In this case, use a separate bowl for soaking and transfer to a donabe to heat when ready to make the dashi. Keep refrigerated if the room is warm or if you're soaking overnight.

2. Once the kombu is reconstituted after soaking in water, use scissors to cut many slits into the kombu. It will infuse more of its flavor this way. Continue to soak longer or start heating to make dashi.

continued

3. When you heat the kombu in the water to make dashi, start with medium-high heat and turn it down to very low once the water temperature reaches 140°F (60°C). Make sure the temperature stays at the same level and let the kombu infuse for 1 hour. That's the optimal temperature for kombu to infuse its rich umami flavor (glutamate). Then remove the kombu and follow the rest of the steps.

Second Dashi

After you've made your *dashi*, what can you do with the used kombu and *katsuobushi*? Many people discard them, but the used solids can be repurposed for making "second *dashi*" (*niban dashi*) or to make tasty treats.

To make "second *dashi*," combine the used kombu and *katsuobushi* from making Kombu and Bonito Dashi with 1 quart (1 L) water in a donabe and bring to a simmer, uncovered, over medium-high heat. Turn down the heat to a low simmer and simmer gently for 10 minutes. Add ⅓ ounce (10 g) unused *katsuobushi* and turn off the heat. Wait until the *katsuobushi* settles in the bottom of the donabe, about 2 minutes.

Remove the kombu and strain the broth into a bowl through a fine-mesh sieve lined with a double layer of damp cheesecloth or a thin cotton cloth. You can press down firmly or squeeze to extract as much of the infused *dashi* as possible. While the "first *dashi*," made with fresh ingredients, is about enjoying the pure, delicate aroma, the "second *dashi*" is more suitable for stews or a type of dish with a richer seasoning.

For other uses, you can cut the used kombu into small pieces and add it to a stew, or place a piece of it on top of rice during cooking to infuse a subtle, elegant flavor into the rice (you can discard the kombu after this use). For the used *katsuobushi*, mince it and dry-sauté in a pan; season with a small drizzle of each of sake, mirin, and soy sauce (or salt) to make a topping for rice. You can also add some sesame seeds.

NOTE:

Cold-infused *dashi* should not be used raw, as it will taste raw. Heat it through once and let cool before using it in a cold soup or sauce.

Kombu Dashi

MAKES ABOUT 1 quart (1 L)

> 5 cups (1.2 L) water, low mineral content preferred (see Note, page 274)
>
> 2 (3 by 6-inch/7.5 by 15 cm) square pieces kombu (about ½ ounce/15 g)

Kombu-only *dashi* has a cleaner flavor compared with *dashi* that includes other ingredients. It's best enjoyed in soup-style dishes. There are two methods for making kombu *dashi*. One of them is cold infusion, which is basically zero fuss and all you need to do is to wait. For a faster version, we also provide a heat-infusion method. As with the Kombu and Bonito Dashi, you can also apply additional methods in order to infuse more flavor (see Enriched Dashi, page 275). Kombu Dashi will keep in the refrigerator for a few days.—Naoko

Cold-infusion method: In a bowl or pitcher, combine the water and kombu. Cover and refrigerate for 18 to 24 hours. Remove the kombu.

Heat-infusion method: Combine the water and kombu in a donabe and let the kombu soak for 30 minutes. The kombu will reconstitute and double in size. Set the donabe, uncovered, over medium heat. Just before the broth comes to a simmer (after about 15 minutes), remove the kombu and turn off the heat.

Kombu and Shiitake Dashi

MAKES ABOUT 1 quart (1 L)

> 1 quart (1 L) water, soft (low-mineral-content) preferred
>
> 1 to 2 (3 by 6-inch/7.5 by 15 cm) square pieces kombu (about ⅓ ounce/10 g)
>
> 4 small to medium dried shiitake mushrooms

This is a standard *dashi* used in Japanese Buddhist temple vegan cuisine (*shojin ryori*). Dried shiitake gives a rich and pronounced flavor, so this *dashi* is ideal for stews or braised dishes, rather than clean-tasting soups. Kombu and Shiitake Dashi will keep in the refrigerator for a few days.—Naoko

Cold-infusion method: Combine all the ingredients in a bowl. Cover and refrigerate for 8 to 12 hours. Remove the kombu and shiitakes.

Heat-infusion method: Combine all the ingredients in a donabe and let soak for 30 minutes. The kombu will reconstitute and double in size. Set the donabe, uncovered, over medium heat. Just before the broth comes to a simmer (after about 15 minutes), remove the kombu. Continue to heat, and as soon as the broth starts to simmer, turn down the heat to medium-low and simmer gently for an additional 10 minutes. Turn off the heat, remove the shiitakes, and strain.

Used dried shiitake mushrooms can also make a tasty treat. Remove the stems and discard; slice the caps and add to soup, stew, or rice.

You can also make a rich chicken- and kombu-infused
dashi. Add a piece of kombu (about 3 by 6-inch/7.5 by
15 cm square) to the donabe with the rest of the ingredients
and remove right before the water comes to a simmer.

If you want to make extra-rich collagen-packed chicken stock,
double the amount of water and simmer very gently for about
4 hours, or until the stock is reduced by more than half. Chicken
wings used for the extra-rich stock should be discarded, as they
become quite exhausted after simmering for so long.

Chicken Dashi

MAKES ABOUT 1 quart (1 L)

1⅓ pounds, (600 g) chicken wings

1 teaspoon sea salt

1 negi (Japanese green onion),
or 2 green onions (green part only)

1 knob ginger, sliced into 3 to 4 pieces
(no need to peel if the ginger is very fresh)

6 black peppercorns

5 cups (1.2 L) water

This is a Japanese-style quick chicken stock, and I
use chicken wings to make it. Because chicken wings
contain many bones, they can release a lot of flavors in a
short time when you make a stock with them. The bonus
is that you can enjoy the meat after making the *dashi* (I
truly love this part!). I often shred the meat and add it to
salad or soup. After straining, you can season the *dashi*
with salt and pepper to enjoy by itself as a soup or serve
with the chicken used to make the *dashi*. I prefer using
the midsection including tips, to make the *dashi*, but
drumettes can work, too. If you need a real short cut, use
Asian chicken stock powder (see Glossary, page 288) to
make the *dashi* instead. Chicken Dashi will keep in the
refrigerator for a few days.—Naoko

Season the chicken all over with the salt. Let the chicken
marinate for 1 hour.

Pat the chicken dry (or rinse and pat dry if there is any
blood) and combine with the rest of the ingredients
in the donabe. Cover and set over medium-high heat.
As soon as the broth starts to boil, turn down the heat
to simmer. Skim as necessary. Cover again and simmer
for 20 minutes. Turn off the heat and let it rest for
15 minutes, or until the stock cools down (about 1 hour).

Transfer the chicken wings to a bowl and save for
another use. Strain the stock through a fine-mesh sieve.

Yuzu Ponzu

MAKES ABOUT 1 cup (240 ml)

¼ cup (60 ml) soy sauce

3 tablespoons sake

3 tablespoons mirin

2 small handfuls (about 0.2 ounce/5 g) katsuobushi (dried bonito flakes)

⅓ cup (80 ml) freshly squeezed yuzu or Meyer lemon juice

1 (2-inch/5 cm) square kombu

There are many different brands of commercial ponzu available, yet I still like my homemade kind the best. My ponzu is very aromatic, with a generous amount of yuzu juice and rich in umami from an overnight infusion of *katsuobushi* (dried bonito flakes) and kombu. If you can't get yuzu juice, Meyer lemon juice will work as a substitute. This ponzu can be kept in a tightly sealed container in the refrigerator for seven to ten days.—Naoko

Combine the soy sauce, sake, and mirin in a saucepan and bring to a simmer over medium heat. Add the *katsuobushi* and immediately turn off the heat.

Add the yuzu juice and kombu. Let the mixture cool down completely. Transfer to a covered container and let rest in the refrigerator overnight. Strain through a fine-mesh sieve.

3-2-1 Ponzu

MAKES ABOUT ⅓ cup (90 ml)

3 tablespoons soy sauce

2 tablespoons rice vinegar

1 tablespoon aromatic freshly squeezed citrus juice (such as yuzu or Meyer lemon)

This is a quick ponzu, which can be made by just combining three ingredients in a bowl. It's good as a dipping sauce or drizzled over grilled fish. This ponzu will keep in the refrigerator, covered, for two to three weeks.—Naoko

Combine all the ingredients in a bowl.

NOTE:

Finished *shio-koji* looks like very thick porridge. You can use it as is or puree it in a blender till smooth when you want to use it for a silky sauce.

Shio-Koji

MAKES ABOUT 1¹/₂ cups (360 ml)

6 ounces (180 g) rice koji (malted rice)

2 ounces (60 g) sea salt

¾ cup (180 ml) water

This is a popular Japanese seasoning or condiment made simply by fermenting rice *koji* (malted rice; see Glossary, page 290), salt, and water together, and it has a delicious combination of salty, sweet, and savory umami flavors. It's very versatile: you can use it as a marinade base, add it to a sauce, or simply replace salt with it in many recipes. It works perfectly as a seasoning for salads, too. After the ingredients are mixed, allow seven to ten days for fermentation at room temperature, stirring once a day. While commercial *shio-koji* is available at Japanese markets, it's very easy to make, so I always make my own. Once fermented, shio-koji will keep, tightly sealed in a container, in the refrigerator for two to three months. The color might turn slightly yellowish, but that's not a problem.—Naoko

If starting with a pressed-type rice *koji*, first break it apart by hand in a large bowl to loosen the grains.

Using both hands, rub the grains for a couple of minutes until slightly fragrant. Add the salt and continue to rub, massaging the salt into the rice for another couple of minutes. Add the water and stir.

Transfer the mixture into a container with a lid. Cover and leave at room temperature for 7 to 10 days to complete the fermentation, stirring the mixture with a spoon once a day for even fermentation.

Negi and Shio-Koji Dipping Sauce

MAKES ABOUT ⅓ cup (80 ml)

1 clove garlic, finely grated

1 teaspoon finely grated peeled fresh ginger

2 tablespoons minced negi (Japanese green onion)
or green onion (white part only)

1 teaspoon raw brown sugar

2 tablespoons toasted sesame oil

1½ teaspoons sake

1 tablespoon Shio-Koji (page 280) or 1 teaspoon sea salt

1 teaspoon Asian chicken stock powder
(optional, see Glossary page 288)

1 tablespoon toasted white sesame seeds (see page 58)

1½ teaspoons freshly squeezed lemon juice or rice vinegar

Pinch of freshly ground black pepper

I like using smoking-hot sesame oil in various recipes, as it flash-cooks the ingredients it touches and enhances the aromatic effect of the dish. In this sauce, when the smoking oil is poured over the aromatics, the texture becomes more round and rich. With the addition of naturally sweet and umami-rich *shio-koji* (page 280), this sauce provides a very complex flavor that can go well with various dishes including steamed meat, vegetables, or *yakiniku* (Japanese-style barbecue of thinly sliced meat). Learn more about Asian chicken stock powder in the Glossary (page 288). The sauce will keep in a tightly sealed container in the refrigerator for up to a week.—Naoko

Combine the garlic, ginger, *negi*, and sugar in a heat-resistant bowl. Heat the sesame oil in a small saucepan over medium-high heat until it starts smoking, about 1 to 2 minutes. Remove from the heat and pour into the bowl immediately to flash-fry the ingredients (be careful because it will sizzle and might splash a little). Immediately add the sake into the same saucepan to cook in the residual heat (be careful again, as it will sizzle). Stir and pour into the bowl. Add the rest of the ingredients to the bowl and stir well.

Naosco

MAKES ABOUT ¼ cup (60 ml)

1 tablespoon yuzu-kosho

2 tablespoons rice vinegar

½ teaspoon Shio-Koji (page 280)

Naosco is "Naoko's hot sauce," and my friends say it's almost addictive. The ingredients are extremely simple—just *yuzu-kosho* (see Glossary, page 295), rice vinegar, and Shio-Koji (page 280)—and all you need to do is just whisk them together. This condiment is good with basically anything you like, regardless of cuisine of origin. Use as a condiment for a hot pot, stir-fry, grilled meat or fish, or even pizza. It's got aroma, saltiness, heat, tartness, and sweetness all integrated in one delicious sauce. It will keep in a tightly sealed container in the refrigerator for three to four weeks.—Naoko

Whisk together all the ingredients in a small bowl until smooth.

Quick-Pickled Kabu in Shio-Koji

serves 4 as a side dish

> 2 medium kabu (Japanese turnips) with greens
>
> 2/3 to 1 tablespoon Shio-Koji (page 280)

I always enjoy these quick pickles, as they're more like a salad and taste very fresh. All you need to do is mix the cut *kabu* (Japanese turnip) and Shio-Koji (page 280), let them rest, and drain. *Kabu*'s crunch and the umami and sweetness from the *shio-koji* make it so delightful. I also love the fact that it's a probiotic dish, as *shio-koji* is never heated.—Naoko

Separate the greens from the *kabu* bulbs and reserve half of them for a later use. For the remaining half, trim off the very thick end of the stems and cut the stems into 2-inch (5 cm) pieces and the leaves into ¼-inch (6 mm) strips. Peel and halve the bulbs and slice into ¼-inch (6 mm) rounds.

In a resealable bag, combine the kabu bulbs with the greens and *shio-koji*. Mix well. Tightly seal by pushing as much air out as possible. Let it marinate in the refrigerator for at least 30 minutes and up to half a day.

Transfer the contents to a colander. Drain and lightly squeeze out the excess moisture before serving.

Karashi Peanut Butter Sauce

MAKES ABOUT ½ cup (120 ml)

> 3 tablespoons peanut butter (chunky or creamy, no salt added)
>
> Up to 2 teaspoons karashi (Japanese mustard)
>
> 2 teaspoons honey
>
> 2 tablespoons soy sauce
>
> 2 tablespoons rice vinegar

This is a quick sauce that you can make from just five simple ingredients. The peanut butter gives it a nice nutty flavor and creamy texture. *Karashi* (Japanese mustard) adds a nice kick to the sauce. Adjust the amount of the *karashi* depending on how hot you want it to be. This sauce is great with simple vegetables, whether raw or steamed. You can keep it in the refrigerator for four or five days.—Naoko

Whisk together all the ingredients in a small bowl until smooth.

Miso-Vinegar Dipping Sauce

MAKES ABOUT 1 cup (240 ml)

⅓ cup (80 ml) red miso (see page 291)

1 tablespoon Saikyo miso or other sweet white miso

2 tablespoons sake

2 tablespoons mirin

2 tablespoons raw brown sugar

2 tablespoons soy sauce

¼ cup rice vinegar

1 clove garlic, finely grated

1 teaspoon finely grated peeled fresh ginger

2 teaspoons tobanjan (fermented chili bean paste), optional

This tangy and slightly spicy miso sauce is great with gyoza dumplings, and as a dipping sauce for shabu-shabu or steamed vegetables. It will keep in the refrigerator, tightly sealed in a container, for seven to ten days.—Naoko

Whisk together all the ingredients in a saucepan and set over medium-low heat. Bring to a gentle simmer and stir constantly with a wooden spatula for 2 to 3 minutes, or until the mixture is slightly thickened and shiny. Turn off the heat and let it cool down completely.

Saikyo Miso Aioli

MAKES ABOUT ¾ cup (180 ml)

¼ cup (60 ml) Saikyo miso

1 very fresh large egg yolk

1 tablespoon freshly squeezed orange or tangerine juice

½ teaspoon finely grated citrus zest

½ cup (120 ml) grapeseed oil

This is an easy way to make a new style of aioli by using Saikyo miso as a base to create an emulsion with the egg yolk and oil. The paste of the miso helps to stabilize the emulsion right from the start, so it is far less likely to "break" than a traditional mayonnaise. The bright acidity from the citrus cuts the richness and balances the salt and umami for use as a dipping sauce or dressing. You can keep a batch in the refrigerator for four or five days.—Kyle

Combine the Saikyo miso, egg yolk, citrus juice, and citrus zest in a metal bowl and whisk to combine. Slowly drizzle in the oil while whisking, just a few drops at the beginning, to create an emulsion. Continue to add all of the oil while whisking constantly. Adjust the consistency and flavor with additional citrus juice or a bit of lemon juice for acidity. An additional 1 to 2 tablespoons water can be added if the aioli is too thick.

Naokochujang

MAKES ABOUT 1 cup (240 ml)

¼ cup (60 ml) red miso

2 tablespoons Hatcho miso or red miso

3 tablespoons raw brown sugar

1½-2 tablespoons coarse ground red chile
(such as Korean gochugaru)

1 tablespoon sake

1 tablespoon Shio-Koji (page 280), or 1 teaspoon soy sauce

2 cloves garlic, finely grated

1½ teaspoons finely grated peeled fresh ginger

¼ cup (60 ml) water

1 teaspoon kurozu (Japanese black vinegar) or rice vinegar

This hot miso and chili paste is my homage to *gochujang* (Korean fermented hot chili paste), and it's a very Japanese version with two kinds of miso as well as Shio-Koji (page 280) in it. While it's quick to make, the paste is rich in umami and is also not too sweet, unlike the commercial kinds of *gochujang* you often find. Although I like to blend two kinds of miso for extra depth and complexity, if you don't have Hatcho miso (malted soybean miso), you can just use red miso. I like to use the paste to mix with rice, or as a topping for grilled meat. You can also incorporate it into a marinade or use it to season soup. It's very versatile. This sauce will keep in a tightly sealed container in the refrigerator for seven to ten days.—Naoko

Whisk together all the ingredients except for the vinegar in a small saucepan and set over medium-low heat. Bring to a gentle simmer and stir constantly with a wooden spatula for about 5 minutes, or until the mixture has thickened to a soft paste and is shiny. Turn off the heat and let it cool down slightly. Add the *kurozu* and stir. Cool down completely.

Umami-Rich Soy Sauce

MAKES ABOUT 1 cup (240 ml)

½ cup (120 ml) soy sauce

¼ cup (60 ml) sake

⅓ cup (80 ml) mirin

2 tablespoons raw brown sugar

1 (2-inch/5 cm) square kombu

This is an extremely versatile sauce with layers of umami flavors including kombu, which is infused in the sauce overnight. You can drizzle it over food, use it as a seasoning for stir-fries, add it to a marinade, or blend it with a little rice vinegar to make a richly flavored ponzu. I also like to use this sauce to season *natto* (Japanese fermented sticky soybeans). The sauce will keep in the refrigerator for up to two weeks.—Naoko

Combine all the ingredients in a saucepan and let the kombu soak for 15 minutes. Set over medium heat. Just before the broth comes to a simmer (after about 4 to 5 minutes), remove the kombu and reserve it. Turn down the heat to a gentle simmer and cook for 4 to 5 minutes, or until the mixture has reduced slightly.

Transfer the sauce to a jar and add the reserved kombu again. Let it cool down completely. Seal the jar and let it rest in the refrigerator overnight. Remove the kombu again and discard. The sauce is ready to use.

Sesame Dipping Sauce

MAKES ABOUT ¾ cup (180 ml)

2 tablespoons ground toasted white sesame seeds (see page 58)

2 tablespoons white sesame paste (tahini is fine)

1 tablespoon miso (see page 291)

1½ teaspoons raw brown sugar

1½ tablespoons soy sauce

1 tablespoon rice vinegar

1 teaspoon toasted sesame oil

3 to 4 tablespoons water or Kombu Dashi (page 277)

I have several different sesame sauce recipes, with variations in flavors and textures for different dishes and purposes. This one is my standard dipping sauce, which is great for shabu-shabu, steamed vegetables, and more. You can adjust the consistency to your preference by the amount of water you add. If you use cold-infused Kombu Dashi, instead of water, make sure the *dashi* is heated once (as it would taste raw otherwise) before it's added to the sauce. The sauce can be kept in a tightly sealed container in the refrigerator for up to one week.—Naoko

Combine all the ingredients except for the water in a bowl and whisk together until smooth. Gradually add the water and whisk thoroughly.

Yuzu-Scented Sweet Vinegar Seasoning

MAKES ABOUT 1½ cups (360 ml)

1 cup (240 ml) rice vinegar

2 tablespoons sugar

2 tablespoons mirin

2 teaspoons sea salt

1 teaspoon usukuchi shoyu (light-colored soy sauce)

4 teaspoons freshly squeezed yuzu or other citrus juice

This multipurpose vinegar seasoning is so tasty that I never let it run out in my kitchen. I add it to soy sauce to make quick ponzu, drizzle it over vegetables with olive oil, or splash it over a stir-fry dish to give it a lightly sweet tang as a finish. You can make quick pickles, such as pickled ginger or radishes, with this seasoning, too. If you don't have yuzu, you can simply omit it or replace it with another citrus juice such as grapefruit or Meyer lemon. This vinegar can be kept in a covered container in a cool, dark place for four or five weeks.—Naoko

Combine the vinegar, sugar, mirin, salt, and *usukuchi shoyu* in a saucepan and bring to a simmer over medium heat, stirring to dissolve the sugar and salt. Turn off the heat. Let it cool down completely and add the yuzu juice.

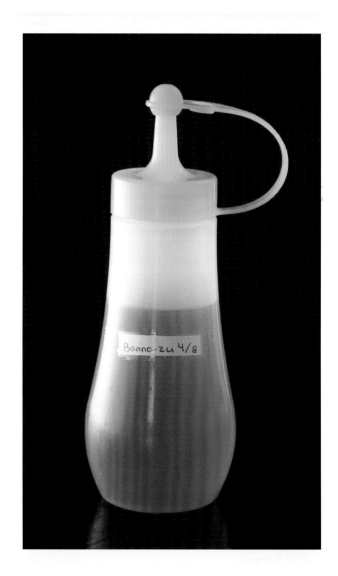

Chunky La-yu

MAKES ABOUT 1 cup (240 ml)

2 cloves garlic

1 small knob (about 1½ teaspoons) ginger

1 medium shallot, quartered

1 green onion (white and green parts separated)

1 generous tablespoon unsalted almonds

1½ tablespoons coarse ground red chiles
(such as Korean gochugaru)

1 teaspoon raw brown sugar

½ teaspoon ground sansho (Japanese
mountain pepper; optional)

1 teaspoon sea salt

½ teaspoon Asian chicken stock powder (optional,
see Glossary, page 288)

1 tablespoon white sesame seeds

½ teaspoon sliced dried red chile or red pepper flakes

¼ cup (60 ml) toasted sesame oil

¾ cup (180 ml) extra-virgin olive oil

1 teaspoon soy sauce

While standard *la-yu* (chili oil) is often used in small amounts to splash over a dish as a condiment, this chunky *la-yu* has layers of flavor and a nice texture. For more on the Japanese ingredients, see the Glossary. It goes well with a wide variety of dishes, from rice and grilled fish, meat, or tofu to dumplings. The flavor is mildly hot and not very salty, so you can use a generous amount as a topping or seasoning. Keep it in a cool, dark place for up to a week.—Naoko

Combine the garlic, ginger, shallot, white part of the green onion, and almonds in a food processor and pulse until very finely minced but not pureed.

Combine the minced mixture with the rest of the ingredients except for the soy sauce in a saucepan and set over medium-low heat. As soon as it comes to a gentle simmer, turn down the heat to low until tiny bubbles appear on the surface and you hear a subtle sound. Slowly cook to infuse (but not fry) the ingredients for 8 to 10 minutes, or until the mixture is aromatic, stirring a few times. Turn off the heat and remove the green part of the green onion. Add the soy sauce and let it cool down completely.

GLOSSARY

ABURA-AGE (ALSO CALLED USU-AGE)

Tofu sliced thinly and fried. *Abura-age* is a popular ingredient in Japanese cuisine, used in soups, salads, fried dishes, and many other recipes. It has a spongy texture and can be opened like a pouch, which can then be stuffed with rice or different ingredients.

AMARANTH

A plant with an ancient origin. Both the leaves and seeds can be consumed. Leaves can be used as a salad green or for cooking, like spinach. They are also rich in calcium and vitamins.

ASIAN CHICKEN STOCK POWDER

An instant stock or soup powder that can also be used as a seasoning for stir-fries and in other dishes to enhance the flavor. I highly suggest you choose a kind that doesn't contain additives such as MSG. Instant chicken stock made from it can be substituted for Chicken Dashi (Japanese chicken stock; page 278)

BLACK SUGAR

Popular in Asia, black sugar is an unrefined raw cane sugar with a high mineral content. The color is very dark brown to black, and it commonly comes in bricks. In Japan, Okinawa black sugar is the most popular.

BURDOCK

Gobo in Japanese. Burdock is a thin, long root vegetable with a strong earthy flavor. It can grow from 2 feet (60 cm) to 3 feet (90 cm) long. If the skin is very dirty, use a scrub brush to clean it. The skin is rich in flavor as well as nutrients, so do not peel it off. If there are very dark and/or hairy spots, use the back side of a knife to scrape them gently off. Once you cut burdock, it discolors quickly. If you want to keep its interior from discoloring and remove its natural muddy flavor, soak in cold water for a few minutes, draining before use. Do not soak for a long time, as a lot of burdock's flavor and nutrients will be lost. If you're making a brothy dish, the brief soaking also helps keep the burdock from getting muddy. You don't need to bother with soaking if you are using it for sautéing or in a dark sauce-based dish (such as one made with soy sauce).

CHINESE FERMENTED BLACK BEANS (DOUCHI)

Also called salted black beans, these are a traditional Chinese seasoning with a strong, pungent flavor. They are made from soybeans that have been dried and fermented with salt. Fermented soybeans are commonly used as a seasoning in stir-fries and in steamed dishes. They are widely available at Asian grocery stores and can be kept in a tightly sealed storage bag in a cool, dry place.

DRIED SHIITAKE MUSHROOMS

An essential ingredient in Japanese cooking, dried shiitake mushrooms are rehydrated and the caps are used in mainly soups and stews. Compared with fresh shiitake mushrooms, dried shiitake mushrooms are higher in umami flavor (guanylate) and meatier in texture. They are also used to make *dashi* in Japanese Buddhist temple vegan cuisine (*shojin ryori*). Choose high-quality dry shiitake mushrooms from Japan with relatively thick caps for the better aroma, flavor, and texture.

GAI LAN

Chinese broccoli. A leaf vegetable with thick stems. Often used in stir-fry dishes.

GOCHUJANG

Korean fermented hot pepper paste, with sweet and savory flavors. Gochujang is used as a condiment or as a seasoning for a variety of dishes including soup and stir fry.

GOCHUGARU

Korean ground red chile pepper. The heat level of gochugaru is milder than Japanese ichimi togarashi.

HATCHO MISO

Type of malted soybean miso that originated in Aichi, Japan. It has a very dark color and a distinctive rich flavor derived from soybeans.

HIJIKI

A type of seaweed, with a dark brown to black color. *Hijiki* is known for its high mineral and fiber content. After the harvest, *hijiki* is commonly cooked (either steamed or boiled) and dried before it is packaged and sold.

HOJICHA

Japanese roasted green tea. Hojicha has a brown color and has sweet nutty to slightly smoky flavor.

ICHIMI TOGARASHI (ALSO CALLED ICHIMI)

Translated as "one-flavor pepper," *ichimi togarashi* is Japanese ground chiles, used as a spice or a condiment to sprinkle over a finished dish.

KABOSU

Kabosu is a citrus fruit related to yuzu citrus. A typical kabosu has a tennis ball size and is picked while it's bright green. Kabosu has a distinctive acidity and often enjoyed with grilled fish, hot pot, and other dishes.

KABU

Japanese white turnip, also called Tokyo turnip in the United States. Its tender yet crisp bulb can be enjoyed fresh or cooked. It can also be grated and added to a soup or sauce. The greens have a mild flavor.

KANZURI

A hot paste specialty condiment from Niigata, Japan. It's made from red chiles, yuzu rind, rice *koji* (malted rice), and salt. Peppers are salt-marinated for several months after harvest, and then left spread over the snow in the wintertime for three to four days in order to remove both saltiness and bitterness. Next, they are mixed with yuzu rind, rice *koji*, and additional salt and then fermented and aged for three years or longer. The flavor of *kanzuri* can be compared to *yuzu-kosho*, as they share main ingredients (chiles, salt, and yuzu rind), but *kanzuri* is richer in umami from the aging process with rice *koji* and less salty. *Kanzuri* can be enjoyed as a condiment for sashimi, grilled meat, fish, hot pots, stews, and more.

KARASHI (ALSO CALLED WAGARASHI)

Japanese mustard with a very sharp and hot flavor.

KATAKURIKO

Japanese potato starch. Commonly used as a thickening agent.

KATSUOBUSHI

Dried, smoked, and fermented bonito loin. It's shaved and used in making *dashi* or as a topping for dishes. To shave a block of *katsuobushi,* you need a special shaving box (*kezuri-ki*). Preshaved kinds are becoming more common among home cooks, and they are available at Japanese grocery stores. If you use the preshaved kind for making *dashi*, the large-shave type (often labeled as *hanakatsuo*) is a good choice.

KOJI

A type of culture/mold; its scientific name is *Aspergillus oryzae. Koji* is traditionally used in a wide variety of Japanese food products such as soy sauce, miso, mirin, vinegar, and sake. Grains are inoculated with *koji* in order to start the fermentation. The most common form is rice *koji* (malted rice). *Koji* is also known for its remarkable health benefits when it's alive in foods such as miso and *amazake.*

KOMATSUNA

A leafy vegetable, often called Japanese (mustard) spinach in English. Komatsuna has a dark green color and slightly meatier texture than spinach. It's enjoyed either raw or cooked.

KOMBU

Kelp. Dried kombu (also called *dashi* kombu) is generally referred as just "kombu," and it's used for making *dashi*. When choosing kombu, the thick, hard kind is preferred. More than 90 percent of kombu in Japan is harvested on Hokkaido (the northernmost island of Japan), and the rest comes from the northern end of Honshu (the main island). There are different varieties of Japanese kombu; Rishiri, Rausu, and Makombu are considered to be the top-quality varieties for *dashi* making. For everyday *dashi* making, relatively reasonable Makombu is recommended.

KOMBUCHA

Japanese Kombu (seaweed) tea powder with salt and other seasonings. It's unrelated to the English word *kombucha*, which refers to a sweetened fermented tea drink, popular as a probiotic health beverage. Japanese *kombucha* can be enjoyed by pouring hot water over it to drink or by using it as a seasoning for a wide variety of dishes.

KONNYAKU

Made from the *konnyaku* (or *konjac*) plant, which is known as devil's tongue in English, *konnyaku* has a jellylike texture and is a popular ingredient in traditional Japanese dishes. Rich in dietary fiber and containing almost zero calories, *konnyaku* is also appreciated as a diet food. *Konnyaku* can be sold in a block shape, as a ball, or as noodles. Noodle-shaped *konnyaku* is called *shirataki* or *ito konnyaku.*

KOYA TOFU (ALSO CALLED KOYA DOFU)

A traditional Japanese freeze-dried tofu that has been appreciated as a preserved food. For its rich protein and vitamins, *koya tofu* has been one of the essential staples in Japanese Buddhist vegan temple cuisine (*shojin ryori*). It's used after being rehydrated in water, growing to about 1½ times its original size.

KUROZU

Japanese dark-colored vinegar with a rich flavor. While Chinese black vinegar is often made from a combination of rice, wheat, barley, and sorghum, most Japanese black vinegar is made purely from rice and has more umami flavor.

KUZUKO (ALSO CALLED KUDZUKO OR KUZU/KUDZU)

Starch made from the kudzu vine, also called Japanese arrowroot starch. It's used as a thickening agent. The most sought-after kind comes from the Yoshino region of Nara Prefecture in Japan. Compared to *katakuriko* (potato starch) or cornstarch, *kuzuko* tends to produce a more delicate texture. If you don't have *kuzuko*, you can substitute with *katakuriko.*

LA-YU

Also known as chili oil or hot chili oil, *la-yu* is of Chinese origin. It is made of vegetable oil that has been infused with chiles. It's a popular condiment for Japanese-style Chinese dishes.

LOTUS ROOT

It's called *renkon* in Japanese. Lotus root is technically not a root, but rhizome of the lotus plant, grown in swamp. It has holes going along the length of the tube. Lotus root is used in a wide variety of Japanese dishes and known for its crunchy texture.

MIRIN

Often translated as "sweet rice wine" in English, mirin is a brewed sweet alcoholic seasoning, made from sweet rice, *koji*, and distilled alcohol. It's an essential seasoning in Japanese cuisine to add glaze and mild sweetness to a dish. The most authentic mirin is called *hon mirin*, which is naturally brewed and has an alcohol level up to 14 percent. I do not recommend any substitute mirin product that contains any added sweetening such as corn syrup.

MISO

A fermented paste made from soybeans, *koji* (malted rice), and salt. Miso is one of the most important traditional staples in Japanese cuisine. Cooked soybeans are mashed and fermented with salt and *koji*, and then aged. While there are easily more than a thousand kinds of miso found in Japan, they can be roughly divided into three basic categories, depending on the ingredients:

> *Kome* miso, the most common style, is made from soybeans, rice *koji* (malted rice), and salt.

> *Mame* miso is made from soybeans, soybean *koji* (malted soybeans), and salt. Most famously represented by Hatcho miso from Aichi Prefecture.

> *Mugi* miso is made from soybeans, barley *koji* (malted barley), and salt.

The color and flavor of the miso depends on various factors: soybean-to-*koji* ratio, whether the soybeans were steamed or boiled, age, and environmental conditions (such as temperature and humidity). In Japan, types and styles of miso still vary widely by region. For example, red (*kome*) miso is commonly used in northern Japan, while *mugi* miso is commonly used in the Kyushu region. Sweet white (*kome*) miso, Saikyo miso, is produced and most heavily consumed in Kyoto.

While the flavor style cannot always be profiled by colors (and they are often defined by regions instead), in general, red miso tends to be aged longer and is saltier in general, and white miso tends to be aged less and has a milder flavor. There is also sweet white miso (such as Saikyo miso), which is much sweeter and less salty than other types of miso. Yellow miso (we don't refer to it as "yellow miso" in Japan; instead we say "pale miso") is often somewhere between red and white, so it has a medium-mild flavor. *Mame* miso is very dark (almost black) in color, but it is often categorized as a red miso.

In Japanese homes, it's common to blend two different kinds of miso (by types or brands) for more complexity. Miso keeps for several months or longer in the refrigerator, but the flavor will change. It's best to consume miso within a few months after opening. Choosing miso can be tricky, especially if you are not familiar with different types or brands. The best way is just to try many different types until you find the one you like. We also suggest choosing miso without additives.

In this book when a recipe calls for just "miso," unless otherwise specified, we generally used the most common style, *kome* miso (with a sodium content of 11 percent to 13 percent), which is not too salty or too sweet. (Because the majority of the miso sold in the market is *kome* miso, it's generally referred as just "miso", unless otherwise specified.)You can use a miso of your choice, ranging from red, light brown or yellow, to white. You can also use a single kind or blend different kinds of miso, if you prefer.

See also Saikyo miso and Hatcho miso.

MITSUBA

Sometimes called Japanese parsley, *mitsuba* is a very popular Japanese herb with a clean aroma that is often used in soup or egg dishes. It has a long stem with three leaves.

MIZUNA

A member of the mustard family, mizuna has tender leaves with a mildly bitter flavor. Baby mizuna is often used in mixed greens. Mizuna can be enjoyed either fresh or cooked.

NEGI

Japanese green onion. It's much taller and thicker than the green onion common in the United States, but green onions can be used as a substitute when *negi* are not available.

NIGARI

The byproduct of sea salt, the extract of seawater. In traditional tofu making in Japan, only *nigari* is used as a coagulator of tofu, while commercial tofu may include different kinds of coagulators. Liquid *nigari* can be found at Japanese grocery stores and some online specialty stores.

NIRA

Also called garlic chives or Chinese chives in English. A plant with long, flat dark-green leaves and a medium-strong flavor.

NORI

Japanese name for a type of edible seaweed. Nori is also commonly referred to as "dry square sheet of nori," made from chopped nori which was made into thin sheets, dried, and cut.

OJIYA (ALSO CALLED ZOSUI)

Japanese quick porridge. It's different from *kayu* (or *okayu*), which is also Japanese porridge. While *kayu* is made from dry rice that is cooked in a large amount of water (or sometimes seasoned broth), *ojiya* is made by adding the cooked rice to a seasoned broth until just heated. *Ojiya* is popular as a way to use the leftover broth as the finishing course of a hot-pot dish.

PONZU

Japanese citrus-based sauce. Although soy-flavored ponzu is technically called ponzu shoyu, it's more commonly referred just as ponzu.

RICE

Our rice recipes (for both white and brown rice) use short-grain rice, unless otherwise noted.

There are different varieties of short-grain rice available at Japanese and other Asian grocery stores and specialty stores. Among the reliable and highly reputed varieties is Koshihikari, which is a premium Japanese type and is now widely cultivated in California and other parts of the world, as well as in its native Japan. The original Japanese kind tends to have a higher moisture content and chewier texture than its Californian counterpart. For brown rice, besides the whole (unpolished) kind, partially polished kinds are also available at Asian grocery stores. While still retaining certain levels of nutrients from bran, partially polished rice can cook in the same way as white rice.

RICE VINEGAR

An essential seasoning in Japanese cuisine, it is a fermented product made from rice, *koji*, and water. Japanese rice vinegar tends to have a very pale color, and the acidity is much milder than Western vinegars in general. For the recipes in this book, use unsalted or unsweetened rice vinegar with no additives.

SAIKYO MISO

This is a type of *malted rice* miso (*kome* miso; made from soybeans, rice *koji*, and salt), which comes from Kyoto, and is also described as sweet white miso. It has a pale cream color with a mild sweetness and a low salt content (about 4.9 percent). The sweetness is due to the high proportion of rice *koji* (malted) used in its production, because *koji* turns the carbohydrate into sugar.

SAKE

Japanese alcoholic drink made from fermented rice. For cooking, we suggest you use good drinking-quality sake (but it doesn't have to be the expensive premium kind), instead of sake that is labeled "cooking sake." Either the *junmai* (made purely from rice and water) or *honjozo* (made from rice, water, and some added alcohol) type is recommended.

SAKE-KASU

Sake lees paste. The leftovers (lees) of sake production, after sake is pressed following the fermentation process. *Sake-kasu* is appreciated for its rich flavor and nutritious value, as it's high in protein and vitamins. It can be used in a wide range of dishes including as a marinade, as flavoring for soup, or even on its own as a snack.

SAKURA EBI

A tiny shrimp with a pinkish body, translated as "cherry blossom shrimp" in English. Dried *sakura ebi* is different from Chinese dried shrimp, as the latter typically requires rehydration before it's used for cooking. Dried *sakura ebi* can be mixed in a dish or enjoyed as a topping. It can be found at Japanese grocery stores in the United States.

SAKURA NO SHIO-ZUKE

Salt-pickled cherry blossoms. These are small cherry blossoms (*sakura*) with stems, freshly picked and pickled in salt to preserve the color and flavor. They're used for making cherry blossom tea, cooked together with rice, used as a garnish for spring-season confections, and more. Salt-preserved cherry blossoms can be found at specialty stores or online shops in the United States.

SALT

Our recipes use sea salt, unless otherwise noted. My top choice is Amabito no Moshio, Seaweed seasalt, made in an ancient manner in a small island of Hiroshima, Japan. This sea salt has an especially round flavor and rich umami from the seaweed. Amabito no Moshio can be found at specialty stores in the United States.

SANSHO

Japanese mountain pepper. It's often dried and ground as a spice, or its fresh green berries can be used in stews or sautéed dishes. Related to Szechuan pepper. *Sansho* belongs to the citrus family.

SATSUMA-IMO

Japanese sweet potato, with purple-red skin and pale interior. It's commonly enjoyed in both dessert and savory dishes in Japan.

SESAME SEEDS

Whether white or black, whole or ground, sesame seeds are used widely in Japanese cuisine. To best enjoy the nutty aroma, it's recommended that you toast them before use to release the aroma, regardless of whether the sesame seeds are nontoasted or already toasted kind.

SHICHIMI TOGARASHI (ALSO CALLED SHICHIMI)

Translated as "seven-flavor pepper," *shichimi togarashi* is a popular chile-spice mix made from seven ingredients. While the seven ingredients and their ratios can be different depending on the producer, the most common ingredients are chiles, ground *sansho*, hemp seeds, sesame seeds, dry orange peel, shiso (perilla) leaves, *aonori* seaweed, and ginger. Yuzu-flavored *shichimi* is also popular.

SHIME

(SHE-meh) Finishing course of a meal. Many hot-pot recipes involve a *shime*. After you finish most of the dish, save enough broth to cook rice or noodles in the fortified liquid. The leftover broth has a rich flavor after it has reduced and been infused with all the ingredients, and many hot-pot lovers look forward to this part of the meal the most.

SHIO-KOMBU

Translated as "salted kombu," *shio-kombu* is kelp that was cut (either into thin shreds or small squares) and cooked with seasonings such as soy sauce and mirin, before being dried and dusted with salt. It's often enjoyed as a topping for *ochazuke* (rice, poured with tea or *dashi*), or as a condiment for various dishes.

SHIRATAKI (SHIRATAKI NOODLES/ KONNYAKU NOODLES)

See konnyaku.

SHIRO SHOYU

Translated as "white soy sauce," but the color is actually pale amber. It's made from mostly wheat as well as soybeans and is fermented for a shorter time to achieve the pale color. *Shiro shoyu* is used in recipes that require a light color. While it has a higher sodium content and is more delicate in flavor compared to dark soy sauce or *usukuchi shoyu*, *shiro shoyu* is naturally sweeter than the others.

SHISO

This herb belongs to the perilla family and is used in a wide variety of Japanese dishes. There is green *shiso* (also called *ohba*) and red *shiso*. It is similar to basil but has a cleaner aroma.

SHOCHU

A Japanese distilled drink. The most common types of *shochu* are barley, sweet potato, and rice. *Shochu* typically contains about 25 percent alcohol, which is much lower than other spirits such as whiskey, vodka, or rum. Therefore, *shochu* can be enjoyed either on its own or more commonly with a meal.

SHOJIN RYORI (SHOJIN CUISINE)

Japanese Buddhist temple cuisine. It typically consists of simple dishes with seasonal vegetables, mushrooms, seaweed, and grains. It is strictly vegan, based on the Buddhist philosophy that forbids killing any living things. Ingredients with a strong aroma, such as green onion, onion, chive, shallot, and garlic, are also not allowed in *shojin* cuisine because they are supposed to stimulate sexual desire. Many popular Japanese home dishes originate from *shojin* dishes.

SHUNGIKU

Chrysanthemum greens. This aromatic plant has soft crisp leaves with stems and can be used fresh or cooked. It's a popular ingredient for Japanese hot-pot dishes.

SOY MILK

Made from dried soybeans that have been soaked, pureed, and cooked in water and pressed. For the recipes in this book, we use pure, rich plain soy milk—it must be the natural kind with no additives (that is, it has to be made only from pure water and soybeans). The soy milk commonly available in paper cartons at US grocery stores is normally not suitable, as even the plain versions have additives or are too thin. *Nigari* liquid won't work properly if the soy milk contains additives or is too thin. Rich plain soy milk can be found at Japanese and other Asian grocery stores; it's normally not labeled as such, but the concentration rate of 12 percent/12 brix or higher, similar to a whole-milk texture, is preferred.

SOY SAUCE

One of the most essential seasonings in Japanese cuisine. Brewed from soybeans, wheat, water, and salt and aged for a few months to several years. For better flavor and quality, naturally brewed soy sauce with no additives is preferred. Soy sauce should be kept in a cool dark place or more preferably in the refrigerator. *See also shiro shoyu* and *usukuchi shoyu*.

SWEET RICE (ALSO CALLED MOCHI RICE)

Glutinous rice. The grain has an opaque white color and becomes very sticky and chewy when it's cooked. This type of rice is widely used in Asian countries for both savory and dessert dishes.

TARO

Known as *sato-imo* in Japanese, taro is a root vegetable used in a variety of Asian cuisines. The skin is rough and fuzzy like a coconut, and the interior is a pale to white color with a slimy texture when it's raw.

TOBANJAN (ALSO CALLED DOUBANJIANG)

Called fermented chili bean paste or sauce in English. Originating in China, it is a fermented paste of beans, chiles, salt, and spices. A small amount is normally used to add hot and spicy flavors and depth to a dish. It's a popular item in Japanese kitchens and is used in a wide variety of dishes including Japanese-style Chinese dishes such as *mabo tofu*.

TOGAN

Winter melon (also called white gourd). Winter melon is vine-grown, has a white interior, and is eaten as a vegetable even though it's called a melon. In Asian cuisines, *togan* is often cooked in soup.

TORORO KOMBU

Kombu that has been seasoned and softened in a vinegar marinade and then shaved into extremely thin shreds. While its usage is versatile, it's most typically used as a topping for soup and noodles.

USUKUCHI SHOYU

Light-colored soy sauce. The aroma and flavor are also slightly lighter than regular (dark-colored) soy sauce. It also has a higher salt content.

WAKAME

Edible seaweed that is a highly popular ingredient in traditional Japanese cuisine. Wakame is most commonly used in soup and salad, as well as in different types of dishes. Wakame is commonly sold in either dried or soft (salt-preserved) form. Dried wakame needs to be reconstituted by being soaked in plenty of water for five to fifteen minutes, depending on type or brand, and then rinsed and drained well. The size will expand by seven to eight times. If the dried wakame is not precut, cut it into the desired size after it's reconstituted. Soft (salt-preserved) wakame is often labeled "fresh wakame," but technically it has been quickly blanched and preserved in salt. This type also needs to be soaked in plenty of water for a few minutes and rinsed well to remove the salt, and then drained well and cut into the desired size before use. The color will become brighter green. If there is a tough rib, it should be cut off. Soft (salt-preserved) wakame expands by about three times. Real fresh wakame is rarely found in stores in the United States. It's dark brown in color. To prepare fresh wakame, blanch it in very hot water (slightly under boiling) for a couple of minutes. The color will turn to bright green. Rinse in cold water and drain well to use.

WASABI

A plant that grows in the beds of mountain streams. Its root is grated and used as a condiment, most typically for sashimi and sushi. It can also be shredded and used as a topping or added to salads and other dishes. It has a hot, refreshing flavor. Wasabi is also sold in powder or paste forms. Although these are not 100 percent wasabi, they are much more accessible and convenient to use.

YAMA-IMO

Also called Japanese mountain yam in English, it's a root vegetable native to Japan. A variety called *naga-imo* is more commonly available at Japanese grocery stores in the United States. The rough skin has a beige color and interior is white and slimy. Yama-imo can be eaten raw or cooked. Raw yama-imo has a crisp texture and is often grated to be used as a topping or a binder for dishes.

YUBA

Tofu skin, also called bean curd sheet in English. When soy milk is heated, a thin layer of film forms on the surface of the liquid. This layer is called *yuba* and is enjoyed as a delicacy in Japan and other Asian countries. *Yuba* is sold fresh, semidried, or dried.

YUZU

A Japanese aromatic citrus. The rind is often sliced and added to dishes as an aromatic garnish. Yuzu has its own distinctive aroma that is often described as elegant, and it's very different from any other citrus. As it's not very easy to find fresh yuzu in the United States, if a recipe calls for yuzu and you don't have it, you can substitute Meyer lemon.

YUZU-KOSHO

An aromatic paste of mashed yuzu rind, salt, and chiles mixed together and fermented. There is both green *yuzu-kosho* and red *yuzu-kosho*. It's a popular condiment that can be used to season sashimi (instead of soy sauce), hot pots, grilled meats or fish, and more.

KITCHEN TOOLS

CERAMIC GRATER

A round ceramic plate that grates ginger and garlic very finely. The ceramic teeth in the center are sharp and long-lasting, and are surrounded by a well where the grated part collects. I have been using the same ceramic grater made by Kyocera for almost fifteen years, and it continues to work great. Kyocera's ceramic grater can be purchased at Japanese markets or online shops.

DAIKON GRATER

While there are various designs of daikon grater, the most convenient style is a rectangular box shape with a draining insert. There is a grate surface with many holes on top, and the grated daikon falls to the insert, which works as a strainer and drains its juice. If you want to drain more juice, you can press on the grated daikon to drain more. If you want more texture in the grated daikon, a Japanese old-fashioned wooden daikon grater (called *onioroshi*) coarsely grates the daikon, and you can enjoy the crunchy texture.

HOROKU (see photo opposite)

A traditional Japanese sesame roaster with a handle and round body for roasting. You can pour the sesame seeds into the open mouth on the top of the body. The handle is hollow and connected to the body, so once the roasting is done, you can simply pour out the sesame seeds from the end of the handle. Nagatani-en, the producer of the *Iga-yaki* donabe used in this book, makes handcrafted *horoku* from Iga clay.

OTOSHIBUTA

Japanese drop lid. It's a flat round piece traditionally made of wood (though it can be made from other materials, such as silicone or metal) that is slightly smaller than the pot's diameter so that it can sit directly on the surface of the cooking contents. *Otoshibuta* causes better circulation of the cooking fluid, which helps even cooking. You can substitute a piece of aluminum foil or parchment paper placed on the surface of the cooking contents. *Otoshibuta* can be purchased at Japanese markets or online shops.

Portable butane gas burner

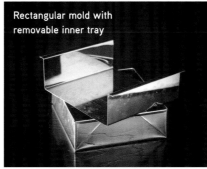

Rectangular mold with removable inner tray

Horoku

PORTABLE BUTANE GAS BURNER (see photo above)

An essential item for the tabletop communal cooking of donabe. It's also an easy solution for cooking with donabe if your kitchen is not equipped with a gas stove top. A portable butane gas burner works with a disposable butane fuel cartridge. Both are available at Japanese or other Asian markets, online stores, and camping stores. My choice is Iwatani brand, whose basic model (BTU 10,000) works just fine. The price for the burner is normally about $30, and a fuel cartridge is about $2 or less. It's an extremely reasonable investment, as I've been using the same burner very frequently for almost fifteen years, and it still works like brand new. A portable burner is also great for an outdoor donabe party.

RECTANGULAR MOLD WITH REMOVABLE INNER TRAY (see photo above)

Called *nagashi-kan* in Japanese, this is a traditional mold that can be used for making *yokan* (steamed sweet azuki jelly), Steam Cakes, *tamago* tofu (steamed egg cakes), and more.

SURIBACHI AND SURIKOGI

Japanese mortar and pestle. *Suribachi* (mortar) is a ceramic bowl with a ribbed interior. *Surikogi* (pestle) is made from wood and is used to crush or grind seeds, herbs, tofu, and more. Various sizes of *suribachi* and *surikogi* can be purchased at Japanese markets or online shops.

WASABI GRATER

At authentic Japanese restaurants, a sharkskin grater is used for grating wasabi. Sharkskin grates the tough root of wasabi very finely. A ceramic grater or metal grater can be used for grating wasabi, too. Sharkskin graters can be purchased at Japanese markets or online shops.

RESOURCES

DONABE, IGA-YAKI PRODUCTS, ETC.
All the donabe products used in this book are made by Nagatani-en, in Iga, Japan, and available online at toiro kitchen in the United States (also ships internationally). Some other Iga-yaki products, kitchen tools, smoke chips, and premium short-grain Japanese variety *koshihikari* rice, made by Tamaki Farms in Uruguay, are also available here.

toiro kitchen
toirokitchen.com

SEAFOOD
High quality sashimi-grade seafood and also caviar is available to ship nationwide in the United States by Kai Gourmet.

www.kaigourmet.com/home

JAPANESE GROCERY
These small chain markets, Nijiya Market, Mitsuwa Marketplace, and Marukai, also offer products from their online shops.

www.nijiyashop.com
www.mitsuwa.com
www.marukaiestore.com

SOYBEANS
Signature Soy is a family-owned farm making non-GMO soybeans.

www.signaturesoy.com

NAGATANI-EN
Nagatani-en is open to visitors. (contact is in Japanese only)

Address: 569 Marubashira, Iga-shi, Mie Prefecture, Japan
Phone: +81-0595-44-1511

VEGETABLES
A family-run business called The Chef's Garden from Ohio offers a wide selection of premium quality vegetables and herbs by home delivery service.

www.chefsgarden.com

ACKNOWLEDGMENTS

We would like to thank the following individuals and organizations.

Our editor, Jenny Wapner, designer, Nami Kurita, and the entire team at Ten Speed Press for working with us throughout the entire process and making such a beautiful book.

Our photographer, Eric Wolfinger, for the most amazing photography, and for making the photo shoots so exciting. Assistant photographer, Alison Christiana, for keeping thing organized.

Our agent, Amy Collins, for believing in us from the very beginning and guiding us all the way.

Jody Eddy, for helping us to start this big project.

Dianne Jacob, for coaching us for over a year and seeing our first book proposal through to success.

Katie Wilson, for copyediting and helping with our draft manuscript.

Asami Tanaka, for assisting us and working long hours every day during the photoshoot in LA.

Our guest chefs for contributing special donabe recipes: David Kinch, Josef Centeno, Nick Balla and Cortney Burns, Shinobu Namae

Ingredients and products sponsors for the photo shoot: Amabito no moshio, Honda Miso, Kai Gourmet, Miyako Oriental Foods Inc., Mutual Trading Co., Inc, Saikai Toki Inc., Takaokaya USA, Takara Sake USA, Tamaki Farms Inc., The Chef's Garden, The Cultured Pickle Shop, Yamasa Corporation USA

Nagatani-en, for bringing their beautiful donabes to the world and for being the story at the heart of our book.

Finally, our families—Jason Moore, Katina, Chloe, and Ava Connaughton for their endless love and support.

INDEX

Copyright © 2015 by Naoko Takei Moore and Kyle Connaughton
Photographs copyright © 2015 by Eric Wolfinger

Published in the United States by Ten Speed Press, an imprint of the
Crown Publishing Group, a division of Penguin Random House LLC,
New York.
www.crownpublishing.com
www.tenspeed.com

Ten Speed Press and the Ten Speed Press colophon are registered
trademarks of Penguin Random House LLC.

Library of Congress Cataloging-in-Publication Data

Moore, Naoko Takei.
    Donabe : traditional and modern Japanese clay pot cooking / by Naoko
Takei Moore and Kyle Connaughton ; photography by Eric Wolfinger.
        pages cm
1. Clay pot cooking. 2. Cooking, Japanese. I. Connaughton, Kyle. II. Title.
    TX825.5.M66 2015
     641.5952—dc23

Hardcover ISBN: 978-1-60774-699-7
eBook ISBN: 978-1-60774-700-0

Printed in China

Design and illustrations by Nami Kurita

10 9 8 7 6 5 4 3 2

First Edition

Flavour Heroes

Gurdeep Loyal

For Dad, who's given me
the flavours of the world.

Flavour Heroes

15 Modern Pantry Ingredients to Amplify Your Cooking

Gurdeep Loyal

Photography by
Patricia Niven

Food styling by
Lucy Rose Turnbull

Quadrille

'Memory is the seamstress, and a capricious one at that.
Memory runs her needle in and out, up and down... Thus,
the most ordinary movement in the world... may agitate a
thousand odd, disconnected fragments, now bright, now
dim, hanging and bobbing and dipping and flaunting...'

Virginia Woolf,
Orlando

'Over picturesque for every day; but then
who wants to eat the same food every day?'

Elizabeth David,
A Book of Mediterranean Food

INTRODUCTION

The secret to flavourful home-cooked food – everyday meals that are easy to make and remarkably delicious to eat – is, when you think about it, quite blindingly obvious. It's *not* what can be achieved by rigidly prescriptive cookbooks, expensive kitchen kit, or closely guarded family recipes. It most certainly *isn't* something you'll discover at a fancy-schmancy deli, where the staff are pretentious and the baffling array of provisions priced up to the nearest hundred. And it *isn't* something you'll necessarily acquire through years climbing the ladder from commis – to sous – to executive head chef.

In truth, the answer to this culinary quandary is so conspicuously unhidden – right on the tip of your very own tongue – that many home cooks unconsciously pass it by. The secret to flavourful food, is quite simply...

to use flavourful ingredients!

As *ta-dah* moments go, I admit that dramatic pause was a trifle unnecessary. But this basic principle of cooking – so elementary it's rarely made explicit – is so often forgotten in our relentless pursuit for flavour as home cooks. In turn, we can find ourselves flustered and flummoxed by the task in hand, overlooking the single most valuable resource we all have at our disposal: the pantry.

'Pantry' doesn't have to mean fancy. In some kitchens it's just a shelf, in others a bijoux corner. Maybe it's a double cupboard, and you're lucky indeed if it's a walk-in 'store' or 'larder'. Whatever guise your pantry takes, it offers the potential to produce fantastically flavourful meals that can thrill your taste buds with salty, sour, umami, bitter and sweet sensations every single day. The key to unlocking those infinite capabilities simply lies in the ingredients you buy, and the clever ways you combine them when you cook.

The virtues of a plentiful pantry have long been celebrated by food writers. Mrs Beeton extolled the merits of a larder filled with preserved ginger, Spanish chestnuts and port wine by the barrel load. Store-cupboard staples of the seventies perked up Fanny Cradock's most iconic dishes – Tabasco sauce in prawn cocktail, Sauternes in trifle and fluorescent-green crystallized angelica on just about everything. For Julia Child, the heart of French cooking could be found through a *bouquet garni* of fresh herbs and canned truffles revived with a splash of Madeira wine. Simon Hopkinson takes joy in umami-rich anchovies, crimson-red saffron, funky blue Roquefort and bitter dark chocolate. Delia Smith showed us *How to Cheat* with jarred lazy ginger, ready-grated Gruyère, and Hartley's lime jelly cubes. And Nigella Lawson's blissful recipes are filled with the marvels of tangy Worcestershire sauce, honeyed Marsala wine, fiery sambal oelek and piquant English mustard.

What their collective wisdom has in common is a desire to empower home cooks (of all abilities) with an armoury of ingredients that deliver big flavour for little effort – creating mouthwateringly tasty food that exhilarates the appetite at every opportunity, for minimal time, energy and cost.

In today's fast-paced information age, getting a head start when it comes to home cooking is more of a necessity than ever before but there's no reason for our routine race to the table to feel like a marathon. Just a few well-selected pantry ingredients can do all the heavy gourmet lifting for us, and the more we lean into these store-cupboard hacks and shortcuts every day, the less effort and expense we need to put in. Embrace this wisdom fully, and we accelerate into the fast lane, because a pantry filled with well-selected flavour superheroes – whose collective powers multiply when thoughtfully entwined – provides the rocket fuel for our daily culinary ride to deliciousness.

This book celebrates the superstar ingredients that can take your daily cooking in countless different directions at the twist of a lid, squeeze of a tube or ring-pull of a can – the flavour heroes of a modern pantry.

Admittedly, the shelves of my own tiny east London kitchen are adorned with hundreds of outlandish products collected on my gastronomic travels across the globe. But I turn to – and repeatedly replenish – just 15 pantry powerhouses again and again and again:

HARISSA

PECORINO ROMANO

GOCHUJANG

THAI GREEN PASTE

YUZU KOSHŌ

TAMARIND PASTE

MANGO CHUTNEY

CHIPOTLE PASTE

TOASTED SESAME OIL

MISO

'NDUJA

CALABRIAN CHILLI PASTE

DARK ROASTED PEANUT BUTTER

INSTANT ESPRESSO POWDER

DARK MAPLE SYRUP

These are *my* store-cupboard favourites that effortlessly turn up the volume of my home cooking every day of the week, no matter what I'm concocting. They are the bedrock of my pantry: delicious in their own right, and astonishingly tasty when combined. I love to cook with these dependable, everyday ingredients as freely as a composer might play with instruments in an orchestra, or a painter with colours on a canvas.

By challenging orthodox 'rules' of how flavours *ought* to be employed or how traditional pairings *must* be observed, I want to showcase each expansive ingredient in a different light. My hope is to empower and liberate you to reach for *any* product on your shelves with boundless confidence *every* time you cook – focusing less on how an ingredient is habitually used, and instead on the full spectrum of tasty potential it holds to enhance the flavours of whatever you happen to be cooking.

My recipes demonstrate how, for instance, smoky-hot **chipotle paste** can amplify the flavours of molten cauliflower cheese (page 130), or be combined with something treacly-fragrant to a make meal out of crispy chicken wings (page 126). How the rounded savouriness of **miso** can bring pleasing umami to creamy mustard baked fish (page 159), or add salty depth to the ganache on a decadent chocolate fudge cake (page 165). How **mango chutney**, stirred into a tangy-sweet glaze with roasted garlic, can transform a few carrots into a superb tarte tatin (page 112), or add tropical-fruit flair to crunchy chicken schnitzels (page 116). And how caramelly **dark maple syrup** can transform a humble tin of butter beans in a citrussy lemon dressing (page 236), or bring vanilla-nectar toffee sweetness to an oat-crumbed rhubarb fool (page 242).

WHAT IS MODERN ABOUT
THESE FLAVOURS?

The 'modern' aspect of these flavour heroes is not so much the diverse commodities themselves – most of which have been celebrated in their cultures of origin for hundreds of years – but our fresh appreciation of them. We have access to more products from around the world – in supermarkets, local diasporic stores, hipster delis, farmers' markets and online – than at any time; and we can travel more easily, frequently and accessibly than ever before. Indeed, the global movement of people has transformed almost all pantry ingredients into 'modern' travellers themselves, morphing and mutating along their own migratory journeys from kitchen to kitchen – flavouring the plates of the planet on their nomadic way.

Moreover, new generations of proudly third-culture cooks – much like myself – are celebrating the culinary narratives of their own 'authentically' hybrid lives; and, thanks to social media, we can be simultaneously connected to the daily *dégustations* of billions of people across the globe, every second of every day. Consequently, through our screens, we can fawn over a café noisette and pistachio croissant in Paris and – in the same moment – join someone brining freshly pressed halloumi in Athens, or sitting down to a Bengali thali and Limca in Kolkata, or tucking into suya skewers with spicy peanut sauce in Lagos, or toasting with Bundaberg palomas and rock oysters in Sydney, or enjoying charred yakitori and Hibiki highballs in Tokyo, or midnight feasting on Korean-style tacos on the streets of LA.

Flavour Heroes reflects and celebrates this gastronomically connected world, and in turn our globally adventurous palates that are becoming curiouser – and curiouser – by the day.

Nonetheless, our emotional experience of flavour is not just what we taste on the tongue, but also what we taste in the mind. 'Flavour' is only *absolutely* felt when we connect the sensations encountered in our mouths – to the aromas that pass from our throats to our noses as we chew – the sights and sounds that feed our hungry eyes and ears – and the memories unconsciously triggered in our thoughts with every bite we take.

I haven't read Proust, but not for lack of trying. As a result, I'm somewhat fluent in the passage about madeleines dipped in tea and if that's as far as I ever get, the sumptuous beauty of those sentences is plenty enough for me. I'm captivated by the idea that taste memories are never lost but perpetually lie in the depths of our unconscious – ghostly spirits of flavour, eternally poised to be unleashed when we least expect them.

The recipes that follow tell the culinary tales of *my* modern taste memories – refracted and retold through flavours that are an expression of *my* life today. In sharing them, I invite you to reimagine *your own* modern memories on a plate, using well-loved ingredients that mirror places you've visited in the past – and still others that reflect where you happen to be right now. But more thrillingly, using new ingredients that are a portal to places you'd like to go to in the future, and to which, through a modern flavour pantry of your very own, you can be magically transported today.

London, 2025

HOW TO SHOP FOR A
MODERN PANTRY

- With genuine curiosity about the cultural context of any new ingredient – and why it's valued by the global communities it's most closely associated with. Shopkeepers in local diasporic stores are the ultimate founts of this knowledge and wisdom – and their shelves a rich cornucopia of flavours just waiting to be explored.

- With understanding of the significance of the ingredient in your hands, precisely what the product is, where it comes from, its individual components, how exactly it's made, and when it's at its seasonal best.

- With mindfulness of the environmental and human footprint, aligning your purchase decisions with your personal ethical values, dietary framework, financial means and sustainability principles.

- With an understanding of what each modern flavour product brings to the table in terms of its flavour and how that can complement other ingredients you cook with.

- With considered intercultural playfulness when adding new products to your shelves – and not being bound by so-called 'rules' when it comes to combining different flavours.

Just as friends meeting for dinner can introduce hilarity, mayhem or drama to the evening, flavourful ingredients bring their own unique personalities and characteristics to a dish. When you add a new pantry ingredient, you're ultimately imparting its *flavour personality* into your cooking... be it tangy sharpness or salty savouriness; nutty cheesiness or smoky spiciness; creamy toastiness or fragrant tartness; citrussy zinginess or caramel sweetness.

The most delicious food, in my opinion, is multi-layered and allows different personalities to sparkle and shine with no one dominating the show.

Cooking is a daily event where every flavour is welcome, and any ingredient from around the world has the potential to be truly delicious in combination with another. It's when culinary worlds collide that you have a truly astronomical party on your plate.

Harissa

smoky and earthy,
piquantly roasted,
complexly spiced,
increasingly building,
chilli heat.

This aromatic oil-based Tunisian chilli paste, rich in hot and tangy red chillies, garlic, roasted peppers, cumin, caraway and coriander seeds, is also strongly associated with Algerian, Libyan and Moroccan cuisines. The word harissa means 'to crush, mash, pound or break' in Arabic – evocative of how it's traditionally made by pummelling the chillies by hand using a pestle and mortar. Popular flavour variations include rose petal, apricot, verbena, preserved lemon, green herb and smoked chilli. Customarily sold in tubes in North Africa, elsewhere it's more commonly found in jars, although you can also buy powdered dry harissa spice blends. Delis also sell freshly blended harissa pastes, which have the most vibrant flavour.

CHARD, HARISSA BUTTERNUT SQUASH & MANCHEGO LASAGNE

Of the infinite things I adore about the Côte d'Azur, my principal magnet is the plethora of *traiteurs gourmets* whose market-side counters offer up Franco-Italian specialities like herby courgette gratins, roasted *oignons farcis*, chicken fat-roasted potatoes, giant *pan bagnat*, anchovy-crossed *pissaladière* and vibrant *pistou*-coated pasta bakes. Adorning those counters you'll often find a sugar-dusted *tourte de blettes* – a Provençal savoury-sweet tart filled with Swiss chard, pine nuts, raisins and parmesan. My recipe brings together that unconventional chard tart with those *traiteur*-baked lasagnes I love so much – using Spanish Manchego cheese for sharp-nutty tang and layers of Tunisian harissa-brushed butternut squash for extra sunny-sweet heat.

SERVES 6

olive oil
1 large red onion, finely diced
4 fat garlic cloves, crushed to a paste
200g (7oz) Swiss chard, finely chopped
250g (9oz) ricotta
15g (½oz) fresh basil, chopped
125g (4 ¼oz) Manchego, grated, plus extra to garnish
1 large egg

1 medium butternut squash (about 750g/1lb 10oz; no need to peel)
3 Tbsp harissa or rose harissa paste
3 Tbsp sun-dried tomato purée (paste)
1 Tbsp Worcestershire sauce
500g (1lb 2oz) tomato passata
15 dried lasagne sheets
125g (4¼oz) fresh mozzarella (1 standard ball)
fine sea salt

Heat a splash of olive oil in a large saucepan, then add the red onion with a pinch of salt. Cook for 5 minutes, then add the garlic and chopped chard. Cook for another 5 minutes until the chard has wilted and most of the water has evaporated. Empty into a bowl and leave to cool completely.

When the chard is at room temperature, add half the ricotta, the basil, manchego, egg and 1 teaspoon of salt. Mix everything well, then set aside. Preheat the oven to 180°C fan/200°C/400°F/ Gas mark 6.

Use a mandoline or sharp knife to very carefully slice the squash into 2–2.5mm (¹⁄₁₆in) rounds or half-moons (any thicker and they won't cook through). When you reach the seeds, remove these with a spoon, discard the fibres and reserve the seeds.

In a separate bowl, make a hot paste by stirring together the harissa, sun-dried tomato purée, Worcestershire sauce and ¾ teaspoon of salt. Liberally brush half of it over the butternut squash slices. Mix the remaining half of the paste with the remaining ricotta, and set aside.

Brush a deep 24 x 30cm/9½ x 12in (or equivalent) baking dish with olive oil. Layer half the harissa-butternut thins over the base, then spread over half the tomato passata. Add a layer of lasagne sheets to cover the base completely – snap the sheets if needed.

Continued...

Smother your first layer of pasta with the manchego-chard mix, spreading it all over thickly. Top this with another layer of lasagne sheets, then repeat: layer on the rest of the butternut slices, then the remaining tomato passata, and cover with a final layer of lasagne sheets. Spread your hot paste-ricotta mix on top in an even layer. Tear over the fresh mozzarella, drizzle liberally with olive oil, then cover the dish tightly with foil.

Place the lasagne on a baking tray to catch any spillage and bake for 1 hour. Remove from the oven, take off the foil and bake for a final 10–15 minutes until golden on top and cooked through. In this last 15 minutes, also bake the butternut squash seeds in the bottom of the oven – spread out over a baking sheet, drizzled with olive oil and a pinch of salt.

Remove the lasagne from the oven, sprinkle over the crunchy seeds, and garnish with extra finely grated manchego if you like.

SWEET POTATO & PUMPKIN SEED GNOCCHI WITH HARISSA MASCARPONE v

Gnocchi and gnudi are labours of love, but their mildly arduous steps to assembly become worth every second as soon as they're ravenously devoured. The former are traditionally made with potatoes and flour which allow them to crisp up wonderfully in a little butter and oil, whereas the latter are made with ricotta for a creamier, pillowy, cloud-like experience. This recipe combines the best of both sensations – the sweet potato dumplings sizzled to a pleasing crisp, the harissa-spiked mascarpone adding a heated velvety creaminess, and toasted pumpkin seeds bringing some obligatory textural crunch.

SERVES 4

30g (1oz) pumpkin seeds, plus extra
    to garnish
350g (12oz) sweet potatoes, peeled
    and chopped
350g (12oz) white potatoes, peeled
    and chopped
4 garlic cloves, crushed to a paste
1 tsp fennel seeds, crushed
½ tsp freshly grated nutmeg
20g (¾oz) butter, plus extra for frying

20g (¾oz) parmesan, freshly grated,
    plus extra to garnish
zest and juice of 1 lemon
275–325g (9¼ –11½oz) plain
    (all-purpose) flour, plus extra
    for dusting
1 large egg yolk
1 Tbsp harissa or rose harissa paste,
    plus extra to serve
1 Tbsp tomato purée (paste)
150g (5½oz) mascarpone
1 tsp finely chopped fresh thyme
fine sea salt

Toast all the pumpkin seeds in a dry frying pan for 1–2 minutes until they just start to pop. Leave to cool slightly, then crush 30g (1oz) using a pestle and mortar to a coarse rubble.

Boil the sweet potatoes and white potatoes in a large pan of well-salted water for 14–15 minutes, then drain through a sieve and leave until the steam escapes completely. Return to the saucepan and mash to a fine purée. If they are still very wet, cook the mashed potatoes in the pan over a low heat for 4–5 minutes, until drier.

Stir through the garlic, fennel seeds, nutmeg, butter, parmesan, half the lemon zest, 1 teaspoon of salt and the crushed pumpkin seeds.

Sift over half the flour, then stir slowly to incorporate fully. Next, add the egg yolk and stir again, before sifting over the rest of the flour. Mix one last time, then very gently knead on a well-floured surface into a soft dough that's not tacky – add a little extra flour if needed – but being careful not to overmix!

Roll the kneaded dough into 2 long sausages 2cm (¾in) thick, then slice into 2cm (¾in) wide nuggets. Gently press each gnocchi with a fork to create indents on the surface.

In a large saucepan, prepare the sauce by whisking together the harissa, tomato purée, mascarpone and lemon juice with 1 teaspoon of salt over a medium heat. Keep warm.

Bring a separate pan of well-salted water to the boil, then drop in the gnocchi in batches – cooking for 2–3 minutes until they rise to the top. Scoop out, then immediately drop into iced water. Repeat with the rest.

When ready to eat, melt a generous knob of butter in a frying pan and add the remaining lemon zest and chopped thyme. Let this sizzle slightly, then add a portion of the well-drained gnocchi. Cook for 4–5 minutes over a medium heat until they're warmed through and start to form a golden brown crust. Repeat with the rest.

Empty into a bowl and spoon over the warm harissa mascarpone sauce. Garnish with toasted pumpkin seeds, a drizzle of harissa and grated parmesan, if you like.

HERBY-HARISSA SHAWARMA
WITH SHALLOT RAITA

Green harissa is very much the 'it' ingredient of the moment: taking the scarlet-red staple our pantries have become accustomed to, and enlivening it with green chillies, verdant herbs and spiky jalapeños. My shawarma recipe takes inspiration from this viridescent trend – also riffing on the classic north Indian *hariyali* chicken, which literally translates as 'green chicken'. The smoked spiciness of harissa blended with the brightness of leafy mixed herbs infuses the meat with flavours that are pleasingly punchy, yet delicate. Dollop liberally with sharp, cooling shallot raita for the full *en vogue* effect.

SERVES 4

60g (2¼oz) fresh mixed green herbs
    (e.g. mint, coriander/cilantro and
    dill), thick stalks removed
4 Tbsp harissa or rose harissa paste,
    plus extra to garnish
7 fat garlic cloves
2 tsp grated fresh ginger root
2 tsp ground cumin
1 tsp ground cinnamon
zest of 1 and juice of 2 lemons
2 Tbsp runny honey

200g (7oz) Greek yoghurt
1kg (2lb 4oz) chicken thighs, skinless
    and boneless (about 8–10)
2 large shallots, very finely diced
½ cucumber
olive oil, for drizzling
fine sea salt

To serve
flatbreads or naans
pickled turnips, chilli peppers
    or pickled onions

First, make the marinade. Add to a small blender the mixed herbs, harissa paste, 6 garlic cloves, the ginger, ground spices, the lemon zest and 6 tablespoons of juice, honey, 50g (1¾oz) of the yoghurt and 2 teaspoons of salt. Whizz together to a thick green paste.

Place the chicken thighs in a large bowl, then pour over the green paste and mix well, smothering the chicken all over. Cover and leave in the refrigerator for at least 8 hours, ideally overnight.

Meanwhile, for the raita, add the finely chopped shallots to a bowl, stir in another tablespoon of lemon juice with a pinch of salt and leave for 10 minutes.

Slice the cucumber in half lengthways, then use a spoon to remove the watery seeds from the middle (keep these for smoothies). Grate the deseeded cucumber into a bowl, stir through a pinch of salt and leave for 10 minutes. Squeeze the water out of the grated cucumber, then mix together with the lemony shallots. Finally stir through the remaining 150g (5½oz) of yoghurt and grate in the remaining garlic clove, seasoning with a pinch of salt if needed.

Preheat the oven to 180°C fan/200°C/400°F/ Gas mark 6. Remove the marinated chicken from the refrigerator and let it come up to room temperature. Skewer the thighs onto two metal or soaked wooden skewers – stacking them one on top of the other to form a large kebab – held in place by the skewers on both sides.

Place the shawarma kebab on a wire rack over a baking sheet, drizzle with olive oil and bake for 1 hour until the chicken is cooked through. Finish cooking under a very hot grill for 2–3 minutes to burnish the top.

Toast the flatbreads and pile in the chicken, sliced, with the shallot raita, an extra drizzle of harissa and some pickles if you like.

HARISSA KEEMA SHAKSHUKA
WITH NAAN SOLDIERS

Savoury spiced breakfasts, flavoured with unapologetic gusto, are a staple of many eastern cuisines. Growing up in Leicester, my own weekend breakfasts were banquets of salted-mooli parathas, masala fried eggs and sour-lime Punjabi pickles – the energy of which is embodied in this Turkish-Punjabi-Tunisian fusion recipe. Here, minced meat (keema) is seasoned with the earthy warmth of cumin, the zesty freshness of sumac and the fiery depth of harissa. Equally delicious for lunch, dinner or a midnight feast.

SERVES 4

olive oil, for frying
1 large red onion, finely diced
2½ tsp cumin seeds, crushed
2 tsp sumac, plus extra to garnish
400g (14oz) minced (ground) lamb,
    at least 10% fat
3 fat garlic cloves, crushed to a paste
2 tsp grated fresh ginger root
1 Tbsp harissa or rose harissa paste,
    plus extra to garnish
3 Tbsp tomato purée (paste)
2 Tbsp dark brown sugar

2 Tbsp white wine vinegar
400g (14oz) canned chopped
    tomatoes
200ml (7fl oz) boiling water
4 eggs
fine sea salt

To serve
150g (5½oz) Greek yoghurt
1 fat garlic clove, crushed to a paste
2 large or 4 mini naans
butter
1 Tbsp chopped dill fronds
pinch of sumac

Heat a splash of olive oil in a deep frying pan, then add the onion with a pinch of salt. Cook over a medium heat for 8–9 minutes until it turns translucent. Next, add the cumin seeds and sumac. Stir through for another 1 minute.

Add the minced lamb and fry for 7–8 minutes until most of the water has evaporated and the meat is just starting to brown. Next, add the garlic, ginger, harissa and tomato purée. Cook for another 1 minute, then stir through the sugar, vinegar, 1½ teaspoons of salt, the canned tomatoes and boiling water. Cover with a lid and continue to cook over a medium heat for 10–12 minutes, stirring occasionally, until the oils start to separate in the sauce.

Remove the lid and cook for another 8–10 minutes to let the sauce thicken.

Make four indents in the keema sauce and carefully crack one whole egg into each cavity. Cover with a lid and cook over a medium heat for 7–9 minutes until the whites are set to your liking.

Meanwhile, in a separate bowl, stir together the Greek yoghurt, garlic and a pinch of salt. Toast the naans, rub over a small knob of butter, sprinkle with sumac and slice into soldiers. Ripple the garlic yoghurt through the keema, sprinkle with dill, an extra drizzle of harissa and a pinch of sumac. Enjoy.

Tip: At the end of step 3, if you can, leave the keema sauce off the heat to rest for 4–5 hours – this allows the flavours to meld together, amplifying the taste significantly. You will need to reheat it to a simmer before proceeding with step 4.

CAMPARI & HARISSA-BRAISED BRISKET
WITH CELERIAC CHAMP

In M.F.K. Fisher's little-known book *A Cordiall Water* (1961), she pontificates over folkloric elixirs and medicinal remedies that she encountered on her travels through California, Mexico, France and Switzerland. Many of them read like alcoholic witch potions infused with meadow plants, liquoriced roots, hot spices and obscure herbal blossoms, reminiscent of Italian amaro. That mélange of flavours is the inspiration behind this recipe, which marries the bitter herbal sweetness of Campari – with its spicy notes of cinnamon, clove and anise – with the piquant heat of harissa. When very slowly cooked together, this celestial pairing of ingredients is quite magical – especially when served with a buttery celeriac champ.

SERVES 4

1.75kg (3lb 14oz) beef brisket
olive oil, for frying
1 large onion, diced
1 large carrot, chopped
2 large celery sticks, diced
1 large red (bell) pepper, diced
8 garlic cloves, crushed to a paste
2½ tsp cumin seeds, crushed
2 tsp ground cinnamon
5 Tbsp harissa or rose harissa paste
4 Tbsp tomato purée (paste)
100ml (3½fl oz) Campari

100ml (3½fl oz) malt vinegar
2 Tbsp dark brown sugar
500ml (17fl oz) beef stock

For the celeriac champ
1 large celeriac, peeled and chopped
    (500g/1lb 2oz peeled weight)
1.25kg (2lb 12oz) floury potatoes
65g (2¼oz) butter
2 large spring onions (scallions),
    finely chopped
fine sea salt and freshly ground black
    pepper
chopped fresh parsley, to garnish

Cut the brisket into 4 or 5 large chunks. Place on a baking sheet, season generously with salt all over, then leave for 30 minutes.

Next heat a splash of olive oil in a large, lidded ovenproof pot over a medium heat, then brown each of the brisket pieces, in batches, for 5–6 minutes – to get a brown crust over the surface of each piece. Place back on the baking sheet and set aside.

Preheat the oven to 180°C fan/200°C/400°F/Gas mark 6. Pour a little more oil into the pot if needed, then add the onion, carrot, celery and red pepper. Cook for 10 minutes until they have reduced in volume by half, then add three-quarters of the crushed garlic, the cumin, cinnamon, harissa, tomato purée and a generous teaspoon of salt. Pour in the Campari and mix well.

Return the browned brisket pieces to the pot and mix well. Finally, add the vinegar, sugar and stock. Bring to the boil, cover with a lid and place in the oven.

Cook for 2½ hours, stirring every 30 minutes. If it's drying out, top up with a little more stock. Remove the lid, then cook for a final 15 minutes. Remove from the oven and rest before serving.

Meanwhile prepare the celeriac champ. Boil the celeriac and potatoes in a large saucepan of salted water for 20 minutes until soft and tender. Drain through a colander over the sink and leave for 5 minutes for the steam to escape.

In the same pan, melt the butter over a medium heat, then add the spring onions and remaining crushed garlic. Sizzle gently for 3–4 minutes, then add the cooked celeriac and potatoes, stirring well. Mash to a smooth purée, then season with salt and pepper. Serve generous dollops of warm champ with the chunks of brisket, lots of Campari-harissa sauce and fresh parsley to garnish.

HARISSA & PINK PEPPERCORN FISH FINGERS WITH DILL PICKLE TARTARE

In their grown-up iterations these often parade themselves on menus as *goujons*, tempura batons or fish tenders – when, in truth, we all know what they really are: posh fish fingers! Harissa and a pink peppercorn-polenta crumb make this version very grown up indeed – bringing warming spice and a lemon-scented crunch. The spiky caper-gherkin tartare is a perfectly discerning accompaniment – although if your preference is for something less mature, then a good squeeze of tomato ketchup never goes amiss.

SERVES 4

325g (11½oz) skinless, boneless
    haddock or sustainably caught
    cod fillets
2 Tbsp harissa or rose harissa paste
1 tsp ground cinnamon
2 tsp onion powder
zest of ½ lemon
olive oil, for drizzling
4 Tbsp cornflour (cornstarch)
1 large egg, beaten

50g (1¾oz) panko breadcrumbs,
    crushed to powder
50g (1¾oz) polenta (cornmeal)
1 Tbsp pink peppercorns, crushed
2 tsp coriander seeds, crushed

For the tartare sauce
2 large gherkins (pickles),
    plus 1 Tbsp brine
2 Tbsp capers, chopped
4 Tbsp mayonnaise
1 Tbsp chopped fresh dill fronds
fine sea salt

Cut the fish fillets into 8–10 thick fish fingers. Next, in a bowl mix together the harissa, cinnamon, onion powder, lemon zest, a pinch of salt and a drizzle of olive oil to form a thick paste. Smother the fish fingers all over and leave for 15 minutes.

Meanwhile, make the tartare by chopping the pickled gherkins into chunky pieces or thin slivers. Add to a bowl and stir in the chopped capers, mayonnaise, dill and 1 tablespoon of the pickled gherkin brine. Put in the refrigerator for the flavours to mingle.

Prepare three shallow bowls for coating the fish fingers: to the first, add the cornflour: to the second, the beaten egg: and to the third, a mixture of the panko breadcrumbs, polenta, pink peppercorns and coriander seeds.

Dip each fish finger first into the cornflour, then into the egg, and then roll in the crumbs to cover on all sides.

Preheat the oven to 200°C fan/220°C/425°F/Gas mark 7. Spread out the coated fish fingers on a baking sheet, drizzle with a little oil and bake for 15–17 minutes until golden on the outside and cooked through. Serve hot with a good dollop of the tartare sauce. Alternatively, pile into well-buttered slices of crusty white bread for the best fish finger sandwiches ever!

Pecorino Romano

sharp and creamy,
saltily grassy,
delicately fruity,
nuttily grainy,
bright cheesiness.

This hard, grainy-textured Italian sheep's-milk cheese dates back to Roman times. Its name reflects this – deriving from *pecora*, meaning 'sheep', and *romano*, referring to its origins in ancient Rome. Traditionally made with animal rennet – although vegetarian versions are available – it's typically aged for between 8 and 12 months. Regional variations include pecorino made in Sardinia, Sicily, Calabria and Tuscany. There are also versions that are younger (3–6 months) and milder, and others that are aged for longer (12-plus months), which have an intensely mature flavour. Specialist delis also sell pecorino cheeses infused with crushed black peppercorns, chamomile petals, pistachios and even decadent black truffle.

BLISTERED SPRING ONION, ZA'ATAR & PECORINO HUMMUS

I don't really like tahini. There, I said it. Don't get me wrong, I love the flavour of sesame – see chapter 9 – but tahini paste is just not something I have a taste for. Tzatziki and taramasalata I'd quite happily bathe in; hummus I can take or leave. Unless that is, it's hummus laden with blackened alliums, citrussy dried herbs and sharp tangy cheese – in which case, turn on the taps! The Pecorino Romano in this recipe brings out the toasted nuttiness of tahini, while somehow mellowing its cloying dominance. I still don't care for tahini, but I do very much adore this hummus.

SERVES 4-6

8 large spring onions (scallions), trimmed (about 175g/6oz)
4 Tbsp olive oil, plus extra for brushing and drizzling
zest of 1 and juice of 2 lemons
3 fat garlic cloves, crushed to a paste
1 Tbsp za'atar, plus extra to garnish
2½ tsp cumin seeds, crushed

2 x 400g (14oz) cans chickpeas, drained (480g/1lb 1oz drained weight)
1 tsp bicarbonate of soda (baking soda)
100g (3½oz) tahini paste
65g (2¼oz) Pecorino Romano, finely grated, plus extra to garnish
¾ tsp fine sea salt
pitta chips or nachos, to serve

Lightly brush the spring onions with olive oil. Warm a frying pan over a high heat, then cook the spring onions for 5–6 minutes, turning frequently, until softened inside and blistered all over.

Put all but one of the charred spring onions, lemon juice and garlic in a food processor, then blitz on high speed for 2 minutes until you have a smooth green purée. Set aside.

In the same frying pan, gently heat the oil, then add the za'atar and cumin seeds. Sizzle for 30 seconds, remove from the heat and set aside.

Next, add the drained chickpeas and bicarbonate of soda to a large saucepan, with enough boiling water to cover well. Simmer over a medium–high heat for 15 minutes until the skins begin to rise to the top, skimming them away carefully.

Drain off the hot water, add cold water, then gently stir with your hands, loosening and gathering the rest of the chickpea skins to discard. Drain completely.

Add the peeled chickpeas and za'atar oil to the food processer, and blitz with the charred spring onions for 1 minute.

Finally, add the tahini, Pecorino, salt and lemon zest and blitz for a final 2–3 minutes until smooth (add 2 tablespoons of ice-cold water if you like your hummus extra silky). Garnish with a drizzle of oil, za'atar, Pecorino and the remaining blistered spring onion, chopped. Enjoy with pitta chips or crunchy nachos.

CACIO E PEPE RISOTTO
WITH BROWN-BUTTER LEMONS

You can 'cacio e pepe' anything it seems, so much so that the phrase almost becomes a verb. You can cacio e pepe shortbread, lasagne, pizza, nachos and even gelato – which, while certainly unique, is probably not something I'll be trying again. Risotto is my favourite thing to 'cacio e pepe' and is, in my opinion, even more satisfyingly delicious than the original cheese-and-black-pepper-pasta dish. The nutty creaminess of Pecorino Romano in this recipe voluptuously coats slow-cooked rice, and the tangle of butter-fried lemon slivers on top surprises the palate with a zing!

SERVES 4

1 unwaxed lemon
85g (3oz) butter
1 Tbsp olive oil
1 large onion, finely diced
2 large celery sticks, finely diced
4 garlic cloves, crushed to a paste
1 Tbsp black peppercorns, coarsely
  crushed

300g (10½oz) arborio or carnaroli rice
200ml (7fl oz) dry white wine
2 tsp Dijon mustard
800ml (28fl oz) hot chicken
  or vegetable stock
75g (2½oz) Pecorino Romano, grated,
  plus extra shavings to serve
½ tsp freshly grated nutmeg

Using a very sharp knife or mandoline, slice the lemon into really thin discs – removing the pips. Heat 50g (1¾oz) of the butter in a saucepan and cook over a medium heat for 5–6 minutes until it just starts to turn toasted brown. Add the lemon slivers and cook for 3–4 minutes, turning regularly, until they are tender. Set aside.

In a separate large saucepan, melt the remaining 35g (1¼oz) of butter with the olive oil, then add the onion. Cook for 7–8 minutes over a medium heat until it turns translucent. Next, add the celery and garlic, cooking for another 3 minutes, adding a splash more oil if needed.

Next, add the crushed black pepper, mix well and then add the rice. Cook for 2–3 minutes, coating the rice with the oil and toasting just slightly – being careful it doesn't burn. Pour over the white wine and add Dijon mustard, cooking for 2 minutes until it has fully dissolved.

Very slowly add 1 ladleful of hot stock to the rice at a time – stirring constantly – and only add another ladleful of stock when the previous one has been absorbed fully. Be patient, and don't be tempted to add it all at once – you want to keep adding stock and stirring for 18–20 minutes over a medium heat until the rice grains are tender and the risotto is creamy.

Remove from the heat and mix through the grated Pecorino – stirring until it's melted. Serve generous dollops of risotto topped with the lemon slivers, brown butter, a grating of fresh nutmeg and extra Pecorino shavings. It shouldn't need any salt but feel free to add more black pepper to garnish.

DEVILLED DATES
WITH PECORINO & ROSE

In one particularly jovial episode of the *Two Fat Ladies*, there's a moment where Clarissa Dickson Wright turns to Jennifer Paterson and flippantly asks: 'Do you go to a lot of parties?' Jennifer stops what she's doing, turns to look Clarissa right in the eye and very sternly replies: 'As a matter of fact I do!' It's an energy I try to channel as much as possible. Parties are serious business and FOMO is not an emotion I've yet learnt to deal with. As a result, much of my adult life has been spent both trying to get invited to, and giving, parties as often as I can. These devilled morsels are the perfect party bite – the fudgy sweetness of baked dates contrasting with the heat of the rose harissa, the smoky char of bacon and salted-creaminess of the Pecorino Romano treasure inside.

MAKES 12

100g (3½oz) Pecorino Romano,
    plus extra to garnish
2 Tbsp harissa or rose harissa paste
1 Tbsp runny honey

¾ tsp rose water
zest of ½ lemon
12 large Medjool dates (or prunes
    or dried apricots)
12 rashers (strips) streaky bacon
2 Tbsp toasted walnuts, crushed

Cut the Pecorino into 12 generous chunks, each large enough to stuff inside the dates.

Make a glaze by stirring together the harissa, honey, rose water and lemon zest in a small bowl. Cut the dates open along one side, remove the stone, then brush the insides liberally with some of the glaze.

Encase the Pecorino inside the glazed dates. Wrap each stuffed date in a rasher of streaky bacon, and pierce with a cocktail stick – all the way through – to hold everything together. Place on a wire rack on a baking tray.

Preheat the oven to 200°C fan/220°C/425°F/ Gas mark 7. Bake the bacon-wrapped devils for 18–20 minutes, turning regularly, until the bacon is cooked through and the cheese is starting to ooze from the middle.

Remove from the oven, brush with the remaining glaze, sprinkle with toasted walnuts and add a grating of fresh Pecorino. Enjoy warm with cocktails or Champagne.

FRENCH ONION SOUP
WITH OATY-PECORINO CRUMBLE

I am a fully-fledged Francophile. French art – Matisse! French music – Ravel! French fashion – Jacquemus! And French food – for which I am passionate about everything from the humble baguette to rotisserie chicken dipped in Dijon mustard; oozing truffled camembert to crème pâtissière-filled choux; and garlic butter drenched escargots to the Pierre Gagnaire pistachio soufflé that changed my life. I love it all, but French onion soup I could eat every day. While a classic Gruyère crouton on top never goes amiss, I'm always looking for extra crunch – and an oaty-Pecorino crumble gives just that. It may not be an especially French adornment, but sure is delicious.

SERVES 4

75g (2½oz) butter
olive oil
6 large onions, sliced
    (about 1kg/2lb 4oz)
1 Tbsp dark brown sugar
1 Tbsp brown or white miso
6 garlic cloves, slivered
1 tsp freshly chopped thyme leaves
1 tsp cracked black pepper
zest and juice of 1 lemon
    (use the zest for the crumble)
2 Tbsp plain (all-purpose) flour
250ml (9fl oz) dry white wine

1.25 litres (44fl oz) stock, preferably
    beef but you can use vegetable too
fine sea salt
double (heavy) cream (optional),
    to serve

For the crumble

100g (3½oz) plain (all-purpose) flour
100g (3½oz) jumbo (rolled) oats
85g (3oz) Pecorino Romano, finely
    grated
1 tsp lemon zest
1 Tbsp onion powder
90g (3¼oz) cold butter, cubed

First, make the soup. Heat the butter in a large saucepan with a splash of olive oil. Add all the sliced onions with a pinch of salt, then cook for 5 minutes, stirring continuously, to get them to just begin to soften. Cover with a lid and cook for another 10–12 minutes.

Add the sugar and miso, cooking for another 15 minutes – without the lid – until the onions are golden brown, but not burnt. Add the garlic, thyme and black pepper, cook for another minute, then add the lemon juice.

Next, stir through the flour. Allow it to cook out for 1 minute, then add the wine. Turn up the temperature and cook until the liquid has been fully absorbed and it just begins to thicken. At this point add the beef stock, bring to the boil, then cover with a lid and leave to simmer for 20 minutes. After 10 minutes, preheat the oven to 200°C fan/220°C/425°F/Gas mark 7.

Meanwhile, make the crumble. In a large bowl, combine the flour, oats, Pecorino, lemon zest and onion powder. Next, add the cubed butter, and use your hands to rub this in completely.

Clump the crumble using your hands into large chunks with some smaller rubble, then spread it out over a baking sheet.

Bake the savoury crumble in the oven for 20 minutes, checking and turning with a spoon every 5 minutes to ensure it does not burn. Remove from the oven and cool completely.

Remove the lid from the onion soup and cook for a final 10–15 minutes – depending on how thick you like it. Serve generous helpings of the soup with a drizzle of cream if you like, and the oaty-Pecorino crumble on top.

PEACH, TALEGGIO &
PECORINO CRINKLE PIE

Peaches and cream are an iconic duo – so much so that there was even an R'n'B song devoted to it in the nineties. I love the combination in all its iterations: from crunchy-apple-like peaches with airy-soft sweet Chantilly, through to soft overripe fig-sweet peaches with salty-rich cream cheese. This picnic-perfect pie combines all of these things – with super creamy and fruitily savoury taleggio cheese, sharp-buttery Pecorino Romano, luxurious crème fraîche and the ripest honeyed peaches you can find. Delicious hot or cold – or anywhere in between for that matter.

SERVES 6-8

125g (4½oz) butter, melted
12 sheets filo pastry
3 large peaches (375g/13oz),
    or use apricots or plums, pitted
200g (7oz) taleggio or scamorza
small handful of basil leaves, finely
    chopped
300ml (10½fl oz) crème fraîche

2 large eggs
80g (2¾oz) Pecorino Romano,
    finely grated
50ml (1¾fl oz) full-fat (whole) milk
1 fat garlic clove, crushed to a paste
2 tsp fennel seeds, crushed
1 tsp lemon zest
1 tsp freshly ground black pepper
1 Tbsp pistachios, crushed

Brush the base and sides of a deep 24 x 30cm/ 9½ x 12in (or equivalent) baking tray with melted butter.

Lay a sheet of filo pastry on a clean work surface or board. Brush liberally all over with melted butter, then pleat the pastry accordion-style from both sides into the middle. Place the crinkled sheet at the top of your baking tray – then repeat with all the filo sheets until you have loosely filled the tray.

Slice the peaches and taleggio cheese into discs approximately 2–3mm (⅛in) thick, then slot these into the pleats of the pastry all over at intervals – aim for a good mix of peaches and cheese throughout – you want to have a bit of both in each bite you take.

Next, slide the chopped basil into the pastry, getting it deep down into the pleats to ensure that it doesn't burn on top.

Preheat the oven to 175°C fan/195°C/385°F/ Gas mark 5½. Add the crème fraîche, eggs, Pecorino, milk, garlic, fennel seeds, lemon zest and black pepper to a large jug. Whisk well, then slowly and evenly trickle all over the pastry, ensuring the cheese sinks into the pleats of the pastry.

Bake the crinkle pie for 25 minutes, then remove from the oven and sprinkle over the crushed pistachios. Bake for a final 5 minutes, remove from the oven and rest for 10 minutes before serving with a green leafy salad.

ABRUZZO APPLE, PECORINO & RAISIN CROSTATA

One summer in the late noughties, I spent a week at a friend's house high in the region of Abruzzo, east of Rome – a characterful cottage built directly into the craggy mountainous rocks, on the edge of a small medieval village that felt like something out of a Chaucerian tale. There was only one store in the village, a cave-like establishment that served many purposes including: post office, bar, laundrette, local gossip hub, card hall, tobacconist, haberdashery, brothel (!) and bakery. I can very vividly remember its oven-warm rustic Italian loaves – on the 'blackened' side of scorched – which had an extraordinarily rich yeasty flavour. Equally vivid are my memories of a white gauze cloche that sat on the counter next to rolls of lottery scratchcards; it housed a lattice-crossed apple tart, that was sharp, sweet and savoury all at once, with salty sheep's cheese baked into the pastry. This recipe is my attempt to relive it, using the delicious charms of Pecorino Romano as my trigger.

SERVES 6

For the pastry crust
zest of 1 lemon (and juice for
   the filling)
100g caster (superfine) sugar
265g (9½oz) plain (all-purpose) flour,
   plus extra for dusting
80g (2¾oz) Pecorino Romano, finely
   grated, plus extra to serve
50g (1¾oz) ground almonds
2 Tbsp coarse semolina
100g (3½oz) cold butter, cubed
2–3 Tbsp full-fat (whole) milk

1 large egg, beaten
2 Tbsp demerara sugar

For the filling
100g (3½oz) raisins
2 large apples (Braeburn or Granny
   Smith)
2 Tbsp caster (superfine) sugar
2 Tbsp lemon juice (see left)
1 tsp ground cinnamon
1 tsp fiori di Sicilia or lemon extract
1 tsp vanilla extract
1 Tbsp cornflour (cornstarch)
mascarpone, to serve

To prepare the crust, rub 1 teaspoon of lemon zest into the caster sugar, then tip it into a food processor. Add the flour, grated Pecorino, ground almonds and 1 tablespoon of the semolina. Pulse to mix everything together and break up any lumps.

Now, pulse in the cold butter cubes until you have a fine sandy rubble. Next, add the milk, very little at a time, pulsing between each drop. You want the dough to just start to come together and hold as one – you may not need all of it.

When ready, empty out onto a well-floured surface, bring together as one. Divide into two pieces – one using a third of the dough for the lattice top, and the other using the remaining two-thirds for the base. Wrap both pieces in cling film and chill for 3–4 hours.

For the filling, soak the raisins in boiling water (or strong Earl Grey tea for an extra kick of flavour) for 30 minutes, then drain very well. Quarter and core the apples (no need to peel) then slice very thinly into 2mm (1/16in) half-moons. Tip the apples into a bowl along with the caster sugar, lemon juice, cinnamon, fiori di Sicilia, vanilla extract and cornflour. Mix well and leave to macerate for 10 minutes.

Remove the pastry from the refrigerator and roll out the larger piece on a piece of baking paper to a 30cm (12in) circle for the base. Slide it onto a baking tray and, using your fingers, dimple the edges up a little around the perimeter. Preheat the oven to 180°C fan/200°C/400°F/Gas mark 6.

Sprinkle the remaining tablespoon of semolina all over the base – this helps to prevent the pastry becoming soggy – then scatter over most of the raisins. Fan out the apple slices on top in overlapping layers to a design of your liking, then scatter over the last of the raisins.

Roll out the pastry for the lattice top and cut into thin strips. Arrange half in straight lines vertically, then weave in the rest on the diagonal – concealing the raisins (if they are close to the surface they can burn). Brush the surface of the pastry with egg, then sprinkle with demerara sugar.

Bake the crostata for 30–35 minutes until golden brown on top and flaky on the bottom. Remove from the oven and allow to cool on the baking tray. Grate over Pecorino to decorate and serve with dollops of mascarpone. Enjoy warm or cold.

Gochujang

bold and spicy,
funkily savoury,
sweetly fermented,
deeply pungent,
crimson chilli.

This Korean chilli paste combines spicy red gochugaru peppers with fermented soya beans, sweet glutinous rice, barley malt and salt. *Gochu* refers to chilli peppers, and *jang* is the term for any fermented soya bean-based condiment. In terms of heat, gochujang ranges from mild to extra spicy and the most delicious versions usually also contain MSG. Variations include *chogochujang* – gochujang that is soured with vinegar – and *ssamjang* – a mix of doenjang soya bean paste, gochujang, garlic, sesame and honey.

VINEGAR-BRINED FRITES
WITH GOCHUJANG-ANDALOUSE SAUCE

I once found myself on a week-long culinary excursion to Brussels, Antwerp and Ghent in pursuit of Franco-Flemish cultural wonders for *Condé Nast Traveller*. Just hours into the trip I was blown away by just how very awesome Belgium is – in everything from art, fashion and design, to music, architecture and food! One of many gastronomic revelations from that trip was *frites with sauce andalouse* – a Belgian speciality that combines mayonnaise with pimento peppers, roasted red peppers and tomato. The addition of gochujang adds an extra kick of fermented Korean heat to the mix; a tasty hot antithesis to all that effortless Belgian cool.

SERVES 4

150ml (5fl oz) cider vinegar
1 Tbsp caster (superfine) sugar
2 Tbsp chopped tarragon leaves
500ml (17fl oz) boiling water
950g (2lb 2oz) floury potatoes,
    preferably Maris Piper or Russet
sunflower or vegetable oil, for frying
fine sea salt

For the sauce

½ large red onion
½ large red (bell) pepper
2 garlic cloves
5 Tbsp mayonnaise
1 Tbsp tomato purée (paste)
2 Tbsp gochujang
2 tsp Worcestershire sauce
    or vegetarian alternative
1 Tbsp caster (superfine) sugar
juice of 1 lemon

Add the vinegar, 1 tablespoon of the sugar, 1 tablespoon of tarragon and 1 tablespoon of salt to a large mixing bowl, then pour over the boiling water. Whisk well to dissolve everything and set aside to cool.

Chop the potatoes into thin long frites with a knife (or a frites cutter if you have one). Place the frites in the vinegar brine ensuring they are fully submerged. Cover and leave for 4–5 hours, ideally overnight.

Meanwhile, make the sauce. Add the onion, red pepper and garlic to a small blender and whizz together into a fine paste. Pour into a frying pan, and over a medium heat, cook for 12–14 minutes – stirring constantly – until much of the water has evaporated and you have an intense thick red purée. Empty into a bowl and leave to cool completely.

Once the purée is cool, add the remaining sauce ingredients and 1 teaspoon of salt. Whisk together well, then leave for 4–5 hours for the flavours to meld – adding extra mayonnaise if you prefer it milder and creamier.

When ready to fry, drain the frites from the vinegar brine into a colander – and shake off all of the excess brine. Spread the drained frites in a single layer onto baking sheets lined with a double layer of paper towels. Pat the frites with more paper to ensure they are as dry as possible above and below.

Add enough oil to a deep-sided saucepan to fill it one-third full. Heat over a medium heat to 165°C/329°F. Fry the frites in small batches for 5 minutes to par-cook, then remove from the heat and place on paper towels to rest for 5 minutes, then return each batch to the oil and cook for another 5 minutes until golden brown. Drain well, sprinkle with salt, 1 tablespoon of chopped tarragon and enjoy hot with the gochujang-andalouse sauce – and extra vinegar, if you like.

KOREAN TUNA &
PICKLED GINGER MELT

If there's a scale for erotic food words, 'melt' is up there at the climactic end of the scale. The patty melt. Melt in the middle chocolate puddings. Fondue – the essence of the word – in hot cheese bucket form. And of course, the tuna melt, which is my culinary kink in every way. This Korean take on the classic combines good canned tuna, with pickled ginger, radish and spring onions, boosted by the flavourful earthy heat of gochujang. Fill the sandwich generously, toast until the bread is golden brown and the cheese oozing pleasingly down the crust, then dive in. Sensual noises when devouring are optional, but greatly encouraged, and feel free to stuff the middle with thickly cut potato crisps if you're that way inclined – I most certainly am.

MAKES 2 LARGE MELTS

2 cans good-quality tuna in oil
   (204g/7oz drained weight)
2–3 tsp gochujang (to your taste)
2 Tbsp Kewpie mayonnaise
zest and juice of ½ lime
1 celery stick, finely diced
1 large spring onion (scallion),
   chopped

2 Tbsp finely diced daikon (mooli)
   or radish
1 Tbsp finely chopped pickled ginger
½ red (bell) pepper, finely diced
30g (1oz) softened butter
4 thick slices of sourdough
gochugaru or shichimi tōgarashi
2 slices strong Cheddar or other hard
   melty cheese
fine sea salt

In a large bowl, mix together the drained tuna, gochujang, mayonnaise, lime juice and zest, celery, spring onion, daikon, pickled ginger and red pepper with a pinch of salt. Set aside for 10 minutes.

Liberally butter the sourdough bread then sprinkle with a pinch of gochugaru or shichimi tōgarashi.

Heat a large frying pan over a medium heat until hot and place one of the slices of bread, butter-side down, into the hot pan. Place a cheese slice on top, then layer on half the gochujang-tuna mix generously. Place another slice of sourdough on top, butter-side up.

Fry and flip the sandwich in the pan – pressing down at the sides with a spatula to contain the filling – for 5–6 minutes until the cheese is melted, and the bread is toasted on the outside but not burnt. Repeat with the remaining ingredients to make a second sandwich. Alternatively, make these using a toastie maker. Enjoy.

BONFIRE-BUTTERMILK
KOREAN FRIED CHICKEN

I am something of a pyromaniac. Not so much for the love of fire per se, but for all those smoky-tobacco, bonfire flavours that I am near-on obsessed with. Barbecued ribs, flame-toasted marshmallows, pan-charred sausages, flambéed crêpes, hot-iron smash burgers – anything that promises the taste of flames makes me salivate! With this in mind, there are two ingredients that I'm never without – oak-smoked sea salt and smoked water from the brilliant people at Halen Môn in Wales. The sweet heat of gochujang, combined with the scorched salinity of smoked salt spark in this fried chicken recipe. An explosion on the tastebuds, without the flames; sometimes you really can have smoke without fire.

SERVES 4

250ml (9fl oz) buttermilk
1 Tbsp smoked salt
1 Tbsp smoked paprika
1 Tbsp onion powder
750g (1lb 10oz) chicken breasts
  (about 4 large ones), cut into
  bite-size chunks
100g (3½oz) plain flour
100g (3½oz) potato starch
50g (1¾oz) cornflour (cornstarch)
2 tsp baking powder
sunflower or vegetable oil, for frying

For the sauce
3 Tbsp gochujang
3 Tbsp tomato ketchup
4 Tbsp dark brown sugar
2 Tbsp dark soy sauce
1 fat garlic clove, crushed to a paste
1 tsp minced fresh ginger root
1 tsp English mustard
1 tsp toasted sesame oil
1 tsp smoked salt

To serve (optional)
sesame seeds
spring onions, finely chopped
red chillies, finely chopped

In a large bowl, whisk together the buttermilk, smoked salt, paprika and onion powder. Add the chicken breast pieces, mix well to coat, then cover and refrigerate for 4–6 hours at least.

Next, prepare the sauce. Add all the ingredients to a saucepan, bring to the boil, then reduce the heat to a low simmer and cook for 6–8 minutes until it has thickened. Set aside.

Remove the bowl from the refrigerator, and place the chicken pieces on a wire rack over a baking tray, reserving the buttermilk in the bowl. Turn the chicken on the rack so the excess buttermilk drips away, then leave for 30 minutes to come up to room temperature.

Meanwhile, prepare the coating by whisking together the flour, potato starch, cornflour and baking powder in a large bowl.

When ready to fry, add enough oil to a medium saucepan to fill it to a third. Heat over a medium heat to 165°C/329°F. Line a baking sheet with a double layer of paper towels and set aside.

Continued...

Dredge the chicken pieces in the flour mix, turning to coat in all the crevices. Shake off the excess flour, dip back into the buttermilk brine, then dredge again in the flour mix. Leave for 1 minute in the flour to ensure the double dredge coating adheres.

Shake the excess flour off the coated chicken and carefully drop no more than 3–4 pieces at a time into the hot oil. Use a slotted metal spoon to turn them in the oil for 5–6 minutes until golden brown on the outside and cooked through. Transfer to the lined baking sheet to drain off the excess oil. Repeat with the remaining chicken pieces.

Toss the fried chicken in the gochujang sauce, then garnish with sesame seeds, spring onions and red chillies, if you like. Enjoy.

CREAMY PARSNIP SOUP WITH
SIZZLING GOCHUJANG OIL & TOFU CROUTONS

Sizzling oils are a secret weapon to keep in mind should you ever find yourself in need of a quick flavour burst. Beloved in Sichuanese and Indonesian cuisines, they deliver maximum punch for minimal effort – with some mildly thrilling theatrics to boot. The method is always similar: mix together aromatics like ginger, spring onions and garlic in a heatproof bowl; add soy sauce, vinegar or citrus juice; then very carefully pour over hot oil, watch it splutter from a distance, and enjoy. The addition of Korean gochujang gives this sizzling oil a sweet-funky flavour and bright crimson colour to really pop against the smooth creamy soup.

SERVES 4

700g (1lb 9oz) parsnips,
    cut into wedges
1 large white onion, quartered
10 garlic cloves, unpeeled
olive oil, for drizzling
1 tsp Chinese five spice
650ml (22fl oz) chicken
    or vegetable stock
100ml (3½fl oz) soured cream
    or coconut cream
zest and juice of 1 lemon
fine sea salt

For the croutons
2 Tbsp onion powder
2 Tbsp cornflour (cornstarch)
200g (7oz) tofu, cut into 1cm (½in)
    cubes

For the oil
1 Tbsp gochujang
1 Tbsp dark soy sauce
2 spring onions (scallions), finely
    chopped
1 Tbsp sesame seeds
1 Tbsp finely chopped coriander
    (cilantro)
4 Tbsp sunflower oil

Preheat the oven to 180°C fan/200°C/400°F/Gas mark 6. Place the parsnips wedges, onion quarters and garlic cloves in a roasting tray. Drizzle with olive oil, sprinkle over the Chinese five spice and 1 teaspoon of salt. Set aside.

For the tofu croutons, combine the onion powder, cornflour and ½ teaspoon of salt in a bowl. Drizzle the tofu cubes with a little olive oil, then dredge in the onion-flour mix. Spread out over a baking sheet.

Bake the vegetables and croutons for 20–25 minutes, turning them halfway through, until the parsnips are just starting to take on a little colour. Check on the tofu croutons every 5 minutes to ensure they don't burn.

For the sizzling oil, whisk together the gochujang and soy sauce in a heatproof bowl, then scatter over the spring onions, sesame seeds and coriander.

Heat the sunflower oil in a small pan over a medium heat until shimmering, then very carefully pour into the bowl – be careful as it can sizzle and splatter. Whisk to combine well and leave the flavours to mingle for 15 minutes.

Meanwhile, add the roasted parsnips and onions to a blender, then squeeze in the roasted garlic cloves from their skins. Add the stock, cream, lemon juice and zest, then whizz to a fine thick purée. If you prefer it a little looser, add a little more stock. Pour into a pan and heat gently.

Serve the parsnip soup warm with tofu croutons and a generous drizzle of sizzling gochujang oil on top. Enjoy.

FENNEL SAUSAGE, GOCHUJANG & VODKA PACCHERI

One of the leitmotifs of my cooking is fennel seeds – a signature ingredient used in both Punjabi and Italian cuisines – in almost everything. I adore the punchy lemony-anise hit they bring to any dish, sweet and savoury. For this reason my usually sparse refrigerator is rarely without Italian fennel sausages – grilled whole to a blackened char for the ultimate sarnies, or split open to sizzle in a pan for dreamy fennel sausage ragus. The spicy-savouriness of gochujang is the perfect note to add to this aniseedy chord, amped up further by the taste-magnifying effects of vodka. With flavours this loud, only very gigantic pasta – like satisfyingly huge paccheri – will do. The bigger the better!

SERVES 2-3

2 Tbsp olive oil
1 large red onion, finely chopped
2 tsp fennel seeds, crushed
350g (12oz) fennel sausages,
    cases removed
2 Tbsp gochujang
200g (7oz) Tenderstem broccoli,
    ends trimmed
2 Tbsp tomato purée (paste)
4 Tbsp vodka
3 Tbsp balsamic vinegar

1 Tbsp caster (superfine) sugar
200g (7oz) baby plum tomatoes,
    halved
125g (4½oz) soured cream
200g (7oz) paccheri or rigatoni
fine sea salt

For the pangrattato topping
35g (1¼oz) butter
2 garlic cloves, crushed to a paste
2 tsp herbes de Provence
50g (1¾oz) panko breadcrumbs
2 Tbsp finely grated parmesan

Heat the olive oil in a large frying pan, then gently fry the onion with a pinch of salt over a medium heat for 4 minutes. Next add the fennel seeds and sausage meat, and cook for 5 minutes until the meat starts to take on a little colour. Stir in the gochujang and cook for another minute.

Next, add the broccoli and 1¼ teaspoons of salt, cooking for 4 minutes until tender. Now stir in the tomato purée, vodka, balsamic vinegar and sugar, combining well.

Add the plum tomatoes, cover with a lid and cook over a medium heat for 5–6 minutes until they start to collapse into the sauce. Finally, stir through the soured cream, and cook over a low heat for 10 minutes. Remove from the heat, cover and leave for 30 minutes to let the flavours develop.

Meanwhile, make a crunchy pangrattato topping. Melt the butter in a frying pan, then add the garlic and dried herbs and fry for 1 minute. Add the breadcrumbs and parmesan, and cook over a medium–high heat for 5 minutes until toasty and golden. Transfer to a bowl and leave to cool completely and crisp up further.

Cook the pasta in a large pan of well-salted boiling water following the packet instructions. Drain, reserving a little of the pasta water.

Reheat the sausage sauce over a low heat, adding a little of the cooking water if needed, then stir through the pasta. Serve in large bowls with a very generous sprinkling of the crunchy pangrattato on top.

GOCHUJANG HISPI &
BACON OKONOMIYAKI

'Whatever takes your fancy. Grilled.' It's a solid mantra for a dish and is the literal translation of *okonomiyaki* – the iconic Japanese pancake, the flavours of which usually fulfil not just something, but everything you fancy! Hispi cabbage and bacon are a classic combination – but the addition of gochujang brings a hit of umami-rich Korean heat that takes the classic to a different dimension. Adorn liberally with toppings, sauces and an extra drizzle of gochujang if you so desire.

MAKES 2 LARGE PANCAKES

60g (2¼oz) plain (all-purpose) flour
2 Tbsp rice flour
1 tsp caster (superfine) sugar
1 large egg
1 tsp fish sauce
vegetable oil, for frying
50g (1¾oz) smoked bacon lardons
175g (6oz) hispi (sweetheart)
   cabbage, finely shredded

1 carrot, grated
30g (1oz) pickled ginger, chopped
2 spring onions (scallions), chopped
2 Tbsp gochujang
fine sea salt

To serve
Kewpie mayonnaise
okonomiyaki sauce (see tip)
nori flakes
katsuobushi (bonito flakes)

Start by making the batter. In a small bowl, whisk together the plain flour, rice flour, sugar and a pinch of salt. Next, whisk in the egg, fish sauce and 4 tablespoons of cold water to make a smooth, thick but pourable batter. Leave aside.

Heat 1 tablespoon of oil in a medium (22cm/8½in) frying pan. Cook the lardons for 4–5 minutes over a medium heat until crispy, then add the shredded cabbage and a pinch of salt. Cook for 6–7 minutes until most of the water has evaporated and it's starting to take on a little colour.

Put the cabbage and lardons into a large mixing bowl with the grated carrot, ginger and spring onions then add the gochujang. Mix to evenly distribute everything, then pour over the batter. Mix again then refrigerate for 30 minutes to rest.

When ready to fry, wipe the frying pan clean and reheat with a little more oil. Stir the mixture one last time, then ladle in enough for a thick pancake into the pan. Cook over a medium heat for 6–7 minutes, cover with a plate to invert, then slide the pancake back into the pan to cook the other side for another 5 minutes until charred and crispy. Turn out onto a plate and keep warm while you repeat with the rest of the mixture to make a second pancake.

To serve, drizzle the pancakes with Kewpie mayo and okonomiyaki sauce. Sprinkle over the nori flakes and katsuobushi to finish. Enjoy.

Tip: If you can't find okonomiyaki sauce, mix equal parts of Worcestershire sauce, dark soy sauce, ketchup and honey for something similar.

Thai Green Paste

fresh and verdant,
intensely fragrant,
vibrantly limey,
harmoniously balanced,
aromatic herbal-ness.

The ubiquitous green cooking paste from Thailand combines ingredients like green chillies, Thai basil, lemongrass, galangal, shrimp paste, shallots, *krachai* (Chinese ginger), lime, fish sauce, cumin seed, coriander and palm sugar. It typifies the Thai approach to balance when cooking, combining elements that are spicy, sour, bitter, salty and sweet. Most often the paste forms the basis for Thai Green Curry – combined with coconut milk – although it's also used as a marinade and dressing. Variations include the hotter red Thai paste, which has fiery bird's eye chillies as its basis, and the milder yellow Thai paste, which features turmeric and curry powder as its core ingredients. There are also vegetarian and vegan versions available.

HAAD TIEN CORN
& CRAB CHOWDER

In Thailand there's a not-so-secret beach sanctuary on the island of Koh Pha Ngan that has a very special place in my heart. I've escaped to it on numerous occasions for both yoga zen-cleansing, and hedonistically raucous partying. Haad Tien is a place where both happen in parallel just yards away from each other – with some extraordinary food being served up to everyone. I have vivid memories of a fragrant limey crab salad and charred corn chowder on one of the more debauched occasions I was there – both were so extremely delicious I couldn't decide which to tuck into first, so amalgamated them into one. Whenever I want to be transported to that moment of bliss, I make this soup.

SERVES 4

4 large or 6 small spring onions
  (scallions)
150g (5½oz) white crab meat
zest of 1 and juice of 2 limes
4 tsp light soy sauce
2 Tbsp Thai green paste
6–8 makrut lime leaves
2 large cans sweetcorn
  (300g/10½oz drained weight)

2 Tbsp olive oil
1½ tsp Chinese five spice
1 tsp ground turmeric
750ml (26fl oz) chicken or vegetable
  stock
30g (1oz) fresh galangal or ginger root
50g (1¾oz) roasted cashews, plus
  extra crushed to garnish
1 tsp fish sauce
1 Tbsp light brown sugar
fine sea salt

Finely chop the spring onions, separating the green and the white parts. Add 2 tablespoons of the greens to a large bowl, then add the white crab meat, lime zest, 1 teaspoon of soy sauce, 1 tablespoon of Thai green paste and a pinch of salt. Mix well, then put in the refrigerator.

Prepare the lime leaves by removing the hard stalks from each leaf. Roll the leaves tightly into a cigar, then very finely shred into chiffonade threads. Set aside.

Preheat the grill to its highest setting. Tumble the well-drained sweetcorn into a large bowl, then add 1 tablespoon of the oil, Chinese five spice, turmeric and a pinch of salt. Mix well to coat the kernels in the spices, then spread out evenly on a baking sheet. Grill for 10–12 minutes until just starting to scorch on top, turning regularly.

Tip most of the grilled corn into a blender (reserve a few tablespoons for garnish), then add the chicken stock. Blend to a fine purée.

In a small grinder, whizz the galangal, cashews and 3 tablespoons of the lime juice into a fine paste, adding a splash of water if needed.

Heat the remaining tablespoon of oil in a large wok or saucepan over a medium heat, then add the spring onion whites and fry for 5–6 minutes until soft. Add the galangal-cashew paste and the remaining tablespoon of Thai green paste. Cook for 4–5 minutes until the paste turns a light golden colour.

Next, add the shredded lime leaves (reserve a little for garnish), fish sauce, sugar and the rest of the soy sauce. Cook for another 2 minutes, then stir through the sweetcorn purée. Bring to the boil, then reduce to a low simmer and cover with a lid. Cook for 15–20 minutes.

To finish, stir through 2 tablespoons of fresh lime juice and season with a pinch of salt if needed. Spoon the chowder into big bowls, and top with the dressed crab meat. Garnish with the reserved charred sweetcorn, crushed cashews and threads of lime leaf if you like.

THAI GREEN AUBERGINE, JALAPEÑO & COCONUT CROQUETTES

The category of foods that can broadly be described as 'orbs of deliciousness, crumbed then deep fried to a golden crisp', is one of my favourites. Dutch *bitterballen*, Belgian prawn croquettes, Indian *masala vada*, Korean *bulgogi goroke*, Spanish jamón béchamel croquetas, Japanese *korokke* – while they all look alike from the outside, inside they're flavour universes apart. These delicious golden globes combine Thai, Mexican and South Indian ingredient notes into something astronomical, with the rocket fuel alchemy of Thai green paste creating that magic.

MAKES 25-30

2 large aubergines (eggplants)
olive oil, for brushing
75g (2½oz) desiccated (dried)
    coconut
75g (2½oz) jalapeños in brine,
    plus 2 Tbsp of the brine
250g (9oz) cooked beluga or
    Puy lentils (drained weight)
4 Tbsp Thai green paste
4 fat garlic cloves, crushed to a paste
zest and juice of 1 lime

20g (¾oz) coriander (cilantro),
    finely chopped
4 Tbsp cornflour (cornstarch),
    plus extra for dredging
200g (7oz) dried breadcrumbs
200g (7oz) canned sweetcorn
    (160g/5¾oz drained weight)
2 large eggs, beaten
75g (2½oz) polenta (cornmeal)
2 Tbsp sesame seeds
sunflower or vegetable oil,
    for frying
fine sea salt

Preheat the oven to 185°C fan/205°C/410°F/ Gas mark 6½. Brush the aubergines with olive oil, and bake whole on a baking sheet for 40–45 minutes until charred outside and soft inside.

Meanwhile, toast the coconut in a dry frying pan over a medium-low heat for 3–4 minutes until golden, but not burnt. Transfer it to a food processor along with the jalapeños plus their brine, cooked lentils, Thai green paste, garlic, lime zest and juice, coriander, cornflour and 2 teaspoons of salt. Whizz for 1 minute until well combined, scraping down the sides as needed.

Cut open the aubergines, scoop out the flesh and discard the charred skins. Add the flesh and 125g (4½oz) of the breadcrumbs to the food processor, and blitz for 1 minute. If the mix is loose, add an extra tablespoon of breadcrumbs. Scrape into a large bowl, stir through the sweetcorn, then chill for 30 minutes.

Prepare three bowls to coat the croquettes: one with the extra cornflour, one with the beaten eggs, and the third containing the remaining 75g (2½oz) of breadcrumbs, the polenta and sesame seeds whisked together.

Continued...

Form the chilled mix into 25–30 croquettes the size of golf balls. To coat, first dredge in cornflour, then coat with egg and finally roll in the crumbs. (For a vegan option, use a plant-based Thai green paste, and just roll straight into the crumbs.)

Add enough sunflower oil to a medium saucepan to fill it to a third. Heat over a medium heat to 175°C/347°F. Fry the croquettes in batches – no more than four at a time – for 4–5 minutes until golden on the outside and piping hot in the middle.

Drain on paper towels and enjoy dipped into the sauce of your choice (see below).

Tip: Thai sweet chilli, horseradish cream and tamarind sauce are great for dipping. Or make a mango-mustard by combining 75g (2½oz) of canned unsweetened mango purée, 2 tablespoons of English mustard and 1 teaspoon of grated ginger root.

THAI FISH PIE WITH
CRISPY TURMERIC POTATOES

This Lancashire hot-pot meets fish pie – by way of Chang Mai – is one of my favourite things to make for a crowd; although I have been known to make it just for myself, dipping into the pie dish gradually for every meal from breakfast to midnight snack over a weekend. It celebrates the affinity of Thai green paste for seafood – a symbiotic marriage of deliciousness that never fails to delight – with a golden yellow crispy crust that's sure to wow an audience. Even if it's an audience of just one.

SERVES 4

50g (1¾oz) desiccated (dried) coconut
30g (1oz) lemongrass
30g (1oz) fresh galangal or ginger root
zest of 1 and juice of 2 limes
3 Tbsp Thai green paste
1 tsp fish sauce
350g (12oz) uncooked fish pie mix, in bite-sized pieces

150g (5½oz) uncooked peeled prawns (shrimp)
2 large celery sticks, finely diced
450g (1lb) floury potatoes
300ml (10½fl oz) coconut milk
2 Tbsp cornflour (cornstarch)
pinch of caster (superfine) sugar
handful of Thai basil leaves, chopped
50g (1¾oz) butter
1 tsp ground turmeric
1 tsp nigella seeds
fine sea salt

Dry-toast the coconut in a frying pan over a medium-low heat for 2–3 minutes until it turns golden brown but not burnt, then tip onto a plate to cool completely.

Next, make a paste in a small grinder or blender by whizzing together the lemongrass, galangal, lime juice and zest and 1½ teaspoons of salt – add a splash of water if needed. Pour into a bowl, then whisk through the Thai green paste and fish sauce.

Add the fish pie mix, prawns, toasted coconut and diced celery. Stir well, then pour into the base of a deep-sided 18 x 22cm (7 x 8½in) pie dish or equivalent. Preheat the oven to 180°C fan/200°C/400°F/Gas mark 6.

Meanwhile, use a mandoline or very sharp knife to slice the potatoes into very thin round discs 1.5–2mm (¹⁄₁₆in) thick, then set aside.

Next, in a large jug whisk together the coconut milk, cornflour and a pinch of sugar, until fully combined. Pour over the fish and prawns in the pie dish, then scatter the chopped Thai basil on top. Layer the potato slices on top, overlapping into a spiral design to cover the filling completely.

Melt the butter in a saucepan along with the turmeric, nigella seeds and a pinch of salt, whisking well. Brush all the turmeric butter over the top of the potatoes.

Place the fish pie on a baking tray to catch any spillage and bake for 35–40 minutes until cooked through and crispy golden on top. Cover with foil if the top is browning too quickly and, if you like it extra-crispy, finish under a hot grill for 3–5 minutes.

Remove from the oven and rest 10 minutes before diving in. Serve with a green salad.

PRAWNS IN BLANKETS WITH THAI-MUSHROOM DUXELLES

I've always something of a thing for those party bites that appear in supermarkets every Christmas – generally based on the trending ingredient of the moment, wrapped in pastry then fried, baked, or both. It could be Chinese five-spiced duck in a spring roll, a concoction of feta and spinach in a spanakopita pastry square, a mini turkey curry pasty, or even little filo-wrapped sausage rolls enlivened with something mustardy-sweet and sickly; whatever they are, I am here for them! My favourites are always those pastry wrapped prawns that have their tails left on for decorative festive campery. This recipe riffs on the many versions of those I've devoured over the years – with the addition of an intense mushroom duxelles, infused with Thai green paste for extra oomph.

MAKES 16

500g (1lb 2oz) chestnut mushrooms
1 large red onion
4 fat garlic cloves
25g (1oz) butter, plus extra, melted, for brushing
2 Tbsp olive oil
2 Tbsp Thai green paste
1 tsp dried thyme
1 tsp lemon zest, plus wedges for squeezing
½ tsp freshly ground black pepper
16 uncooked, unpeeled king prawns (jumbo shrimp), about 600–650g/1lb 5–7oz
1 pack filo pastry (270g/9½oz)
fine sea salt

Put the mushrooms into a food processor and pulse to very fine pieces – being careful not to turn them into a purée. Empty into a bowl, stir through ½ teaspoon of salt and leave for 10 minutes. Next, add the onion and garlic to the processor and pulse to very fine pieces.

Empty the salted mushrooms onto a cheesecloth or muslin and squeeze out as much of the water as you can over a bowl – save the mushroom water for stock or risotto.

Heat the butter and oil in a large frying pan, then add the chopped onion, garlic and drained mushrooms. Cook over a high heat, mixing continuously for 12–14 minutes. By this stage the mixture should be starting to dry out but cook for a couple of extra minutes if needed.

Next, add the Thai green paste, thyme, lemon zest, black pepper and ½ teaspoon of salt. Cook for another 5–6 minutes, stirring continuously, then empty into a large bowl to cool completely.

Use your hands to carefully remove the heads and shells from the king prawns, keeping on the tail-ends as a decorative handle.

Preheat the oven to 200°C fan/220°C/425°F/Gas mark 7. Unroll the filo pastry sheets and slice each sheet into long thin strips the height of your prawns. Brush with melted butter, then dollop 1 tablespoon of the chilled Thai-mushroom duxelles at one end. Place a raw prawn on top of each strip with the tail-shell pointing out, then fold over the strips in a square three or four times – brushing with butter each time you fold, wrapping the prawns completely. Brush with butter again, and place on a baking sheet.

Bake the wrapped prawns for 12–13 minutes until crispy on the outside, and cooked through in the middle. Eat immediately with a squeeze of lemon, or dipped into garlic mayonnaise.

AROMATIC CHICKEN
PAD THAI

Bangkok is probably my favourite city in the world and devouring freshly made pad Thai – cooked over fire and served on paper plates from a roadside wooden cart – is one of the things I love most about the city. The skilful mastery of Thai street-food vendors to create sublime flavours in a flash is something I've never been able to replicate. My attempt here uses Thai green paste as a marinade to magnify the flavours of the chicken – with the unconventional addition of cardamom to bring out the fragrant mystique of lemongrass and lime leaves in the paste and tamarind that also features in the dish. Not a patch on the backstreets of Siam Square, but tasty nonetheless.

SERVES 2

seeds from 10 cardamom pods
1 Tbsp minced fresh galangal
    or ginger root
zest and juice of ½ lemon
3 Tbsp Thai green paste
2 tsp toasted sesame oil
300g (10½oz) chicken breasts (about
    2, skinless), cut into thin strips
20g (¾oz) dried shrimp
185g (6½oz) medium rice noodles
1 Tbsp vegetable oil
2 large or 4 small shallots, finely
    chopped

4 fat garlic cloves, slivered
2 eggs
100g (3½oz) beansprouts
handful of chives or garlic chives,
    finely chopped
30g (1oz) roasted peanuts, crushed
fine sea salt

For the sauce
1 Tbsp tamarind paste
2 Tbsp dark soy sauce
1 Tbsp sriracha sauce
1 Tbsp fish sauce
2 Tbsp palm sugar or dark brown
    sugar

Use a pestle and mortar to pound the cardamom seeds and 1 teaspoon of salt to a fine powder. Spoon into a large bowl, then add the galangal, 1 teaspoon of lemon zest, the Thai green paste and toasted sesame oil. Mix well, then add the chicken, stirring to coat all over. Cover and leave to marinate in the refrigerator for at least 3–4 hours.

Prepare the pad Thai sauce by whisking together the tamarind paste, soy sauce, sriracha, fish sauce and sugar, with a splash of water. Set aside.

Next, soak the dried shrimp in boiling water for 10 minutes. Also cook the rice noodles for 3–4 minutes until al dente but not cooked through. Drain the noodles and set aside.

Heat a large wok over a medium–high heat and add the oil, then the shallots, stir-frying

for 2–3 minutes until they take on a little colour. Drain the soaked dried shrimp, add to the wok and stir-fry for another minute, before adding the chicken with all of its aromatic marinade and the garlic. Cook for 5–6 minutes, stirring continuously until the strips are brown on the outside and just cooked in the middle. Move the chicken to one side of the wok, crack in the eggs, then use a spatula to break up into big chunks.

Next, add the beansprouts, cook for another minute before adding the pad Thai sauce. Stir-fry for 3 minutes, then mix through the cooked noodles and lemon juice. Garnish with chives and crushed peanuts.

Serve in large bowls with Thai crackers on the side for extra crunch, if you like.

SEARED STEAK TAGLIATA WITH THAI GREEN BÉARNAISE

I could quite happily enrobe everything I eat in rich buttery béarnaise sauce – and I have indeed tried it with most things. It's especially delicious with fried chicken, perfect for dipping pizza crusts into, and I've even spooned it into the middle of *masala keema* samosas: a gastronomic triumph that I will one day turn into a supper club. What I love most about this sauce is how the indulgent, tangy cream is balanced to allow tarragon to sing through at full volume. This riff on the classic amplifies those aniseedy tarragon notes with the addition of aromatic Thai basil and green paste. Served here with a seared Italian-style steak tagliata, but equally delicious with anything else that takes your fancy.

SERVES 2

2 bavette or rump steaks
(225g/8oz each)
135ml (4½fl oz) white wine vinegar
2 Tbsp finely chopped tarragon
leaves, plus extra to garnish
2 Tbsp finely chopped Thai basil
leaves
1 large stalk of lemongrass, bruised
then finely chopped

2 medium shallots, very finely
chopped
1 tsp black peppercorns, crushed
175g (6oz) butter, plus 15g (½oz)
for frying
2 Tbsp Thai green paste
3 large egg yolks
squeeze of lime juice
vegetable oil, for frying
fine sea salt and freshly ground black
pepper

Season the steaks liberally with salt and pepper on both sides then leave at room temperature for 30 minutes.

Add the vinegar, three-quarters of the chopped herbs, the lemongrass, shallots and black peppercorns to a saucepan. Bring to the boil, then reduce the heat and simmer until it's reduced to a volume of 3 tablespoons – you want an intensely concentrated infused vinegar.

Drain the vinegar through a sieve into a medium, heatproof bowl, pressing on the herbs and lemongrass to extract as much flavour as possible (keep these for flavouring stocks and stir-fries).

Melt the butter in a saucepan or microwave. Pour into a jug, then add the Thai green paste and whisk well.

Add the egg yolks to the bowl with the concentrated vinegar and whisk well. Place the bowl over a pan of barely simmering water (do not allow the base of the bowl to be in contact with the water) over a very gentle heat –

and start to whisk. When it starts to froth a little, very slowly start to trickle in the melted butter, a little at a time, whisking constantly – you want to form an emulsified sauce so don't go too quickly. If it's thickening too fast, remove from the heat as needed – always whisking. You're aiming for the texture of thin mayonnaise.

Once all of the melted butter has been incorporated, add ½ teaspoon of salt, the remaining chopped herbs plus a squeeze of lime juice. Whisk well and set aside.

On a high heat, heat a heavy-based frying pan to the hottest it will go, then add the 15g (½oz) butter and a splash of oil. Sear the steaks on one side for 3 minutes, then flip and cook for another 2 minutes (for rare), or 4–5 minutes (for medium) or 6–7 minutes (for well done).

Slice the steaks thinly into strips, then drizzle over the Thai béarnaise, and garnish with some tarragon leaves. Serve with some wilted spinach or salted frites. Enjoy!

Yuzu Koshō

zesty and refreshing,
intensely fragrant,
sourly zingy,
saltily floral,
chillied citrussiness.

This classic Japanese seasoning is a blend of aromatic yuzu peel, hot green chillies and salt, which is then fermented. 'Yuzu' refers to the small citrus fruit it's made from, and 'koshō' translates as 'pepper'. There are several versions: red yuzu koshō uses milder red chillies, and black yuzu koshō includes bamboo charcoal. Another is *kanzuri* – an aged red yuzu koshō blended with fermented koji grains. Yuzu koshō is usually sold in tubes or jars, sometimes labelled as 'Yuzu chilli paste' or 'spicy Japanese citrus paste'. It is a local speciality on Japan's island of Kyushu, where it is used in soups, hotpots and served as a dipping sauce for sashimi.

YUZU KOSHŌ PRAWN & PEANUT RICE PAPER DUMPLINGS

If your Instagram algorithm is a window to your soul, then mine is a quarter crème pâtissière-filled choux buns; a quarter expensive tasselled brogues from French cobblers; a quarter bearded personal trainers in Berlin called Jendrik who like to flex into mirrors; and a quarter dumpling-folding techniques as taught by skilled matriarchs from different culinary cultures around the world. Rice paper dumplings – a social media sensation – are some of the easiest dumplings to make. I love their satisfying chewy-crunchy-crispy texture, which, paired with the flavours of yuzu koshō and peanuts, for me make them a viral hit!

MAKES 18

225g (8oz) white cabbage,
    finely shredded
500g (1lb 2oz) uncooked peeled
    prawns (shrimp)
1 heaped Tbsp yuzu koshō
2 tsp light soy sauce
2 Tbsp runny honey
1 tsp toasted sesame oil
zest and juice of 1 lemon
2 garlic cloves, crushed to a paste
1 tsp grated fresh root ginger
65g (2¼oz) roasted peanuts, crushed
2 Tbsp finely chopped chives
2 Tbsp cornflour (cornstarch)
sunflower oil, for greasing
36 circular rice paper wrappers,
    16cm (6¼in) diameter
fine sea salt

Put the cabbage in a mixing bowl, sprinkle with 1 teaspoon of salt, and massage for 1 minute. Leave for 10 minutes, then squeeze out the cabbage into a sieve over the sink, pressing out as much liquid as possible. Return to the bowl, leave for 5 more minutes then squeeze again.

Cook the squeezed cabbage in a dry frying pan over a medium heat for 5 minutes, until most of the water has evaporated and the edges start to brown. Remove from the heat and set aside to cool.

In a food processor, blitz the prawns, yuzu koshō, soy sauce, honey, sesame oil, lemon zest and juice, garlic and ginger to a paste. Add the cooled cabbage, peanuts, chives and cornflour. Blitz again to combine, scraping down the sides as needed. Empty the filling into a bowl and chill for 10 minutes.

Preheat the oven to 200°C fan/220°C/425°F/Gas mark 7 and liberally brush a large baking tray with oil.

Fill a large bowl with warm water. To make the dumplings, you need two rice paper wrappers per dumpling. Take the first wrapper and place in the bowl of warm water for 30 seconds to bloom, then remove and spread it flat on a board. Pile a heaped tablespoon of the prawn filling into the middle, then pull up all four sides into the middle, forming a square box. Place, seam-side down, on the oiled baking sheet, and repeat to make a total of 18 dumplings.

For the second layer, bloom a rice paper wrapper in the warm water, spread it flat on a board, then place one of your prepared dumpling boxes in the middle – seam-side down. Pull up the sides of the wrapper and twist it around the dumpling, pinching the edges together on top. Repeat for all the dumplings and put them back on the baking sheet.

Bake in the oven for 25–30 minutes until crispy on the outside, with a chewy layer inside. If you like them extra crispy, brush with a little oil, then finish under a grill or sizzle in a pan of hot oil until golden brown. Serve with a sweet chilli sauce or ponzu – watch out, the filling will be very hot!

CRINKLE CRISP & YUZU KOSHŌ
TOMATO FRITTATA v

Ferran Adrià's potato crisp (chip) tortilla has sparked countless variations over the years. This is my own: more a grill-baked frittata than a pan-fried tortilla, which uses thick-cut crinkle crisps (chips) for added texture. Yuzu-koshō roasted tomatoes dotted over the top add intense bursts of tangy citrussy umami. This dish is extremely simple to make, but deliciously complex in eat

SERVES 4-6

300g (10½oz) cherry tomatoes, halved
1 heaped Tbsp yuzu koshō
3 Tbsp olive oil, plus extra for frying
2 garlic cloves, crushed to a paste
zest of ½ lemon
20g (¾oz) butter
1 large onion, thinly sliced
small handful of sage leaves, finely chopped
small handful of chives, finely chopped
12 large eggs
1 tsp coarsely ground black pepper
125g (4½oz) crinkle-cut potato crisps (chips)
fine sea salt

Preheat the oven to 170°C fan/190°C/375°F/Gas mark 5. Spread out the cherry tomatoes on a baking sheet, cut-side up. Whisk together the yuzu koshō, olive oil, garlic, lemon zest and ½ teaspoon of salt in a small bowl. Spoon a little drizzle over each cut tomato.

Bake the tomatoes for 30 minutes until soft and slightly charred on top. Remove from the oven and set aside to cool completely.

Melt the butter in a large, deep, ovenproof frying pan along with a splash of olive oil. Add the sliced onion with a pinch of salt and slowly cook over a medium heat for 10–12 minutes, until starting to caramelize. Add the sage and chives, cook for another 1 minute, then empty into a bowl and leave to cool. Wipe out the pan.

Crack the eggs into a large bowl. Whisk well then add ¾ teaspoon of salt, the black pepper, the cooled onion, and the crinkled potato crisps. Mix to coat everything well, then leave for 5 minutes for the crisps to absorb the egg.

Preheat the grill to its highest setting. Meanwhile, add a splash of oil to the pan used to fry the onion and place over a medium–high heat. Carefully spoon in the egg mix, spreading it to form an even layer. Spoon the tomatoes over the eggs, dotting them around evenly. Cook for 6–7 minutes until the bottom is sealed and it's just starting to cook in the middle.

Place the pan under the preheated grill and cook for another 4–5 minutes until the top is golden brown. Check the frittata is cooked in the middle by inserting a skewer – it should be a little soft but not wet. If needed, give it another 1–2 minutes, both on the hob and under the grill.

Serve warm out of the pan or cold with a side salad.

Tip: The yuzu koshō tomatoes are equally delicious on their own or on toast!

GARLIC & YUZU KOSHŌ BUTTER CIABATTA v

British comedian Peter Kay's line about garlic bread being 'the future' is a mantra I like to live by. Over the years I've made excessively cheesy versions folded into calzone, masala-onion versions cooked into parathas, and even a version that was essentially a sausage roll with a garlic bread exterior. This rendition keeps things relatively classic by comparison, with the fragrant flair of yuzu koshō adding a surprising – but very welcome – flourish of lemony citrus to the holy trinity of bread, butter and garlic.

SERVES 4-6

6 fat garlic cloves
small handful of sage leaves
small handful of flat-leaf parsley
zest of 1 large lemon
100g (3½ oz) very soft butter

1 Tbsp yuzu koshō
1 Tbsp olive oil, plus extra for drizzling
1 large ciabatta loaf or 4 small ones
1 tsp nigella seeds
grated parmesan (optional)
½ tsp fine sea salt and 1 tsp freshly
     ground black pepper

Preheat the oven to 190°C fan/210°C/410°F/Gas mark 6½. In a small grinder or food processor, whizz together the garlic, sage, parsley, 1 teaspoon of the lemon zest, the salt and pepper until finely minced, but not puréed.

Transfer the mixture to a bowl along with the softened butter, yuzu koshō and olive oil – then mash everything to a zesty garlic paste.

Halve your ciabatta horizontally or alternatively make slits along the top – and place on a well-oiled baking sheet. Spread liberally with the garlic butter – getting it into all of the slits and grooves. Sprinkle over the nigella seeds and drizzle with a little oil.

Bake the ciabatta for 10–12 minutes, checking it after 8 minutes. Serve warm, sprinkled with the remaining lemon zest, and some grated parmesan, if you like.

SALMON POKE WITH
YUZU KOSHŌ TIGER MILK

Leche de tigre is a classic Peruvian marinade that balances citrus juices with chilli, salt, herbs and spices in a way that packs a powerful punch. It's most commonly used as the cure for fresh fish and seafood in ceviches but is equally delicious drizzled over fresh tropical fruits or seared barbecued meats. The most delicious versions I've ever tasted don't rely on just lemon and lime, but add passion fruit, pineapple or even tart-tangy soursop pulp to the mix. The Peruvian–Japanese- (*nikkei-*) inspired tiger milk in this poke recipe has coconut milk for indulgent velvety creaminess, and yuzu koshō for unsubtle hits of floral chilli heat.

SERVES 2

zest of 1 and juice of 3 limes
2 tsp yuzu koshō
2 tsp grated fresh ginger root
4 makrut lime leaves, stalks removed
120ml (4fl oz) coconut milk
1 tsp toasted sesame oil
2 Tbsp ponzu or light soy sauce
2 Tbsp caster (superfine) sugar
150g (5½oz) sustainably caught
    or wild sashimi-grade salmon,
    cut into 1cm (½in) cubes
cooked rice or grains, as the base

2 Tbsp chopped mango
    (1cm/½in cubes)
2 Tbsp pickled ginger
2 Tbsp edamame beans
1 small carrot, julienned
4 breakfast radishes, sliced
fine sea salt

To garnish
4 sheets nori
sesame seeds
finely chopped spring onions
    (scallions)

In a small blender, whizz together the lime zest and juice, yuzu koshō, ginger, lime leaves, coconut milk, sesame oil, ponzu, sugar and ½ teaspoon of salt to make a completely smooth creamy milk.

Add the salmon to a bowl, pour over the tiger milk and leave to marinate for 10–15 minutes.

Create a bed of cooked rice or grains in two large serving bowls, then top with the mango, pickled ginger, edamame, carrot and radishes.

Pile on the marinated salmon, and spoon over lots of the zingy tiger milk as a dressing to coat the rice. Garnish with nori, sesame seeds and spring onions. Enjoy!

MOULES MARINIÈRE WITH YUZU KOSHŌ & SMOKY BACON

It had never occurred to me that mussels could be a brilliant vehicle for celebrating delicately refined flavours until I had a dish of mussels with saffron at The Sportsman in Whitstable on England's Kent coast a few years ago. The way the salty sweetness of the shellfish magnified the earthy honey notes of the saffron was truly magical. In my recipe, the mussels seem to bring out the citrussy aromas of the yuzu koshō and the herbal accents in the vermouth – with charred bits of smoky bacon adding a touch of bonfire for good measure.

SERVES 4

1.75kg –2kg (3lb 12oz–4lb 7 oz) fresh
    mussels (allow about 450g/1lb
    per person)
100g (3½oz) smoked bacon lardons
50g (1¾oz) butter
1 large onion, finely chopped
1 large leek, chopped
4 fat garlic cloves, crushed to a paste

1 tsp grated fresh ginger root
2 tsp coriander seeds, crushed
3 Tbsp yuzu koshō
125ml (4fl oz) dry vermouth
    or white wine
zest and juice of 1 large lemon
150ml (5fl oz) double (heavy) cream
big handful of flat-leaf parsley,
    chopped
fine sea salt

Inspect the mussel shells, discarding any that are cracked, or ones that are open and won't close when lightly tapped on the work surface. Wash thoroughly under cold running water, pulling out the rough beards.

Select a large pan (big enough to hold all the mussels) in which to fry the lardons over a medium–high heat for 4 minutes until they are starting to crisp up and have rendered a lot of their fat. Next, add the butter, onion and leek and cook for 8–9 minutes until they are reduced by two-thirds, and the onion starts to take on a little colour. Add the garlic, ginger, coriander seeds, yuzu koshō and a good pinch of salt. Stir well and cook for another minute.

Now, add the washed mussels, stirring well so they are covered in the aromatics. Add the vermouth or wine, mix one last time, then cover with a lid, turn up the heat to high and cook for 4 minutes until the mussels have steamed open – shake the pan a couple of times to mix everything up.

Stir through the lemon zest and juice, and the cream. Cook, uncovered, over a high heat for a final minute, then sprinkle over the chopped parsley and serve immediately – discarding any mussels that have not opened. Enjoy with plenty of crusty bread to soak up the citrussy sauce.

YAKITORI WITH
CITRUSSY HOT HONEY

I first encountered Mike's Hot Honey in Williamsburg, New York a decade ago – when it seemed like every food establishment in the neighbourhood had bottles of the stuff on their tables, regardless of the cuisine they were serving. Hot honey's popularity has sky-rocketed in recent years; there are now entire aisles devoted to the stuff in hipster delis around the world. In this recipe, I've combined honey's nectar sweetness with Japanese flavours – adding the citrussy notes of yuzu koshō and moreish burn of red chilli. Drizzled over freshly charred yakitori, it's easy to see what all the fuss is about.

MAKES 12-14

3 Tbsp dark soy sauce
1 tsp toasted sesame oil
2 tsp grated fresh ginger root
2 fat garlic cloves, crushed
    to a paste
1 Tbsp rice wine vinegar
1 Tbsp caster (superfine) sugar
750g (1lb 10oz) skinless, boneless
    chicken thighs or pork loin,
    cut into bite-sized chunks

6 large spring onions (scallions),
    sliced into 2.5cm (1in) lengths
vegetable oil, for drizzling
shichimi tōgarashi, to sprinkle
fine sea salt

For the hot honey
30g (1oz) butter
1 large red chilli, slivered
2 Tbsp yuzu koshō
zest of ½ lemon
100g (3½oz) runny honey

First, marinate the chicken or pork. Whisk together the soy sauce, sesame oil, ginger, garlic, vinegar, sugar and 1 teaspoon of salt in a large bowl. Stir in the meat to cover on all sides and refrigerate for at least 4–6 hours.

To make the hot honey, melt the butter in a saucepan, then add the chilli, yuzu koshō and lemon zest. Sizzle over a medium heat for 1 minute, then add the honey and ½ teaspoon of salt. Warm through for 1–2 minutes, whisking well, then pour into a bowl and leave to cool.

Preheat the grill to its highest setting. Thread spring onion and marinated meat alternately onto metal or pre-soaked wooden skewers. Place on a baking sheet and drizzle with a little oil.

Cook under the hot grill for 5 minutes, then turn and cook for another 5 minutes. Turn again and cook for a final 4–6 minutes until charred and cooked through.

Finally brush over a little of the hot honey, and cook for a final 1 minute until scorched and sticky on top. Serve piled high onto plates with more hot honey on the side and a sprinkle of shichimi tōgarashi to garnish.

Tamarind

tart and fruity,
darkly viscous,
ripely apricotty,
cuttingly sour,
puckering tanginess.

This tree fruit, native to tropical Africa and naturalized in parts of Asia, is now widely cultivated in tropical and sub-tropical regions around the world. The bulbous bean-like pods of the tamarind tree have a brittle brown outer shell, which contains hard seeds surrounded by sticky, plummy, tangy-sweet pulp. Tamarind paste combines this pulp with water and sometimes a little salt and sugar, whereas tamarind concentrate is the pulp boiled down to an intense treacly black tar. Wet tamarind is nothing more than the semi-dried seeds and their pulp compacted into a block, that can be boiled with water and strained to produce fresh tamarind paste. Its natural acidity makes tamarind an excellent tenderizer of meat and other proteins.

HỘI AN GREEN MANGO, TAMARIND, MINT & CASHEW SALAD

Hội An in Vietnam is a miraculous place – an ancient town of winding canals, ornate temples, pagodas, bridges and beautiful stretches of paddy fields that you can cycle through all the way to the blissfully sandy shores of An Bang beach. Street-food vendors set up shop daily along the banks of Hội An's canals, selling such delights as *bánh xèo* (crispy pancakes), *cơm tấm* (broken rice), *gỏi cuốn* (shrimp summer rolls) and delicious *gỏi xoài* (green mango salad), which is sold in plastic bags with pouches of tangy chilli-tamarind dressing on the side. This recipe evokes my memories of that special place, and those very special bags of joy.

SERVES 2-3

10g (¼oz) dried shrimp (optional)
1 large green (unripe) raw mango
 or raw papaya, peeled
1 large carrot
1 large red shallot
2 Tbsp vegetable oil
2 garlic cloves, very finely chopped
1 small red chilli, finely chopped
2 Tbsp caster (superfine) sugar

5 teaspoons of warm water
1 Tbsp tamarind paste
zest of 1 and juice of 2 limes
2 Tbsp fish sauce or vegan alternative
small handful of mint leaves
fine sea salt

To garnish
20g (¾oz) roasted cashews, crushed
crispy onions

Put the dried shrimp (if using) in a small bowl, pour over boiling water and soak for 10 minutes.

Use a julienne peeler to shred the mango flesh from the large seed and the carrot into long thin threads. Chop the shallot into thin rings. Tumble together into a large bowl.

For the dressing, heat the vegetable oil in a frying pan, then add the garlic and very gently sizzle over a low heat for 3–4 minutes until it just takes on a little colour. Next, add the drained shrimp and chopped chilli. Sizzle for another 1 minute.

Now, add the sugar, 1 teaspoon of salt and the warm water, mixing until the sugar and salt dissolve. Remove from the heat, then whisk through the tamarind paste, lime zest and juice, and fish sauce. Pour into a bowl and leave to cool completely.

Once cool, whisk the dressing one last time, then pour over the shredded mango and carrots, tossing to coat everything well. Tear in the fresh mint, mixing again, then garnish with roasted cashews and crispy onions. Enjoy.

IMLI HASSELBACK HALLOUMI
& CHICKPEA CHAAT v

My friend Georgina Hayden's whole baked halloumi with Greek honey, thyme and lemon zest is something that I'll never forget eating – and is a recipe I improvise on very often. In this manifestation it takes form as an Indian-Greek(ish) chaat – masala-coated halloumi grilled to a char in hasselback stripes, then smothered in a tangy-sweet tamarind (*imli*) chutney with spiced chickpeas. Adorn with crunchy bits and extra toppings to your heart's content.

SERVES 2

400g (14oz) can of chickpeas, drained
    (240g/8½oz drained weight)
2 Tbsp vegetable oil, plus extra
    for drizzling
225g (8oz) block of halloumi
1 Tbsp tamarind paste
3 Tbsp runny honey
1 tsp finely chopped mint leaves

For the masala
1 tsp Kashmiri chilli powder
2 tsp amchoor (mango powder)
2 tsp ground cumin
1 tsp ground coriander
2 tsp caster (superfine) sugar
1 tsp fine sea salt

To garnish
crunchy sev, puffed rice
    or Bombay mix
red onion, finely chopped
pomegranate seeds
finely chopped coriander (cilantro)
finely chopped mint

Make the masala by mixing all the ingredients together in a small bowl.

Preheat the grill to its highest setting. Tumble the drained chickpeas into a large bowl, then add the vegetable oil and 2 tablespoons of the masala powder, mixing well to coat all over. Spread out on a baking sheet and grill for 10–12 minutes until slightly scorched, turning regularly.

Meanwhile, score the halloumi block every 1–2cm (½–¾in) hasselback-style, being careful not to slice all the way through. Drizzle over a little oil then sprinkle with 1 teaspoon of the masala powder, getting it into the slits. Place in an ovenproof dish and grill for 4–5 minutes until the top starts to char.

Next, whisk together the tamarind paste, honey and mint in a small bowl. Remove the charred halloumi from the grill and drizzle with the tamarind-honey sauce. Grill for another 5 minutes, basting every minute or so.

Scatter the chickpeas into the dish, then serve garnished with some crunchy sev, red onion, pomegranate seeds, fresh coriander and mint and a final sprinkle of the masala powder.

TANGY TERIYAKI MEATBALLS
WITH PAK CHOI UDON

Tamarind is a truly versatile source of sourness – marrying with almost any flavours from across the world as if it's meant to be there. Which, in my opinion, it always is. I love to combine it with Japanese ingredients in particular, as in these teriyaki meatballs, where its tangy fruitiness brings out the salty-sweetness of teriyaki sauce. While delicious over noodles, these meatballs are equally heavenly as sub sandwiches – either with some iceberg lettuce or try them toasted with a slice of cheese and a squeeze of mustard for an extra kick. They are also very good served on their own with drinks.

SERVES 2-3

1 large onion
500g (1lb 2oz) minced (ground) beef, at least 5% fat
1 Tbsp brown or white miso
3 Tbsp polenta
2 Tbsp finely chopped coriander (cilantro), plus extra to garnish
vegetable oil, for frying
3 Tbsp tamarind paste
3 Tbsp black treacle
5 Tbsp dark soy sauce
2 garlic cloves, crushed to a paste
1 tsp grated fresh ginger root
3 tsp toasted sesame oil
2 Tbsp cider vinegar
2 Tbsp runny honey
200g (7oz) pak choi (bok choy), chopped
400–600g (14oz–1lb 5oz) cooked udon noodles (200g/7oz per person)
zest and juice of ½ lime
fine sea salt

Using a small blender or food processor, blitz the onion to a fine paste then put into a large bowl along with the beef, miso, polenta, the chopped coriander and a generous pinch of salt.

Use your hands to combine the mixture evenly, then form into 22–24 meatballs just smaller than a golf ball. Pile them up in the bowl, cover and refrigerate for 1 hour to firm up.

Heat a splash of oil in a large deep frying pan over a medium heat, then slowly sear the meatballs, in batches, for 5–6 minutes to brown all over, turning regularly to seal completely (you're just browning the outsides, not cooking them through). Set aside on a plate.

To the same pan, add the tamarind paste, treacle, soy sauce, garlic, ginger, 2 teaspoons of the sesame oil, the vinegar and honey. Bring to the boil, then reduce the heat to medium and cook for 3 minutes, to reduce the sauce a little.

Next, drop in the meatballs. Mix well so they are coated all over, then stir in a splash of water, cover with a lid and cook over a medium heat for 4–5 minutes.

Meanwhile, heat another splash of vegetable oil with the remaining teaspoon of sesame oil in a wok over a medium–high heat. Add the pak choi, stir-fry until tender, then add the cooked udon noodles and a splash of water to heat them through.

Remove the lid from the meatball pan, and allow them to cook for another 3–4 minutes to allow the sauce to thicken. Finally, stir through the lime zest and juice.

Serve the meatballs on a bed of pak choi and noodles, sprinkled with chopped coriander.

SALT & PEPPER PANEER PITTAS
WITH SWEET & SOUR SLAW v

Salt and pepper are not used enough as headline flavours in my opinion. It's key when they are the stars, not simply background seasonings, that you should use them very generously and give them space to shine among the other ingredients. With this in mind, they are the perfect flavour-pairing to zhuzh up anything deliciously creamy and plain – say mozzarella, burrata or, as here, paneer – especially if contrasted with something pleasingly sweetly sour. This tangy tamarind slaw is just the ticket – and a worthy superstar on its own for that matter.

SERVES 4

For the slaw
3 Tbsp caster (superfine) sugar,
 plus an extra 1 tsp
1 teaspoon of salt
zest and juice of 1 lime
2 tablespoons of boiling water
2 Tbsp tamarind paste
1 Tbsp olive oil, plus extra for drizzling
1 fat garlic clove, crushed to a paste
400g (14oz) red cabbage
2 large carrots
½ large white onion

For the pittas
300g (10½oz) paneer, cut into
 2cm (¾in) cubes
2 tsp coarsely ground black pepper
1 tsp amchoor (mango powder)
1 tsp onion powder
2 tsp cornflour (cornstarch)
4 pitta breads
small handful of coriander (cilantro),
 chopped

Tabasco or hot sauce (optional)

Put the sugar and salt in a large bowl, along with the lime juice and boiling water. Whisk well until the sugar and salt have dissolved, then add the tamarind paste, oil, lime zest and garlic. Whisk well again.

Use a mandoline or very sharp knife to shred the cabbage, carrots and onion as thinly as possible. Add the vegetables into the bowl with the dressing, mix well to coat and set aside for the flavours to mingle for at least 15 minutes.

Preheat the oven to 200°C fan/220°C/425°F/ Gas mark 7 and line a baking sheet with baking parchment.

Put the paneer in a separate bowl and cover with boiling water. Leave to soak for 5 minutes.

Meanwhile, in another bowl, whisk together 1 teaspoon of salt, the black pepper, amchoor, the remaining teaspoon of sugar, the onion powder and the cornflour.

Drain the paneer, then pat completely dry with a clean tea towel or paper towels. Drizzle the cubes with oil so they are coated all over, then one by one tumble them into the salt and pepper coating.

Spread out the coated paneer on the lined sheet and bake for 10–12 minutes until the cubes are just starting to turn brown on the outside.

Warm the pitta breads, slit down one side and stuff with the tangy coleslaw and warm crunchy paneer. Sprinkle with the coriander and enjoy with a drizzle of Tabasco or hot sauce if you like.

SPICY TAMARIND & CORIANDER
CHICKEN ADOBO

Suka Pinakurat is an extraordinary ingredient, elegantly sweet with an unapologetic kick of spice, and a staple in Filipino cuisine. This fermented vinegar, made from coconut sap, is often the bold flavour in chicken adobo, the country's unofficial national dish. On a similar vibe, during a trip to Antigua, I became hooked on another vinegar – Baldwin Bamboozle – made from almonds, with that has a juicy tropical tartness that's addictive. This recipe attempts to capture the essence of both these flavours using tamarind. Its fruity, tangy sourness works wonderfully with the molasses sweetness of dark brown sugar, and the scorched-earth spice notes of cumin and black pepper.

SERVES 4

1.25kg (2lb 12oz) chicken thighs,
  bone in and skin on (8 thighs)
vegetable oil, for frying
10 garlic cloves, slivered
2 tsp grated fresh root ginger
1 tablespoon cracked black pepper
6 bay leaves
1 Tbsp coriander seeds, crushed
2 tsp ground cumin

1 tsp chilli powder
175ml (5¾fl oz) white distilled vinegar
  or white wine vinegar
125ml (4fl oz) dark soy sauce
4 Tbsp tamarind paste
4 Tbsp dark brown sugar
handful of coriander (cilantro),
  chopped
zest of ½ lime
fine sea salt

Slash the chicken thighs through the skin to the bone a couple of times, then rub a little salt onto each one, getting it deep into the slits. Put on a plate and set aside for 15 minutes.

Heat a splash of vegetable oil in a large wok, then fry the chicken thighs over a medium–high heat for 7–8 minutes, skin-side down at first, until they brown. Carefully spoon off the excess fat, leaving just enough to coat the pan.

Next, add the garlic, ginger, black pepper and bay leaves to the wok. Stir well and cook over a medium–high heat for 2 minutes, ensuring the garlic doesn't burn. Next, add the coriander seeds, cumin and chilli powder and cook for 1 more minute – add a splash of water if they start to burn.

In a small jug, whisk together the vinegar, soy sauce, tamarind paste and sugar. Pour this over the chicken, bring to the boil and cook for 2–3 minutes, stirring to deglaze the base of the wok. Cover with a lid and cook over a medium–low heat for 25 minutes, stirring occasionally.

Remove the lid, add 1 teaspoon of salt and cook, uncovered, for another 15–20 minutes until you have a thick, intensely concentrated and syrupy sauce.

Plate up the chicken and sauce and garnish with coriander and lime zest. Serve with warm jasmine rice or a cucumber salad.

PLUM & TAMARIND
CHAR SIU BAO BUNS

'Tart' is one of my favourite food words. I'm not sure what that says about me – but I am drawn to any ingredients that can be grouped under this heading. Both plum and tamarind are very much in this camp, offering up different ends of the tart spectrum – from cherry-nectar sweet, through to raspy-sour tropical. The glaze in this char siu recipe embraces both ends of that spectrum – and is equally wonderful with baked chicken, fish or vegetables.

SERVES 4

550–650g (1lb 4oz–1lb 7oz) pork
    tenderloin
2 tablespoons boiling water
8 bao buns

For the marinade
3 Tbsp plum sauce
2 Tbsp tamarind paste
2 tsp Chinese five spice
2 Tbsp tomato ketchup

2 Tbsp dark brown sugar
2 Tbsp white rice vinegar
2 Tbsp dark soy sauce
1 Tbsp toasted sesame oil
2 tsp smoked salt

To serve
Kewpie mayonnaise
2 spring onions (scallions), finely
    chopped
pickled cucumbers or daikon (mooli),
    sliced

Whisk together the marinade ingredients in a bowl.

Place the pork loin in a deep roasting tray, then smother with the marinade – covering it all over. Leave to marinate in the refrigerator for at least 3–4 hours, or ideally overnight, basting regularly.

Remove the pork loin from the oven to bring to room temperature.

Preheat the oven to 175°C fan/195°C/390°F/Gas mark 5½. Bake the pork loin for 35–40 minutes, basting every 10 minutes, and ensuring that the sauce is not burning. If it is, cover the tray with foil.

Remove the tray from the oven then transfer the cooked pork loin to a separate baking sheet – and keep the sauce in the tray.

Preheat the grill to high. Grill the pork for 5–7 minutes until charred on top but not burnt. Remove from the grill, slice into 1cm (½in) discs and spread out on a serving plate.

Add a couple of tablespoons of boiling water to the roasting tray to deglaze the pan and whisk vigorously. If the sauce is too thin, warm on the hob to reduce to more of a thick syrup.

Heat the bao buns in a microwave or a steamer. Fill with slices of pork and drizzle over the sauce. Serve with mayo, spring onions, pickles of your choice and extra sauce on the side if you like.

Mango Chutney

sticky and vinegary,
burstlingly tropical,
flamboyantly spiced,
succulently juicy,
mellow sweetness.

The classic Indian chutney is made from ripe mango pulp, garlic, ginger, chilli and spices like cumin, cloves, fenugreek and nigella seeds. The ingredients are simmered to a thick jammy relish with sugar and vinegar, which both preserves and amplifies the flavour of the mangoes. There are mild, hot or extra-hot versions, and ones infused with extra garlic, turmeric, pomegranate or other fruits like raisins and apple. Not to be confused with mango pickle, which is not the same thing at all, being made with unripe green mangoes preserved in savoury mustard oil, vinegar and salted spices.

ZESTY LEMON &
MANGO TARKHA DAL v

As a kid, I hated dal – the daily staple on our Punjabi table was, to me, a culinary enemy I had to endure to be allowed anything sweet to finish. I was truly perplexed when it became hip in the late noughties – although that trend was predominantly driven by the appearance of butter-rich black dal makhani. What's not to love about that! At the opposite end of the flavour spectrum are yellow tarkha dals, far closer to those I grew up eating. This one is enriched with the sweetness of mango chutney, coconut milk for creamy depth, and lifted by sizzling curry leaves, warm spices and fresh lemon. I not only love this dal, I'd happily have a second serving for dessert.

SERVES 4-6

300g (10½oz) red lentils
2 Tbsp ghee
2 tsp cumin seeds, crushed
2 tsp coriander seeds, crushed
1 large red onion, finely chopped
2 tsp grated fresh ginger root
2 tsp garam masala
1 tsp ground turmeric
3 Tbsp tomato purée (paste)
200g (7oz) mango chutney, plus more
    to serve

400ml (14fl oz) coconut milk
400ml (14fl oz) water
zest and juice of 1 large lemon
fine sea salt

For the tarkha
2 Tbsp ghee
1 tsp nigella seeds
4 fat garlic cloves, finely slivered
1 tsp chilli powder
2 Tbsp desiccated (dried) coconut
20 fresh curry leaves, chopped

Rinse the lentils in a sieve under the cold tap until the water runs clean, then leave to soak in a bowl of cold water for 30 minutes.

Melt 2 tablespoons of the ghee in a deep frying pan over a medium heat, then add the cumin and coriander seeds and allow to sizzle for 1 minute. Next, add the chopped onion, and fry for 6–7 minutes until it turns translucent, then add the ginger and fry for 1 minute. Next, add the well-drained lentils, stirring these through to coat them in the oniony oil.

Mix the garam masala and turmeric with 3 tablespoons of water, then add this to the pan, then the tomato purée and mango chutney. Cook for another 2 minutes before adding the coconut milk, water and 1½ teaspoons of salt.

Bring to the boil, then reduce to a simmer and cook for 20–25 minutes until the lentils are tender. Add a splash more water if it's drying out and stir regularly so the dal doesn't catch on the bottom. Stir through the lemon juice once it's cooked, adding more salt to season if needed.

For the tarkha, heat 2 tablespoons of ghee in a small frying pan over a medium heat, then add the nigella seeds, 2 teaspoons of lemon zest, the garlic slivers, chilli powder and desiccated coconut. Sizzle for 2 minutes until the garlic just starts to show some colour, then add the curry leaves (be careful, they will spit!). Sizzle for 1 minute, then drizzle the tarkha over the dal, and spoon over more mango chutney if you like. Enjoy with warm rotis, flatbread or rice.

MANGO, RAINBOW ROOTS & ROASTED GARLIC
TARTE TATIN v

This summery tart is my go-to dish whenever I'm cooking for vegetarians – and is the first thing meat eaters around the table flock towards as well. The mango chutney glaze adds zesty, tropical tang to the festival of rainbow-coloured roots – with fudgy-sweet roasted garlic slathered over the pastry adding an additional layer of intrigue. Delicious hot, cold or even lukewarm. Just be sure to make two, as everyone around the table will want a piece.

SERVES 4-6

320g (11¼oz) sheet ready-rolled puff
  pastry (prepared pie dough)
plain (all-purpose) flour, for dusting
2 small heritage carrots
  (1 purple, 1 orange)
2 small heritage beetroot (1 yellow,
  1 candy striped or purple)
2 small parsnips

10 whole garlic cloves, unpeeled
olive oil, for drizzling
1 tsp nigella seeds, crushed
20g (¾oz) butter
1 tsp finely chopped fresh rosemary
1 Tbsp dark brown sugar
1 Tbsp white wine vinegar
4 Tbsp mango chutney
1 tsp English mustard
fine sea salt

Preheat the oven to 180°C fan/200°C/400°F/Gas mark 6. Roll out the pastry slightly on a floured surface. Using a large (28–30cm/11¼–12in) ovenproof frying pan as your guide, cut around the pastry in a circle allowing an extra 1cm (½in) overhang. Transfer the pastry to a baking sheet and refrigerate to chill.

Peel and chop the carrots, beetroot and parsnips into discs 1.5cm (⅝in) thick and spread out on a second baking sheet – along with the unpeeled garlic cloves. Drizzle with olive oil, season with fine sea salt and sprinkle over the nigella seeds.

Bake the vegetables in the oven for 20 minutes then remove the garlic cloves, leaving the roots to roast for another 5–7 minutes. Remove from the oven and set aside to cool completely (keep the oven on).

Squeeze the garlic cloves from their skins into a small bowl and mash to a fine paste.

In your large frying pan, melt the butter over a medium heat then add the rosemary, sugar and ½ teaspoon of salt. Whisk well then, just as the

sugar starts to caramelize, add the vinegar – whisk well until it starts to form a caramel glaze. Next add the mango chutney and English mustard, cooking for 2 minutes until it thickens slightly.

Spoon half the mango glaze into a bowl, and spread the remainder into an even layer across the base of the pan. Arrange the roasted roots in a single-layer on top, totally covering the base of the pan. Spread the rest of the glaze on top. Take your puff pastry disc out of the refrigerator and spread the roasted garlic paste over it. Place the pastry disc over the roots – garlic side-down – tucking in the overhang to encase the roots.

Bake in the oven for 24–26 minutes, turning halfway and checking regularly to ensure the top doesn't burn. Carefully remove from the oven using oven gloves (the handle will be hot!) then loosen the pastry from the sides with a spatula. Cool for 5 minutes, then carefully invert onto a plate. Enjoy with a dressed green salad.

HALLOUMI, MANGO, COURGETTE & TARRAGON PIZZETTES v

I love a scissor-cut Roman-style pizza slice, especially one that's charred at the bottom, chewy in the middle and liberally topped with a plethora of things, which could be anything as long they include fennel sausage! Bonci in Rome, MyPixxa and Malleti in London are bastions of brilliance in this genre – all of which have taught me that a tomato base really is not essential when it comes to very good pizza. This recipe is my globally remixed ode to those joints – using mango chutney for its sweet tang, melted halloumi for chewy saltiness, charred yellow courgettes for bitter freshness and tarragon for that essential herbal hit of anise.

MAKES 6

220ml (7¾fl oz) warm water
1 Tbsp caster (superfine) sugar
2 tsp onion powder
3 Tbsp olive oil, plus extra for brushing
150g (5½oz) plain (all-purpose) flour, plus extra for dusting
200g (7oz) strong white flour
1½ tsp nigella seeds
2¼ tsp fast-action dried yeast

2 large yellow or green courgettes (zucchini), sliced into 1cm (½in) discs
6 heaped Tbsp sun-dried tomato purée (paste)
6 Tbsp mango chutney, plus optional extra to serve
225g (8oz) halloumi, grated
handful of fresh tarragon leaves, finely chopped
fine sea salt

Whisk together the warm water, sugar, onion powder and oil in a small jug. Separately, in a large mixing bowl, whisk together both flours, 1½ teaspoons of salt and the nigella seeds.

Tip half of the dry mix into the bowl of a stand mixer fitted with a dough hook, then whisk through the yeast. Begin mixing at a slow speed. Slowly trickle in the liquid – scraping down the sides of the bowl as needed – until fully incorporated. You will have a very loose, slack dough at this point.

Keep the mixer running slowly and add the rest of the flour, a third at a time, until you have a tacky dough ball that comes away from the sides of the bowl. Turn out onto a floured surface and knead for 10–12 minutes until the dough is smooth and elastic.

Form into a ball, place in a bowl, brush with oil, cover and leave to prove for 1 hour. Punch down the dough, knead in the bowl for 1 minute, then cover and leave for another hour.

Meanwhile, brush the courgette slices with a little oil. Heat a griddle or frying pan over a medium–high heat and sear on one side for 4–5 minutes until they brown. Set side.

Punch down the rested dough again, knead for 1 more minute, then divide and roll into six large dough balls (about 110g/3¾oz each). Preheat the oven to 200°C fan/220°C/425°F/Gas mark 7.

Brush two baking sheets liberally with olive oil. Using your fingers and knuckles, form each ball into roughly a 15cm (6in) circle and place three on each sheet, spaced apart. Spread the pizzette with a tablespoon of tomato purée, a tablespoon of mango chutney, then sprinkle with the halloumi and tarragon.

Bake one sheet at a time for 18–20 minutes (or, if you want to bake all the pizzette at once, swap the trays over halfway through the cook time) until puffed and golden brown on top. Enjoy hot or cold with extra mango chutney, if you like.

MANGO CHICKEN SCHNITZEL WITH LIME-LEAF SMASHED PEAS

Schnitzels and mushy peas both have a nostalgic seventies Fanny Cradock-meets-Wimpy-diner charm that I'm always drawn to – crying out for the addition of pineapple rings to garnish, piped green mashed potato and silver jugs of parsley sauce on the side. My flavour elevated take on these culinary relics uses mango chutney to add tropical pizzaz to the chicken, and lime leaves to bring Southeast Asian fragrance to the smashed peas. Arguably so retro it's back, although in my opinion these two culinary superheroes will never be out of vogue.

SERVES 2

5 Tbsp mango chutney, plus extra
   to serve
3 fat garlic cloves
1 Tbsp Worcestershire sauce
2 Tbsp apple cider vinegar
500g (1lb 2oz) chicken breasts
   (2 large ones), boneless and
   skinless
cornflour (cornstarch), for dredging
1 large egg
60g (2¼oz) panko breadcrumbs
1 Tbsp nigella seeds
2 Tbsp sesame seeds

sunflower or vegetable oil, for frying
fine sea salt and freshly ground
   black pepper
lemon wedges, to serve

For the peas
400g (14oz) frozen peas
12–14 fresh makrut lime leaves
about 30 fresh mint leaves
zest and juice of 1 small lemon
20g (¾oz) butter
splash of olive oil, for frying
2 whole spring onions (scallions),
   finely chopped

Put the mango chutney, garlic cloves, Worcestershire sauce, vinegar, 1 teaspoon of salt and 1 teaspoon of black pepper in a small blender and whizz to a fine paste.

Place one of the chicken breasts between two sheets of baking paper and use a rolling pin to gently flatten into a thin steak approximately 3–4mm (⅛in) thick. Don't bash hard or the meat will tear! Repeat with the other breast.

Transfer them to a large bowl and smother both breasts all over with the mango marinade, then leave for at least 30 minutes.

Prepare the smashed peas. Boil the peas in a pan of salted water for 3 minutes, then drain and set aside. Use a small blender to whizz together the lime leaves, mint, lemon juice and 1 teaspoon of zest to a very fine paste.

Melt the butter in a pan with a splash of oil, then add the green paste, frying over a medium heat for 2 minutes. Next, add the spring onions, cook for another minute, then add the cooked peas,

plus 1 teaspoon of salt. Cook for a final minute, then either smash chunkily with a potato masher, or use a hand blender to turn into a mushy pea purée. Keep warm.

To coat the schnitzels, prepare three large bowls: one with cornflour, one with beaten egg, and one with a mix of breadcrumbs, nigella seeds and sesame seeds.

Dredge one marinated chicken schnitzel in the cornflour, flipping it to coat all over. Leave for 30 seconds, then dredge again so the surface is completely covered. Shake off the excess, then dip into the egg, and finally into the breadcrumbs, coating liberally all over. Repeat with the second schnitzel.

Heat 2cm (¾in) of sunflower or vegetable oil in a deep frying pan to 165°C/329°F. Cook the schnitzels, one at a time, over a medium heat for 6–7 minutes – turning occasionally – until crunchy and golden brown on the outside and cooked through. Serve with the smashed peas, lemon wedge and extra mango chutney on the side.

JAFFNA-SPICED CHICKEN WITH COCONUT GRAVY

Paradise is one of my favourite restaurants in London – celebrating the multifaceted cuisine of Sri Lanka at full volume in their own unique way. It's given me a taste for fragrant Jaffna spice mixes – rich in fennel, coriander and mustard seeds, curry leaves, cinnamon and cloves. This roast chicken recipe offsets the earthy depth of those spices with the sweet tang of mango chutney and richness of coconut milk. The flavour alchemy that results is astonishingly delicious, and unapologetically loud!

SERVES 4

1 whole free-range chicken
    (1.75kg–1.95kg/3lb 12oz–4lb 3oz)
zest and juice of 2 lemons
seeds from 10 green cardamom pods,
    crushed to powder
2 tsp amchoor (mango powder)
2 tsp coriander seeds
2 tsp fennel seeds
2 tsp mustard seeds
6 whole cloves

30 fresh curry leaves
4 Tbsp mango chutney
30g (1oz) fresh root ginger, roughly
    chopped
2 large red chillies
1 tsp ground cinnamon
1 tsp ground turmeric
400ml (14fl oz) coconut milk
2 Tbsp Greek yoghurt
fine sea salt
coconut shreds, to garnish

To spatchcock the chicken, place it breast-side down, legs facing you, on a chopping board. Use poultry scissors to cut either side of its backbone and remove. Turn the bird over then press down firmly with your palm to flatten the breast bone and make all one thickness. With a sharp knife, slash through the skin along the legs, thighs and breasts, then splay out the spatchcocked bird in a deep roasting tin that the chicken fits snugly into.

Whisk together 6 tablespoons of lemon juice, 2 teaspoons of salt, the powdered cardamom seeds and amchoor in a jug until well combined. Spoon this lemony brine over the chicken, using your hands to get it deep into the cavities and slashes. Set aside to brine for 30 minutes.

Meanwhile, in a dry frying pan, toast the coriander, fennel, mustard seeds and cloves for 1–2 minutes until they release their aromas. Grind to a fine powder using a pestle and mortar.

Shallow fry six curry leaves for 45 seconds in vegetable oil. Set aside for the garnish.

Into a small blender, add the mango chutney, ginger, red chillies, the remaining curry leaves, cinnamon, turmeric, the ground spice powder,

plus the lemony brine from the roasting tin. Blend to a fine paste, then slather all over the chicken, getting it deep into the slashes. Leave to marinate in the refrigerator for 4–6 hours.

Once marinated allow the chicken to return to room temperature. Preheat the oven to 190°C fan/210°C/410°F/Gas mark 6½. Roast the chicken for 30 minutes. Remove from the oven and baste with the juices and oils in the bottom of the tin. Next, add the coconut milk into the tin, pouring it around the chicken not over the top. Cook for 30–35 minutes until the chicken is cooked through and golden brown, whisking the gravy every 10 minutes.

Remove the chicken from the roasting tin to a serving board and rest for 10 minutes. Meanwhile, stir in the lemon zest and a squeeze of juice into the gravy, along with the Greek yoghurt and cooking juices from the resting chicken – using a whisk to deglaze the bottom of the roasting tin.

Place the rested chicken back into the tin and baste with a little of the gravy. Garnish with fried curry leaves and coconut shreds if you like.

BALINESE MANGO-PORK
CRISPY ROLLS

After a week of yoga, juicing and chanting at a Balinese jungle retreat in Ubud a few years back –
I made the executive decision to undo all of that 'wellness' by booking into The Slow in Canggu.
It is without doubt one of the most chic, stylish and cosmopolitan places I've ever stayed with
beautiful boho interiors, a magical cocktail list of dreams and a Balinese-leaning, culture crossing
menu that reads like poetry. These Balinese spiced-pork crispy rolls are inspired by my stay there –
mango chutney, lemongrass, fish sauce, peanuts and lime creating flavour acrobatics on the palate.
Forget the yoga, cooking these is my kind of meditation.

**MAKES 10 LARGE
OR 20 MINI ROLLS**

8 whole makrut lime leaves,
    stalks removed
20g (¾oz) lemongrass, roughly
    chopped
10g (¼oz) knob of fresh ginger root,
    roughly chopped
6 garlic cloves
1 Tbsp fish sauce
20g (¾oz) roasted peanuts
1 tsp ground cinnamon
½ tsp freshly grated nutmeg
1 tsp chilli flakes
3 Tbsp vegetable oil, plus extra
    for brushing
1 large red onion, finely diced
500g (1lb 2oz) minced (ground) pork,
    at least 5% fat
100g (3½oz) mango chutney
zest and juice of 2 limes
10 sheets filo pastry
nigella seeds, to sprinkle
fine sea salt

In a blender, whizz together the lime leaves, lemongrass, ginger, garlic, fish sauce, peanuts, cinnamon, nutmeg, chilli flakes and a splash of water to a very fine paste.

Heat the oil in a large pan over a medium heat, then fry the onion for 5–6 minutes. Add the pork and cook for 10–12 minutes until a lot of the water has evaporated and it's starting to brown.

Next, add the lime-leaf paste, and cook for 3 minutes before adding the mango chutney and cooking for another 3 minutes. Finally, stir through the lime juice, 1 teaspoon of zest and 1½ teaspoons of salt. Set aside to cool to room temperature.

Preheat the oven to 200°C fan/220°C/425°F/Gas mark 7. Lay the first sheet of filo pastry on a board, then cut in half – use half a sheet of filo per roll. Spread 2 heaped tablespoons of the mince in a thick line down one side of the cut sheet. Fold down at the sides, then roll up into a cigar. Brush the join with oil to seal, then place, seam-side down, on a baking sheet. Repeat with the remaining pastry and mince. Brush the tops liberally with more oil, then sprinkle over the nigella seeds.

Bake for 14–16 minutes until crispy on the outside and piping hot in the middle. Enjoy the rolls as they are with drinks or as a starter – served with dips or chilli sauce.

Chipotle Paste

scorched and caramelized,
spicily fruity,
bitter chocolatey,
peppery hot,
rich smokiness.

Native to Mexico, chipotle chillies are actually just very ripe, dark red jalapeños that have been smoke-dried until black. To make chipotle paste these medium–hot chillies are blended with onions, garlic, vinegar, tomato concentrate, salt and spices like cumin and smoked paprika. The paste is most often found in jars, although in Mexico it is usually sold in cans or tubes. Variations on the paste include: chipotle salsa sauces, which are diluted with extra vinegar to make a pourable condiment; chipotle chillies in adobo, which are the whole chillies in a tangy sauce; and dry chipotle spice-salt rubs.

CHIPOTLE-HOI SIN CHICKEN WINGS

As Mae West famously said: 'Too much of a good thing can be wonderful'. This applies to many facets in life, including flavour, and – in my opinion – there's nothing more thrilling than pairing two extremely delicious, loud and out-there flavours. Sweet, sticky hoi sin and smoky dark chipotle are ingredients that I especially love to intermingle. Together, they are the perfect adornment for crispy-skinned chicken wings. Just wonderful!

MAKES 14 WINGS - ENOUGH FOR 3-4 PER PORTION

6 Tbsp baking powder
1 tsp Chinese five spice
2 Tbsp fine polenta (cornmeal),
    ground to a powder
1 Tbsp onion powder
14 chicken wings, skin on
    (about 1.25kg/2lb 12oz)
6 Tbsp hoi sin sauce
3 Tbsp chipotle paste
3 fat garlic cloves, crushed to a paste
3 Tbsp apple cider vinegar

Preheat the oven to 180°C fan/200°C/400°F/Gas mark 6.

Prepare a coating by whisking together the baking powder, Chinese five spice, ground polenta and onion powder in a bowl.

Pat dry each of the chicken wings using paper towels so that no moisture remains on the skin. Dredge in the coating, ensuring that they are covered all over and in the crevices. Place on two baking sheets, spaced well apart, and bake for 40–45 minutes until crispy.

Meanwhile, prepare a glaze by whisking together the hoi sin sauce, chipotle paste, garlic and vinegar in a bowl.

Remove the cooked wings from the oven, brush liberally with the glaze, then bake for a final 3 minutes. Serve hot from the oven, brushing with more glaze if you like.

CHIPOTLE & BURNT ORANGE
TIGER PRAWNS

I first tried an Amer Picon Bière in Paris on the courtyard of the Palais de Tokyo overlooking the Eiffel Tower one scorching-hot August day, and it's quickly become one of my favourite summer tipples. This bitter-orange aperitif is mixed with blonde beer for the French version of a shandy – and also makes a killer Negroni Sbagliato. It's given me a taste for the flavour of burnt orange peel, which I've combined in this recipe with smoky chipotle paste and salty butter. Here, I've used prawns (shrimp) but this treatment is equally delicious with other fresh seafood like squid, crayfish or whole grilled fish. If you're feeling lavish, it's especially tasty with barbecued lobster.

SERVES 2–3

500g (1lb 2oz) uncooked, unpeeled
    tiger or large king prawns
    (jumbo shrimp)
2 large oranges
1 Tbsp chipotle paste
4 Tbsp olive oil

1 Tbsp minced fresh ginger root
1 tsp ground cumin
1 Tbsp runny honey
1 Tbsp white wine vinegar
50g (1¾oz) butter
fine sea salt
finely chopped coriander (cilantro),
    to garnish

Carefully peel away the shell from the body of the prawns and devein – but keep the heads and tails on for flavour.

Using a vegetable peeler, take off the peel from the oranges in large pieces, aiming to include as little as the white pith as possible. Juice the oranges and set the juice aside.

Preheat the grill to its highest setting. Spread the orange peels – orange exterior-side up – on a baking sheet, and grill for 2–3 minutes until they just start to char and blacken at the edges. You want the surface of the peels to be gently scorched and blackened in a few places, but not totally burnt. Remove but keep the grill on high.

Add the scorched peels to a small blender or grinder along with the chipotle paste, oil, ginger, cumin, honey, white wine vinegar, 2 tablespoons of orange juice and 1½ teaspoons of salt. Blitz to a coarse paste that still has a little texture – you don't want it completely smooth.

Melt the butter in a frying pan over a medium heat, then add the chipotle-orange paste. Cook for 1–2 minutes to let the flavours mingle together.

Spread out the prawns on a baking tray, then pour over the chipotle-orange butter, evenly covering each prawn.

Grill for 6–7 minutes until the prawns turn coral pink and are cooked through but not burnt on top. Remove the prawns, scatter with coriander and serve with good crusty bread to mop up the chipotle-orange oils.

CHEESY CHIPOTLE & FENNEL SEED
BUTTERMILK SCONES v

During university, I was sous chef at a twee tearoom in Clifton Village, Bristol, called the Rainbow Café. It was famous for three things: its technicolour door handle, its transistor radio that was permanently tuned to Radio 4, and its fresh handmade scones. By the time I left, I'd become quite expert at crafting those crumbly-cakey delectations. For someone with 'hot hands', it's a skill that I proudly flaunt to this day. These savoury scones combine the smoky heat of chipotle, the lemony freshness of fennel seeds and the rich robustness of sharp cheeses. The method utilizes the refrigerator at every step – so these should turn out perfect no matter how hot your palms.

MAKES 12-14

325g (11½oz) plain (all-purpose) flour,
    plus extra for dusting
1 Tbsp baking powder
½ tsp bicarbonate of soda
    (baking soda)
2 tsp fennel seeds, crushed
1 tsp coarsely ground black pepper
1 Tbsp caster (superfine) sugar
125g (4½oz) cold butter, cubed

100g (3½oz) mixed strong-flavoured
    melting cheeses (I like a strong
    Cheddar, vintage Red Leicester
    and manchego), grated, plus
    extra to finish
2 Tbsp very finely chopped chives
1 egg, separated
125ml (4fl oz) buttermilk,
    plus an extra 1 Tbsp
3 tsp chipotle paste
fine sea salt

Add to a large mixing bowl the flour, baking powder, bicarbonate of soda, fennel seeds, ½ teaspoon of salt, the black pepper and sugar. Whisk to mix well.

Add the cubed butter and rub into the dry mix until you have a fine sandy rubble speckled with just a few slightly larger flecks of butter still in the mix (these bigger flecks help the scones to rise!). Mix through the grated cheese then the chives. Put the bowl in the refrigerator for 15 minutes.

In a small jug, whisk together the egg white, buttermilk and 2 teaspoons of the chipotle paste until fully combined. Remove the bowl from the refrigerator and gradually add the wet ingredients to the dry ingredients, using a round-bladed knife to cut these in slowly.

Start to knead the dough with your hands in the bowl, then turn out onto a floured surface and knead for 1–2 minutes until it just starts to spring back and is smooth on the outside. Compress the dough into a very tight ball, cover with cling film and return to the refrigerator for 15 minutes.

Roll the chilled dough into a circle approximately 3cm (1¼in) thick. Use a 5 or 6cm (2–2½in) round cutter to stamp out your scones – press firmly straight up and down without twisting. Gather the trimmings together to make the last ones – you should have 12 or 14 scones depending on the cutter size. Flip each scone upside down onto a baking sheet, then chill the tray for 15 minutes.

Preheat the oven to 190°C fan/210°C/410°F/ Gas mark 6½. Make a glaze by whisking together the egg yolk, the remaining teaspoon of chipotle paste and the tablespoon of buttermilk. Brush the chilled scones with the glaze and if you like, sprinkle over extra grated cheese.

Bake for 15–16 minutes on the middle shelf of the oven until cooked, risen and dark golden on top. Transfer to a wire rack to cool completely. Enjoy with lots of butter.

NACHO CAULIFLOWER CHEESE
WITH JALAPEÑO RELISH

Of all the restaurants we used to frequent as children on fortnightly Sunday treat days, none had my affection quite like the faux Tex-Mex restaurants that were found in shopping malls on the outskirts of Leicester – where the staff wore oversized sombreros, the cowboy interiors looked like a Disney theme park ride and all the food tasted of Tabasco. My lasting memories of those places are mouth-blisteringly warm cauliflower cheese served in red-hot skillets, salsa-drenched nachos with dollops of cold guacamole, and vinegar-spiked jalapeño rings adorning everything. I've combined all of those things for this playful recipe – with chipotle paste adding a touch 'genuine' Mexicana, to counter all that Latino fakery.

SERVES 3-4

1 large cauliflower, chopped
    into bite-sized florets
1 tsp ground cumin
2 garlic cloves, crushed to a paste
1 tsp smoked paprika
3 Tbsp olive oil
1 Tbsp chipotle paste
100g (3½oz) butter
90g (3¼oz) plain (all-purpose) flour
1 tsp freshly grated nutmeg
750ml (26fl oz) full-fat (whole) milk

1½ tsp English mustard
175g (6oz) mature Cheddar, grated
80g (2¾oz) jalapeños in brine
    (drained weight), plus extra
    to garnish
1 Tbsp runny honey
1 Tbsp apple cider vinegar
salt
small handful of coriander (cilantro),
    finely chopped, plus optional extra
    to garnish
65g (2¼oz) tortilla chips, crushed,
    plus extra to garnish

Boil the cauliflower florets in a large pan of salted water for 5 minutes until tender. Drain in a colander and leave to cool, allowing the steam to escape completely. Preheat the oven to 190°C fan/210°C/410°F/Gas mark 6½.

Make a paste by whisking together the cumin, garlic, smoked paprika, oil and chipotle paste in a large bowl.

Add the cooled cauliflower to the bowl and stir to coat all over in the paste. Spoon into a deep-sided 18 x 22cm (7 x 8½in) ovenproof dish, scraping in any remaining paste from the bowl.

Melt the butter in a saucepan, then add the flour and nutmeg. Stir well and cook for 3–4 minutes until you have a golden roux. Add the milk and mustard, then whisk for 4–5 minutes over a medium heat until you have a thick sauce. Finally, stir through the Cheddar, mixing well until melted through.

Pour the cheese sauce over the cauliflower, filling all the cracks and crevices. Bake in the oven for 15 minutes.

Meanwhile, make a relish by blending the jalapeños, honey, vinegar and chopped coriander to a coarse paste.

Remove the cauliflower cheese from the oven, drizzle over the relish and top with crushed tortilla chips.

Return to the oven and bake for a further 6–8 minutes until bubbling, golden and crunchy on top. Garnish with extra jalapeños, crushed tortilla chips and coriander if you like.

CUMIN & GARLIC CHICKEN
WITH CHIPOTLE REMOULADE

Celeriac may be the ugly duckling of the vegetable world, but beneath its gnarly exterior is one of the most exquisitely flavoured of all vegetables – especially when its nutty hard flesh is transformed into a mayonnaise-rich remoulade. The addition of chipotle paste adds fragrantly smoky undertones that accentuate the aniseedy flavour of the root. Chicken marinated in cumin and garlic is a fitting taste bomb to match all that flavour-overload, although the chipotle-spiked remoulade is equally tasty in a sandwich with some sharp tangy cheese.

SERVES 4

4 Tbsp olive oil
2 tsp cumin seeds
8 garlic cloves, crushed to a paste
zest and juice of 1 lemon,
    plus an extra squeeze to serve
1 tsp ground cinnamon
1 tsp ground cumin
1 tsp ground coriander

4 chicken legs, bone in skin on
    (about 1kg/2lb 4oz)
fine sea salt

For the remoulade
350g (12oz) celeriac (peeled weight)
2 large carrots
2 Tbsp apple cider vinegar
4 Tbsp mayonnaise
2 tsp Dijon mustard
1 Tbsp chipotle paste
1 tsp caster (superfine) sugar

Mix together the olive oil, cumin seeds, garlic, 2 teaspoons of salt, 1 teaspoon of the lemon zest and all of its juice, the ground cinnamon, cumin and coriander in a large bowl.

Slash the skin of the chicken legs three or four times through the fleshiest parts. Add the legs to the bowl and smother all over with the paste, getting it deep into the slashes and crevices. Cover and leave to marinate in the refrigerator for at least 6 hours, ideally overnight. Remove from the refrigerator an hour before cooking so the chicken comes up to room temperature.

Preheat the oven to 175°C fan/195°C/385°F/Gas mark 5½. Spread out the marinated chicken legs on a baking tray, spooning over the remaining marinade, with the garlic and cumin seeds on top. Bake for 45–55 minutes, until the legs are nicely charred and cooked through – cover with foil if the tops are browning too quickly.

Meanwhile, make the remoulade. Use a mandoline, julienne peeler or sharp knife to slice the celeriac and carrots into very thin matchsticks. Cover with 1 teaspoon of salt and sprinkle over the cider vinegar. Mix well and set aside for 10 minutes.

Next, add the mayonnaise, mustard, chipotle paste and sugar. Mix again and set aside for another 10 minutes.

Remove the chicken from the oven and leave to rest for 5 minutes. Serve the warm chicken piled onto generous spoonfuls of the chipotle remoulade – with a squeeze of lemon and some peppery leaves on the side.

CRISPY RICE WITH
CHIPOTLE KOFTAS & TAHINI SAUCE

Much like the scorched cheesy corner is the very best bit of a lasagne, and the molten fudgy middle the best bit of a brownie, it's the brown crispy bottom that's most treasured in the Persian baked rice dish known as tahdig. My intercultural take is dotted with chipotle-marinated koftas – fried until golden to render their chilli rich **lamb** fat, which is then used to create that perfect crunchy rice crust. The technique of mixing the bottom layer of rice with soured cream and using a non-stick pan makes it almost foolproof, but don't fret if it doesn't hold its shape in one crackled piece – broken crunchy rice is just as delicious.

SERVES 4

500g (1lb 2oz) minced (ground) lamb,
    at least 20% fat
1 large red onion, grated
1 Tbsp chipotle paste, plus optional
    extra to serve
1 Tbsp pomegranate or sour cherry
    molasses, plus optional extra to
    serve
generous handful of coriander
    (cilantro), finely chopped

1 tsp ground cumin
375g (13oz) basmati rice
150ml (5fl oz) soured cream,
    plus 4 Tbsp for the rice
2 Tbsp tahini
1 garlic clove, crushed to a paste
zest and juice of 1 large lemon
20 saffron threads, soaked in 1 Tbsp
    hot water
1 Tbsp olive oil, plus extra for drizzling
fine sea salt

In a large bowl, mix together the lamb, onion, chipotle paste, molasses, coriander, cumin and 1½ teaspoons of salt. Cover and leave for 30 minutes.

Rinse the rice under the cold tap until the water runs clear, then soak in a bowl of cold water for 30 minutes.

Meanwhile, make a tahini sauce by whisking together the 150ml (5fl oz) of soured cream with the tahini, garlic, lemon juice, 1 teaspoon of zest and ½ teaspoon of salt – add a splash of warm water if it stiffens up.

Using your hands, form the minced lamb into 16–18 small oval koftas – wear disposable gloves for safety and be careful not to get chilli in your eyes. Set aside.

Boil the soaked rice in a large pan of very well salted water for 6 minutes, then drain and immediately rinse under the cold tap. Shake off the excess water, tip the rice back into your pan (off the heat), then stir through the saffron and its soaking water. Set aside, uncovered.

Heat a drizzle of oil in a large, deep non-stick frying pan or non-stick skillet pan. Add the lamb koftas then cook for 10–12 minutes, turning regularly, until charred on the outside and just cooked through. Transfer the koftas to a plate to rest, then drain the rendered fat in the pan through a sieve into a bowl, and set aside. This fat will be used to make the rice crispy.

Continued...

In a separate bowl, stir together 4 tablespoons of soured cream with 1½ cups of the cooked rice. Mix well so the rice is fully coated in the cream.

Return 3 tablespoons of the lamb fat to the non-stick frying pan, along with 1 tablespoon of oil, and reheat the pan. Spoon in then spread out the cream-coated rice in an even layer over the base of the pan. Top this with a third of the remaining rice, then spoon over the koftas. Finally, spoon over the remaining rice, compacting it with a spatula. Use the back of the spatula to make six indents in the rice to let the steam escape.

Cook, uncovered, over a medium–high heat for 12 minutes, or until a crust has started to form on the base and sides. Use a spatula to pull away the rice from the sides, then reduce the heat to low and cook for another 13–15 minutes until the base moves as one crispy piece.

Carefully invert the crispy rice onto a serving board or plate, and serve immediately with the tahini sauce – rippled with molasses or chipotle paste, if you like.

Toasted Sesame Oil

aromatic and smoky,
deeply roasted,
delicately bitter,
burnt buttered,
amber nuttiness.

Sesame oil is made using raw sesame seeds that are sun-dried then pressed to extract their flavourful oil. These recipes call for toasted sesame oil, for which the dried sesame seeds are roasted before being pressed. Different producers brown the sesame seeds to different degrees – some just lightly tinting them to a pale tawny with a delicate nutty flavour, whereas others take them to a dark coffee brown with a more robust smoky flavour. Another is black sesame oil, which is made using earthier black sesame seeds.

SESAME PRAWN COCKTAIL TOSTADOS
WITH CHARRED CORN

During my short stint 'living' in Chicago as a writer in residence, I somehow found myself residing in a rooftop apartment that I still dream about to this day. It was eye-wateringly cool – kitted out with a covetable collection of pretentious coffee-table books, an uber-stylish record player with LPs including the Taylor Swift back catalogue, and a gigantic terrace that looked out over the streets of West Town – home to some of the very best taquerías in the city. One of these was Diego, a neon-painted establishment specializing in Baja cuisine from Tijuana, that fused Mexican and Japanese flavours with bold Chicagoan finesse. I returned often for their shrimp-avocado taco, becoming hooked on its piquant-creamy sauce and pleasingly loud crunch. My rendition of that taste memory adds the complex nuttiness of toasted sesame and charred corn to the mix – and every bite takes me back there.

SERVES 4

340g (12oz) can of sweetcorn
    (285g/10oz drained weight)
2 Tbsp toasted sesame oil
1 Tbsp sesame seeds, plus optional
    extra to garnish
1 tsp fine sea salt
1 Tbsp onion powder
8 corn or flour tortillas
vegetable oil, for brushing
1 tsp sweet paprika, plus extra
    for sprinkling

300g (10½oz) peeled cooked large
    prawns (shrimp)
1 Tbsp Worcestershire sauce
5 Tbsp tomato ketchup
5 Tbsp Kewpie mayonnaise
1 Tbsp cognac or brandy
    (optional)
2 tsp Tabasco sauce
zest and juice of 1 lemon
½ large iceberg lettuce, finely
    shredded

Preheat the grill to high. In a large bowl mix together the drained sweetcorn, 1 tablespoon of the sesame oil, sesame seeds, salt and onion powder. Set aside.

Use a 10cm (4in) cookie cutter or a glass to stamp out eight tostadas from the tortillas (keep the scraps for making breadcrumbs). Brush with a little vegetable oil, sprinkle with a little paprika, then space apart on a baking sheet.

Grill over a high heat for 5–6 minutes, turning regularly until toasted but not burnt. Leave to cool completely; they will crisp up as they do.

Using the same baking sheet, spread out the sweetcorn and grill for 6–7 minutes, turning regularly, until charred. Set aside.

Pat dry the cooked prawns with paper towels, then chop into large chunks and add to a bowl. Drizzle over the Worcestershire sauce, mix well, then drizzle over the remaining tablespoon of toasted sesame oil.

Make a sauce by stirring together the ketchup, mayonnaise, cognac (if using), Tabasco, lemon zest and juice, and the teaspoon of paprika. Add to the prawns and mix well.

Pile the tostados high with finely shredded lettuce, the dressed prawns and charred sweetcorn. Garnish with paprika and more sesame seeds if you like.

SESAME CHICKEN
PARMIGIANA

The renaissance of Italian–American 'mom-and-pop' restaurants in London is something I'm wholeheartedly behind – primarily for the flavour-forward chicken dishes they've revived. Chicken piccata with its lemon-buttered caper sauce I could eat every day; chicken cacciatore with its base of intense tomatoes, onions and mushrooms is a delicious hug; and chicken scarpariello, rich in Italian sausage, vinegar and pickled peppers, is palate-tingling heaven. Chicken parmigiana is the undisputed star of this culinary canon – crunchily coated with parmesan, smothered in sauce, loaded with mozzarella then baked. My version includes toasted sesame for a layer of smoked nuttiness that's totally unnecessary – but totally delicious.

SERVES 2

2 large chicken breasts, boneless and skinless (350g/12oz)
2 tsp onion powder
2 Tbsp toasted sesame oil, plus extra for drizzling
olive oil, for frying
½ large onion, finely chopped
5 fat garlic cloves, crushed to a paste
1 tsp dried oregano
400g (14oz) can Italian chopped tomatoes
1 Tbsp tomato purée (paste)

2 Tbsp red wine vinegar
20g (¾oz) butter
6 Tbsp plain (all-purpose) flour, for dredging
2 eggs
95g (3½oz) dried breadcrumbs
60g (2¼oz) parmesan, very finely grated
1 tsp coarsely ground black pepper
sunflower or vegetable oil, for frying
125g (4½oz) fresh mozzarella ball
2 tsp sesame seeds
3–4 basil leaves, finely chopped
fine sea salt

Use a rolling pin to flatten the chicken breasts between two sheets of baking paper into thin steaks approximately 1.5cm (⅝in) thick. Sprinkle over 1 teaspoon of salt and the onion powder then leave for 15 minutes. Next, drizzle with the toasted sesame oil, coating the breasts all over, then set aside.

Meanwhile, make the sauce. Heat a splash of olive oil in a large saucepan, add the onion and sizzle over a medium heat for 5–6 minutes until it turns translucent. Next, add the garlic and oregano, and sizzle for another 2 minutes, before adding the chopped tomatoes. Cook over a medium heat for 3–4 minutes, then add the tomato purée, vinegar and 1 teaspoon of salt. Simmer for 15 minutes over a medium heat, until it reduces into an intense thick sauce. Add the butter, simmer for a final 5 minutes and set aside.

Prepare three bowls for coating the chicken: add the flour to the first; whisk the eggs in the second; and fill the third with a mix of breadcrumbs, 30g (1oz) of parmesan and the black pepper.

Dredge the chicken breasts in the flour, coating all over. Shake off the excess then dunk into the egg, and finally into the parmesan breadcrumbs. Toss to coat all over.

Heat 1cm of sunflower or vegetable oil in a large frying pan to 170°C/338°F. Sizzle the coated chicken breasts, one at a time, for 6–7 minutes, turning every few minutes, until golden brown on the outside and cooked through. Transfer to a baking sheet.

Preheat the grill to its highest setting. Spoon the tomato sauce over the breaded chicken, then sprinkle with the remaining 30g (1oz) of parmesan and tear over the mozzarella. Grill for 5 minutes until the cheese starts to melt and bubble.

Remove from the grill, drizzle with a splash of toasted sesame oil, top with sesame seeds and chopped basil. Return to the grill and cook for 3–4 minutes until golden brown. Enjoy with buttered spaghetti.

BLUEBERRY & SESAME PANCAKES
WITH APPLE PIE BUTTER v

My love of Americana is entrenched in recollections of epic family road trips from Orlando to Miami in the early nineties. They cemented my childhood love of fluffy, syrup-soaked American-style pancakes with sweet jammy compote for breakfast – especially when served up in a stack at one of those retro roadside diners that seemed to be a living manifestation of both *Grease* and *Happy Days*. When it comes to pancakes nowadays, I like to add in grown-up flavours like toasted sesame – and then undo all that adulting by being just as freehand with the syrup as I was back then.

SERVES 3-4

200g (7oz) plain (all-purpose) flour
75g (2½oz) caster (superfine) sugar
¼ tsp bicarbonate of soda
    (baking soda)
1 tsp baking powder
2 Tbsp toasted sesame seeds,
    plus extra to serve
150ml (5fl oz) buttermilk or kefir
135ml (4½fl oz) full-fat (whole) milk
1 large egg
2 Tbsp toasted sesame oil, plus extra
    to serve
150g (5½oz) blueberries
fine sea salt

For the apple pie butter

50g (1¾oz) butter, plus extra for frying
1 tsp ground cinnamon
½ tsp ground allspice
1 tsp ground ginger
1 Tbsp caster (superfine) sugar
125g (4½oz) Granny Smith apples
    (about 2 small ones), peeled and
    diced
250g (9oz) apple purée
Greek yoghurt or thickly whipped
    double (heavy) cream, to serve
maple syrup, to serve (optional)

In a large bowl, whisk together the flour, sugar, bicarbonate of soda, baking powder, sesame seeds and a pinch of salt.

Next, in a jug, whisk together the buttermilk, milk, egg and toasted sesame oil.

Gently whisk the wet ingredients into the dry until just combined – don't overmix. Tumble in the blueberries, mix once more, then refrigerate for 30 minutes to let the batter rest.

For the apple pie butter, melt the butter in a saucepan, then add the ground spices and sugar. Whisk well, then add the diced apples. Cook for 2–3 minutes over a medium heat until they start to become tender, then add the apple purée. Simmer over a medium heat for 10–12 minutes, stirring continuously, until reduced by a third into a thick apple butter. Set aside and keep warm.

To cook the pancakes, heat a large frying pan over a medium–high heat – not too high or they can burn. Add a knob of butter to the pan, then spoon over a ladleful of batter. Cook for 1 minute until bubbles start to appear on the surface, then flip and cook for another 1 minute. Cook for a final 2 minutes, flipping regularly, until the pancake is golden on the outside and cooked through. Keep warm and repeat with the rest of the batter to make 12 pancakes.

Stack the pancakes on a plate, layered with warm apple pie butter, and dollops of Greek yoghurt. Scatter with sesame seeds, a drizzle of toasted sesame oil and maple syrup, if you like.

BLOOD ORANGE, SESAME
& MARZIPAN POLENTA CAKE v

Along with the Taj Mahal, Rachmaninov's 3rd Symphony, Bach's 4th cello suite, *Anna Karenina*, and the cult movie *Death Becomes Her*, it is my strong-held opinion that the invention of marzipan is one of the pinnacle achievements of humankind. For this reason, I'm suspicious of people who say they don't like it – because they are not only wrong but almost certainly lying. Pairing this gastronomic triumph with sesame intensifies its nutty, toasty aromas and the addition of tart blood orange further perks up the flavours. This cake is equally delicious made with clementines, mandarins, lemons or ruby grapefruit; however, omitting the marzipan is strictly prohibited.

SERVES 8

225g (8oz) caster (superfine) sugar
100g (3½oz) light brown sugar
2 blood oranges or oranges
1 lemon
35ml (7 tsp) toasted sesame oil
225g (8oz) very soft butter, plus
    an extra 25g (1oz) for the glaze
4 large eggs
100g (3½oz) Greek yoghurt,
    plus extra to serve
175g (6oz) polenta (cornmeal)
150g (5½oz) ground almonds
2 Tbsp poppy seeds
1½ tsp baking powder
½ tsp fine sea salt
100g (3½oz) marzipan, small diced
2 Tbsp sesame seeds

Preheat the oven to 175°C fan/195°C/385°F/Gas mark 5½ and place a baking sheet on the middle shelf. Line a 20cm (8in) round cake tin with greaseproof paper.

Add 100g (3½oz) of the caster sugar and all of the brown sugar to the bowl of a stand mixer, then grate over the zest of both oranges and the lemon. Use your hands to rub the zest into the sugar, then add the toasted sesame oil and whisk well.

Add the soft butter to the bowl, and beat with the paddle attachment for 4–5 minutes, scraping down the sides as needed until everything is combined.

In a jug, whisk together the eggs and Greek yoghurt. In a separate bowl, combine the polenta, almonds, poppy seeds, baking powder, ½ teaspoon of salt and the marzipan.

Very slowly pour the egg mix into the stand mixer bowl, and continuously beat slowly with the paddle until it has just combined. Tip in the dry ingredients in one go and continue mixing until everything is fully combined, scraping down the sides as needed. Carefully pour the batter into the lined tin.

Place the tin on the hot baking sheet and bake for 50–55 minutes until the cake is coming away from the sides. Check after 30 minutes, and cover with foil if browning too quickly.

Make the syrup. Squeeze out 150ml (5½fl oz) of orange and 3 tablespoons of lemon juice. Melt the 25g (1oz) of butter in a pan, then add the sesame seeds. Sizzle for 2–3 minutes over a low–medium heat, then add the remaining 100g (3½oz) of caster sugar, the orange and lemon juice. Cook over a medium heat for 10–12 minutes until reduced by half into an intense syrup. Take the cake out of the oven, and cool in the tin for 10 minutes. Prick the top all over with a cocktail stick, then spoon over the citrussy syrup and sesame seeds. Leave for 1 hour for the syrup to soak in. Serve with Greek yoghurt or crème fraîche.

SALTED-SESAME
BASQUE CHEESECAKE v

A few years ago, I spent a week in San Sebastián for the Gastronomika congress – one of the most mind-blowing culinary experiences of my life. The number of times I ate the iconic Basque cheesecake from La Viña during that trip goes into double figures – and was fully worth every extra gym class in the months that followed. While a masterpiece in its own right, adding toasted sesame oil, being extra liberal with the sea salt and baking it in a loaf tin brings in a few layers of complexity that enhance its extreme pleasure just that smidgen more.

SERVES 8

olive oil, for brushing
300ml (10½fl oz) soured cream,
 at room temperature
3 Tbsp runny honey, plus extra
 to drizzle
7 tsp toasted sesame oil, plus extra
 to drizzle
zest from ½ lemon
2 tsp fine sea salt
1¾ tsp vanilla bean paste
5 large eggs, at room temperature
290g (10¼oz) caster (superfine) sugar
3 Tbsp cornflour (cornstarch)
750g (1lb 10oz) mascarpone,
 at room temperature
toasted sesame seeds, to decorate

Preheat the oven to 210°C fan/230°C/450°F/Gas mark 8 and place a baking sheet on the middle shelf to get hot.

Oil a large narrow loaf tin (30 x 13 x 8cm/ 12 x 5 x 3¼in) or 2 litre (68fl oz) volume rectangular tin. Line with crumpled baking paper, leaving plenty of overhang on each side.

In a large bowl, slowly mix together the room temperature soured cream, honey, sesame oil, lemon zest, salt and vanilla bean paste. Set aside.

Crack the room temperature eggs into a small jug and whisk. Separately, whisk together the sugar and cornflour in a bowl ensuring there are no lumps.

Add the mascarpone to the bowl of a stand mixer with a paddle attachment and beat for 1 minute until soft. Scrape down the edges, then pour in the soured cream mix. Beat for another minute until combined, scraping down the sides again.

Add the sugar and beat slowly for another 1 minute until fully combined – scrape down the sides again. Then, with the mixer running as slowly as possible, very slowly trickle in the eggs – you want to add as little air as possible.

Give it a final mix with a spatula – again scraping down the sides – and then pour everything into the lined tin, allowing a gap at the top of at least 1cm (½in) for it to rise. Tap the filled tin gently on your work surface to release any bubbles.

Place the tin on the baking sheet in the oven and bake for 30 minutes until it puffs up, is burnished on top but still wobbly in the middle. If not burnished enough, give it another 3–5 minutes but do not overbake or you won't get a smooth creamy texture.

Remove from the oven and let it cool completely in the tin – it continues to cook as it cools. Refrigerate for at least 3–4 hours to set fully.

Using the paper to help you, transfer the cheesecake to a plate and decorate with a drizzle of honey, toasted sesame oil and sesame seeds. Serve with some tart berries if you wish.

DAME BLANCHE WITH
SESAME-COFFEE TOFFEE v

It was a true pleasure to discover that the relatively mundane-sounding 'vanilla and chocolate ice-cream sundae' has a fabulously extravagant title in Belgium: a 'Dame Blanche'. The original all-white dessert was created by French chef Escoffier, and named after an 1825 comic-fantasy opera. My take enriches the fudge sauce with the toasted nuttiness of sesame oil, and adds essential crunch via bitter-sweet coffee brittle. Pile high with whipped cream and top with a maraschino cocktail cherry if you're feeling extra frou-frou (which I always am).

SERVES 4

8 scoops good-quality vanilla
   ice cream
8 chocolate wafer rolls
cocktail cherries, to decorate

For the toffee
10g (¼oz) butter
1 Tbsp toasted sesame oil
125g (4½oz) light brown sugar
1 Tbsp ground coffee beans
1 Tbsp toasted sesame seeds,
   plus extra to decorate

For the fudge sauce
25g (1oz) butter
100g (3½oz) light brown sugar
200ml (7fl oz) double (heavy) cream,
   plus optional 100ml (3½fl oz)
   extra, whipped, to serve
1 Tbsp toasted sesame oil
2 tablespoons cocoa powder
   (Dutch processed)
1½ tsp fine sea salt
100g (3½oz) dark chocolate
   (minimum 60% cocoa),
   finely chopped

First, make the toffee. Line a baking sheet with a silicone mat or use baking paper brushed with a little neutral oil.

Heat the butter and toasted sesame oil in a frying pan over a medium heat, whisk well, then add the sugar. Gently warm it to 150°C/300°F, swirling the pan, but not stirring too much as the sugar can seize up. Carefully pour out the molten sugar onto the lined sheet, and spread out in a thin (2–3mm/⅛in) layer using a spatula.

Sprinkle over the ground coffee and toasted sesame seeds then, using another piece of baking paper or the spatula, gently press these into the hot sugar. Leave to harden completely for 20 minutes, then snap into shards.

For the fudge sauce, heat the butter in a small saucepan over a medium heat with the sugar, cream, sesame oil, cocoa and salt, whisking continuously. Bring to just below boiling point, then take off the heat.

Add a third of the chopped chocolate, and whisk until it's melted through. Repeat with another third and then the final one. You should have a thick luscious sauce. If any oil has separated, add 1 tablespoon of cold water and whisk through vigorously – this will bring everything together.

To assemble, scoop the vanilla ice cream into sundae glasses and, if you like, pile on some extra whipped cream. Spoon over the warm fudge sauce and sprinkle over shards of toffee. Decorate with wafer rolls and a cocktail cherry.

Miso

swalty and umami,
invitingly funky,
complexly full-bodied,
subtly sweet,
creamy savouriness.

This Japanese paste is made by fermenting soya beans and grains – such as rice, barley or oats – with koji fungus and salt. White miso, the mildest in terms of salty-savouriness, is fermented for just three months, which gives it a rounded sweetness, whereas yellow miso, fermented for a year, has a slightly earthier flavour and a more subtle sweetness. Red miso, fermented for one to two years, develops a mellow savoury depth, and brown miso, fermented for at least two years, is the strongest with a rich, pungently salty savouriness. 'Extra Aged Miso' is fermented for more than three years, allowing the flavours to mature slowly to even more intense levels of umami funk. Flavoured versions of miso are combined with ingredients like seaweed, yuzu, chilli, dashi, ume plum and even cocoa beans. The best-quality miso pastes are sold refrigerated.

MISO-MUSTARD, CORNICHON & SAMPHIRE BAKED HADDOCK

During 2020's global mayhem, I found myself quite suddenly in limbo in France for ten days. As one who revels in moments of unforeseen providence, I took this as a sign that the universe wanted me to explore – and so embarked on a solo journey from Nice to Paris, taking in Grasse, Lyon, Grenoble and Dijon along the way. My penultimate stop was the city of Beaune in the heart of Burgundy: its cobbled streets, renaissance grandeur, some very garlicky escargots, and wineries at every turn utterly bewitched me. However, the sight that made me most happy was the Edmond Fallot moutarderie – where I tasted every mustard variety they make – from blackcurrant, basil and tarragon, to walnut, red wine and gingerbread! I was astonished by how intricately complex and savoury each one was – something I now replicate in my cooking. The trick is to accentuate whatever mustard I happen to be using with a spoonful of miso – the alchemy of which this simple but delicious recipe will reveal.

SERVES 2

100g (3½oz) samphire
2 haddock or hake fillets, pin-boned
    and skinned (about 300g/10½oz)
175g (6oz) crème fraîche
2 heaped Tbsp brown or white miso
1 Tbsp English mustard
2 tsp capers, chopped

30g (1oz) cornichons, chopped
    (about 4)
small handful of dill fronds, finely
    chopped, plus extra to garnish
2 garlic cloves, crushed to a paste
zest and juice of ½ lemon
1 Tbsp light brown sugar
1 tsp coarsely crushed black pepper
fine sea salt

Preheat the oven to 180°C fan/200°C/400°F/ Gas mark 6.

Select a baking dish, large enough to comfortably accommodate the size of your fish fillets. Pile a high bed of samphire into the dish and place the fillets on top as a single layer to cover the samphire as far as you can.

In a large bowl, whisk together all the remaining ingredients, adding a pinch of salt. Spoon this miso-mustard crème over the haddock and samphire, covering them completely in a thick layer.

Bake in the oven for 14–16 minutes until the fish is cooked through and the crème is starting to turn golden on top.

Serve with some watercress or other peppery green leaves. Garnish with some dill fronds.

Tip: If you like, you can sprinkle over some breadcrumbs and finish under a hot grill for 2 minutes to burnish the top.

GARAM MASALA, MISO & FENNEL CHICKEN TRAYBAKE

The intercultural marriage of any Indian spices with miso is something that I am perpetually experimenting with in the kitchen. Be it a South Indian *sambhar masala*, a Kashmiri *basaar masala*, a Punjabi *tandoori masala* or Bengali *panch puran masala,* there seems to be no regional spice blend that isn't deliciously augmented by the savoury charms of miso. Garam masala is the one most widely used in northern India – and it's become something of a trend in recent years, appearing in everything from popcorn to pizza, chocolate to gelato! My slightly more conventional recipe is for a tasty quick and easy mid-week meal – made even more effortless as it can be served from the tray.

SERVES 4

zest and juice of 2 lemons
½ tsp cardamom seeds (removed
    from the husks), crushed
8 chicken thighs, bone in but skinned
    (about 1.25kg/2lb 12oz)
2 Tbsp garam masala
1 tsp ground turmeric
3 Tbsp brown or white miso
6 garlic cloves, crushed to a paste

1 tsp grated fresh ginger root
1 tsp freshly ground black pepper
2 Tbsp apple cider vinegar
2 fennel bulbs, sliced in wedges
1 large red onion, sliced in wedges
2 yellow (bell) peppers,
    deseeded and sliced
olive oil, for roasting
2 tsp cumin seeds, crushed
a few dill fronds, chopped
fine sea salt

In a large mixing bowl, whisk together the lemon juice, 1½ teaspoons of salt and crushed cardamom seeds. Slash the chicken thighs two or three times through to the bone, then add them to the lemony brine, mixing well to ensure it gets in all of the slashes. Set aside to brine for 30 minutes.

Next, make the spice paste. Whisk together the garam masala, turmeric, miso, garlic, ginger, black pepper, lemon zest and vinegar. Pour the paste over the brined chicken, mixing well with your hands to ensure it gets deep into the grooves. Put into the refrigerator to marinate for 1–2 hours.

Preheat the oven to 180°C fan/200°C/400°F/Gas mark 6. Spread out the fennel, onion and yellow peppers in a large roasting tray. Drizzle liberally with oil, sprinkle with salt and the crushed cumin seeds. Place the marinated chicken on top, spooning out all the spice paste to cover the thighs completely.

Roast for 45–50 minutes until the chicken is cooked through, charred on top and the vegetables are tender – cover everything with foil if it's browning too quickly. Sprinkle over chopped dill, another drizzle of oil and a final squeeze of lemon juice to finish. Enjoy.

CHICKEN FRICASSÉE
WITH MISO MUSHROOMS

School-dinner dishes from the 1990s have become something of an internet sensation lately –
particularly rainbow-sprinkled tray cake with custard, deep-fried Spam fritters, classic cheese flan
and Arctic roll. I have nostalgic reverence for them all... however, it's blandly creamy and suspiciously
gloopy chicken fricassée that I pine for most. Properly made, this classic French country stew is rich
in browned butter, slow-cooked mushrooms, creamy stock and herbs. I've added miso to amp up the
mushrooms with yet more savoury oomph. It's as far from school dinners as you can get, but just as
comforting nonetheless.

SERVES 4

4 chicken breasts, bone in, skin on
    (about 850g/1lb 4oz total weight)
60g (2¼oz) butter
olive oil, for frying
400g (14oz) chestnut mushrooms,
    sliced
2 heaped Tbsp brown or white miso
6 garlic cloves, slivered
1 large onion, diced
2 large celery sticks, diced

1 Tbsp finely chopped thyme, plus
    extra to garnish
1 tsp freshly grated nutmeg, plus extra
    to garnish
250ml (9fl oz) dry white wine
250ml (9fl oz) chicken stock
150ml (5fl oz) crème fraîche
1 large egg yolk
1 Tbsp cornflour (cornstarch)
zest and juice of 1 lemon
fine sea salt and freshly ground black
    pepper

Make three or four cuts on each chicken breast
using a sharp knife, cutting right through the
skin. Add a generous seasoning of salt and pepper,
getting it deep into the slits. Leave for 30 minutes.

Melt 20g (¾oz) of the butter with a splash of olive
oil in a large pan over a medium–high heat. Add
the chicken breasts, two at a time, skin-side down.
Brown on all sides for 8–10 minutes – you're not
cooking the chicken through, just ensuring it has
a dark golden brown colour all over. Remove from
the pan and set aside on a baking sheet.

Add another 20g (¾oz) of butter to the pan with
a splash of oil, then add the mushrooms and a
pinch of salt. Cook for 10–12 minutes, until they
have reduced in volume by half. Add the miso
and garlic, then cook for another 5 minutes.

Add the remaining butter, a final splash of oil,
the onion and celery. Fry for 6–7 minutes, then
stir in the thyme and nutmeg. Once the onions

have started to turn translucent, add the browned
chicken breasts back to the pan, mixing well
to coat all over.

Pour the white wine into the pan, mix well
and simmer until the liquid has fully evaporated.

Next, add the chicken stock, stir again, cover
with a lid and simmer over a medium–high heat
for 10 minutes.

In a small jug, whisk together the crème fraîche,
egg yolk, cornflour and lemon zest. Remove the
lid from the pan, stir in the creamy mixture and
simmer for 12–15 minutes – uncovered – until
the sauce is thick and creamy.

Season with a good pinch of salt, stir through the
lemon juice, then simmer for a final minute. Taste
and add more salt or lemon if needed. Garnish
with extra thyme and nutmeg.

STICKY LEMONGRASS-MISO LAMB RIBS WITH ZINGY CARROT SALAD

I knew Andi Oliver and I were kindred spirits when, on a visit to Antigua, she suggested we explore the St John's farmers' market... at 5.30am. As a fellow early-riser who loves nothing more than a bazaar, this was music to my ears. I won't forget the sight of buttery orange pumpkins piled high; freshly caught grouper and iridescent mahi mahi; cassava and plantain in every hue; spiky soursop and breadfruit; guava jam, tamarind pulp and, much to my surprise, lemongrass. In Antigua, where lemongrass is known as fever grass, the leafy green stalks are brewed into aromatic teas to calm all ailments. This recipe evokes the delights of that trip – amplifying the fragrant lemongrass lamb-ribs with rounded savoury miso.

SERVES 3–4

8 meaty lamb ribs (1.25kg/2lb 12oz)
65g (2¼oz) lemongrass,
    stalks bruised
85g (3oz) finely chopped fresh
    ginger root
3 Tbsp brown miso
3 fat garlic cloves
3 Tbsp apple cider vinegar
2 tsp Chinese five spice
2 Tbsp runny honey
2 Tbsp dark brown sugar
fine sea salt

For the salad
zest and juice of 1½ limes
½ tsp toasted sesame oil
1 tsp fish sauce
1 tsp sriracha sauce
2 tsp dark brown sugar
400g (14oz) carrots, ribboned
small handful of coriander (cilantro),
    chopped
1 Tbsp toasted sesame seeds

Put the lamb ribs in a large saucepan, then add half the lemongrass, two-thirds of the chopped ginger, 1 tablespoon of the miso and enough boiling water to just cover the ribs fully. Bring to the boil, then reduce to a simmer, cover with a lid and cook for 55 minutes–1 hour until the ribs start to become tender.

Meanwhile, use a small grinder to blitz together the remaining lemongrass and ginger, the garlic and vinegar to a very fine paste. Pour into a bowl then mix in 2 tablespoons of brown miso, the Chinese five spice, honey, sugar and 1 teaspoon of salt. Set aside.

Preheat the oven to 200°C fan/220°C/425°F/Gas mark 7 and line a roasting tray with foil. Remove the ribs from the broth (use this for soups or casseroles) and place on the tray, spaced well apart. Bake for 15 minutes, then remove from the oven and drain off some of the lamb fat (keep this; it's great for roast potatoes!).

Spread the glaze very liberally over the ribs, then return the tray to the oven and cook for a further 15–20 minutes, turning and basting halfway through, until they are sticky, charred and tender in the middle. Cover with foil they are browning too quickly.

For the salad, whisk together the lime zest and juice, sesame oil, fish sauce, sriracha, sugar and a good pinch of salt in a jug. Add the ribboned carrots, coriander and sesame seeds to a bowl and toss with the dressing. Serve the ribs hot from the oven with the carrot salad on the side.

MISO GANACHE FUDGE CAKE

There was this cream-covered chocolate cake from an Italian bakery, Brucciani's, in Leicester Market that was the candle-lit epicentre of every family celebration of my childhood. I've been searching for the sensory thrill of its rich sponge and whipped cloud-like icing (that was as salty as it was sweet) – for almost twenty years, but never quite found the full sensation of it in anything. Then, about a year ago, sipping on a bowl of miso soup in a sushi bar in Soho, something in my mind was triggered: suddenly it was one of my childhood birthday parties again. That evening, I got to work on a sponge cake that was as chocolatey as possible, with a luscious ganache icing made salty-savoury with a little miso. With this cake, it can forever be my ninth birthday.

SERVES 8

125ml (4fl oz) sunflower oil, plus extra
    for brushing
75g (2½oz) cocoa powder
    (Dutch processed)
1 heaped Tbsp instant espresso
    powder
4 Tbsp black treacle
125ml (4fl oz) boiling water
200g (7oz) plain (all-purpose) flour
1 tsp bicarbonate of soda
    (baking soda)
1½ tsp baking powder
½ tsp fine sea salt

200g (7oz) golden caster (superfine)
    sugar
100g (3½oz) butter
2 large eggs, plus 1 yolk
125ml (4fl oz) double (heavy) cream
1 Tbsp apple cider vinegar

For the ganache
325g (11½oz) white chocolate,
    snapped into small pieces
200ml (7fl oz) double (heavy) cream
2 Tbsp white miso
1 tsp vanilla bean paste
50g (1¾oz) butter

Preheat the oven to 175°C fan/195°C/385°F/ Gas mark 5½. Brush a deep-sided 20cm (8in) springform cake tin with a little sunflower oil and line the base with a disc of baking paper.

Put the cocoa powder, espresso powder and treacle in a jug. Pour over the boiling water, whisk well and set aside to cool. Sift the flour, bicarbonate of soda, baking powder and salt into a large bowl.

Add the sugar and oil to the bowl of a stand mixer fitted with a paddle attachment and mix well. Melt the butter in a saucepan over a medium heat and brown for 5–6 minutes – swirling gently – until nutty and dark golden. Pour the butter into the stand mixer bowl and beat well, scraping down the sides as needed.

Next, add the whole eggs, egg yolk and cream, beating for 1 minute to combine. Pour in the cocoa-treacle mix, beating for 1–2 minutes.

Stop the motor, tip in half the flour mix, then very slowly beat until everything is combined, scraping down the sides as needed. Repeat with the remaining flour mix, then add the vinegar, beating on medium speed for 30 seconds to combine everything evenly.

Continued...

Place the lined cake tin on a baking sheet. Pour the batter into the tin, scraping the bowl clean with a spatula. Tap the tin on the work surface to release any bubbles, then transfer the tin (on its sheet) to the middle rack of the oven. Bake for 45–50 minutes or until a cocktail stick inserted into the centre comes out clean.

Remove from the oven and let the cake cool in the tin for 15 minutes. Then, very carefully, invert upside down onto a wire rack to cool completely.

Meanwhile, make the ganache. Put the chocolate in a large heatproof, microwavable bowl. Add the cream, white miso, vanilla bean paste and butter

to a small saucepan and whisk over a low heat until just below boiling point. Pour this over the chocolate pieces and whisk to combine. If needed, put the mix in the microwave for a few seconds

Chill the ganache for 10 minutes, whisk vigorously, then chill for another 20–25 minutes until it's the texture of spreadable butter. Mix again, then spread over the cake with a palette knife to cover the top in a very thick layer – or both the top and sides in a medium-thick layer. Alternatively, pipe the ganache using a fancy nozzle if you like. Chill for 30 minutes to set completely. Enjoy.

BUTTERSCOTCH-MISO
& CANDIED LEMON COOKIES

The salty miso-enriched cookie is a modern gastronomic powerhouse in every one of its guises. My contribution to this genre counters the savoury depth of miso with zesty candied lemon peel and the nostalgic sugary crunch of hard butterscotch candies. A brush of lemony syrup adds an extra hit of tang, ensuring that these cookies will ignite every tastebud in your mouth at once. From my experience, they are moreish in a way that can become all consuming – so it's probably best to make a double batch from the get-go.

MAKES 18

2 unwaxed lemons
235g (8½oz) caster (superfine) sugar,
     plus extra for coating the pee
4 Tbsp waterl
240g (8½oz) very soft butter
2–3 Tbsp white miso (to taste;
     I like more!)
125g (4½oz) light brown sugar

50g (1¾oz) demerara sugar,
     plus extra for rolling and
     decorating (optional)
1 large egg
1½ tsp vanilla bean paste
375g (13oz) plain (all-purpose) flour
1 tsp bicarbonate of soda (baking
     soda)
½ tsp fine sea salt
75g (2½oz) hard butterscotch candies
     (about 15)

Preheat the oven to 120°C fan/140°C/275°F/Gas mark 1 and line a baking sheet with baking paper. Using a sharp knife or vegetable peeler, carefully remove the peel from the lemons with as little of the white pith as possible. Slice the peels into very thin (matchstick) strips.

Measure into a small saucepan 85g (3oz) of the caster sugar, 4 tablespoons of lemon juice and the 4 tablespoons of water. Place over a medium–high heat until fully dissolved. Add the strips of lemon peel and simmer for 10–12 minutes until the peel turns translucent.

Drain into a bowl through a sieve – keeping the lemony syrup – and pressing down to remove as much liquid from the peel as possible. Spread out over the lined sheet and bake in the low oven for 20–22 minutes until completely dry – tossing and

turning halfway through. Remove from the oven, dust with extra caster sugar and leave to cool completely.

In the bowl of a stand mixer fitted with a paddle attachment, beat together the butter, miso, the remaining 150g (5½oz) of caster sugar, the soft brown sugar and the demerara sugar until completely smooth. Add the egg and vanilla bean paste to the bowl, then beat for another minute, scraping down the sides to ensure everything is fully combined.

In a separate bowl, whisk together the flour, bicarbonate of soda and salt. Use a rolling pin to bash the butterscotch candies into small shards, then add these to the bowl.

Chop most of your candied lemon peel into small chunks (keep a few strips whole to decorate) and mix these through the flour mix.

Add half the dry ingredients to the butter mixture and beat until fully incorporated. Tip in the rest of the dry ingredients, beating for 30–45 seconds until there are no dry patches. Compact the dough into 18 tight round balls (about 60g/2¼oz each), roll in demerara sugar, then refrigerate for 30 minutes.

Preheat the oven to 175°C fan/195°C/385°F/Gas mark 5½. Place no more than six balls on two baking sheets, well spaced apart – they will spread as they cook. Bake for 17–18 minutes – rotating the sheets halfway through – until golden brown.

Remove from the oven. Use a round glass or pastry cutter to shape the warm cookies while they are still soft into perfect circles if you like. Leave to cool on the baking sheets for 10 minutes, then transfer to a wire rack to cool completely, while you cook the remaining six. The cookies harden as they cool, becoming crunchy on the outside.

The lemon syrup will have transformed into a loose jelly by this point. Give it a quick whisk, then brush over the cooled cookies. Decorate with the reserved strips of candied peel and extra demerara sugar, if you like. Enjoy.

Tip: If you don't have any butterscotch candies, use toffee chunks or white chocolate chips instead.

'Nduja

cured and complex,
addictively fiery,
satisfyingly lardy,
bitingly spiced,
smooth meatiness.

The crimson-red, spiced, cured, spreadable pork sausage from southern Italy combines minced (ground) cuts of pork meat – jowl, leg, shoulder and belly – with a high proportion of lardy fat, herbs, salt and fiery, sun-dried Calabrian chillies. The spiced sausage meat is packed into an intestinal casing, smoked lightly, then left to cure naturally for anything between four weeks and six months, which imparts a delicate sour funk. You can buy 'nduja as a bulging fresh sausage still inside its casing, or in glass jars where its spreadable centre has been scooped out of the casing. Sobrasada is a Spanish alternative to 'nduja, which is made from Iberian pork and flavoured with paprika. Vegan alternatives are also available.

'NDUJA-BAKED
RATATOUILLE-NATA

I'm fascinated by 'synaesthesia' – where the senses connect in ways that can lead to people hearing colours, seeing aromas, or tasting music. The Disney movie *Ratatouille* (2007), about a rat called Remy with a flair for flavour, played right into my intrigue, fusing visuals with sound – the screen erupting in a flurry of Kandinsky-esque swirls and swooshes whenever Remy's internal taste world was aroused, most thrillingly when he crafted a meticulous ratatouille. My version of that dish adds the heat of 'nduja and vinegary spike of a caponata. The end result tastes, smells, looks, sounds – and feels – delicious.

SERVES 4

2 Tbsp balsamic vinegar
2 Tbsp runny honey
2 Tbsp capers
3 Tbsp raisins
3 Tbsp pitted black olives, chopped
500g (1lb 2oz) tomato passata
100g (3½oz) 'nduja (4 Tbsp)
4 garlic cloves, crushed to a paste

1 tsp dried oregano
2 large courgettes (zucchini),
    one yellow, one green
1 large aubergine (eggplant)
1 large red (bell) pepper, deseeded
1 large red onion
olive oil, for drizzling
100g (3½oz) mascarpone
fine sea salt

In a small bowl, whisk together the balsamic vinegar and honey, then add the capers, raisins and olives, ensuring they are fully submerged. Set aside to macerate.

Next, set a large saucepan over a low heat and add the passata, three-quarters of the 'nduja, the garlic, oregano and 1 teaspoon of fine salt. Gently heat until the 'nduja has melted into the tomatoes. Increase the heat to medium and simmer for 10–12 minutes to concentrate the sauce. Pour into the base of a round 24cm (9½in) diameter ovenproof dish.

Slice the courgettes, aubergine, red pepper and red onion into discs or half-moons 2mm (1⁄16in) thick, making them roughly the same height.

Arrange the slices alternately in a spiral on top of the 'nduja sauce – working from the outside in to form a single multicoloured layer.

Preheat the oven to 180°C fan/200°C/400°F/Gas mark 6. Drizzle the vegetables liberally with olive oil, sprinkle over a pinch of salt and place the dish in the oven on top of a baking sheet to catch any spills. Bake for 30 minutes.

Remove from the oven and spoon over the capers, raisins and olives, plus all the honeyed vinegar. Return to the oven and cook for another 15 minutes until cooked through, bubbling and very slightly burnished on top. Place some foil over the top if it's browning too quickly.

Remove from the oven and let it rest for 10 minutes. Meanwhile, mix together the mascarpone with the remaining 'nduja. Spoon dollops of the 'nduja cream on top of the dish – letting the cream melt in. Serve with crusty bread.

'NDUJA & ROQUEFORT
MAC 'N CHEESE

A few summers ago, I spent a few days in Luxembourg. During my stay I took in some very memorable culinary delights, including a tour of crémant wineries in Alsace over the French border; a very nineties 'fine-dining' restaurant where everything came with a coulis; and a rustic brasserie that served lardy choucroute laced with Riesling, and a cardiac arrest inducing fondue made with blue cheese. That sharp cheese and smoky pork combination is imprinted on my taste memory. It's encapsulated (somewhat less extravagantly) in this easy weekday recipe for classic mac 'n cheese – enlivened by the spiced meatiness of 'nduja and the creamy bite of Roquefort.

SERVES 6

300g (10½oz) macaroni pasta
500ml (17fl oz) full-fat (whole) milk
1 tsp freshly grated nutmeg
1 garlic clove, crushed to a paste
1 egg yolk
2 tsp English mustard

65g (2¼oz) butter
75g (2½oz) plain (all-purpose) flour
85g (3oz) 'nduja (3 heaped Tbsp)
150g (5½oz) mature Cheddar, grated
100g (3½oz) Roquefort, crumbled
Herby Pangrattato (page 59),
    or 6 Tbsp breadcrumbs
salt

Par-cook the macaroni pasta in a large pan of salted boiling water for 6 minutes until al dente. Drain well and set aside. Preheat the oven to 200°C fan/220°C/425°F/Gas mark 7.

In a small jug, whisk together the milk, nutmeg and garlic. Then, in a small bowl, whisk together the egg yolk and mustard.

Heat the butter in a large saucepan, add the flour and whisk vigorously over a medium heat for 1 minute to start cooking out the raw flour. Whisking continuously, add the milk, a little at a time, until you have a thick creamy sauce.

Next, stir through the 'nduja, whisking well, then add the mustardy egg yolk. Finally, stir through the Cheddar cheese and cook for 1 more minute until it's melted.

Stir the pasta through the 'nduja-cheese sauce, then pour into a 23cm (9in) square deep-sided baking tin (or equivalent).

Crumble the Roquefort all over, then cover in herby pangrattato or breadcrumbs. Bake for 18–20 minutes until golden on top and cooked through – cover with foil if it's browning too quickly on top. Serve hot with a green salad.

TOASTED ALMOND & 'NDUJA COD
WITH CAPER-COURGETTE ORZO

'Crust' is one of those sensually alluring words that promises mouthwatering deliciousness, conjuring up thoughts of something crunchy, crispy, flaky or crumbly to bite into. Whether topping a pie, the rim of a pizza, edges of a pasty or encasing a beautiful piece of fish, if I read 'crust' on a menu, I'm in. Toasted almonds, 'nduja and breadcrumbs make a superb baked crust, especially when flecked with bold spices like fennel seeds and black pepper. In this recipe, it tops firm-fleshed cod but is as good over other flaky fish, slow-roasted vegetables – or simply baked on a tray to serve as a crunchy nibble with drinks.

SERVES 2

200g (7oz) orzo pasta
650ml (22fl oz) chicken or
    vegetable stock
1 large courgette (zucchini)
25g (1oz) butter
olive oil
6 anchovies (canned or jarred),
    finely chopped
2 Tbsp capers, chopped
zest and juice of ½ lemon
large handful of basil leaves, chopped

For the crusted cod

25g (1oz) flaked almonds
1 tsp fennel seeds, crushed
4 Tbsp panko breadcrumbs
1 tsp coarsely crushed black
    peppercorns
1 fat garlic clove, crushed to a paste
85g (3oz) 'nduja (3 heaped Tbsp)
300g (10½oz) sustainably caught cod
    (2 fillets)

First, boil the orzo in the stock for 6–7 minutes until al dente. Drain (keep the starchy stock for soups or stews) then leave to cool.

Using a julienne peeler, peel the courgette into thin strips – or peel with a standard vegetable peeler, then slice into thin strips.

Heat the butter with a splash of oil in a large frying pan, then add the anchovies. Cook for 2–3 minutes until they have mostly dissolved. Add the capers, cook for another minute, then add the courgette strips and cook for 1 more minute. Stir through the drained orzo, cook for another minute then finish with the lemon zest and juice, and chopped basil.

Preheat the oven to 180°C fan/200°C/400°F/Gas mark 6.

In a separate frying pan over a medium heat, toast the almonds for 1–2 minutes until they brown a little – being careful not to burn them. Empty into a mixing bowl. Next, toast the fennel seeds for 1 minute, adding these bowl. And finally add the panko breadcrumbs.

Mix in the black pepper, garlic and 'nduja, adding a splash of olive oil if needed – you want the crust to be of a damp consistency that holds together when clumped in your hands.

Place the cod fillets on a baking sheet, then press the 'nduja crust in a thick layer over both fillets. Drizzle with olive oil and bake for 12–14 minutes until cooked through and golden brown on top. Serve straight from the oven on a bed of the orzo.

'NDUJA CRAB CAKES WITH ROASTED PINEAPPLE SALSA

'Nduja has a special affinity with shellfish, be that prawns, lobster, mussels or crab. There's something about pairing its spicy meatiness with the sweet salinity of seafood that just works – emitting all the charms of 'surf and turf' in a deliciously subtle way. This flavour-packed crab cake recipe celebrates their kinship, with a roasted pineapple salsa as an overstated flourish.

SERVES 4

400g (14oz) floury potatoes, peeled and chopped
300g (10½oz) cooked fresh or canned white crab meat
85g (3oz) 'nduja (3 heaped Tbsp)
2 tsp fennel seeds, crushed
zest and juice of ½ lemon
2 spring onions (scallions), very finely chopped
2 Tbsp plain (all-purpose) flour
1 tsp freshly ground black pepper
2 eggs
95g (3½oz) coarse polenta (cornmeal)
sunflower oil, for frying
fine sea salt

For the salsa

500g (1lb 2oz) fresh ripe pineapple (peeled and cored weight)
vegetable or sunflower oil, for brushing
2 Tbsp Worcestershire sauce
1 small white onion
1 red (bell) pepper, deseeded
2 Tbsp apple cider vinegar
2 Tbsp grated fresh ginger root
caster (superfine) sugar (to taste)
small handful of coriander (cilantro), finely chopped

lime wedges, to serve

For the salsa, preheat the oven to 200°C fan/ 220°C/425°F/Gas mark 7. Chop the pineapple into 2cm (¾in) cubes then spread over a baking sheet. Brush with oil, then roast for 20–22 minutes.

In a blender, whizz together the roasted pineapple, Worcestershire sauce, onion, red pepper, 1½ teaspoons of salt, vinegar, ginger and a good pinch of sugar to a fine paste.

Pour into a saucepan and simmer over a medium heat for 10–12 minutes until it reduces to a thick fruity salsa. Empty into a bowl, set aside to cool completely, then chill.

Meanwhile, boil the potatoes in a separate pan of well-salted water for 16–18 minutes until soft. Drain, letting the steam escape fully, and return the potatoes to the pan. Mash to a fine purée.

Reheat the mash gently for 3–4 minutes, stirring continuously until it is smooth and dry. Stir through the crab meat, 'nduja, fennel seeds, lemon zest and juice, spring onions, flour and a teaspoon of salt and the black pepper. If the mix is very loose, add a touch more flour.

Press a 6cm (2½in) cookie cutter or baking ring into the mix to form small cakes roughly 2.5cm (1in) thick. Place on a baking tray and refrigerate for 15 minutes to firm up.

Beat the eggs in a bowl and tip the polenta into another. One at a time, dip the chilled crab cakes first into the egg, then into the polenta, coating on all sides. Heat 2cm (¾in) of sunflower oil in a deep frying pan to 170°C/340°F. Fry the crab cakes in batches for 8–10 minutes, until golden brown on the outside and piping hot inside.

Stir the coriander through the salsa, adding salt, vinegar or sugar if needed. Serve the crab cakes warm with the pineapple salsa and lime wedges.

CHICKEN MARBELLA WITH 'NDUJA & PICKLED WALNUTS

I'm a magpie when it comes to classic American food writing in vintage bookshops. Tracking down works by James Beard, Edna Lewis, Craig Claiborne, Julia Child, Richard Olney and – my favourite of all – M.F.K. Fisher, is something of an obsession. I'm equally drawn to cookbooks from iconic American restaurants – a rabbit hole that led me to *The Silver Palate Cookbook*. Its main pull is its fusion of French, Mediterranean, Asian and American styles, epitomized by its most famous recipe – Chicken Marbella – the height of sophistication in the eighties. My Hackney-ed (literally!) remix adds 'nduja for a spice kick, and pickled walnuts for extra tang.

SERVES 4

8 large chicken thighs and legs,
  skin on and bone in
  (1.4–1.6kg/3lb 2oz–3lb 8oz)
130ml (4fl oz) olive oil
150ml (5fl oz) red wine vinegar
6 Tbsp dark brown sugar, plus extra
  for sprinkling
150g (5½oz) prunes, pitted
50g (1¾oz) capers

75g (2½oz) pickled walnuts, chopped,
  plus 2 Tbsp brine
125g (4½oz) pitted green olives
10 garlic cloves, finely chopped
1 tsp dried oregano
2 tsp black peppercorns, coarsely
  crushed
85g (3oz) 'nduja (3 heaped Tbsp)
200ml (7fl oz) dry white wine or
  dry vermouth
2 rosemary sprigs
fine sea salt

Slash the chicken pieces two or three times in the fleshiest parts, right through the skin.

In a large bowl, whisk together the olive oil, vinegar, 4 tablespoons of dark brown sugar, prunes, capers, walnuts and their brine, olives, garlic, oregano, 2 teaspoons of salt and the black pepper so everything is well combined.

Add the chicken pieces, stir to coat all over, cover and put in the refrigerator to marinate for at least 8 hours – ideally overnight – stirring every few hours.

Remove the chicken pieces from the marinade, shaking off the juices, and place on a baking sheet. Pat dry on top with kitchen paper and sprinkle each piece with a little salt and brown sugar. Spread 1 heaped teaspoon of 'nduja liberally over the top of each piece in a generous layer.

Preheat the oven to 175°C fan/195°C/385°F/Gas mark 5½. Add all the marinade (including the olives, prunes, etc) to a large deep roasting tin, and pour in the wine or vermouth. Whisk well.

Place the coated chicken pieces on top of the marinade – skin-side up – without submerging the part coated in 'nduja in liquid. If needed, remove a little of the marinade juices from the tin – the top of the chicken should bake not boil. Nestle the rosemary sprigs among the pieces.

Bake in the oven for 30 minutes without opening the door. Remove from the oven and baste well, then cook for another 20–30 minutes – basting regularly with the pan juices – until nicely charred on top and the meat is cooked through with the juices running clear. Cover with foil if burning too quickly on top.

Remove from the oven and leave to rest for 15 minutes. Enjoy with good crusty bread.

'NDUJA & GRUYÈRE
CORNBREAD MUFFINS

My love of cornbread was cemented on a culinary safari to Portland, Oregon, a few years ago that took in countless artisanal bakeries in the food-obsessed city. Along the way, we encountered every iteration of cornbread imaginable: thick, Southern-style skillet-baked loaves cooked in bacon fat, cornbread cookies, cornbread waffles, cornbread doughnuts, American biscuit style cornbread scones and endlessly inventive cheese-crusted cornbread muffins. These 'nduja-loaded muffins amalgamate my favourite elements – enriched with delicious Gruyère for a completely unnecessary but totally delicious extra flavour boost.

MAKES 12

275g (9¾oz) coarse polenta
   (cornmeal)
125g (4½oz) plain (all-purpose) flour
2 tsp baking powder
1 tsp fine sea salt

1 tsp dried oregano
150ml (5fl oz) soured cream
3 large eggs
2 Tbsp runny honey
185g (6½oz) butter, melted
100g (3½oz) Gruyère cheese, grated
85g (3oz) 'nduja (3 heaped Tbsp)

Preheat the oven to 200°C fan/220°C/425°F/Gas mark 7.

Place a 12-hole muffin tray on a baking sheet then line with silicone muffin cases. (If using paper cases, brush these on the inside with olive oil otherwise the batter will stick.)

In a large mixing bowl, combine the polenta, flour, baking powder, salt and oregano.

In a large jug, whisk together the cream, eggs and honey, then slowly whisk through the melted butter.

Add the wet ingredients to the dry ingredients and whisk slowly to combine everything together – being careful not to overmix. Finally, stir through the Gruyère.

Spoon 1 heaped tablespoon of the muffin batter into the base of each muffin case, then spoon 1 teaspoon of the 'nduja in the middle of each. Spoon over a heaped tablespoon of the batter, encasing the 'nduja completely.

Transfer the tray (on top of the baking sheet) to the oven and bake for 18–20 minutes, until the muffins are golden brown on top.

Remove from the oven and leave the muffins in the tray to cool for 15 minutes, before transferring to a wire rack to cool completely. Enjoy!

Calabrian Chilli Paste

explosive and lively,
intensely volcanic,
cherry fruited,
crimson oiled,
sharp chilli-fire.

Like 'nduja, this bright-red chilli paste hails from Calabria where it is known as *crema di peperoncino* or *peperoncino calabrese*. It's also made using the same dried fruity *diavoletti rossi* ('red devil') chillies native to southern Italy, which are combined with olive oil and salt. Some styles coarsely chop the chillies into fiery red slivers that speckle the oil with their seeds; others blend the ingredients together into a smooth scarlet paste. Flavoured versions include ones infused with ingredients like basil, fennel seeds or garlic, and you can also buy jars of whole Calabrian chillies, brined in vinegary-oil.

WHIPPED FETA WITH CALABRIAN CHILLI-HONEY BUTTER v

Avant-garde 19th-century French pianist Erik Satie was famous for his unconventional musical compositions that closely allied him with Surrealism. Equally eccentric were his diary entries. In one account about a day in the life of a musician, he shares his 'white food only' diet, which included pale turnips, chicken cooked in water, coconuts, salt, camphorated sausage, grated bones and white cheeses. I've always thought it sounded delicious – especially if it warranted copious servings of white burrata, camembert and feta. Try as I might to emulate Satie's monochrome originality, my flavour universe leans towards the technicolour. The slick of crimson Calabrian chilli-honey butter through whipped feta in this recipe might not have been Satie certified, but is delicious music to me.

SERVES 4-6

200g (7oz) Greek feta
75g (2½oz) soured cream
zest and juice of ½ lemon
1 fat garlic clove, crushed to a paste
1 tsp dried mint

1 tsp coarsely ground black pepper
40g (1½oz) butter
1 tsp fennel seeds, crushed
1 Tbsp Calabrian chilli paste
2 Tbsp runny honey
¾ tsp smoked salt

Crumble the feta into a food processor, then add the cream, lemon zest, garlic, mint and black pepper. Blend for 1–2 minutes, scraping down the sides, until whipped very smooth. Season with extra pepper if needed. Spoon into a serving bowl.

Next, heat the butter in a frying pan over a medium–high heat for 2–3 minutes until it just begins to turn golden brown.

Add the fennel seeds and sizzle for 45 seconds, before spooning in the Calabrian chilli paste, runny honey and smoked salt. Warm everything through for 1 minute, mixing well then, add the lemon juice to finish.

Drizzle the warm Calabrian chilli butter over the whipped feta. Serve with toasted pittas, corn tortilla chips, radishes or crudités.

PIEDMONTESE PEPPERS
WITH CALABRIAN CHILLI & FENNEL

Elizabeth David's Piedmontese peppers have been revered by everyone from Delia Smith to Simon Hopkinson – and now it's time for a Punjabi home cook from Leicester to offer up his own hero worship – though adding the masala touch to the Elizabeth David classic feels like sacrilege even to me! My take brings in the kick of Calabrian chilli and the liquorice bite of diced fresh fennel. Culinary blasphemy maybe, but undeniably delicious nonetheless.

SERVES 4

250g (9oz) baby plum tomatoes
1 fennel bulb, finely diced
1 Tbsp Calabrian chilli paste,
    plus extra to serve
4 red (bell) peppers
olive oil, for drizzling
4 garlic cloves, slivered

2 Tbsp pitted black olives, chopped
zest of ½ lemon
1 Tbsp torn basil leaves
8 anchovies (canned or jarred),
    drained
fine sea salt
parmesan shavings, to serve
    (optional)

Cut a cross on the tip of each baby tomatoes with a sharp knife, then plunge into a bowl of boiling water for 30 seconds. Drain in a colander and rinse under cold running water to loosen the skins. Remove all the skins from the tomatoes and set aside.

Next, mix together the finely diced fennel and Calabrian chilli paste. Halve the red peppers vertically through the stalks from top to bottom, remove the seeds and place on a well-oiled baking sheet. Preheat the oven to 190°C fan/210°C/410°F/Gas mark 6½.

Spoon 1 teaspoon of the Calabrian chilli-fennel mix into each pepper cavity, then add a couple of tomatoes, slivers of garlic, a few olives, a good glug of olive oil and a generous sprinkle of salt. Finish by adding more of the Calabrian chilli-fennel mix on top.

Bake the peppers for 45 minutes, until cooked through, covering with foil if they are browning too quickly.

Remove from the oven, sprinkle with lemon zest, add torn basil leaves, place anchovies on top of each pepper half, then bake for a final 5–10 minutes.

Drizzle over a little more Calabrian chilli paste and olive oil. Serve with parmesan shavings if you like, and some good crusty bread.

CARROT & SAGE LATKES WITH CALABRIAN CHILLI OIL v

The most memorable house party I've ever been to – at a friends' in Brooklyn – was a life-lesson in the effectiveness of doing just a few things… but doing them really well! To drink, she served up three meticulously made cocktails – a Manhattan, a Margarita and a Harvey Wallbanger – pre-batched into giant Mason jars. To groove, the speakers were locked into a playlist of Erykah Badu and Lauryn Hill on repeat. And to eat, she had just three platters of Russ & Daughters latkes, topped with dill-flecked crème fraîche, smoked salmon, pearly roe and lemon. I'm now obsessed with latkes, although my flavour kleptomania doesn't allow me to keep them quite so classic. Carrots and sage add sweetness and herbal-anise notes – which, combined with fiery Calabrian chilli oil – really get the tastebud party started.

MAKES 16-18

100ml (3½fl oz) olive oil
loose handful of sage leaves,
    stalks removed, plus extra
    to garnish
2 Tbsp Calabrian chilli paste
zest and juice of ½ lemon,
    plus extra for squeezing
1 tsp caster (superfine) sugar
850g (1lb 14oz) floury potatoes

275g (9¾oz) carrots
1 large white onion
2 eggs
1 tsp coarsely ground black pepper
1 tsp baking powder
4 Tbsp plain (all-purpose) flour
sunflower oil, for frying
fine sea salt
crème fraîche or soured cream,
    to serve

Heat the oil in a frying pan over a medium heat until just starting to bubble, then add the sage leaves (including some extra if you would like to have some as a garnish). Sizzle for 2–3 minutes until they turn dark green. Lift the leaves onto paper towels to dry.

Meanwhile, add the Calabrian chilli paste to the sage oil, along with the lemon juice and sugar. Remove from the heat and stir well. Cool slightly, then add the lemon zest. Set aside.

Coarsely grate the potatoes, carrots and onion. Tip everything into a large mixing bowl, spoon over 1 teaspoon of salt and mix well. Leave for 10 minutes then, using a cheesecloth or muslin, squeeze everything through the cloth over another large bowl to catch the starchy liquid. Do this in batches extracting as much liquid as possible.

Put the squeezed vegetables back into a clean bowl, spoon over another 1 teaspoon of salt, leave for another 10 minutes, and squeeze for a second time – again catching the starchy liquid in the bowl. Spread the twice-squeezed vegetables on a baking sheet lined with paper towels or a clean tea towel. Press on top with another towel to remove any last moisture.

Leave the starchy liquid to settle for 10 minutes, then pour off the water – you'll be left with a very thick white starch residue at the bottom of the bowl which will help to bind the latkes. Crack the eggs on top of this starch residue and whisk well to combine, then add the black pepper, all the grated vegetables and the crispy sage. Mix well, then add the baking powder, then the flour, a tablespoon at a time – being careful not to overmix. Leave the mixture to rest for 10 minutes.

When ready to cook, add 3cm (1¼in) of sunflower oil to a wide deep frying pan and heat to 180°C/350°F. Use your hands to make 16 or 18 portions of the mixture the size of a golf ball then press them between your palms – thinly flattening the balls and creating craggy edges. Carefully drop them into the oil, no more than four at a time. Cook for 3–5 minutes on each side, flipping regularly until crispy brown and cooked through.

Drain the latkes on paper towels, then serve with a squeeze of lemon juice, some crème fraîche or soured cream, a drizzle of the sage-Calabrian chilli oil and extra crispy sage if you like.

CALABRESE CHICKEN CAESAR
WITH GIANT CROUTONS

If there's Caesar salad on the menu, I will be ordering it. The alchemy of anchovies, parmesan, egg yolks and oil, dressing stalks of crunchy Romaine strikes a perfectly harmonious chord. Almost nothing could be more perfect... aside that is, from the adding a little chilli heat, a touch of aniseed, fried bacon and some giant crunchy croutons that look comedically oversized on a plate. This recipe does all of those things with gusto – intense Calabrian chilli paste adding sharp, fiery heat to the pan-charred chicken, and fennel seeds infused throughout for their delicious flavour.

SERVES 2

2 large chicken breasts, skinless
   and boneless
100g (3½oz) smoked bacon lardons
200ml (7fl oz) olive oil
4 garlic cloves, crushed to a paste
1 tsp fennel seeds, crushed
1 small sourdough loaf, cut into very
   large cubes
8 anchovies (canned or jarred),
   drained

2 large egg yolks
zest and juice of ½ lemon
1 Tbsp white wine vinegar
1 tsp black peppercorns, coarsely
   crushed
25g (1oz) parmesan, finely grated,
   plus extra to serve
2 Tbsp sun-dried tomato purée
   (paste)
1 Tbsp Calabrian chilli paste
2 heads of Romaine lettuce
fine sea salt

Place the chicken breasts between two sheets of baking paper and flatten with a meat tenderiser until 1.5cm (⅝in) thick. Sprinkle with salt and set aside.

In a large frying pan, cook the lardons over a medium–low heat until they turn crispy. Remove from the pan and set aside, keeping the bacony oils in the pan.

Very gently heat the olive oil in the same pan. Add the garlic and fennel seeds, sizzling very gently for 2–3 minutes – don't let the garlic take on any colour. If needed, remove the pan from the heat. Strain the oil into a measuring jug, reserving the garlic and fennel seeds – keep the pan handy. Preheat the oven to 200°C fan/220°C/425°F/Gas mark 7.

Tip the sourdough cubes onto a baking tray and liberally brush with the garlic-infused oil. Bake in the oven for 8–10 minutes until golden and crunchy.

Meanwhile, make the dressing. Pulverize the anchovies to a very fine paste in a large bowl using a pestle. Add the egg yolks and whisk to combine. Slowly whisk through the lemon juice and vinegar.

Next, very gently trickle 100ml (3½fl oz) of the garlicky oil into the dressing, whisking the whole time. It will start to thicken as you add more oil.

Stop after 100ml (3½fl oz) of oil has been incorporated and add the parmesan. Whisk well, then continue slowly adding another 50ml (1¾fl oz) of the oil (more if you prefer it even thicker). Whisk through the reserved garlic and fennel seeds, along with the lemon zest and peppercorns. Check for seasoning, adding salt, lemon juice or parmesan to suit your taste.

Heat the remainder of the infused oil in the large frying pan, along with the tomato purée and Calabrian chilli paste. Over a medium heat, sizzle the chicken breasts, one at a time, in the tomato-chilli oil for 6–7 minutes, turning regularly, until cooked through and charred on the outside.

To assemble, tear the Romaine leaves into a large bowl and toss through the Caesar dressing – any leftover dressing will keep in the refrigerator for up to three days. Slice the chicken and place over the leaves with the tomato-chilli oil from the pan. Sprinkle over the lardons, croutons and more parmesan, if you like.

TOULOUSE SAUSAGES WITH CALABRIAN CHILLI-OREGANO LENTILS

One of the more extravagant days of my early thirties was when three friends and I had lunch at the House of Lords. (It's a little-known secret that the Peers' Dining Room opens to the public a few times a year for a three-course luncheon.) It progressed over 5 hours: from sherry aperitifs with crab vol-au-vents, all the way to delicious port with bijoux petits fours. The course I still taste in my memory was some extremely good rustic Toulouse sausages with a tomato-lentil ragout. My modern pantry take – enlivened by Calabrian chilli paste – is fit for any Lord or Lady in my opinion.

SERVES 4

olive oil
85g (3oz) smoked bacon lardons
2 large celery sticks, finely diced
1 large red onion, finely diced
2 carrots, finely diced
4 fat garlic cloves, crushed to a paste
2 Tbsp Calabrian chilli paste
handful of oregano leaves, chopped
4 Tbsp tomato purée (paste)
300g (10½oz) dried Puy or green
  lentils
700ml (24fl oz) rich beef or lamb
  stock
8 Toulouse or other coarse ground
  sausages
2 Tbsp English mustard
2 Tbsp apple cider vinegar, plus
  an extra 1 tsp
200g (7oz) prepared butternut
  squash, cut into 1cm (½in) dice
2 Tbsp caster (superfine) sugar
fine sea salt

Heat a splash of oil in a large deep saucepan, add the lardons and fry off for 3–4 minutes until they start to brown. Add the celery, onion and carrots with a pinch of salt, cooking over a medium–high heat – stirring regularly so they don't catch – for 16–18 minutes until they have reduced in volume by half. Add a little more oil if drying out.

Now add the garlic, Calabrian chilli paste, half the chopped oregano and the tomato purée to the pan. Stir well then mix through the lentils – mixing to coat them all over. Finally add the stock. Bring to the boil, then cover with a lid and cook for 30 minutes, stirring regularly.

Preheat the oven to 200°C fan/220°C/425°F/Gas mark 7. Make three or four diagonal cuts across each of the sausages.

Mix together the English mustard and 1 teaspoon of vinegar in a small bowl. Brush the sausages with this glaze, including into the cuts.

Place the sausages on one side of a baking sheet and sprinkle over a little of the oregano. Scatter the butternut squash on the other side of the baking sheet, drizzle with a little oil, a pinch of salt and the rest of the chopped oregano.

Bake in the oven for 30–35 minutes, turning the sausages a few times – and basting with more of the mustard mix – until they are brown all over and cooked through.

After 30 minutes, stir the lentils well then add the sugar, the 2 tablespoons of vinegar, and a good pinch of salt. Stir well, then cook, uncovered, for a final 5 minutes – seasoning as needed. Serve the lentils and sausages with a drizzle of oil and some good crusty bread.

BROKEN LASAGNE WITH
CALABRIAN SHORT RIB RAGU

When my friends Phil and Marco asked me to be a groom's man at their wedding but disclosed only that it would take place in Florence, I knew it was going to be spectacular. The evening before the big day, we all congregated outside the Uffizi before being ushered towards the river where we were guided into a dark shuttered chamber – the headquarters of the Firenze rowing club. A shimmering door suddenly burst open to expose flower-covered steps, leading down to a spectacular banquet on the banks of the Arno beneath Ponte Vecchio. Minutes later, the grooms arrived by boat, as we all cried tears of joy. The dish I kept returning to that evening was a rich beef ragu served with fresh pappardelle. This recipe elicits that treasured night before the wedding day – the spectacle of which is another story altogether...

SERVES 4

olive oil, for frying
1.5–1.75kg (3lb 5oz–3lb 12oz) beef
    short ribs (about 6 large ones)
1 large onion, finely diced
2 celery sticks, finely diced
2 carrots, finely diced
6 garlic cloves, crushed to a paste
8 anchovies (canned or jarred),
    finely chopped
1 Tbsp Calabrian chilli paste,
    plus extra to serve

2 Tbsp tomato purée (paste)
2 Tbsp caster (superfine) sugar
1 rosemary sprig, finely chopped
small handful of oregano, finely
    chopped
750ml (26fl oz) beef stock
250ml (9fl oz) red wine
400g (14oz) can chopped Italian
    tomatoes
12–14 lasagne sheets
fine sea salt
parmesan, finely grated, to serve

Heat 1 tablespoon of olive oil in a large, lidded pan, then sear the short ribs in batches for 7–8 minutes, turning regularly, until nicely charred brown on the outside. Set aside on a plate.

Add the onion, celery, carrots and garlic to the same pan with a splash more oil if needed. Cook for 10–12 minutes over a medium heat until really soft and just starting to turn golden.

Next, add the anchovies, Calabrian chilli paste, tomato purée, sugar and 2 teaspoons of salt. Mix well and cook for another minute, before adding the chopped herbs.

Return the ribs to the pan, mixing well, then add the stock, wine and chopped tomatoes. Bring everything to the boil, simmer for 3 minutes, then reduce the temperature to low.

Scrunch up a sheet of greaseproof paper and use it to cover the surface of the ragu. Put the lid on the pan and leave to cook over a low heat for 2½ hours. Check it every 30 minutes, topping up with a little stock if needed.

Remove the ribs from the pan and place on a baking sheet. Use two forks to shred the meat from the bones in big chunky shreds, discarding any excess sinew or fat.

Return the shredded meat to the sauce, then simmer, uncovered, over a medium heat for 15 minutes. Check for seasoning – adding a little more salt, sugar or wine if needed.

Break the lasagne sheets in half directly into the pot, then cook for a final 13–15 minutes until the pasta is cooked through – add a splash of stock or water if needed to submerge the pasta fully in the liquid.

Serve with a generous sprinkling of parmesan and more Calabrian chilli paste, if you like.

Dark Roasted Peanut Butter

rich and burnished,
earthily savoury,
lusciously crunchy,
moreishly cloying,
creamy toastiness.

'Regular' peanut butter is made from peanuts that are blitzed into a smooth or crunchy spreadable butter, seasoned with a sprinkle of salt. To become 'dark roasted' peanut butter, the nuts are first roasted to a scorched chocolate brown before being ground. For the best quality, look for at least 95 per cent peanut content. Typically, it is sold in jars although in some stores you can buy it freshly ground to order. Variants include butters made from almonds, walnuts, pecans or pistachios – and flavoured versions where ground peanuts are combined with ingredients like cocoa beans, honey, chilli, cinnamon or dates.

CHARRED LEEKS WITH
SMOKY PEANUT ROMESCO v

In Spain, the annual Gran Festa de la Calçotada heralds the beginning of calçot (spring onion) season in Catalonia. Calçots are charred to a crisp over a fire of vine branches, then wrapped in newspaper to steam. I have a 'thing' for charred alliums, so much to my delight, one freezing-cold January day I was invited to lunch at Parillan in London's Borough Market where I experienced my own calçot fiesta – and the ritual of dipping the blackened onions in romesco with your hands, holding them above your mouth, then swallowing down in one. My ode to that ceremony uses sweet leeks charred to a crisp, dolloped with peanut butter-enriched romesco. Cutlery optional.

SERVES 2

2 large or 3 medium leeks
4 Tbsp olive oil, plus extra for drizzling
2 tsp smoked salt
8 garlic cloves, unpeeled
1 thick slice of crusty white bread
350g (12oz) jar roasted red (bell)
    peppers, drained

3 Tbsp dark roasted peanut butter
2 Tbsp red wine vinegar
1 tsp pul biber or chilli flakes
2 tsp smoked paprika
zest and juice of ½ lemon
60g (2¼oz) roasted peanuts, coarsely
    crushed, plus extra to garnish

Preheat the oven to 180°C fan/200°C/400°F/ Gas mark 6. Wash the leeks well, particularly between the green leaves and pat dry. Using a sharp knife, make a slit down the middle of each leek, starting 1cm (½in) up from the bottom to just before the green parts fan out. Place on a baking sheet, drizzle liberally with oil and sprinkle over 1 teaspoon of the smoked salt. Add the garlic cloves to the same sheet and drizzle with oil.

Bake the leeks and garlic for 15–17 minutes until the leeks are starting to just char and the garlic is soft.

Meanwhile, toast the slice of bread to a deep golden colour. Roughly tear it into pieces.

Remove the leeks and garlic from the oven. Set the leeks aside on the baking sheet and squeeze the garlic cloves out of their skins into a food processor. Next, add the roasted red peppers, the dark roasted peanut butter, vinegar, pul biber, paprika, 1 teaspoon of smoked salt, the lemon zest and juice, oil, toasted bread and roasted peanuts.

Pulse at first to get it going, then blitz for 1–2 minutes until you have a coarse thick purée. Check for seasoning, adding more smoked salt or a splash of vinegar if needed, and a little more oil if you prefer a thinner romesco. Leave the flavours to mingle for 15 minutes, then pour into a bowl.

Meanwhile, heat the grill to its highest setting. Drizzle the par-cooked leeks with more oil, then cook under the grill for 6–8 minutes until soft in the centre and charred on top (if the green tops are burning too quickly, cover with foil).

Serve the warm charred leeks with dollops of the peanut romesco, and garnish with more crushed peanuts, if you like.

SUN-DRIED TOMATO-CAULIFLOWER, PEANUT & OLIVE PAPPARDELLE

Dining alone is my favourite pastime. I love to take myself for lunch – somewhere nice but not fancy where I can lean into every sensory stimulus the culinary outing offers. The first time I went to Chez Panisse in Berkeley, California, I sat in the upstairs café, perched solo at a wooden table, at the other end of which a gaggle of tipsy New Yorkers seemed both intrigued and perplexed by my state of bliss. The cause of my pleasure was a plate of Sicilian pasta with cauliflower, raisins, walnuts, chilli, saffron, herbs and lemony breadcrumbs. This recipe loosely takes inspiration from that lunch, made indulgent with creamy peanut butter and salty pops of bittersweet black olives. Perfect for a family meal or just for one.

SERVES 2-3

40g (1½oz) sultanas (golden raisins)
5 Tbsp boiling water
300g (10½oz) small cauliflower
  florets, roughly chopped
5 Tbsp olive oil
3 Tbsp sun-dried tomato purée
  (paste)
80g (2¾oz) pitted black olives,
  chopped
200g (7oz) pappardelle or malfadine
  pasta

1 onion, finely chopped
2 garlic cloves, crushed to a paste
large handful of basil leaves, chopped
50g (1¾oz) dark roasted peanut
  butter
2 Tbsp white wine vinegar
1 tsp lemon zest
fine sea salt
grated parmesan or Herby Pangrattato
  (page 59), to garnish

Put the sultanas in a small bowl with the 5 tablespoons of boiling water. Leave to soak for 15 minutes.

Heat 3 tablespoons of oil in a large, deep-sided frying pan over a medium–high heat. Add the cauliflower florets and ½ teaspoon of salt and cook for 10–12 minutes until they take on some colour.

Next, add the sultanas and their soaking water, the tomato purée and olives. Cook for 2 minutes until the cauliflower is tender, then empty everything into a bowl. Keep the pan handy.

Bring a large pan of well-salted water to the boil and drop in the pasta, checking the cook time on the packet.

Add the remaining 2 tablespoons of oil to the frying pan and fry the onion over a medium heat for 6–7 minutes until translucent. Add the garlic and basil and fry for another minute before stirring through the dark roasted peanut butter, 1 teaspoon of salt, the vinegar and lemon zest.

Once the pasta is cooked, drain through a sieve into a bowl or jug and measure off 150–200ml (5–7fl oz) of the cooking water. Pour this into the frying pan, whisking for 2 minutes until you have a thick glossy sauce – add more water if needed.

Swirl the cooked pasta through the peanut butter sauce, then tumble in the cooked cauliflower, mixing everything well. Serve in big bowls topped with parmesan or Herby Pangrattato, if you like.

SINGAPORE SATAY CHICKEN WITH ROASTED-PEANUT SAUCE

I'm regularly catapulted in my dreams to the hawker centres of Singapore – most frequently to a particular stand that sold *chwee kueh* (steamed rice cakes) with salty preserved radish in Ghim Moh Market, and another in Little India that served the best satay chicken I've ever had. I've no idea how their peanut sauce got the level of smoky depth and intense flavour that it did – the peanuts almost certainly wood-fire roasted, with an abundance of aromatic spices infusing it from within. My take on that memory combines the rich smokiness of deep roasted peanut butter with a plentiful blend of heady spices, fragrant lemongrass and tangy tamarind for the full effect.

MAKES 12-14

2 tsp coriander seeds
1 tsp cumin seeds
2 tsp fennel seeds
1 Tbsp dark brown sugar
1 tsp ground turmeric
1 tsp ground cinnamon
zest and juice of ½ lemon
40g (1½oz) fresh ginger root,
    roughly chopped
1 Tbsp light soy sauce
1 Tbsp vegetable oil
750g (1lb 10oz) chicken breasts
    (about 4), skinless and boneless
fine sea salt

For the peanut sauce

4 large shallots (100g/3½oz)
25g (1oz) lemongrass
2 Tbsp vegetable oil
1 Tbsp Kashmiri chilli powder
200ml (7fl oz) coconut milk
4 Tbsp dark roasted peanut butter
2 Tbsp dark brown sugar
1 tsp fish sauce
50g (1¾oz) dry-roasted peanuts,
    crushed
1 Tbsp tamarind paste

First, make a marinade for the chicken. Toast all the seeds in a frying pan over a medium heat for 1–2 minutes, then use a pestle and mortar to grind them to a powder. Add to a small blender along with 1 tablespoon of dark brown sugar, the turmeric, cinnamon, lemon zest and juice, ginger, soy sauce, 1 teaspoon of salt and the oil. Whizz together to a fine paste.

Cut the chicken breast into 12–14 long strips, transfer to a bowl and smother with the marinade. Cover and leave to marinate in the refrigerator for 4–6 hours.

Next, make the peanut sauce. Blend the shallots and lemongrass with a splash of water to a fine paste. Heat the oil in a saucepan, add the paste and cook over a medium heat for 4–5 minutes. Add the Kashmiri chilli powder, coconut milk and dark roasted peanut butter and cook for

3 minutes. Add the 2 tablespoons of dark brown sugar, fish sauce and the peanuts, cook for another 2–3 minutes. Finally, add the tamarind paste with 1 teaspoon of salt. Cook for another minute, whisking well, then leave to cool.

Remove the chicken from the refrigerator and bring to room temperature.

Preheat the grill to its highest setting. Skewer the chicken pieces onto pre-soaked wooden skewers. Grill for 6 minutes, turn, then grill for another 6 minutes. Turn again and finish cooking for another 4–5 minutes until charred on the outside and cooked through.

Serve the satay chicken with the peanut sauce drizzled over or in a small bowl for dipping. Enjoy.

BAJA FISH TACOS WITH PEANUTTY SALSA MACHA

Few things are more wonderful than freshly fried seafood – first doused in malt vinegar then dipped in mayonnaise – and devoured on a windy but sunny beach somewhere in Britain – the pleasure of it is always exemplary. I'm equally drawn to the Mexican take on this culinary tradition – fried fish tacos smothered in salsa! While tangy *pico de gallo* or *salsa fresca* are more common pairings, I'm hooked on *salsa macha* – a rich chilli oil made with dried chillies, roasted spices, nuts and seeds. My peanut butter laced version brings extra crunch using whole spices like cumin and coriander, and is unashamedly heavy on the vinegar. Imagine the taste of Tijuana tacos but from a Brighton Pier chippy and you're heading in the right direction.

MAKES 6 LARGE TACOS

2 Tbsp Dijon mustard
1½ tsp smoked paprika
400g (14oz) sustainably caught cod,
   hake or haddock (3 large fillets)
150g (5½oz) plain flour
1½ tsp baking powder
165–185ml (5¼–6fl oz) Mexican beer
sunflower or vegetable oil, for frying
fine sea salt

For the salsa
25g (1oz) dried guajillo chilli
25g (1oz) dried ancho chilli

2 tsp cumin seeds
2 tsp coriander seeds
2 tsp sesame seeds
125ml (4fl oz) vegetable oil
4 garlic cloves, slivered
2 tsp dried oregano
4 Tbsp dark roasted peanut butter
4 Tbsp apple cider vinegar
zest and juice of 2 limes

To serve
taco tortillas
iceberg lettuce, shredded
lime wedges

Whisk together the Dijon mustard and smoked paprika with a pinch of fine sea salt. Cut each fish fillet in half, put in a bowl, smother in the mustard mix and marinate for 30 minutes.

Meanwhile, prepare the salsa. Gently toast the guajillo and ancho chillies in a dry frying pan for 1–2 minutes until they start to release their aromas. Place them in a small bowl, cover with boiling water and leave to hydrate for 20 minutes.

Using the same frying pan, gently toast all the seeds for 1 minute – being careful that they don't burn. Transfer to a pestle and mortar, then bash a couple of times just to break them up a little – you want to keep their texture. Set aside.

Return the frying pan to a low–medium heat, add the vegetable oil, then gently sizzle the garlic for 3–4 minutes ensuring it does not take on too much colour. Next, add the dried oregano and dark roasted peanut butter, cooking for another 2 minutes.

Scrape everything into a blender, then add the drained rehydrated chillies, vinegar, lime zest and juice with 1½ teaspoons of salt. Blend to a semi-smooth paste, empty into a bowl, then stir through the toasted seeds. Set aside.

Continued...

Prepare the fish coating by whisking together the plain flour, baking powder and 165ml (5¼fl oz) of Mexican beer in a large bowl to make a thick pancake batter – only adding the extra beer if needed. Rest for 15 minutes.

When ready to fry, add enough oil to a medium saucepan to fill it to a third and heat to 165°C/329°F. Give the batter a quick whisk, then dip the marinated fish into it. Shake off the excess, and lower the fish, no more than two pieces at a time, into the hot oil. Fry for 4–5 minutes until golden brown on the outside and cooked through. Remove from the pan with a slotted spoon and drain well on paper towels. Repeat with the remaining pieces.

Serve the hot fried fish on taco tortillas, with shredded lettuce, a good dollop of the peanutty salsa macha and a squeeze of fresh lime.

Tip: You can also make these using tofu or paneer in place of the fish.

PEANUT BUTTER PIE WITH
A CINNAMON CEREAL CRUST

There's a particularly funny line by Henry James in *Washington Square*. Taking a gentle swipe at his plus-sized protagonist Catherine Sloper, James proclaims that she was 'something of a glutton... [She never] stole raisins out of the pantry; but she devoted her pocket-money to the purchase of cream-cakes.' It's something I fully identify with; in my teens, I too spent much of my pocket money on chocolate éclairs, custard slices and cream-filled buns. As an adult, the habit has endured, although these days, I'm more likely to bake an indulgent treat for myself. This peanut butter cream pie is unashamedly gluttonous – one of the tastiest creations I've dreamt up.

SERVES 10-12

vegetable or sunflower oil,
    for brushing
120g (4¼oz) very soft butter
80g (2¾oz) light brown sugar
2 tsp ground cinnamon
100g (3½oz) cornflakes, crushed
24 Oreos or other chocolate
    sandwich cookies (265g/9½oz)
fine sea salt
whipped double (heavy) cream,
    to decorate
roasted peanuts, crushed, to decorate
    (optional)

For the pastry cream
6 large egg yolks
125g (4½oz) caster (superfine) sugar
65g (2½oz) cornflour (cornstarch)
2½ tsp powdered gelatine
500ml (17fl oz) full-fat (whole) milk
2 tsp vanilla bean paste
150g (5½oz) very soft butter
275g (9¾oz) dark roasted peanut
    butter, plus extra to decorate

First, make the pastry cream. In a large mixing bowl, whisk together the egg yolks, caster sugar and cornflour into a very thick yellow paste. Set aside.

Measure 4 tablespoons of water into a small heatproof bowl, then sprinkle the gelatine on top (it's important to do it this way round!). Mix well and leave the gelatine to bloom for 10 minutes. Then gently warm in a microwave, or place the bowl over a pan containing a little simmering water until the gelatine has fully melted.

Heat the milk and vanilla paste in a saucepan to just below boiling. Pour a quarter of the hot milk over the egg-yolk paste, whisking vigorously. Add another quarter and whisk again. Then pour everything back into the saucepan of milk.

Cook over a high heat for 1–2 minutes, whisking continuously until it resembles thick custard, then whisk through the gelatine. Pour it into the bowl

of a stand mixer, cover with cling film pressed onto the surface to prevent a skin forming and put in the refrigerator for 2 hours to set.

Next, make the crust. Preheat the oven to 200°C fan/220°C/425°F/Gas mark 7 and brush a 22cm (8½in) fluted loose-bottomed deep-sided pie tin with oil.

Melt 80g (2¾oz) of the butter in a large saucepan, then add the light brown sugar. Cook over a medium–high heat for 3–4 minutes, whisking well until it forms a runny caramel. Stir through the cinnamon, then remove from the heat and quickly stir through the crushed cornflakes. Tip them into a large mixing bowl – reserving 2 tablespoons to decorate – and allow to cool.

Continued...

Blitz the Oreo cookies in a food processor, then add to the cooled cornflakes with a pinch of salt. Melt the remaining 40g (1½oz) of butter, pour into the bowl and mix everything to form a damp rubble.

Scrape the mixture into the tin then use the bottom of a flat-sided cup to compress and very tightly pack the crust into the base and sides of the tin – you want a thick rim with a deep cavity for the cream. Place on a baking sheet and bake for 10 minutes. If the crust has sunk a little, very carefully use the bottom of the cup to compress back into shape while warm. Leave to cool completely in the tin – it will harden as it does.

When ready to assemble, remove the chilled pastry cream from the refrigerator – it will be the texture of set jelly. Whisk in the stand mixer for 2 minutes to loosen, then gradually whisk in the very soft butter, dark roasted peanut butter and a teaspoon of salt.

Spoon the peanut butter cream into the cooled crust, smoothing over the top. Put in the refrigerator for 8 hours to set. Top with whipped cream, drizzle over extra peanut butter and decorate with the remaining cornflake crumbs and extra peanuts, if you like.

BLACKCURRANT 'PBJ'
CUSTARD TARTS v

I once spent New Year's Eve in Hong Kong with my friend Mark – a trip filled with more delicious revelations every minute than I'd ever experienced. Despite all that we scoffed in our time there, every day we ensured our stomachs had space for three things: in the morning an extraordinary Chinese egg tart from an unassuming vendor next to Victoria Park; in the afternoon a mind-blowing raspberry-peanut butter shaved ice from a dessert bar in Causeway Bay and, just before bed, another egg tart from the same vendor. This recipe elicits my memories of that trip – with blackcurrant jam giving a pleasingly tart contrast to the indulgent peanut butter and just-set sweet vanilla custard.

MAKES 12

2 x 320g (11¼oz) sheets ready-rolled
  shortcrust pastry (prepared pie
  dough)
vegetable or sunflower oil, for
  brushing
8 large egg yolks
80g (2¾oz) caster (superfine) sugar
2 Tbsp cornflour (cornstarch)
500ml (17fl oz) double (heavy) cream
1 tsp freshly grated nutmeg
1½ tsp vanilla bean paste
12 tsp dark roasted peanut butter
12 tsp blackcurrant jam (jelly)

Unroll the pastry, then use a 10cm (4in) cooking cutter or baking ring to stamp out 12 discs. Brush a 12-hole muffin tray lightly with oil, then carefully line with the discs, using your fingers to press into the base and sides, right up to the top, ensuring there are no air bubbles. Chill the tray in the refrigerator for at least 30 minutes.

Meanwhile, make the custard. In a large heatproof jug, whisk together the egg yolks, caster sugar and cornflour. Set aside.

Next, put the cream, nutmeg and vanilla paste in a saucepan over a low heat and gently bring up to 90°C/194°F – just below boiling. Very slowly, whisk the hot cream into the egg yolks, then cover the surface with cling film to prevent it forming a skin. Set aside.

Preheat the oven to 240°C fan/260°C/500°F/Gas mark 10 (you want it very hot!) and place a baking sheet on the middle shelf to heat up.

Take the chilled muffin tray from the refrigerator, and carefully spread 1 teaspoon of dark roasted peanut butter into the bottom of each pastry case, and top with 1 teaspoon of blackcurrant jam.

Give the custard a quick whisk, then carefully pour into each tart case to fill up to the top. Place the muffin tray on top of the hot baking sheet and bake for 11–12 minutes until the pastry is cooked through and the custard is scorched dark brown on top. Check on the tarts after 8 minutes, and cover with foil if they are darkening too quickly.

Remove from the oven and let the tarts cool in the muffin tray for 30 minutes – the custard will continue cooking in this time, so this is important. Transfer to a wire rack to cool completely, and enjoy.

Instant Espresso Powder

dark and roasted,
acidically chocolatey,
smokily charcoaly,
burnt caramel,
tannic bitterness.

Made from dark roasted, rich and intensely flavoured coffee beans that are coarsely ground and then brewed. A concentrated espresso elixir is extracted from this solution, then dehydrated to remove all the liquid to become the fine water-soluble espresso powder you buy in jars. The best-tasting versions will use single-origin, Rainforest Alliance or Fairtrade coffee beans. Strong instant coffee powder is a suitable alternative, and you can also buy concentrated espresso syrups.

KOPI-SAMBAL SEARED SALMON
WITH PISTACHIO DUKKAH

Breakfast in Penang, Malaysia, is a multisensory street feast of flavours that truly bang. Early one morning on my last visit there, I gorged on *nasi lemak* (coconut rice) topped with crispy anchovies, peanuts and a sour chilli sauce – washed down with strong Malaysian coffee (*kopi*) that was bitterly rich but mellowed by sickly sweet condensed milk. The combination of coffee, fish, nuts and chilli was surprisingly marvellous and is the inspiration behind this unconventional recipe. It combines sambal oelek – a sharply vinegary chilli paste – with the scorched flavour of instant espresso powder, and pistachio dukkah for some essential crunch.

SERVES 2

2 Tbsp sambal oelek or sriracha
2 Tbsp kecap manis
1¼ tsp instant espresso powder
1 tsp grated fresh ginger root
2 garlic cloves, crushed to a paste
1 tsp toasted sesame oil
2 Tbsp runny honey
zest and juice of ½ lime
olive oil, for frying

2 x 150g (5½oz) sustainably caught
    or wild salmon fillets, skin on
fine sea salt

For the dukkah
1 Tbsp cumin seeds
1 Tbsp coriander seeds
1 Tbsp fennel seeds
1 Tbsp sesame seeds
50g (1¾oz) toasted pistachios,
    crushed
1 tsp smoked paprika

First, make the dukkah. Toast the cumin, coriander and fennel seeds in a dry frying pan over a medium heat for 2 minutes until just golden. Add the sesame seeds and toast for another minute. Allow to cool, then coarsely grind using a pestle and mortar. Mix together with the crushed pistachios, smoked paprika and 1 teaspoon of fine sea salt. Set aside.

Next, in a small bowl, whisk the sambal oelek, kecap manis, instant espresso powder, ginger, garlic, toasted sesame oil, honey, lime zest and juice with 1 teaspoon of salt to form a glaze. Leave for 10 minutes for the flavours to mingle.

When ready to cook, drizzle a little olive oil into a cold frying pan to lightly coat the base, then place the salmon fillets, skin-side down, into the cold pan. Slowly increase the temperature to medium and cook for 2–3 minutes until the skin is crispy. Flip over carefully, and cook for 45 seconds to sear the top, then flip back again.

Spoon in all of the glaze, spreading it over the salmon, then cook for another 1–2 minutes, basting with the glaze continuously – watch out; it can burn if the heat is too high! Continue cooking until the glaze has warmed through and the salmon is perfectly cooked in the middle.

Serve the salmon on a bed of rice, grains or Asian greens. Drizzle over the remaining glaze, sprinkle with the dukkah and enjoy.

COFFEE-COLA BBQ
PORK CARNITAS

Every time I'm in San Francisco, I gorge myself on as many tamales, tacos and pupusas as I can. One especially memorable establishment in the Mission neighbourhood serves up slow-cooked pork carnitas with dark chocolate on fresh corn tortillas and tomatillo salsa. The flavours are remarkable! Earthy, rich, meaty, sweet and syrupy like cola, with a heady mix of aromatics: intense cinnamon, burnt cumin and bitter coffee. This recipe attempts to capture those flavours, contrasting the sweet-spice of cola with the complex intensity of espresso coffee to magnify the effect.

SERVES 4-6

1.75–1.85kg (3lb 13oz–3lb 4lb) pork
    shoulder
2 Tbsp instant espresso powder
¾ tsp cayenne pepper
2 tsp smoked paprika
4 tsp smoked salt
5 Tbsp dark brown sugar
2 Tbsp onion powder
1 tsp black peppercorns, coarsely
    crushed
15 allspice berries

1 Tbsp cumin seeds
1½ tsp dried oregano
1½ tsp ground cinnamon
1 large red onion, sliced
330ml (11¼fl oz) cola (full sugar,
    not diet), plus extra if needed
zest and juice of 1½ limes
fine sea salt

To serve
cooked rice or corn tacos
iceberg lettuce, shredded
jalapeños

Remove the thick rind from the pork shoulder, leaving a small layer of fat left for flavour. Score the fat in a cross-hatch with a knife, then very carefully cut a deep flap horizontally into the middle of the joint.

Make a rub by grinding together the instant espresso powder, cayenne pepper, smoked paprika, smoked salt, dark brown sugar, onion powder, black pepper, allspice, cumin seeds, oregano and cinnamon – you want a fine powder.

Spread the onion slices over the base of a deep roasting tin. Butterfly out the pork on top of the onions, then sprinkle very liberally with the rub so it entirely covers the surfaces. Fold up the joint again, cover with the last of the rub and put in the refrigerator to marinate for 2 hours.

Remove the pork from the refrigerator and allow to return to room temperature. Preheat the oven to 190°C fan/210°C/410°F/Gas mark 6½. Pour the cola into the base of the roasting tin, cover tightly

with foil and cook for 3 hours, basting every 45 minutes or so. If it's drying out too quickly top up with a little more cola to prevent the sauce from burning, and if there's excess fat in the bottom of the tin, spoon this off.

After 3 hours, remove the tray from the oven and increase the temperature to 220°C fan/240°C/475°F/ Gas mark 9. Spoon any further excess fat from the tray, then use two forks to pull the pork into chunky shreds, mixing it through with the spiced cola-coffee juices.

Add the lime zest and juice, mix well and season. Cook for a final 15 minutes in the hot oven until the shredded meat is charred and the sauce is treacly sticky – adding an extra splash of cola or water to prevent the sauce from burning.

Serve with rice, or on corn tacos with shredded lettuce and jalapeños.

BROWN TOAST & MALTED-COFFEE
RIPPLE ICE CREAM v

I adore breakfast ice creams in every guise. Humphry Slocombe in San Francisco is famous for its Drunken Breakfast – a delicious combination of cornflakes and bourbon. I'm always mesmerized by the menu at Morgenstern's in Greenwich Village, New York, which has flavours like almond croissant, chocolate granola and blueberry-maple pancake. And the one time I ate at Heston Blumenthal's Fat Duck, its bacon and egg ice cream was a true highlight. My all-time favourite was a brown toast ice cream served at an unassuming dessert bar on London's Brick Lane. My riff on it adds a syrupy malted-coffee ripple... ice cream for breakfast with an espresso kick!

SERVES 8

200g (7oz) sliced brown bread
    (about 5 thick slices)
4 Tbsp dark brown sugar
4 Tbsp milk powder
50g (1¾oz) butter
300ml (10½fl oz) soured cream
2 Tbsp liquid glucose syrup

397g (14oz) condensed milk
1 tsp fine sea salt
600ml (20fl oz) double (heavy) cream
4 Tbsp runny honey
2 heaped Tbsp instant espresso
    powder
5 Tbsp malt extract
2 Tbsp olive oil
1 teaspoon of boiling water

Preheat the oven to 200°C fan/220°C/425°F/ Gas mark 7. Toast the bread until golden brown, tear into pieces then put in a blender or food processor. Pulse until you have coarse breadcrumbs, then tip into a large mixing bowl, along with the sugar and milk powder. Melt the butter, then pour over the breadcrumbs, mixing well to form a damp sandy rubble.

Spread the crumbs over a large baking sheet in a single layer, pressing them into small clumps as you do. You want a mix of chunky clumps and smaller rubble. Bake for 5 minutes, tossing once with a spoon, then bake for a final minute until golden brown but not burnt. Remove from the oven and set aside to cool completely.

Meanwhile, in another large mixing bowl, whisk the soured cream and glucose syrup until completely combined. Add the condensed milk and salt, whisking again to combine.

In a separate bowl, whisk the double cream to stiff peaks. Pour a little of the soured cream mix into the whipped cream to loosen, then fold through the rest, a little at a time, until completely combined – keep in as much of the air as possible.

Tip most of the cooled breadcrumbs into the cream (reserve a few spoonfuls for decoration) and fold through gently. Pour everything into a lidded freezerproof 1.5 litre (52fl oz) container.

For the ripple, whisk together the runny honey, instant espresso powder, malt extract, olive oil and the boiling water. Drizzle in swirly patterns over the cream, then use a cocktail stick to swirl it through to the bottom of the container.

Freeze for 4 hours for a creamy soft-set ice cream, longer for a harder-set ice cream. Remove from the freezer 15 minutes before eating to soften. Serve generous scoops in bowls or cones with the extra breadcrumbs on top.

CARDAMOM, COFFEE & ORANGE NOUGAT v

Slices of dreamy white, almond-flecked nougat, stacked on silver platters in a Florentine confectioner is a sight to behold. Conversely, making nougat in a home kitchen – with a sugar thermometer and a stand mixer – is probably not. But don't be put off: the unbelievably tasty reward more than warrants the brief period of culinary chaos – just take it one step at a time, trust in the process and smile! The flavours of cardamom, espresso coffee and orange work wonderfully together; but feel free to remix whatever trio of ingredients suits your fancy.

MAKES 18-20 PIECES

vegetable oil, for brushing
icing (confectioner's) sugar,
    for dusting
2 sheets edible wafer paper,
    cut to the tin size
400g (14oz) mixed whole roasted
    nuts
seeds from 10 green cardamom
    pods, crushed

2 Tbsp orange zest
3 Tbsp instant espresso powder
125g (4½oz) egg whites (about 4),
    at room temperature
½ tsp cream of tartar
500g (1lb 2oz) caster (superfine)
    sugar
500g (1lb 2oz) runny honey
¼ tsp orange extract

Brush the sides of a 22cm (8½in) square baking tin with oil. Generously dust the base of the tin with a thick layer of icing sugar, then place one square of edible wafer paper on top.

In a large bowl, mix together the nuts, crushed cardamom seeds, orange zest and 2 tablespoons of the instant espresso powder. Set aside.

Using a stand mixer fitted with the whisk attachment, whisk the eggs whites and cream of tartar for 3–4 minutes until they form medium peaks.

Gently warm the caster sugar and honey in a saucepan, stirring constantly until the sugar dissolves. Increase the heat to get the mix to 125°C/257°F, stirring constantly. At this point, stop stirring but keep cooking over a high heat until the temperature is 160°C/325°F – this will take 4–6 minutes; you must get it up to this 'hard crack' temperature for the nougat to set. Remove from the heat, then VERY carefully pour into a heatproof jug.

With the stand mixer running at medium–high speed, very slowly pour the hot honey mix into the egg whites – the volume will increase, rising to the top of the bowl. Once all the hot honey is in, keep the mixer running on high for another 3–4 minutes and add the orange extract; your nougat will sink down in the bowl as it starts to cool.

Now move quickly. Take the bowl off the stand mixer and tip in the bowl of nuts. Stir very quickly with a silicone spatula – the nougat will immediately turn sticky but soon become cool enough to touch.

Spoon half of the nougat into the bottom of the prepared tin, using your hands to press down (wear disposable gloves or dust your hands with icing sugar to make this easier). Sprinkle over the remaining tablespoon of instant espresso powder, then spoon over the rest of the nougat. Lay the second sheet of edible wafer paper on top and press everything into an even layer. Dust generously with icing sugar.

Place in the refrigerator to set for at least 4–6 hours. Slice into bite-sized nuggets. Enjoy.

MARASCHINO-CAPPUCCINO TRUFFLES v

I still recall when Thorntons Chocolates opened in Leicester in the late nineties. 'Posh chocolate' had officially arrived and with it the social status of our city shot up a notch. The first time I tried their Continental Viennese Truffles remains lodged in my memories. The mix of sugar-coated milk and white chocolate enrobing a whipped mousse was bliss. Years later, I worked with the world's most exquisite chocolatiers at Harrods who revealed the *true* craft of fine chocolate, yet the taste of those ersatz-sophisticated Thorntons truffles lingered. This recipe is my ode to them: coffee and cherry striking a chord that's bitter and sweet, to appeal to both the teenager and grown-up in you.

MAKES 30-35

30 maraschino cherries plus
    4 Tbsp of syrup from the jar
    (or use Amarena)
2 Tbsp cognac or brandy
425g (15oz) dark chocolate
    (at least 60% cocoa),
    snapped into small pieces
3 Tbsp instant espresso powder
175ml (5¾oz) double (heavy) cream

½ tsp fine sea salt
50g (1¾oz) butter
125g (4½oz) roasted almonds,
    crushed

To decorate
180g (6¼oz) white chocolate
    (optional)
instant espresso powder
cocoa powder (optional)

Chop the maraschino cherries into small pieces, then put into a bowl along with the cherry syrup and cognac. Leave to macerate for 15 minutes.

Put the dark chocolate pieces in a large heatproof bowl along with the instant espresso powder, cream and salt. Place over a pan of simmering water to melt completely, stirring occasionally to ensure everything emulsifies as one.

Add the butter to the melted chocolate, stirring through until completely melted. Then stir through the crushed almonds, chopped cherries and their cognac syrup. Refrigerate for at least 4 hours.

Take the chilled chocolate mix out of the refrigerator and, using a spoon dipped into hot water, spoon out truffles the size of a hazelnut.

If using, snap the white chocolate into pieces and melt in a heatproof bowl over a pan of simmering water.

Dip each truffle into the chocolate, ripple over a little of the cherry syrup and then sprinkle with instant espresso powder. Place the truffles on a tray and refrigerate for at least 2 hours until the chocolate coating has hardened. Alternatively, simply roll the truffles in cocoa powder, then sprinkle over a little instant espresso powder. These are delicious served after dinner and make a great edible gift.

TREACLE MOCHA & BLONDE CHOCOLATE BROWNIES v

The distinction between cookies and brownies is often blurred, with soft, melt-in the-middle cookies – and light, fluffy, cakey-at-the-edges brownies having become equally popular. The morphing of the two is a culinary travesty: cookies should revel in crunchy-crinkly chewiness, whereas brownies should be unapologetically dense! I want a brownie with a texture so rich it's like biting into a cold block of butter, with obscenely concentrated cocoa that coats the mouth with it's cloying flinginess These intensely gooey, chocolatey and treacly brownies do all of these things – with the flavour enhancing magic of bitter espresso amplifying the effect.

MAKES 16

olive oil, for brushing
5 large eggs
200g (7oz) caster (superfine) sugar
250g (9oz) dark chocolate (at least
    60% cocoa), snapped into pieces
225g (8oz) butter
2 heaped Tbsp instant espresso
    powder

65g (2¼oz) cocoa powder
    (Dutch-processed)
125g (4½oz) black treacle (molasses)
125g (4½oz) blonde or white
    chocolate
75ml (2½fl oz) soured cream
150g (5½oz) plain (all-purpose) flour
¼ tsp bicarbonate of soda
    (baking soda)
1 tsp fine sea salt

Preheat the oven to 175°C fan/195°C/385°F/Gas mark 5½. Brush a deep-sided 23cm (9in) baking tin with olive oil, then line with baking paper.

In a stand mixer fitted with the whisk attachment, beat together four of the eggs and the sugar for 5–6 minutes until the mixture has doubled in volume.

Put the dark chocolate, butter and instant espresso powder in a heatproof bowl over a pan of simmering water to melt together, stirring to combine. Remove the bowl from the pan, then stir through the cocoa powder and treacle. Leave to cool for 2 minutes.

Meanwhile, melt the blonde chocolate in another heatproof bowl over the same pan of hot water. Remove the bowl from the heat then stir through the soured cream. Cool for 2 minutes, then crack in the remaining egg, whisking thoroughly. Set aside.

Slowly pour the dark chocolate-butter into the stand mixer bowl, gently folding it by hand into the whisked eggs using a spatula to retain as much air as possible.

In a separate bowl, whisk together the flour, bicarbonate of soda and salt. Add a quarter of the dry ingredients to the batter, folding it through fully, then add the rest, a quarter at a time.

Pour half of the batter into the lined tin, drizzle over half the blonde chocolate cream and swirl with a cocktail stick. Then pour in the rest of the batter, drizzle with the remaining blonde chocolate cream, again swirling into a nice pattern.

Place the tin on top of a baking sheet and bake for 25 minutes until cakey on the rim and puffed up in the middle. Remove from the oven and leave to cool in the tin to room temperature. Then chill for at least 12 hours, allowing it to turn from molten-gooey to fudgy. Slice into 16 squares and enjoy!

Dark Maple Syrup

robust and oaky,
treacly vanilla'd,
richly woody,
herbally smoky,
toffee sweetness.

Syrup made from the rising sap of maple trees native to northeast North America – including the red, black and sugar maples – was first discovered centuries ago by the Algonquian people of present-day Canada who developed the technique of 'tapping' the trees to extract the sap. The sap is boiled to concentrate its flavour – with around 40 litres of sap being required to make a litre of maple syrup. 'Light golden' and 'Amber' maple syrups are harvested earlier in the season and have a more delicate flavour than the 'Dark' syrups harvested later in the season, which are richer and more robust. 'Very dark' maple syrups, harvested at the very end of the season, develop an intense, burnt toffee-caramel flavour and dark brown colour.

MAPLE-ÉPICES CHICKEN WITH BALSAMIC-ROASTED GRAPES

One summer in southern France, I came across a spice mix in a yellow box with its label portraying a chef in a toque holding a knife to a pig. It was *Épices Rabelais,* a seasoning from Marseille dating from 1880 who's blend of spices and herbs, including rosemary, cloves, nutmeg, fennel and bay, is unchanged. I used it to make a deliciously spiced garlic butter into which I dipped rotisserie chicken. This recipe evokes those flavours, with dark maple syrup amplifying the sweet woody notes of the spices, contrasted by sharp balsamic-roasted grapes.

SERVES 4

400g (14oz) baby shallots
75g (2½oz) softened butter
1 tsp freshly grated nutmeg
¼ tsp ground cloves
2 tsp fennel seeds, crushed
   to a powder
1 tsp ground cinnamon
20 strands of saffron, crushed
1 orange, zested then halved
1 lemon, zested then halved
4 garlic cloves, crushed to a paste
1 Tbsp Dijon mustard
3 Tbsp dark maple syrup
1.75–1.95kg (3lb 13oz–4lb 3oz) chicken
4 sprigs rosemary
500g (1lb 2oz) seedless black grapes
olive oil, for drizzling
2 Tbsp balsamic vinegar
fine sea salt

Peel the baby shallots, keeping whole, then tumble into a large deep roasting tin. Preheat the oven to 180°C fan/200°C/400°F/Gas mark 6.

In a small bowl, mash together the softened butter, nutmeg, cloves, fennel seeds, cinnamon, saffron, 2 teaspoons of salt, the orange and lemon zest, garlic, mustard and 2 tablespoons of the dark maple syrup to make a paste.

Using your hands, loosen the skin from the breast of the chicken, then stuff most of the spiced-maple paste into the gap – smoothing along with your fingers. Smother the rest over the outside of the chicken. Stuff the cavity with the orange and lemon halves and rosemary sprigs.

Place the chicken on top of the shallots in the roasting tin. Drizzle over 1 tablespoon of maple syrup, then sprinkle with fine sea salt.

Bake the chicken in the oven for 1½ hours. After the first 30 minutes, remove from the oven and baste, then baste again after 1 hour. If blackening on top, cover loosely with foil.

When 20 minutes of the total cook time remain, place the whole bunch of black grapes on a separate baking tray. Drizzle with olive oil and balsamic vinegar, then sprinkle generously with fine sea salt. Place the tray in the oven on a shelf beneath the chicken.

When the chicken is cooked remove from the oven – along with the grapes. Spoon the grapes onto a serving platter and place the chicken on top. Leave to rest for 10 minutes while you make a gravy.

Place the roasting tray over a low heat, then whisk to deglaze the pan, adding a splash of wine if you like. Stir in the chicken's resting juices, then squeeze in the juice from the orange and lemon halves that were inside the chicken's cavity into the gravy and finely chop in the rosemary sprigs. Serve the chicken and balsamic grapes with roast potatoes and extra gravy on the side.

CRISPY KALE & BUTTER BEANS WITH
SALTY LEMON-MAPLE DRESSING v

The very best salads, in my opinion, are those that have a canvas of contrasting leaves and vegetables on to which are added flavourful adornments that combine extremes of textures and flavours on one plate. Key to tying everything together is a surprising dressing that's sour, savoury, salty and sweet at the same time. The three-ingredient combination in this recipe is just the thing, a simple mingling of good fruity olive oil, woody caramel-sweet dark maple syrup and sharp preserved lemon with a fruity or tangy brine. Crispy kale and creamy butter beans provide the backdrop, but this dressing can enliven even the most unexciting limp lettuce leaves if that's all you have.

SERVES 2

6 Tbsp olive oil
1 tsp sumac, plus extra to garnish
1 tsp cumin seeds
1 tsp dried mint
400g (14oz) canned butter (lima)
    beans (240g/8¾oz drained
    weight)
125g (4½oz) kale, chopped

200g (7oz) heritage tomatoes, sliced
50g (1¾oz) feta (optional)
1 Tbsp toasted pumpkin seeds
fine sea salt

For the dressing
50g (1¾oz) preserved lemon, pips
    removed, plus 2 Tbsp of the brine
2 Tbsp olive oil
4 Tbsp dark maple syrup

Preheat the oven to 190°C fan/210°C/410°F/Gas mark 6½. In small bowl whisk, together the oil, sumac, cumin seeds, dried mint and 1 teaspoon of salt.

Tip the butter beans into a roasting tray and drizzle over half the spiced oil, mixing well to coat them all over.

Put the kale on a separate roasting tray, then drizzle over the other half of the spiced oil. Use your hands to scrunch and massage the oil into the kale, ensuring it's coated fully.

Bake the butter beans for 10 minutes in the top of the oven and the kale for 5–6 minutes in the bottom of the oven, tossing both halfway through – check the kale regularly and cover with foil if it's browning too quickly.

Meanwhile, make the dressing. Whizz together the preserved lemon and brine, the oil and dark maple syrup in a small blender. Taste for seasoning, adding a little extra salt or brine if needed – it should be tart, salty, sweet and tangy in equal measure.

Serve the crispy kale on a platter, pile on the warm butter beans and tomatoes, crumble over the feta, if using, and scatter the pumpkin seeds. Drizzle the maple-lemon dressing liberally and finish with a sprinkling of sumac. Enjoy.

MAPLE-CHORIZO
EGG MUFFINS

Cheeky's is a Palm Springs institution – famous for serving up Californian sunny-side up breakfasts all day, every day, and some of the very best brunch-tails in America. Every time I've visited, their new additions to the menu have been a revelation. Even so, I always order the same thing – their iconic 'flight of bacon', which includes a line-up of applewood-smoked, honey, apricot and BBQ bacon. Right at the end of this ensemble is their jalapeño bacon, for which maple syrup is an essential accompaniment. These breakfast muffins are a Spanish-style take on that spicy-chilli-sweet sensorial experience, with coriander seeds adding a lemony crunch to contrast the spiced-maple meatiness.

MAKES 2

80g (2¾oz) cured chorizo, diced small
1 tsp coriander seeds, crushed
2 Tbsp pumpkin seeds
zest and juice of ½ lemon
¾ tsp smoked salt
2 Tbsp dark maple syrup,
  plus extra for drizzling
knob of butter
2 large eggs
2 English muffins, split in half
2 tsp English mustard
2 slices of American cheese or Edam

Heat a small frying pan over a medium heat, then add the diced chorizo. Cook for 5–6 minutes until a lot of the oil has rendered and it's just starting to turn crispy on the outside. If there is enough in the pan, remove 1 teaspoon of the chorizo oil to cook the eggs later.

Next, add the coriander seeds, pumpkin seeds and lemon zest to the pan. Cook for 1 minute, then add the smoked salt and dark maple syrup, cooking for another 1–2 minutes until you have a sticky sweet glaze. Finally, add the lemon juice and cook for a final minute. Empty out into a bowl.

Add the reserved chorizo oil back into the pan with half the butter, and place a baking ring the diameter of your muffins in the middle.

Crack an egg into the ring and cook for 1 minute. Splash a little water into the pan, cover with a lid and cook for another 2 minutes. Then, very carefully remove the baking ring and flip the egg over to cook on the other side for 1–2 minutes until sealed but soft in the centre. Repeat with the second egg, adding a little more butter to the pan.

Toast the English muffins and spread liberally with English mustard. Then, sandwich each muffin with a slice of cheese, a spoonful of the maple-glazed chorizo, an egg, and a drizzle of dark maple syrup to finish, if you like. Enjoy.

SAUTERNES STRAWBERRY TIRAMISU
WITH MAPLE MASCARPONE v

The cookbook *Wild Raspberries*, illustrated by Andy Warhol and co-authored with New York socialite Suzie Frankfurt, is a riot of foodie frivolity and culinary campery in the best of ways. The more extravagant sketches include an ornate pink Torte à la Dobosch, a majestic green jelly of Greengages à la Warhol and a gravity-defying Gateau of Marzipan. I've had a taste for 'more is more' desserts since I discovered the book, hence this strawberry tiramisu. Dark maple syrup-enriched mascarpone adds a toasted nectar quality, while the Sauternes brings notes of peach, honey, butterscotch, toasted brioche and cinnamon! With all that going on, the hazelnut praline is somewhat excessive – but I think Andy would have approved.

SERVES 8-9

vegetable oil, for brushing
100g (3½oz) chopped roasted
  hazelnuts
200g (7oz) light brown sugar,
  plus an extra 1 Tbsp
500g (1lb 2oz) strawberries
175ml (5¾fl oz) Sauternes or sweet
  muscat wine, plus an extra 3 Tbsp
pinch of fine sea salt
200g (7oz) strawberry jam (jelly)

zest and juice of 1 lemon
250g (9oz) mascarpone, at room
  temperature
2 tsp vanilla bean paste
4 large egg yolks
175ml (5¾fl oz) dark maple syrup,
  plus extra to serve
300ml (10½fl oz) double (heavy)
  cream
350g (12oz) savoiardi (sponge or lady
  fingers), 50 small or 25 large ones

Start by making the praline. Line a baking sheet with baking paper then brush with oil, or better still use a silicone mat. Sprinkle half the chopped hazelnuts in an even layer.

Heat the sugar in a frying pan over a medium heat for 5–6 minutes, swirling gently, until it's a runny liquid. Very carefully pour the molten sugar over the nuts on the sheet, then sprinkle the rest of the nuts on top. Use a spatula to press them into the sugar as it cools. Set aside for 15 minutes to harden completely, then snap into shards and grind using a pestle and mortar (or put in a sandwich bag, then crush with a rolling pin) to a coarse praline powder – reserve a few shards to decorate.

Next, slice the tops off the strawberries, stand on a board and slice into heart shapes about 3mm (⅛in) thick. Add to a bowl then pour over 3 tablespoons of Sauternes, the extra tablespoon of sugar and the salt. Set aside to macerate for 15 minutes.

Drain the strawberries through a sieve, catching the juices in a bowl. Add to the bowl the 175ml (5¾fl oz) of Sauternes, the strawberry jam, lemon zest and 4 tablespoons of juice. Whisk well and set aside.

In a second bowl, mix the mascarpone and vanilla bean paste together. Make sure it's at room temperature (otherwise it can clump when added to the egg yolks in the next step).

Using a stand mixer fitted with the whisk attachment, whisk the egg yolks and maple syrup for 7–8 minutes until frothy and tripled in size. With the motor still going, slowly add the mascarpone, a little at a time.

In another bowl, whip the cream to stiff peaks. Fold a little of the egg-mascarpone mix into the whipped cream to loosen, then gently fold in the rest until you have a smooth consistent mix – being careful not to lose too much air.

To assemble, select a deep 23cm (9in) square dish or equivalent. One by one, dip enough savoiardi into the Sauternes mixture, rolling them around to fully soak, to form a layer in the base of the tin.

Cover the soaked savoiardi with a layer of mascarpone, top with half the strawberries, then sprinkle over half the praline powder. Repeat the layers of savoiardi, mascarpone and strawberries. Transfer to the refrigerator to set for at least 12 hours. Decorate with the remaining praline, the reserved praline shards and a drizzle of dark maple syrup. Enjoy.

Tip: For an alcohol-free version, replace the Sauternes with 150ml (5fl oz) orange juice and use 3 tablespoons of elderflower cordial for macerating the berries.

RHUBARB & PASSION FRUIT FOOL
WITH MAPLE CRUMBLE v

Shrikhand is a decadent Indian dessert that catapults me back to childhood summers spent being fattened up by auntie-jis in Punjab. It combines thick strained yoghurt with whipped cream, saffron, cardamom and jaggery, either eaten as is, or rippled with a very nineties coulis of crushed raspberries, mango or lychees. This recipe transforms that memory into a fruit fool – with rich dark maple syrup sweetening the yoghurt-cream, and adding a toasted oakiness to the crumble. Use whatever fruit are in season. Just don't be shy with the whipped cream – Punjabi auntie-ji desserts are never restrained.

SERVES 4

300g (10½oz) full-fat Greek yoghurt
525g (1lb 3oz) rhubarb, chopped
zest and juice of ½ orange
50g (1¾oz) caster (superfine) sugar
1 Tbsp cornflour (cornstarch)
4 Tbsp dark maple syrup, plus extra
    to drizzle
300ml (10½fl oz) double (heavy)
    cream

1 tsp vanilla bean paste
4 passion fruit, halved

For the crumble
125g (4½oz) jumbo oats (rolled oats)
1 tsp ground cinnamon
65g (2¼oz) caster (superfine) sugar
fine sea salt
100g (3½oz) plain (all-purpose) flour
2 Tbsp dark maple syrup
100g (3½oz) cold butter, in small
    cubes

Place the Greek yoghurt in a cheesecloth, gather the sides and squeeze over a sink to remove as much water as you can. Tie to enclose the yoghurt, place in a sieve over a bowl and set a heavy weight on top. Refrigerate for 3–4 hours until a lot of the liquid has drained away.

Meanwhile, make the crumble. Preheat the oven to 180°C fan/200°C/400°F/Gas mark 6. Put the oats, cinnamon, flour, 65g (2¼oz) of sugar and ½ teaspoon of salt in a large bowl and mix well. Add the maple syrup and cubed butter and rub them into the dry ingredients to form a clumpy crumble mix.

Spread the crumble on a baking sheet and bake on the bottom oven shelf for 20–25 minutes until golden and toasty. Check regularly and shake every 5 minutes so it doesn't burn.

At the same time roast the rhubarb. Put it in a deep roasting tin with the orange zest and juice, 50g (1¾oz) sugar and the cornflour. Mix well.

Cover the tin with foil and bake for 20 minutes. Remove the foil and bake for another 6–8 minutes until the rhubarb is cooked through and jammy. Set aside the crumble and the rhubarb to cool.

Once the Greek yoghurt has fully drained, transfer the strained curds to a large bowl and mix with the maple syrup. Stir vigorously, then set aside to come up to room temperature.

Gently whip the cream – with the vanilla bean paste – to soft peaks, being careful not to overwhip. Add a little of the cream to the room-temperature maple-yoghurt curds to loosen, then gently fold through the rest until you have a smooth and consistent fool.

To assemble, take four glasses of your choosing, carefully layer in the jammy rhubarb, maple-yoghurt fool and the passion fruit pulp, adding lots of crumble on top. Drizzle with extra syrup, if you like.

PECAN-COGNAC CARROT CAKE
WITH MAPLE GLAZE v

While my culinary education at Harrods lasted seven years, my schooling on fine cognac was a just few days of intense immersion in the middle of that magical chapter. Our team was invited to Hennessy's Château de Bagnolet in France for 36 hours of distillery touring, very fine dining and imbibing on some of the most exquisite cognacs ever made. The very first sip of its rose-scented, honeyed fig, ripe plum, golden-amber nectars transformed my palate forever – a taste I'm eternally trying to recreate through cooking. This spicy, cognac laced carrot cake with a dark maple infused brown-butter glaze is the closest I've got.

SERVES 10-12

5 Tbsp cognac or brandy
100g (3½oz) sultanas (golden raisins)
450g (1lb) carrots, grated
285ml (3¾fl oz) olive oil, plus extra
    for brushing
325g (11½oz) plain (all-purpose) flour,
    sifted
2 tsp ground cinnamon
1 Tbsp ground ginger
1 tsp baking powder
½ tsp bicarbonate of soda
    (baking soda)

150g (5½oz) toasted pecans, chopped
½ tsp fine sea salt
150g (5½oz) caster (superfine) sugar
100g (3½oz) dark brown sugar
2 Tbsp orange zest (from about
    3 large oranges)
4 large eggs

For the glaze
65g (2¼oz) butter
5 Tbsp dark maple syrup
1 Tbsp cognac or brandy
150g (5½oz) icing (confectioner's)
    sugar

Over a low heat, gently warm 5 tablespoons of cognac in a medium saucepan for 1–2 minutes – careful as the alcohol can catch. Take off the heat and stir in the sultanas. Steep for 10 minutes before mixing in the grated carrots. Set aside.

Preheat the oven to 175°C fan/195°C/385°F/Gas mark 5½ and brush a 24cm (9½cm) ring cake or bundt tin with oil. In a large mixing bowl, combine the flour, cinnamon, ginger, baking powder, bicarbonate of soda, pecans and salt. Set aside.

Add the caster sugar, dark brown sugar and orange zest to the bowl of a stand mixer. Use your hands to rub the zest into the sugar, then add the eggs. Beat with the paddle attachment for 2–3 minutes until the mixture just starts to become frothy.

With the mixer running slowly, gradually drizzle in the oil until incorporated. Add the carrots, sultanas and cognac, then beat for another 1 minute until well combined.

Next, with the mixer on slow, add the dry ingredients one-third at a time, beating just until the flour has been incorporated fully, scraping down the sides as needed.

Pour the batter into the prepared tin and tap it on the surface to release any bubbles. Place the tin on top of a baking sheet and bake for 55–60 minutes on the middle rack until a skewer into the centre comes out clean. Remove from the oven, leave the cake in the tin for 20 minutes, then turn out onto a wire rack to cool completely.

For the glaze, heat the butter in a saucepan over a medium heat for 5–6 minutes, swirling continuously until the butter turns nutty brown. Pour into a heatproof bowl, then whisk in the dark maple syrup and cognac. Leave to cool for 2 minutes, then whisk in the icing sugar until you have a thick smooth glaze. Add a drop of cognac if too thick or extra icing, if runny. Drizzle the glaze over the cake, letting it drip down the sides. Leave to set for 15 minutes. Enjoy!

ABOUT THE AUTHOR

Gurdeep Loyal is an award-winning food, restaurant and travel writer based in East London. He was winner of the *Jane Grigson Trust Award* for his debut cookbook, *Mother Tongue – Flavours of a Second Generation* (4th Estate, 2023) which celebrated third-culture British Indian culinary identity through recipes, personal memoir and humorous essays; and was named the *Observer Food Monthly's* 'new favourite cookbook of 2023'. He is a monthly columnist for *Olive Magazine* and frequent guest on the *Olive Podcast*, as well as regularly appearing on BBC1's breakfast TV show *Saturday Kitchen*. Gurdeep is also a culinary trends expert, having built his career at gourmet institutions including Harrods' Food Halls,

Marks & Spencer and Innocent Drinks. He has written about food, travel and diasporic cuisines for *Condé Nast Traveller, Delicious Magazine, Suitcase, Borough Market, The Food Almanac* and *The Independent*; as well as featuring in the likes of *The Times, Guardian, New York Times, The Telegraph, Financial Times, Harper's Bazaar, Elle Decoration* and *Stylist Magazine*. Gurdeep also curates a Substack newsletter called *The Pudding Menu* – a light-hearted online journal following his gastronomic explorations and discoveries around the world.

Follow him @gurd_loyal.

ACKNOWLEDGEMENTS

It takes a village to cook a book. With loving thanks...

To **Sarah Lavelle**, my Managing Director of Publishing at Quadrille, for believing in me and this book so assuredly. I'll never forget waking up on a freezing cold November morning in Chicago to a very exciting message from you, and our joyful transatlantic phone call a few hours later, that sparked this book into being. Thank you for everything.

To **Patricia Niven**, whose exquisitely beautiful photographs grace these pages. Our summer bubble of creativity was just so special; I loved every second. Every picture in this book is a sublime pleasure on the eye – your skilful brilliance captured the sentiment of each recipe just perfectly. So much love for you and for our wonderful new friendship.

To **Lucy Rose Turnbull**, whose food styling is extraordinary in ways I could never have even imagined. I was in awe of your talent every single day of our shoots – and your calm, clever, considered commitment to perfecting every dish until it shone in *the* most delicious way it possibly could.

To **Eila Purvis**, for your virtuosic editing and seamless coordination as the connector of every piece in this flavour-filled book puzzle. It couldn't have happened without you. Your dedication to this becoming the best book it possibly could be – and being uncompromisingly true to my vision – has meant so much.

To **Stacey Cleworth**, whose commissioning editorship shaped this book from the chaotic ugly duckling it began life as, to the discerningly polished swan it has become.

To **Emily Lapworth**, whose art direction and design mastery has made every page of this book so understatedly chic, refined and elegant. You got the aesthetic *so* right – in every way. I love it all so much.

To **Luke Bird**, whose cover design embodies everything this book is about with such stylish, playful and artistic panache. Every time I look at those dancing Hockney splodges of flavourful joy, I smile.

To **Katie Smith**, for bringing your superb talents to this book as Lucy's food styling assistant. You contributed so much to every single photograph, brought sunshine energy to set every day and have technical baking knowledge like no one else I know.

To **Ruth Samuels**, for your gleaming expertise as Patricia's photography assistant, and for the infectious fun you brought to our shoot days. It was such a delight to have you be a part of this book.

To **Charlie Philips**, for your prop styling selections that were immaculately on point every single time – and to your lovely assistant **Anita Gohil** for getting everything to us in one piece.

To **Stephanie Evans**, for copy editing this book with such precision – and ensuring my somewhat overly verbose tone of voice was never compromised. And to **Kathy Steer**, for your help with proofreading.

To the PR, Marketing, Sales and Production teams at **Quadrille** and **Penguin Random House** who've contributed in any way to this book getting onto the shelves of bookshops or into minds, hearts and homes of flavour-loving home cooks around the world.

To **Lulu Grimes**, **Janine Ratcliffe**, **Alex Crossley** and all of the team at **Olive Magazine** for their continued patronage over the last 4 years – and for giving me such a fun monthly platform to share my culinary discoveries with gourmet readers everywhere.

To all the **magazine/newspaper editors**, **TV producers** and **casting directors** who've have commissioned or chosen to work with me in recent years – particularly at Saturday Kitchen, Condé Nast Traveller, Delicious, Waitrose Weekend and Borough Market. I'm eternally grateful for your support.

To **Yotam Ottolenghi**, **Anna Jones**, **Rachel Khoo**, **Nik Sharma**, **Andi Oliver**, **Matt Tebbutt**, **Helen Goh**, **Phil Khoury** and **Georgina Hayden** for your incredibly generous endorsements of this book. I have such admiration for all of you, and your collective backing means so much.

To my **closest friends** and **cousins** for so being my biggest cheerleaders throughout this big culinary adventure – that feels in many ways like it's only just beginning! Particularly those that tested recipes. Thank you for sticking by me – even when I'm not replying to WhatsApp because I'm too busy '*with the book*' – but still finding time to post selfies on Instagram trying on expensive coats in Liberty ¯_(ツ)_/¯

To **Nayan**, **Anaiya**, **Reeva** and **Neev** – my squad of little champions – who fill me with joy every day. Especially when you say things like: "*Uncle, why did you wear that weird shiny shirt on TV?*"

To **Sunny**, **Shreya**, **Jasmin** and **Kully** for always supporting me and my tangential career whims so resolutely.

To **Mum**, who I love more than words... but who got the honour of my first cookbook... and so...

Finally, to **Dad, *my* hero.** This one is for you. Your boundless love for me is the only reason any of this has happened. Love you always. Cheers... and cheers again... and maybe just one more for the road... x

INDEX

INDEX

Quadrille, Penguin Random House UK,
One Embassy Gardens, 8 Viaduct Gardens,
London SW11 7BW

Quadrille Publishing Limited is part of the
Penguin Random House group of companies
whose addresses can be found at global.
penguinrandomhouse.com

Published by Quadrille in 2025

www.penguin.co.uk

A CIP catalogue record for this book
is available from the British Library

ISBN 978-1-83783-258-3

10 9 8 7 6 5 4 3 2 1

Managing Director, Publishing: Sarah Lavelle
Senior Commissioning Editor: Stacey Cleworth
Senior Editor: Eila Purvis
Design and Art Direction: Emily Lapworth
Cover Designer: Luke Bird
Photographer: Patricia Niven
Photography Assistant: Ruth Samuels
Props Stylist: Charlie Philips
Props Stylist Assistant: Anita Gohil
Food Stylist: Lucy Turnball
Food Stylist Assistant: Katie Smith
Copy-editor: Stephanie Evans
Proofreader: Katie Birr
Indexer: Cathy Heath
Production Manager: Sabeena Atchia

Colour reproduction by F1

Printed in China by C&C Offset Printing Co., Ltd.

The authorised representative in the EEA is
Penguin Random House Ireland, Morrison
Chambers, 32 Nassau Street, Dublin D02 YH68.